OUTCAST CAPE TOWN

Published with assistance from the Roger E. Joseph Memorial Fund for greater understanding of history and public affairs, a cause in which Roger Joseph believed.

Outcast
Cape Town

John Western

UNIVERSITY OF MINNESOTA PRESS □ MINNEAPOLIS

Published by the University of Minnesota Press,
2037 University Avenue Southeast,
Minneapolis, Minnesota 55414
Printed in the United States of America

Library of Congress Cataloging in Publication Data

Western, John.
    Outcast Cape Town.

    Bibliography: p.
    Includes index.
    1. Cape Town (South Africa) — Description.
2. Segregation — South Africa — Cape Town. I. Title.
DT848.C54W47   968.7   81-14640
ISBN 0-8166-1025-8   AACR2

The University of Minnesota
is an equal-opportunity
educator and employer.

For

Ernie and Catherine
Joey and Yvonne
 on the Cape Flats

Pat and Val
 now in Australia

The Society of Friends' Cape Town meeting

and in memory of
Victor Wessels

A report by Stanley Uys from Cape Town in the
Guardian Weekly, 7 September 1974.

Racial Love at the End of the Line

The suicide of a 20-year-old Coloured boy in Cape Town has brought to light an apartheid tragedy almost unparalleled in South Africa's history.

The boy threw himself under a train at a suburban station when he learnt that his white girlfriend was pregnant. He could not marry her, because the Mixed Marriages Act prohibits marriage across the colour line.

He left his girlfriend all the money he had—30 rand—to help her to buy clothes for the baby. He asked her in a suicide note to name the baby after him if it was a boy. The girl's father took the money and used it to pay for an abortion—a legal abortion could be obtained because the father was Coloured.

The girl then tried to commit suicide by cutting her wrists, but failed. She was unaware that her boyfriend was Coloured. She heard of his death after he failed to arrive that evening to take her to a cinema.

The girl, Sonya Shepherd, 17, said afterwards: "I did not know my boyfriend was Coloured. The first I knew was when the police told me. It would not have made the slightest difference. If only he had known that. We could have run away to another country and got married and lived a normal life away from apartheid."

The boy's identity is not being revealed, because his family is leading an illegal try-for-white existence. The father, who is white, met the mother, who is Coloured, in 1950—the year in which the Mixed Marriages Act was passed. They lived together, defying the Immorality Act of 1951, which prohibits sexual relations across the colour line.

They have five children, and the family lived as whites in a white suburb. They could not send the children to school, because their birth certificates classified them as Coloured and they would have been refused admission to a white school. This would have begun events that would have led to their exposure, their expulsion from the white suburb, and the loss of their white friends.

Whenever there was a knock at the door during the mornings, she would hide the children at the back of the house, in case it was a school inspector. "We are so frightened," the mother said. "Everytime there is a knock on the door we think they have come to arrest us." (They are contravening the Immorality Act by co-habiting.)

The mother said there were frequent family rows as a result of the strain under which they lived. "The final and fatal row came on the morning my son died. In a moment of anger, I threatened to telephone Sonya's parents and tell them he was Coloured. My son walked out of the house and I never saw him alive again. I feel so guilty."

She also tried to take her life, unsuccessfully. The son, in dying, bequeathed another problem. Because he was Coloured, he could not be buried in a white cemetery — friends would have asked why he was buried in a Coloured cemetery and the family secret would have been revealed. So he was cremated and the ashes put in an urn.

"I have hidden my son's ashes in the house," the mother said, "so that our friends won't ask embarrassing questions."

Sonya said her parents had forbidden her to see her boyfriend's family again. "I don't know much about politics," she said, "but if only he had told me. If only these laws that caused all this had not existed all this would have been avoided. I can't forget what happened. I have nightmares."

Foreword

Robert Coles

I first met John Western in Cape Town, a city whose mixture of natural beauty (I know no place anywhere quite so dramatically appealing) and terrible human tragedy is the subject of this remarkable and important inquiry. The year was 1974; I had come to the city at the invitation of the students at the University of Cape Town, South Africa's oldest educational institution. During my stay in the city, I began to hear, naturally, of the various racially connected injustices that, in sum, are South Africa's exceedingly heavy burden — heavy to the point that one wonders how long it will be until an awful Armageddon is faced by the millions of human beings who live in cities such as Cape Town, Johannesburg, Durban, and Port Elizabeth, not to mention the countless towns and villages of South Africa. Among the students I met during that rainy August I spent in Cape Town was a rangy and obviously bright and discerning Englishman who struck me as being brilliantly informed, not only about the people of South Africa and its history and cultural life, but about my own country as well, especially about the difficulties America's blacks and Indians have faced as they have tried to obtain an all too elusive political and economic equity with their powerful, white fellow citizens.

Since 1974 I have stayed in touch with John Western and his South African wife, Wendy Western; I have watched a research project get done, a couple realize how hard it would be for them morally to live in South Africa, and two "foreigners" take up residence in the United States and contribute significantly to its educational assets. I have also watched this book gradually take shape: the careful and knowing observations, the interviews, the statistical data — all assembled into a clear, strong, and suggestive prose. With this effort accomplished, a young professional man has embarked upon a promising career indeed.

ix

John Western is a social geographer, a member of a profession not especially well known to the American public. He is interested in the contours and the complexities of the human landscape—in this book, the South African one. Who lives where, and why? Who lives how, and why? Who started living here and ended up living there, and, again, why? There are elements of sociology, history, anthropology, legal theory and practice, psychology, economics, and politics, since all of these disciplines bear upon the way people live. But the social geographer emphasizes the textures of *place*: the neighborhood or the city district or the rural province as something to be examined deeply and widely. For a person like John Western, the lines on a map pulsate with life. Wars, expeditions of plunder, schemes, sleights-of-hand, accommodations, acquiescences, victories and defeats, maneuvers and more maneuvers of various principalities and powers have conspired over time to make those lines no abstract exercise in cartography but rather for men and women and children, so very many of them, an expression of hard, concrete reality.

The reality of South Africa's Cape Town is, of course, the matter this book takes up, scrupulously, thoughtfully, and worriedly. The author is a first-rate scholar, but he is also a person of compassion and moral reflection. He knows a living nightmare when he sees one. He can spot evidence of human brutality, greed, and selfishness. He responds to the sight of suffering and pain, to the spectacle of hunger, malnutrition, faulty housing, inadequate sanitation, and job-lessness among a majority while a minority does right well for itself, buttressed always by its overwhelming military power. His reaction, though, is not an easy or smug self-righteousness. This is a book about a human tragedy by an author who understands—with the ancient Greeks, with the Tolstoy of *War and Peace*, with the George Eliot of *Middlemarch*, with the Faulkner of the American South, and with the Alan Paton of South Africa—that history is not made in dark, conspiratorial meetings attended by Satan and a few of his mortal agents but that fate is a terribly complex affair. John Western under-stands that chance, accident, and unpredictable circumstance play roles in every nation's, people's, and continents's history (hence, the requirement of a capacity for irony and ambiguity among those who would understand how societies work).

It is all too easy, I fear, for many Americans to turn the present-day situation in South Africa into a convenient occasion for moral scapegoating—with that nation's evil compared to America's virtue. I will never forget what I heard from a black child I came to know in South Africa (1979): "We weren't put here by those white people over there. They were born into this mess, and so were we!" He was pointing at some white people, parents and their children, sitting on a park bench in Johannesburg; he was also showing an exceptional capability, a willingness to take a long, wry, and broad-minded view of how things work in a given history. Not that the youth lacked moral or political indignation; he was no servile product of a repressive regime, handing to the white master sweet pieties in exchange for a pat on the head and a stick of candy. He was a tough survivor of Soweto's riots letting an American sympathizer know that pity can be cheap and empathy meaningless to someone who has to ready himself for a long, tough fight *and* that his is a fight (so I have heard from many such "children") not by any means confined to the Republic of South Africa. I wanted to hand that "child" a few sympathetic words, but he had no use for the wordy self-justifications or the sly self-exaltations of my kind.

I rather think that "boy" would have enjoyed a bit more the line of inquiry and argument pursued in the following pages—straightforward, unapologetic, clearheaded, and morally alert, yet unsentimental. When the reader has finished this book, he/she will understand how South Africa's outcasts live, at least those part of one important city: Cape Town. Cape Town's coloureds are accidents of history, no doubt! One can only hope and pray that there is time enough for those who probably will never read this book—South Africa's impoverished, politically disenfranchised, ever so vulnerable "coloured" and "black" people, and its whites—to come to their collective senses, lest one awful, murderous series of confrontations furnish us with yet another example of the cursed nature of life so many men and women simply must take for granted, it seems, "world without end." Meanwhile, we have a factual sermon of sorts, a study done by a man who writes like an experienced and astute essayist and thinks in the tradition of wise and original-minded social inquiry. His is no small or common gift; it is one to be acknowledged with gratitude. We ought to read the following pages attentively and celebrate them among our colleagues and friends as an encouraging sign for the intellectual life of a profession, of a community of readers—though not, alas, a sign that the question under discussion will soon be academic.

Robert Coles
Harvard University

Preface

In 1968, having just completed my undergraduate education in England and having no clear notion of what career path I should follow, I applied to Voluntary Service Overseas, the British equivalent of the Peace Corps. By chance, they sent me to teach in the rural interior of Burundi. During my two years there, I traveled quite widely in central and east Africa and began to sense that there was another very powerful Africa, a sort of *éminence grise*, "south." It was not often mentioned outright by the Africans I knew and worked with, but a few of its products were to be found on the shelves at the marketplace. In parts of Kenya especially, I found indications of how things might be ordered farther to the south: when I rode in the Mercedes of a white farmer from Naivasha, who had picked me up hitch-hiking "because I don't like to see our chaps standing by the side of the road" and who was bluffly cursing his black farm workers (the "boys" who were in the livestock truck following us); when I saw the shrubs and lawns, manicured by so many "garden-boys," of Nairobi's quiet, leafy suburbs; when I noticed in a railway station at Londiani, in the Highlands, a platform urinal that had been once divided down the middle into "European" and "Non-European" sections, the offending terms painted over, but still visible because they were sunken in the concrete wall.

In early 1972, I began my doctoral studies at the University of California at Los Angeles, hoping somehow that I could return to Burundi for fieldwork. Four months later, one of the ugliest and least known episodes of the decade began—what René Lemarchand has correctly called the "selective genocide" of the Hutu people in Burundi, an African Holocaust that weeded out *all* the formally educated and even minimally literate people among the Hutu. Perhaps one of every fifteen in the nation's population was killed. (This included some of the 13- and 14-year-old schoolboys whom I had taught, as I discovered during a grim visit in 1975.) Clearly, then, any field research in Burundi was absolutely out of the question. It was at about this time that I had the good fortune to meet Leo and Hilda Kuper, who began to make me aware of the possibilities of research in South Africa. I had difficulty deciding whether I should even consider doing my fieldwork there. Eventually, sheer curiosity won out over ill-informed and unfocused moral misgivings—I wanted to find out for myself about apartheid. So, in July 1974, I flew to South Africa . . . and found that I had put myself in the way of more experience than I had ever anticipated. I encountered the most superlative landscapes of any country I have ever seen, more lovely even than the hills of Burundi. I made friends who seem to me to be among the most courageous and resilient people I know, battling to retain their humanity and humor under a system that grinds away at them daily, whether they are black or white. And, in a country I came to love, I came to abhor what apartheid has been doing to its people. Because of the nature of my fieldwork in the black (mainly "Coloured") areas of Cape Town, I do believe I was "fortunate" enough to gain a taste of legislated racial discrimination, even though I was always a white foreigner.

In a study involving work of this nature in present-day South Africa, it is not possible to acknowledge certain people by name, whether they are the ex-residents of Mowbray who took great trouble to help me in my investigations or other interested parties. However, there are some whom it *is* possible to thank by name, and I find this a pleasure: first, Prof. Leo Kuper, to whom I am immensely indebted, for it was he who was able to find a way for me to get to Cape Town in the first place and it was he who helped guide some of my interpretations on my return; Prof. H. W. van der Merwe, to whom I am also greatly indebted, for his Centre for Intergroup Studies at the University of Cape Town supported me through a research scholarship while I did my fieldwork from 1974 to 1976; Dr. Oscar Wollheim, who freely gave me the benefit of his years of concerned experience of the Cape Flats and for whom I should like to express my admiration. Professors George Ellis and Martin Putterill (the latter now living in New Zealand) of the University of Cape Town also gave of their time and provided me with much information, as did Johann Maree and Paul Andrew. Thanks are also due to the Rev. D. P. Botha of the Dutch Reformed Mission Church, to Richard Rosenthal, to Vernie and Beryl Domingo, to Mark Povall, and to Margaret Vane (Bonteheuwel's first housing manager). Most of all of those I feel I can name in Cape Town, I wish warmly to thank Prof. Michael Whisson (now at Rhodes University in Grahamstown), whose knowledge and perceptively acerbic observations on the situation of "Coloured people" in the Cape Peninsula were indispensable. On my return to UCLA for the 1976-1977 academic year, I benefited from the advice and criticism of Professors J. E. Spencer, Gerry Hale, and, especially, Ed Soja, whose supervision made completing my doctoral dissertation exigent but enjoyable. A good portion of this present work has been drawn from that work. After I gathered further information in Cape Town in July and August 1978, I was asked to consider writing what has become *Outcast Cape Town*. I would like to thank Dr. Leonard Guelke, a Capetonian now living in Ontario, for some very constructive suggestions at that juncture. Then, I would like to thank Gloria Basmajian for her energetic typing once I got started on the book, and Mark Mattson and Joe Ochlak for the fine maps they drew in Temple University's cartographic laboratory. I would also like to thank Prof. Nick Patricios, a Johannesburger now living in Florida, for his thoughtful observations from time to time; and Dr. Carolyn Adams for some crisp criticism as the work approached its final form.

I would like to thank Human and Rousseau for permission to quote Adam Small's poem "Ons't gewag vi die Hanoverstraat se bus" and a portion of his "Die bulldozers, hulle't gakom"; the South African Institute of Race Relations for permission to quote excerpts from a number of their publications; and Okpaku Communications Corporation for permission to quote Dollar Brand's "Blues for District Six," reprinted from *New African Literature and the Arts*, Vol. I, edited by Joseph Okpaku, copyright 1970 by The Third Press. I am grateful to Chris Jansen for his permission to publish Figure 3; to Struan Robertson for Figures 30 and 38; to Terence McNally for Figure 34; and to *Die Burger* and the *Argus* for Figures 37, 1 and 39, respectively. Mark Povall provided me with Figure 6; George Ellis, Paul Andrew, and the Urban Problems Research Unit at the University of Cape Town with Figures 29, 41, 42, 47, and 48. The remaining photographs are mine.

Since this is my first major piece of published work, it does not seem inappropriate to go a little into the past to thank Mr. E. Paget, Fellow of Jesus College, Oxford, in whose fine tutorials I first had my social geographic imagination stimulated. Also, my debt to my senior geography master and history master at Chatham House Grammar School in Ramsgate, to my elder sister and brother, and to my parents is immense. Finally, Wendy—a native of Cape Province and a proofreader extraordinaire—has given profound aid throughout.

There are no doubt some errors of fact that have crept into this study; for these I apologize. Whatever guidance I may have received from those persons mentioned, the factual and interpretative errors must clearly remain my responsibility. One last point: all those "Coloured" persons who are not public figures but who are quoted by name in this study have been given pseudonyms. The pseudonyms were chosen randomly from surnames common among "Coloured" Capetonians, such as Koopmans, Davids, Fortuin, and Petersen.

Contents

PART I
INTRODUCTION

CHAPTER ONE

Introduction: Themes and Actors

The trouble is, to understand a place like . . . the Republic [of South Africa], it is no good looking coolly from outside. You have to experience the paranoia, the adolescent sentimentality, the neurosis. Experience—then retreat into a cool look from the outside. Most politicians and journalists do their judging from outside only. And most of the people on the spot are lost in violent emotionalism.

> Doris Lessing,
> in a May 1967 postscript to *Going Home* (1957)

THE DIALECTIC OF PERSON AND PLACE

There is no city whose morphology has evolved at random. Neither is there at work an omnipotent "hidden hand" totally independent of human control. To a greater or lesser degree, human intent, past and present, permeates every city's constructed form. Pointed evidence for this fact can be found in contemporary South African cities, for these cities clearly manifest the intentions of those in power.

A rigidly segregationist racial policy—apartheid—has been imposed upon the city of Cape Town, South Africa, over the last thirty years. Although the roots of segregation go back almost to the time of the first arrival of European settlers in southern Africa over three and a quarter centuries ago, Cape Town's case is of particular interest because, before apartheid's institution in 1948, it was by far the *least* racially segregated city in southern Africa, and perhaps even in all of sub-Saharan Africa. The contrast between Cape Town's past and present is striking and instructive; the city has been transformed.

In remaking the city, apartheid has also remade Cape Town's citizens. That there is a complex and inextricable link between a person's identity and his or her place is one of the basic themes of this book. Although this link may be complex, it is neither vague nor insubstantial. It is real and demonstrable; it is molding the present and the future of Cape Town. It unavoidably mediates the everyday experiences of all Capetonians, whether they are White, Brown, or Black, whether they are at home, at work, or at leisure, whether it is day or night. Recognizing the dialectic of person and place is central to an appreciation of the texture of life in Cape Town today.

Consider the first half of this dialectic: the familiar proposition that people create places, that the structure of society is inevitably mirrored in the form of the city, although probably with a time lag because social relations can metamorphose more quickly than concrete and clay. In this commonsensical position it seems that social relations are the active component: spatial relations simply come to reflect passively the qualities already mapped out for them by social relations. (By "spatial relations" is meant the organizational concept that subsumes such oppositions as here/there, near/far, up/down, front/back, and left/right and in which a person is inevitably placed at the center of his or her world and cannot but accord that spatial center with affective qualities.)

If social is active and spatial is passive, then geographers—whose disciplinary focus is particularly concerned with spatial relations—are really rather unimportant. All they can do is describe the effects of forces that are the concern of other social scientists, and their contribution can be "little more than pedantic area delimitations, or the maps and diagrams to illustrate the data gathered by others" (Pahl, 1965, p. 87). As mere chorologists they concentrate on a dependent variable—spatial relations—that has frequently been "controlled out," ignored with ease, by theoreticians in the social sciences. Soja (1976, p. 1) among others, has complained that "studies of social stratification, for example, as well as those of class formation, are occasionally conducted as if human societies lived on the head of a pin rather than in differentiated and socially meaningful spatial systems." Soja was attacking the conventional view that there is little to inform social science in the study of the spatial variable per se. Pitirim Sorokin averred in *Sociocultural Causality, Space, Time* (1964) that spatial location derives from position in society rather than vice versa. *Space is merely the mirror of society.* If the intent is to influence people's behavior, then policy-makers should concentrate upon inducing looked-for changes via the structure of social relations. It is *there* that the independent, causative variable resides: "Plans and policies aimed at changing people's behavior cannot be

implemented through prescribing alterations in the physical community or by directives aimed at builders; they must be directed at
the national sources and agents which bring about the present behavior" (Gans, 1972, p. 40), or "Because problems appear in space, this
does not mean that solutions are to be found by spatial means. This I
would term 'The Spatial Fallacy' " (Marris, 1977).

There is a reason for quoting Gans and Marris, who were chosen
from a score of social commentators who have written more or less
the same thing. Both Gans and Marris are *not* adherents to the space-
as-mere-mirror point of view but are recognized for their understanding of the spatial dimension active in the molding of society. This
apparent contradiction leads us to the second half of the dialectic. Is
there any validity in attempting to reverse Sorokin's dictum ("Position
in society derives from spatial location")? *Can society be the mirror
of space?* Gans's work in the West End of Boston and Marris's work
in Lagos have both underscored the central importance of place to
low-income people, people who, when obligatorily moved by slum-
clearance schemes, found as a result that their place in society had
been changed, often against their wills. In Cape Town a similar
record stands.

In claiming that spatial relations can mold social relations, social
scientists must be careful not to overstate their case. Certain ethol-
ogists—for example, Lorenz (1966)—have tried to extend their
findings on animal territorial behavior to human territoriality. Montagu (1968) carefully reviewed and then discounted many such exten-
sions. However, the rejection of ethological determinism in human
group behavior does not mean the total rejection of the applicability
of the concept of territoriality[1] and the influence of spatial relations.
Wary of being accused of propounding spatial determinism, I can,
nevertheless, posit that space *does* have a certain power of its own
that acts, among other ways, through territoriality. Suttles (1972,
p. 17), marshaling evidence from the West Side of Chicago, has
written:

> Sociologists have persistently attempted to portray territorial groups as
> something else: as the result of ethnic clannishness, or of associational net-
> works, or of attempts to segregate income groups and the like . . .
> [rather than taking] territorial distinctions themselves as a basis for associ-
> ational distinctions.

In sum, human social relations may be *both* space forming *and*
space contingent.[2] From such a stance, the changing social geography of Cape Town can be observed.

Suppose that one accepted the idea that society can be shaped through the organization of space, that a physical planner can mold society. Suppose also that we are not considering the liberal, ameliorative, commonweal-directed values of planners such as Gans and Marris, but the attempts of a racial oligarchy to maintain its hegemony by as many means as possible—including spatial means. This goal, I would claim, is explicit in the attempt to manipulate space for more effective domination expressed in the Group Areas Act. Chapter 4 will investigate in detail the chilling subtlety of such manipulation, which has resulted in the apartheid city of South Africa today. The word "subtlety" is important, for nothing could be more misleading than to imagine that apartheid is simply irrational racism. A sadistic Hitler ordering the razing of Warsaw after the unsuccessful 1944 uprising of Slavic *untermensch* cannot be compared to a Dr. Verwoerd[3] coolly conceiving apartheid plans to keep Nonwhite *untermensch* in *their* subordinate station (except, of course, in the amount of human pain their actions caused). Heribert Adam wrote in *Modernizing Racial Domination* that

> the Apartheid system has been viewed as simply the most outdated relic of a dying colonialism, yet possibly it is one of the most advanced and effective patterns of rational, oligarchic domination. . . . This pragmatism . . . is oriented solely toward the purpose of the system: the smooth, frictionless, and tolerable domination over cheap labor and political dependents as a prerequisite for the privileges of the minority (Adam, 1971, pp. 16, 53).

The apartheid spatial planners could be attempting to influence the relationship between space and society in two ways. The spatial apartheid of the Group Areas Act could be an appreciation of the fact that, by the manipulation of space, society can itself be modified; *human social relations are space contingent.* This constitutes one way.

Considering the second way involves approaching the group areas conception from the other tack, returning to the viewpoint of space as mirror. In Cape Town the majority of the people who have been forced to leave their homes and go to new racially homogeneous residential areas are those who are by the government termed "(Cape) Coloured" persons. An investigation of their position in South African society over the past thirty or more years shows that in political, economic, and social spheres the people of "mixed blood" have lost their limited, second-class constitutional incorporation with the ruling Whites and that much of their erstwhile economic and social overlap with Whites has been eroded by laws made by Whites. Not coincidentally, at the same time Coloureds were being distanced in social relations, their place in spatial relations was changing, also: from limited overlap with White residential areas to distanced ghettoization. From this we could infer that space has been the passive reflection of social change or that *human social relations are also space forming.*

There is another element to consider: time. It has already been noted in passing that social organization and spatial organization get out of step, the former tending to run ahead of the latter. Thus, in inner-city Cape Town racially integrated working-class housing tracts no longer mirror the prevailing social reality as they did under British imperial rule until 1910. The Group Areas Act is expunging these tracts, attempting to bring social organization and spatial organization into congruence so that they may the better *reinforce* each other in maintaining the present pattern of White minority hegemony.

However, the complex dialectic of social structure and spatial structure can encompass elements of *contradiction* just as well as elements of reinforcement. Consider, then, this expunction of the interracial housing tracts whereby space is being overtly manipulated and Nonwhites (that is, Coloureds, Asians, and Black Africans) are being distanced from the now-White city centers for strategic reasons. At the moment of expulsion and resettlement, the White government has achieved its aim: a cowed and atomized mass of Nonwhites has been placed at a "safe"distance. Still, the situation is dynamic. With the passage of time the Nonwhites may of their ghettoized space create a solidarity, a territoriality, a powerful, self-supportive force in reaction to the distancing forced' upon them. Such a power, as Soweto has demonstrated, is a threat to the desired territorial omnipotence of the White government, so the most effective policy for the government has to be one of *continual* removal, one that does not permit the appearance of place-specific solidarity. Otherwise, the hand that endeavored to manipulate space may find it has used an uncontrollable tool. A contradiction can arise in time: society's rulers create an apartheid space, and space is used for domination; yet, subsequently, the dominated may begin to find in space an ally in challenging the domination.

From all these intertwining strands one is led to ask whether it is society or space that is being created. The answer is that it is both. This surely leads to another question: are society and space indeed separable, or are they not different facets of the same complex sociospatial (or spatiosocial) reality? This second alternative I take to be the case and would try to illustrate my contention by applying the phrase "knowing one's place" to the experience of the majority of Capetonians who are Coloured people. "Knowing one's place" implies more than an awareness of one's station in the social hierarchy of South Africa and more than just a knowledge of one's geographical situation within the varied physiography of the Cape Peninsula. Its witting ambiguity also implies that there is some pregnant meshing of these two meanings, and from this meshing can arise a third meaning. To "know one's place" can imply an appreciation of its possibilities, to know its potential creativity for social action. All these three meanings are inherent in a study of apartheid in Cape Town.

THE PEOPLE OF CAPE TOWN

The Power of Definition

The first interpretation of "knowing one's place" involved the Coloured people's awareness of their position in the structure of South African society. What has this position been, and who exactly *are* the Coloured people?

This last question is not, as it might seem at first, one that straightforwardly seeks after information. It brings us immediately to a fundamental aspect of the act of naming: "The nature or essence of an object does not reside mysteriously within the object itself but is dependent upon how it is defined by the namer. . . . Justification lies in the perspective, not in the things" (Strauss, 1959, p. 20).

This universally valid assertion is especially germane to the various terms employed in South Africa for the various population groups. The fact that I have chosen to use such terms as "Whites," "Coloureds," and "Black Africans" in my explication of the cleavages within the South African population immediately and inevitably propels my analysis in a different direction from that of another social geographer using the terms "bourgeoisie" and "proletariat." The power of definition is enormous and can have a dynamic of its own. This power of definition has in South Africa been held almost completely in the hands of the Whites, during this century at least, and it inescapably structures the world for both Nonwhites and Whites—in and on the latter's terms. The very use of the term "Nonwhite" and the well-known, somewhat sardonic South African aphorism "a Coloured is one who has failed to pass for White" both imply the positive value of Whiteness. In fact the "Coloured" people of "mixed blood" are defined by apartheid laws in a *doubly* negative manner as those who are both non-White and non-Black African. The wording of the Group Areas Act of 1950 (as amended in 1966) is an example.

2. (I) For the purposes of this Act, there shall be the following groups:

    (a) a white group . . . [whose diagnostic characteristics are then stated]

    (b) a native group . . . [whose diagnostic characteristics are then stated]

    (c) a coloured group, in which shall be included:

        (i) any person who is not a member of the white group or of the native group; and

        (ii) any woman, to whichever race, tribe, or class she may belong, between whom and a person who is, in terms of sub-paragraph (i), a member of the coloured group, there exists a marriage, or who cohabits with such a person;

        (iii) any white man between whom and a woman who in terms of sub-paragraph (i) is a member of the coloured group, there exists a marriage, or who cohabits with such a woman.

Understandably, "Coloured" people's reactions to this merely residual categorization of themselves are mostly less than enthusiastic. Yet, to claim that there is no such entity as "a Coloured person," as some "Coloured" intellectual leaders do, is not to dispose of the issue.

It is not only a question of other-definition, for there *is* some impalpable collectivity that partakes of "Colouredness," although such "Colouredness" does not appear to be definable, nor does it match perfectly those whom the government has legally classified as "Coloured." The dilemma remains because an awareness exists, among many of those with whom I talked, of "we Coloured people" or, more frequently, simply "us." The "we-ness" may well exist because almost since 1652, when the first White settlers came to South Africa, the Whites have considered "persons of colour" to be different from themselves. To be treated as "separate" for 300 years would presumably engender a measure of objective separateness in the nature of a self-fulfilling prophecy. Whether or not this "we-ness" is strong enough to impart any conscious solidarity to persons in the "Coloured" category, with both its remarkable range of ethnic origins and yet its overall cultural identity with the Whites, is most problematic.

Given that White policies impose a legal definition of a "Coloured" person, I am perhaps justified, endeavoring as I am to describe the present reality of Cape Town, in accepting the expository validity of the term "Coloured." By this I am admitting the terminological validity of "Coloureds" merely as an expediential category but *not* as the "nation in the making" to which South Africa's White government is sometimes pleased to refer. This may seem to us an overly nice distinction, but it is a matter of great sensitivity to the highly educated of those classified as "Coloured," many of whom refer to themselves as "so-called Coloured." "So-called Coloureds" is a term that hobbles the tongue. To employ it away from South Africa seems a conceit, although in Cape Town it seemed to me defensible. To have used "so-called Coloured" or to have put the word "Coloured" always in quotation marks in this study would have been an imposition upon the reader, and so such a style was not used, even though I might have wished to do so for ideological reasons.

Similarly, I use the term "Nonwhite," rather than "Black," to refer to all those who are not White in South Africa. Although I am aware of the negative "flipside" identity (as Afrikaner writer André Brink neatly called it) inherent in the White-fabricated term "Nonwhite," using the term "Black" might be confusing. A large part of this study deals with those "Blacks" who are called "Coloureds" by the government. Those whom the *government* terms "Blacks" are not *all* the "Nonwhites" in South Africa but are *only* those whom until 1978 the government termed "Bantu" (and before that "Natives") and whom I call "Black Africans." Thus, in government parlance, both "Blacks" and "Coloureds" are subsets of "Nonwhites." The differentiation made by law between Black Africans and Coloureds in South Africa renders their experience of apartheid dissimilar. Therefore, the terminological difference is real to them. For this reason, I differentiate between them and do not use the term "Black" in its broader sense to mean either or both of them. There is also the question of clarity. Although "Black" is preferable to "Nonwhite," "Nonwhite" is not ambiguous, whereas "Black" can be. As with "Coloured," I might have wished to put the word "Nonwhite" in quotation marks throughout this study to indicate my distaste for the term; but this would also have been an imposition upon the reader, and so it was not done. When, occasionally, the term "Black" *is* used by me in this study, it does mean all those who are not White; but it is only used where it does not impair clarity. Lest all this appear to be a digression, I must point out that we must be aware that to name is to attempt to control or, as James Baldwin (1963, p. 62) put it, "the power of the White world is threatened whenever a Black man refuses to accept the White world's definitions."

Definition and nomenclature in the South African situation include latent as well as overt meanings. Consider the oversensitivity that could prompt a strong reaction like mine in Cape Town over, of all things, a British publisher's blurb on the back of a cookbook: "Carrier has travelled, eaten, and cooked in every civilised country in the world." In North America an objection to the use of the word "civilized" would perhaps be considered an extreme and self-conscious reaction to the ethnocentrism of the Western world. In South Africa, however, "civilised" has a latent meaning: "White." The word "civilised" has been used as a bland and fraudulent euphemism for the legitimation of the Whites' appropriation of the power, prestige, and goods of the total society, as in, for example, the "Civilised Labour policy" of 1924 onwards, which reserved during a period of economic depression a specified proportion of jobs in various occupations for those who could attain "civilised" living standards; in meaning, and in practice, this requirement meant "for Whites only."

A similar word is "traditional," as frequently used in the phrase "our traditional South African way of life." "South African" here, of course, refers to *White* South African, and "traditional" refers to the superordination of White over Nonwhite. The use of "traditional," through its intimation of custom long abided by, is an attempt to validate by reference to history the right of Whites to superordination, be it the right to have Nonwhite servants or segregated restaurants or residential segregation. With regard to residential segregation, some White South African academics offer the apologia that the "fact is that the races in South Africa's urban areas have traditionally segregated themselves, and the Group Areas Act was adopted rather to consolidate the existing traditional pattern of racial separation, and to ensure that it be maintained in future, than to enforce something new" (Nel, 1962, p. 207), or that "the Group Areas Act cannot be considered as the instrument whereby this separateness was initiated. The pattern is traditional . . ." (W. J. Davies, 1971, p. 227). It is not necessarily the facts that are in question here—W. J. Davies's study of Port Elizabeth's racial geography is clear and well documented—but the artful imputation that there is really nothing disagreeable in the Group Areas Act because it is merely an expression of something accepted throughout South African history as normal and indeed desirable by all component population groups who ". . . traditionally segregated *themselves* . . ." Is this ghettoization by consensus?

The History of the "Coloured People"

The current population of South Africa (including the "independent" homelands) is over 27 million, of which 19.5 million are Black Africans, 4.4 million are Whites, 2.5 million are Coloureds, and 0.75 million are Asians (of which 99 percent are Indians and 1 percent are Chinese). Essentially, the Coloureds are the products of miscegenation among Whites (who established themselves in South Africa after 1652 and moved toward the interior from the Dutch fort of Cape Town), their slaves (who were imported mainly from Madagascar and the East Indies), and the autochthonous Khoisan peoples (otherwise known as Hottentots and Bushmen) who have been almost completely wiped out.[4] Through their slavery and subsequent dependence, the Coloureds involuntarily took on a culture that in nearly all respects is the same as that of White South Africans; an important exception is the Muslim religion of a subgroup of about 160,000 Cape Malays.

Among the most celebrated of the slaves who provided the Cape Malays with a prideful myth of origin were the political exiles from the Dutch East Indies. The leaders of resistance there were transported to the Cape and used as domestic slaves, and, because of their skills in cabinetmaking and building, their Dutch masters valued them highly as craftsmen. The Malay slaves brought with them their Islamic culture, and Islam apparently was accepted eagerly by slaves of other origins (Shell, 1975). Thus, "the term 'Malay' came in the Cape to denote a religious rather than an ethnic group" (Patterson, 1953, p. 17). Sheikh Joseph, one of the exiled Indonesian political leaders, was buried at Macassar (note the use of the East Indian place-name) 25 miles from Cape Town, and his grave became a shrine for the Cape Muslims.

The main ingredients in the "mix" that is the Coloured people today were these Madagascan, East African, Ceylonese, Bengali, and Malayo-Indonesian slaves, all taken from areas on the Dutch trade routes during the seventeenth and eighteenth centuries. Again, apart from the fact that one in seventeen Coloured people professes Islam, nearly all the cultural traits the Coloured people possess are of European origin, learned through the 176-year-long experience of slavery and thereafter through their subordination to Whites. Because of this history, in 1971 Adam Small, a Coloured playwright, could state in *A Brown Afrikaner Speaks*, "I mean everybody who is Afrikaner [formerly 'Boer'] in South Africa, and this means the Coloured there too." Similarly, the first Coloured political organization, formed on the diamond diggings at Kimberley in 1883, called itself the Afrikaner League (Coloured). E. J. Doman, a journalist classified as Coloured, informed us in 1975 (p. 138) that "a few years ago a committee set out to establish a Coloured cultural museum but had to abandon the project because it could not discover a single artefact which was specifically 'Coloured.' "

This last statement bears examination. Clearly artifacts that are specifically Khoikhoi or San could have been found, but they would not have been considered Coloured. When, then, did the term "Coloured" come into use? Patterson (1953) has claimed that it was after the emancipation of the slaves in 1834 that "Coloured" became a general term for ex-slaves, for formally free "apprenticed" Khoikhoi and San farmworkers, for "free Blacks" (Asiatic slaves who, having been adjudged guilty of some offense against Dutch rule in Asia, had been permitted to work off their sentences in the Cape and then go free there), and for various other groups, such as the Basters and the Griquas, products of frontier miscegenation between Boer and Khoikhoi.

After the emancipation of South Africa's slaves, as in the United States of America, only a very limited amount was done to discriminate positively in favor of the Coloureds once they were formally free. Coloureds were no longer slaves, but they remained servants. The Masters and Servants Ordinance of 1841 (the successors of which were only taken off the statute book in 1975), whereby criminal sanctions could be imposed when a servant broke his or her contract, was a piece of legislation that did not explicitly mention race, although it applied mainly to Coloureds. When a degree of self-government was conferred upon the Cape Colony in 1853, the constitution established the parliamentary franchise based on age (over twenty-one), sex (male), and property ownership or income to Whites, Coloureds, and Black Africans indifferently. There was no impediment to a Coloured man sitting in the Cape Parliament, but none ever did, for the qualified franchise naturally favored the Whites. When, however, the Coloureds had made some economic progress and had thereby increased their proportion of voters and it seemed likely that the Muslim leader H. N. Effendi would be returned to Parliament in 1893, Cecil Rhodes, then the prime minister of the Cape Colony, tinkered with the electoral law in order to forestall this undesirable occurrence. In the Colonial Office in London a few years later, sentiments were not markedly different. In the minutes of a meeting on 22 May 1902, which reports the discussion over what terms of surrender to offer the Boers of the South African Republic (the Transvaal) and the Orange Free State, the assistant undersecretary proposed that "if the franchise is given to Nonwhites it will be so limited as to preserve the just predominance of the white race as in the Cape Colony" (Pakenham, 1979, p. 598).

In the educational field, similar attitudes are encountered among the colonial administrators. After emancipation, the Coloured children went to mission schools, and government schools were provided for Whites. Marais (1939, p. 270) claimed that "it is quite impossible to assess the damage suffered by the Coloured people through their children being confined to the inferior mission schools." Sir Langham Dale, then superintendent-general of education at the Cape, said in 1889:

The first duty of the Government . . . [is] . . . to see that the sons and daughters of the colonists . . . should have at least such education as their peers in Europe enjoy, with such local modifications as will fit them to maintain their unquestioned superiority and supremacy in this land. Traditions, religion, custom all demand this as essential to the stability of the Government and the material progress of this Colony and the neighbouring states.

Coloured persons also customarily received lower wages than Whites; in 1859 through 1861 in Cape Town the standard wage for White carpenters, masons, bricklayers, joiners, and mechanics was 7s6d a day; for Coloureds with the same skills, it was 6s0d a day. Simons and Simons (1969, p. 27) reported an illuminating incident that occurred in 1865.

White navvies employed on railway construction . . . refused to work alongside Coloured, and abandoned their jobs for this reason when set to work on the line at Tulbagh Kloof in the Western Cape. They "spoke about the Kloof in very strong navvy language" and said they were not going to mix with the Coloured, or teach them the way to work for the same rates of pay. Though the contractors offered higher wages to skilled men if they would stay and instruct the labourers, they refused and left for New Zealand.

During the 1890s the celebrated South African woman of letters and feminist Olive Schreiner (1923, p. 129) noted that, after emancipation sixty years earlier,

> . . . the slave has been set free, the Half-caste has multiplied, and now forms a more or less distinct section of society. . . . Nevertheless, socially his position remains much what it was. Without nationality, tradition, or racial ideals . . . robbed of racial self-respect. . . . The Englishman will swear to you on the word of an Englishman, and the Bantu on the word of the Bantu, but no Half-caste ever yet swore on the honour of a Half-caste. The world would break into cackling laughter did he do so: "The *honour* of a *Half-caste!* "

"God's Stepchildren": "Gambling, Drink and Lechery"

Olive Schreiner's jarring assertion[5] of the Coloureds' moral worthlessness—utterly typical of its time—leads directly to a topic parallel to "naming." The Whites have been the rulers of the Cape for a long time. There, their ideas have been the ruling ideas, their perceptions the ones upon which policies have been framed, their vision of Nonwhites the one with which Nonwhites have been forced to deal. How have Whites viewed Coloureds? Jan van Riebeeck, the first Dutch governor of the Cape (1652-1662) referred to the "proto-Coloured" Khoikhoi as "savages," as a "lazy stinking people." When the British took over the Cape in 1795 and again in 1806, an earnest paternal tone was added to such judgments. From such roots present-day White attitudes toward Coloureds have grown.

I would claim that a first element in any stereotype that whites may have of Coloureds revolves around the theme of white possession. The use of the Afrikaans phrase "ons bruinmense"—"*our brown people,*" a usage I would call "the imperial possessive"—is widespread among Whites in South Africa. In the liberal *Cape Times* newspaper of 21 May 1976, an article concerning "our traditional washerwomen, the Cape Malays," reads

> As one devotee of the wash-house[6] put it: "They've been part of my life for the past 25 years and are really a part of Africana of the city. I'll certainly never give up my washer-woman, unless she gives me up. It is not only a question of getting the washing done, but there is this relationship that enriches my life, and I like to think does so for her. I know my Fatima, her family, her children, her problems. And over our long association she knows everything about my household."

Many Whites only know Coloured people as domestic servants, as subordinate laborers, or as office messengers, the ones who make the tea for the workbreaks. In the middle of the Coloured rioting in Cape Town, on 15 September 1976, the *Cape Times* cartoonist Grogan pointedly drew a cartoon that shows a White boardroom conference at which a worried chairman is asking other concerned members of the board, "Gentlemen, the Prime Minister might not think the situation critical, but organised commerce is seriously concerned and I ask you, who on earth is going to make the tea?"!

White possession is even evident in the names of Coloured people in Cape Town today. There are many surnames such as Januarie and November. Slaveowners were not prepared to essay the pronunciation of, say, Madagascan names, which seemed to them outlandish. Thus, slave children were sometimes assigned the Afrikaans name for the month in which they were born and sometimes the day of the week on which they were born. Classical names were also given to some slave babies; Cupido—from Cupid—was common. Finally, in Afrikaans the suffix *-se* denotes possession, analogous to the apostrophe *s* in English. Hence, numerous Coloured names—for example, Carelse, Hendrikse, and Pieterse—reflected the possession of objects (the slave babies) that belonged to masters named Carel, Hendrik, and Pieter.

The second feature of the Coloured stereotype is the group's "bastardy." A well-known poem, "Cape Coloured Batman," by South African Guy Butler (1959), dwells on the mixed ancestry and casual mating that produced the subject of the poem: "bought for brandy, sold for doubloons." Other stanzas voice a common White myth that uses itinerant seamen as scapegoats—after all, without *some* White "blood" there would be no Coloureds. Why not "blame" passing *matelots* coming ashore at the Tavern of the Seas[7] and not the local White South Africans? O'Toole (1973, p. 47) has written that "bastardy is very nearly the only element of cultural folklore that the Coloured people have," and Olive Schreiner (1923, pp. 126-27) wrote:

> The Half-caste came into the world as the result of the most undifferentiated sex instinct. . . . To his father he was the broken wineglass left from last night's feast or as the remembrance of last year's sin—a thing one would rather forget—or at best, he was a useful tool. . . . He belonged to neither [White nor Black] —the very breast he had sucked was not of the same colour as himself. . . . The Half-caste alone of all created things is at war with his own individuality.

It would appear symbolic that the most feared gang of Coloured *skollies* (lower-class ruffians) in the then ill-famed Cape Flats public housing project of Hanover Park in 1974-1975 called themselves the "Mongrels" (*Cape Times*, 26 May 1975). A comparison that springs to mind is with the derogatory appellation "Sabines" for those of mixed Amerindian-White ancestry in southern Louisiana (presumably a reference to the ancient Romans' rape of the Sabine women).

Not only are Coloureds themselves supposedly "damned" by the great disgrace of having "a touch of the tar-brush" in their faces (again, phrases that occur in "Cape Coloured Batman"), but many Whites have felt that the very existence of the Coloured people is a disgrace to Whites, also (hence, the need to use the seamen as scapegoats). Olive Schreiner (1923, p. 141) again:

> He is here, our own; we have made him; we cannot wash our hands of him. When from under the beetling eyebrows in a dark face something of the White man's eye looks out at us, is not the curious shrinking and aversion we feel somewhat of a consciousness of a national disgrace and sin?

One reaction of Coloured people to such imputations is righteous anger. In August 1976 a Mr. Pop, an elected member of the Johannesburg Coloured Management Committee, evaluated the psychological effects on Coloured people of the Whites' concern for their own "purity" as reflected in the laws against interracial marriage and sexual relations:

> The so-called Coloured is the product of racial mixing as affirmed in the law that declares us Coloured. This self-same law, the White man's law, also declares that this sort of mixing is illegal and therefore abhorrent . . . the specific law outlawing the activity that created us is called the Immorality Act. This repugnant law makes us feel that we as Coloureds are immoral creations. I make bold to say that never in the history of mankind has a group been forced to live under such legislated humiliation.

Another reaction to such imputations is to mock them; humor is one way to deal with pain. Coloured humor is also a subtle form of protest in a situation in which more overt protest would be met with White *kragdadigheid* (crushing, uncompromising power).

The third fundamental characteristic in the Whites' image of the Coloureds is drunkenness, which maybe goes back to the alacrity with which some Khoikhoi traded livestock for Dutch brandy and which undoubtedly has a basis in the tot system. In the tot system, Coloured farm laborers are in part paid in wine, as a sort of "fringe benefit." The system makes sure that the workers are kept partially drunk and therefore more tractable with swigs of wine taken through-out the working day. Astonishingly, this degrading system is still practiced openly today by some White farmers around Cape Town.

The White stereotype has been internalized by many Coloureds. Dickie-Clark (1966) found that the most common negative trait that Coloureds felt themselves to have (28 percent of his sample) was drinking too much. An ex-Mowbrayite I interviewed (one of the few who was not "respectable" and had been in and out of prison) said in August 1975: "There've been two things that are the downfall of the Coloured people: too much drink and too little education." I received the lowest number of responses and the most evasive ones of any to the 130-plus questions in my questionnaire on the question "Where do/did you go for a drink?" Van den Berghe's research into racial stereotyping in Durban at the beginning of the 1960s found that the second most common Black African stereotype of Coloureds was that they were "alcoholic," with fifteen mentions; "colour conscious" received fifty-one mentions. Similarly, Indian stereotypes of Coloureds included nineteen "alcoholic," second only to twenty-seven "colour conscious." "Alcoholic" was the third most common stereotype Whites held of Coloureds, with nineteen mentions, after "gay, happy" with twenty-four and "musical" with twenty-eight.

This brings us to the fourth feature of the stereotype, that Coloureds are musical. As in the American South, in South Africa a quintessential task of Coloured servants was making music for the masters. Captain James Cook, on his third voyage (1776), reported that

> we left Stellenbosch next morning, and arrived at the house . . . [of]
> . . . Mr. Cloeder . . . [who] entertained us with the greatest hospitality.
> He received us with music, and a band also played while we were at dinner;
> which, considering the situation of the place, might be considered elegant.
> He showed us his winecellars, orchards, and vineyards.

Mr. Cloeder's band was probably composed of Coloured servants, since they played through dinner and did not sup with the farmer and his guests. The "musical" image received a boost from the visit to the Cape of an American "darky minstrel" troupe during Queen Victoria's Jubilee in 1887. The troupe's style, apparently, was copied and parodied by Coloureds, who lampblacked their faces, sported flashy silk costumes, straw hats, canes, and tailcoats, and strutted through the streets of District Six and Woodstock at the New Year Holiday, which was called the Coon Carnival.

It is also interesting that one of the few indubitably Coloured/

Malay cultural traits that might have found a place in the stillborn Coloured museum Doman mentioned is the association with the Confederate raider *Alabama*, which sailed into Table Bay during the American Civil War. The Cape folksong "Daar kom die Alibama" is perhaps the best-known symbol of the Coloured people in the Cape (other than District Six). Alan Paton (author of *Cry, the Beloved Country*) used this folksong as such a symbol at a presentation he gave in St. George's Cathedral, Cape Town, in July 1975.

The musical image is greatly resented by politically aware Coloureds, as Patterson noted during the 1949-to-1951 period and as I personally found in 1975. A Coloured high school's production of the musical *Irma La Douce* was disdained and avoided by some people with very close ties with the school because, unlike, say, a Shakespearean production, it was considered not only trivial but also supportive of the White stereotype. (Lest this be thought a trifling detail, it should be mentioned that the theater has often tweaked such sensitivities. A riot greeted the first performance at the Abbey Theatre in Dublin on 26 January 1907 of J. M. Synge's *The Playboy of the Western World*. The Dublin audience felt that Synge, himself an Irishman, was portraying a negative stereotype of the Irish people. When the play came to America, Irish Americans demonstrated against it for the same reason.)

With the musical image goes the image of the happy jester, which Stone (1972) aptly speculated is a subtle and ritualized form of protest made by those without power. Playing the jester is also a means whereby White superordinates can be manipulated without their being aware of it. André Brink (1975) captured this situation delightfully when he described scenes in which Coloured professional actors are stopped by a White traffic policeman when they are driving their battered Volkswagen out in the country.

A fifth theme of the stereotype revolves around the hopelessness and powerlessness of the Coloured people, who have been discounted as a serious threat to White hegemony for at least the last 100 years. As Doman (1975, p. 131) wrote, "In many ways their position in the evolution of postwar politics has been overlooked or understated." An English-language White newspaper (the Natal *Daily News*) editorialized after the riots in 1976: "There has been an unreal tendency to see the mixed-race people of the Cape as rather carefree, colourful, and amusing appendages of the White establishment. A kind of quaint Gamat[8] version of those faithful Amos 'n' Andy retainers beloved of the American South. . . ." The Coloureds have been those who have been ignored with impunity, the bystanders to White action.

Figure 1. "Knowing One's Place." "Shannon Greenway, 19, of Mowbray, finds the colourful fallen autumn leaves in Wynberg Park hard to resist as she runs through piles raked up by a municipal worker, Mr. Henry Phillips, of Retreat" (*Argus*, 7 May 1976).

The situation is strikingly symbolized by the Coloured workman's place in the Cape Town *Argus* newspaper photograph of May 1976 (Figure 1).

Another equally striking example of how Coloured people seem to have become the easily overlooked "invisible men" of South African life can be found in something as prosaic as the Cape Town street directories for 1936 and 1946 (Figure 2). These examples are from the inner Cape Town suburb of Mowbray, which is described in a case study in Chapters 7, 8, and 9. Note that those who were not named, but were designated as Coloured in 1936, were not even mentioned in 1946. In John Street, by 1946, there was apparently one household at number 7, that of Mrs. A. Harris, and number 12 was perhaps standing empty. Otherwise, John Street could have been an uninhabited wasteland. Of course, it was not; it was just that people of the twenty-five or more households who were living there were Coloured. There is perhaps a partial explanation for this situation in the fact that such directories probably were compiled from voters' rolls; Coloured people held limited parliamentary suffrage at that time. Nevertheless, the point remains: Whites were people and had personal names; Coloureds had only a label in 1936 and were nonexistent in 1946.

The arrogance with which Whites ignore nonexistent Coloureds and their aspirations—the Coloureds apparently powerless and thus discountable—has been demonstrated throughout South African history. A recent example in the political sphere concerns the announcement in August 1977 of an ill-defined tri-parliamentary constitutional plan providing for separate representation for Whites, Coloureds, and Indians. The plan totally excluded Black Africans. After considering the proposals, the leading formal voice of the Coloureds, the Labour party (which is limited to membership by Coloureds only, by law), rejected the proposals. The Indian Council rejected it at the beginning of November. However, the proposition made one thing clear: the Coloureds are, as ever, having their political dispensation impressed upon them by the Whites. P. W. Botha (who became prime minister in 1978) said in October 1977 that, "even if the Coloureds and Indians do not accept the new constitution, the government will go ahead and implement it until they do accept it."

The hapless and powerless image has easily permeated academic writing, also. Some educated Coloured people strongly resent the tone of social science investigators in South Africa, most of whom, whether from the republic or from abroad, seem to be White. "Colonialist-minded" social anthropology is naturally a favorite target; a

1936

JOHN STREET
(Mowbray).
Ward 10).—Map 12, F 12.

Left Side.

___Station Road.
2-8 Coloured.
___Durban Road.
10 Coloured.
12 Daniels, A. J., painter, "St. John's Cottage."
14 Davids, H., signwriter, "Majiedia." Mission Hall.
___Victoria Road.

Right Side.

___Station Road.
1-5 Coloured.
7 Harris, Mrs. A., dressmaker.
9-13 Coloured.
15 Jacobs, E.
17 Coloured.
19 Ishmaiel, Miss J.
21-23 Coloured.
___Durban Road.
25-31 Coloured.
Stable.
33 Siann, M.
___Victoria Road.

1936

AYRES STREET
(Rosebank).
(Ward 10).—Map 12, H 13.

Left Side.

___Liesbeek Road.
5 Harvey-Smith, Mrs. L., "Leyton Cottage."
7 Wright, W. L., "Dover Cottage."
9 Connolly, M., "Lassodie."
13 Müller, W.
15 Beattie, R.
17 Blanckenberg, H.
19 Harris, H., "Eureka."
21 Norris, Mrs. A.
___River Street.
23 Morton, C. P.
25-31 Coloured.
33 Whitehead, J. G.
35 Hendricks, K.
___Unnamed Road.

Right Side.

___Liesbeek Road.
Ayres Nurseries.
Mowbray Presbyterian Mission Hall.
4-8 Coloured.
10 Kariem, O., gen. dlr.
___River Street.
12-24 Coloured.
___Unnamed Road.

1946

JOHN STREET
(Mowbray).
(Ward 10).—Map 12, F 12.

Left Side.

___Station Road.
___Durban Road.
12 ___.
___Victoria Road.

Right Side.

___Station Road.
7 Harris, Mrs. A.
___Durban Road.
___Victoria Road.

1946

AYRES STREET
(Rosebank).
(Ward 10).—Map 12, H 13.

Left Side.

___Liesbeek Road.
5 Winch, H. F.
7 Wright, W. L.
___River Street.
23 Morton, C. P.
___Unnamed Road.

Right Side.

___Liesbeek Road.
Ayres Nurseries.
___River Street.
10 ___.
___Unnamed Road.

Figure 2. Cape Town Street Directory Listings for Mowbray, 1936 and 1946.

reading of the work of O'Toole—an American social anthropologist who worked in Cape Town ten years ago—gives some indication why this should be so. Even in his preface (1973, p. xi) he wrote: ". . . [Coloured] people quickly confided in me when word spread that I had 'come from Oxford' to find out about their problems." A Coloured friend "banned" under the Suppression of Communism Act mockingly accused me once of having "come to watch the zoo."

Such condescension is an easy trap for the "sympathetic" White investigator who is legally and *automatically* placed in a superior position, who observes the apparent impotence of Coloured people—until the Cape riots of 1976?—to do anything to ameliorate their own situation, and whose first impression is that any Coloured participation in politics has been mere reaction to White action. Adam calmly described reality (in 1971, p. 81) when he wrote:

> These superficial changes in race relations do not indicate a greater tolerance of the South African system, but rather the complete absence of alternatives for the ruled. The control of the state machinery is so absolute, and the certainty of this total dependence so universal, that no individual dares to claim what ought to be his rights. The state official, therefore, can afford to demonstrate a generous benevolence.

Their apparently quiescent impotence has meant that Coloureds have frequently been portrayed by White liberal historiographers as devastated victims, rather like American Blacks until the mid-1960s: "They could deal with the Negro as a symbol or a victim but had no sense of him as a man" (Baldwin, 1963, p. 54). The celebrated phrase "God's Stepchildren" used by Sarah Gertrude Millin in 1924 or Hilda Kuper's "marooned community" (1947) or Sheila Patterson's (1953) well-modulated voice, tend to see the Coloureds as a hard-done-by minority deserving of sympathy; this is the "devastated victim" paradigm. In such voices—not shared by the majority of the people of South Africa, the Black Africans, above whom apartheid laws slot the Coloureds—may perhaps be heard the echoes of White paternalism and patronage, voices seemingly convinced of their own magnanimity.

A sixth theme, which runs parallel to the first ("White possession"), is that of White sentimentalism for the "child-like" qualities of Coloureds: they are assumed to be ignorant, fecklessly irresponsible, and vulnerable. Such imputation of childlike qualities to subordinates by superordinates is common, whether the latter are Tutsi in Ruanda or Whites in the Deep South of the United States. In Cape Town I once gave an elderly Coloured churchwoman a ride to the home of the ailing Scots wife of a Mowbray minister. On hearing that

I had done this, the Scots woman gave me a stern but not unfriendly look and said, within the hearing of her Coloured guest and with no attempt at concealment, "You mustn't spoil them, you know. They'll only take advantage of you."

Another trait of immaturity unilaterally ascribed to Coloureds was mentioned in a sober London newspaper. The Theron Commission, established by the South African government to look into the present and future status of the Coloured people, made limited positive recommendations in its June 1976 report. After deliberation, the government announced in April 1977 that it found many of the commissions's recommendations unacceptable. The reaction of the Coloureds to this was characterized in the (London) *Daily Telegraph* (13 April 1977) as small-minded pique: "What Coloureds want is full White acceptance of them as social, economic, and political equals and, *like rejected lovers*, they are reacting to this latest rebuff with extreme bitterness" [my emphasis]. One might ask also whether indeed all Coloureds now desire "acceptance" from Whites.

A seventh part of the stereotype is the Coloureds' involvement in crime and violence. As is sometimes true of stereotypes, there may be an element of truth in this supposed characteristic of Coloured people. No matter how chary one is of official criminal statistics and no matter how many intervening variables there may be, the information provided by the minister of prisons on 16 June 1976 on the average number of prisoners per 100,000 of each population group during the year 1974-1975 should be noted: Asian, 74.82; White, 92.87; Black African, 397.50; Coloured, 785.89. The violent image of Coloured South Africans is given currency by the sensationalism of the White-owned and White-edited (until 1977) newspaper for Coloured Cape Town, the *Cape Herald*, "the paper that cares." Taking a copy at random, that of 7 September 1974, I found in the center of the front page the heading "Twelve die in weekend of violence." For each of the twelve the paper began a new paragraph in staccato style: "A man was stabbed to death in Elsie's River [or Hanover Park or Guguletu] on Saturday." The three men who died in Guguletu were presumably Black Africans—Guguletu being an African rental township—but the other nine were presumably Coloured people. Private citizens of both population groups are not allowed to carry firearms; hence, death by stabbing is commonplace.

Such journalism is resented by educated Coloureds. A letter one such friend wrote to me in October 1976 mentioned with cynicism "the *Herald* (School teacher raped by six youths typical headlines)." Parallels with the United States can be perceived, for as Ley (1974, p. 33) noted:

the White press tends to be preoccupied with what is dysfunctional in the inner city; in the words of a New York Times correspondent, "I agree . . . we tend to cover Harlem as a police beat." And again, "The press has played up Watts, so as to isolate it from the black community as a whole. But Watts is only some 30,000 of the 250,000 black people in south Los Angeles."

Similarly, White Capetonians' ideas of the enormous and extremely varied Coloured residential areas of the metropolis are usually based on their inexact memories of what they perceived the "slum" of District Six to have been like (see Chapter 6) and their negative image of the Cape Flats townships (the newer council rental projects on the city's sand-dune periphery to which most working-class Coloured people were removed by the Group Areas Act). Of the total population of around 600,000 in all the Coloured residental areas, the name "Bonteheuwel" (population around 45,000) epitomizes for many Whites the perceived nature of Cape Flats life: violent, unknown, and to be avoided. An educated young Jewish woman from Sea Point, Cape Town, was astonished to hear that I was pursuing research on the Cape Flats: "Ooh, how fascinating! And you go out there *at night*?!" I might as well have been an anthropologist visiting the pygmies of the Ituri Forest, so exotic to her seemed the fauna of this terra incognita less than 15 kilometers from her home.

Such images of the Cape Flats public housing townships may be shared by "respectable" middle-class Coloured people, also: "I don't go out to those quarters like Bonteheuwel,"[9] a woman living in the lower Wynberg Coloured home-ownership area of Cape Town said to me, "It's rough out there." Such images held *among* the Coloured people—as opposed to the White images of the Coloured people outlined here—will be discussed in detail in Chapter 9.

The last of the components of the Whites' image of the Coloured people is their sexual profligacy. I suspect that this image was gained from two complementary sources, both of them based on impressions of the exotic and the unknown. First, middle-class and upperclass persons—those who form and control most of the image creation in the society through their greater activity in scholarly and popular writing and through their access to the communications media—have often experienced the nagging suspicion that they might in their "refinement" be missing out on some rambunctious, earthy, or even sensuous qualities of *real* life, which the "red-blooded" working classes enjoy unashamedly. If to the unknown (life for the working classes) is added another exotic ingredient (a different, darker skin color), we might find the phenomenon Ralph Ellison portrayed in Harlem during the interwar years: well-to-do whites coming to the colored sections of town of an evening to "let their hair down." These two ingredients have been present in Cape Town, also; working-class, Coloured District Six was known as a nighttime resort for White males. In Coloured Mowbray, too, a number of the people I interviewed let it be known that there had been a house of ill repute in the Valley. (See Chapter 7.) Also, in the Malay Camp area of Coloured Mowbray, there was (according to an unassailably reliable White source) such a "high-class" house to which members of Parliament came to take their pleasure with Coloured and Malay girls. Olive Schreiner (1923, pp. 124-25, 130) wrote:

> It is always asserted that he [the "Half-caste"] possesses the vice of both parent races and the virtues of neither;[10] that he is born especially with a tendency to be a liar, cowardly, licentious, and without self-respect. . . . Three-fourths of the prostitutes who fill our brothels and lock-hospitals are "coloured," or Half-caste; only the remaining fourth are of pure breed [that is, Black Africans] (except in Johannesburg). In the smaller criminal cases tried in our Magistrates' Courts, the "coloured man" figures out of all proportion to the pure-blooded Europeans, Bantus, or Malays. . . . [However, in order to explain this there is no] necessity of appealing to a theory of inborn depravity . . . but rather to social conditions. . . . But one is undoubtedly justified in stating that, generally speaking, the Half-caste is less sexually self-respecting than the white woman, or even than the black woman is till she has been totally severed from her own social surroundings and therefore practically reduced to much the same condition as the Half-caste.

I am reminded of the Brazilian saying "a white woman for marriage, a black woman for work, a mulatto for bed."

In Cape Town only rarely do the ongoing White male/Coloured female commercial liaisons become public. One instructive instance occurred in 1975 and 1976. A certain Mr. McKey was charged (*Argus*, 15 January 1976) with keeping a brothel, in that he used his house for lewd and indecent purposes, and with attempting to obstruct the course of justice. Describing himself as an entrepreneur, he explained how it came to be that the parties attended by "professional people with influence—farmers and businessmen—and on two occasions [his] father" took place. "I wanted to put on something that another impresario had not thought of—a cabaret show with various acts *and a Cape Coloured flavour* [my emphasis]. . . . I told them [the girls] it would mean stripping in some acts. . . . I decided to put on a show in the lounge of my Tokai[11] home. I in-

vited 23 men—payment was an impromptu thing—and introduced
the show as Arthur's Afro-Asian Cabaret. After the show there was
dancing and the girls mixed with the guests." To this the public pro-
secutor commented drily that "it is the first time I have heard that
nudity is an element of Cape Coloured life." The accused was subsequently found guilty.

THE INSTITUTION OF APARTHEID

I have attempted to convey some sense of the context, some sense of
the place of Coloureds in Cape Town, some sense of what the texture
of their lives has been. Any Afro-American reading about the experience of the ex-slave Coloureds probably would find a great deal that
parallels the Black experience in the United States. He or she would
have found even more thirty years ago in Cape Town. One most
evident difference today between life for Coloureds in Cape Town
and for Blacks in, say, Philadelphia is the difference between de jure
and de facto segregation. Yet, until 1948 de jure segregation in Cape
Town was limited, and the socioeconomic-cum-racial gradients of
the city's residential pattern were in the broadest sense similar to
those in the cities of the northern United States. It has been since the
imposition of the watertight segregative apartheid laws from 1948
that there has been a marked divergence in city morphology between
the Cape and the United States.

PART II
PLACE

CHAPTER TWO

Cape Town before Apartheid:
Urbanization and Urban Ecology

A fourth-rate provincial town full of the most awful cads.

> O. Walrond,
> Private secretary to Sir Alfred Milner
> (lieutenant-governor of Cape Colony),
> 25 June 1897

In the Capetonian's mind poverty is associated with "Coloured blood" . . . [and with] a swarthy skin.

> Graham Watson,
> *Passing for White: A Study of Racial Assimilation*
> *in a South African School,* 1970

DE FACTO SEGREGATION IN CAPE TOWN

When it was founded in 1652, De Kaap was not meant to become a city at all. By 1652, more than 160 years had passed since the first European sailors en route to the Indies rounded the Cape of Good Hope. Table Bay had become known as a safe anchorage just 50 kilometers north of the often wild seas of the Cape, where fresh water could be found, but where the local inhabitants might not always be welcoming. (In 1510 the viceroy of Portuguese India and fifty-seven compatriots were killed in a clash with Khoikhoi tribesmen on the beach of Table Bay, the site of the future city.)

By the seventeenth century, the Netherlands had supplanted Portugal as the predominant European maritime power trading with the Indies. The average journey from the Netherlands to the Indies took six months, and the losses from scurvy among the seamen were heavy. Supplies of fresh fruit, meat, vegetables, and water could have prevented such losses.

Eventually, the directors of the Dutch East India Company sent out a small expedition under Jan van Riebeeck, which arrived at the Cape on 6 April 1652 to set up a provisioning station at the halfway point in the long journey—Table Bay. A fort was built as a defense against the Khoikhoi, and a vegetable garden was planted. Through barter with the Khoikhoi—whom the Dutch called "Hottentots," expressing their incomprehension of the Khoikhoi's click language, which they thought resembled a stutter—sheep and cattle were to be obtained. Apparently, there was no intention of establishing a permanent settlement. The orientation of the fort was wholly toward the outside world: toward supplying passing ships and providing medical help for the ships' crews.

Bartering proved to be an uncertain method of getting fresh meat, and so, after five years, to ensure a reliable supply of foodstuffs, a few Dutchmen were permitted to become "freeburgher" farmers on the lower slopes of Table Mountain immediately adjacent to the fort. The first slaves were imported during the following year, 1658, to work on the farms. The small streams of the Salt and Liesbeek rivers were established as the "permanent" boundary between Khoikhoi and company domains. However, once this acquisition of Khoikhoi land by White slaveowning farmers had begun, it proved impossible to check, despite directives from the administrators at the fort. The White farmers' firepower was more than a match for the Khoikhoi spears or San (Bushman) arrows. So too were the diseases the Whites carried; a smallpox epidemic in 1713 decimated the Khoikhoi. Hence, the White frontier expanded. As it did so, Cape Town grew falteringly to be an administrative and marketing center for a growing agricultural hinterland of, as it turned out, rather unimpressive wealth. By the end of Dutch East India Company control in 1795, Cape Town had achieved only moderate size, with about 1,200 houses. These houses had slave quarters in their yards, as did the nearby farms. By the time of the second British occupation of the Cape in 1806, there were more slaves than White settlers in the colony. There was also a small group of Free Blacks in the city. Of Black Africans, who had been encountered by settlers since the mid-eighteenth century at the eastern frontier of the Cape, some 750 kilometers distant, there was but a handful.

After the emancipation of the slaves in 1834, ex-slaves established humble dwellings on the fringes of Cape Town—for example, in Kanaaldorp[1] and in Schotsche's Kloof[2] —and next to the farms where they continued to labor, including those by the village of Drie-koppen, later renamed Mowbray. In the slow-paced style of colonial

Cape Town, the ex-slaves "found their own level"[3] of indigence, and an officially color-blind administration tolerated their poverty without disquiet. Coloured slaves had become servants; they had been involuntarily acculturated to "Western civilization" through 176 years of slavery; and they appeared to be subservient people whom the Whites "have never feared . . . , accepting them as the docile, non-competitive counterparts of themselves" (Meer, 1976, p. 19). Indeed, to the White rulers on the Cape during this period, "all [that] the Coloured people seemed to represent . . . [was] . . . the mere question of the poor" (Marais, 1939, p. 256). There were so few of the potentially outnumbering and culturally foreign Black Africans in Cape Town that the Whites felt confident enough to manifest a certain bounded liberality toward those who were not White, and the British administration espoused equality before the law. It did not by any direct legislation restrict Nonwhites to ghettos, for it was not necessary. Cape Town was a small city, its population only 27,000. In 1859 there were just fifty-six brickyards, lime kilns, foundries, breweries, corn and snuff mills, soapworks, candleworks, fish-curing houses, and printing works in the whole area.

Over the next few years, the first railways were constructed, bringing with them a potential for revolutionizing land transportation in the Cape, which until then had had only very poor roads that made bringing produce to Cape Town very onerous. A more important factor than railways facilitating agricultural development, however, was soon to jerk Cape Town out of its provincial torpor and into the mainstream of British imperial concern: the mineral finds. With the discovery of the diamond- (1867) and goldfields (1886), the city became the point of entry for the interior. The Cape Town docks were constructed in 1870. As the Cape main line pushed inland, Cape Town's Salt River railway workshops became the largest in South Africa. The struggle for control of the goldfields brought further economic buoyancy to Cape Town at the time of the Anglo-Boer War. The population rose from 33,239 in 1875 to 77,668 in 1904 and on to 168,257 in 1911. Rapid capitalist industrialization took root.

Especially since the mineral discoveries of the late 1800's the ownership of the means of production has remained largely in private hands, and . . . an exploitative opportunity-seeking style, assisted by government, has dominated the approach of private enterprise to economic development in South Africa. In turn, urban development as it affects whites has been largely subject to no more than the usual health, amenity, and town planning controls . . . displaying a natural tendency to do nothing

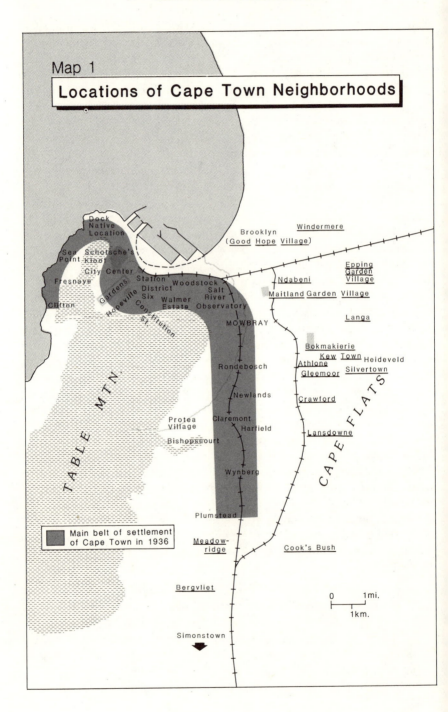

Map 1

Locations of Cape Town Neighborhoods

Dock
Native
Location

Brooklyn
(Good Hope Village)

Windermere

Sea
Point
Schotsche's
Kloof

Epping
Garden
Village

City Center

Fresnaye

Station

Gardens

Hopeville

Constitution St.

Woodstock
District
Six   Walmer
Estate   Salt
River
Observatory

Ndabeni

Maitland Garden Village

Clifton

MOWBRAY

Langa

Bokmakierie
Kew Town
Athlone   Heideveld
Gleemoor   Silvertown

Rondebosch

Newlands

Crawford

Protea
Village   Claremont
Harfield

Bishopscourt

Lansdowne

Wynberg

TABLE MTN.

CAPE FLATS

Plumstead

Main belt of settlement
of Cape Town in 1936

Meadow-
ridge

Cook's Bush

Bergvliet

0   1mi.

1km.

Simonstown

until undesirable dysfunctions are seen to demand corrective action (Fair and R. J. Davies, 1976, p. 60).

In Cape Town such unconstrained urban growth did not apply merely to the White section of the population, for there was almost no legislated racial segregation here, as there was in the Transvaal and the Orange Free State. Plots that were desirable by virtue of their amenity and aspect in Cape Town were sold to the highest bidders; persons of lesser means obtained what was not wanted by the others. After emancipation:

> those of the Coloured who could pay for it purchased housing accommodation in the ordinary way. Though no Municipality in the Cape had (or has) the power to compulsorily segregate its Coloured from its European inhabitants, the Coloured People quite naturally tended to live together in the poorer quarters of the towns. Some of them, however, live interspersed with the Europeans (Marais, 1939, p. 257).

However, there were no regulations inhibiting the inclusion of restrictive covenants on properties to ensure their sale to Whites only. There also can be no doubt that various informal ploys were also used, such as not publicly advertising a property for sale lest a Nonwhite attempt to purchase it.

Still, few Nonwhites would even have been in the market, since most were too poor to purchase property. Most Nonwhites lived in high-density working-class housing close to the industrial areas developing along the docks-Observatory rail axis. (See Map 1 for these and all subsequent Cape Town localities mentioned in the text.) The older working-class tracts were multiracial; there, the socioeconomic statuses of Whites, Coloureds, Indians, a few Chinese, and even sometimes Black Africans were similar. On such streets White alternated with Nonwhite (predominantly Coloured) in haphazard fashion, and it was not a question of spatial microsegregative sorting, for example, with one end of a street being all-White. This kind of mixing could with reason be termed *integration,* the first of three types of residential patterns in preapartheid Cape Town.

RESIDENTIAL PATTERNS
IN PREAPARTHEID CAPE TOWN

Integration

Residential integration in South Africa was not peculiar to Cape Town, but it was most extensive there: 37 percent of the residential area of the city in 1936 was "mixed."[4] Other South African cities —Johannesburg, Durban, Port Elizabeth, and East London—also had their "mixed" zones before apartheid, although these zones tended to be more obvious exceptions to a general pattern of racial segregation. Thus, in this matter the difference between Cape Town and the other cities was more one of degree than of kind.

One of the interesting symmetries of social and spatial structure in preapartheid Cape Town is that in this city, to a far greater extent than in any other in South Africa, there was and is a continuum of pigmentation or "race," like Brazil's, with no unambiguous break between White and Black. This phenotypic continuum was also paralleled, in this city to a far greater extent than in any other in South Africa, by a continuum, or a gradient, of space (that is, extensive areas of residential mixing among Capetonians with slightly different shades of skin color and appearance). Even more striking is the fact that, when some of the residential areas gradually changed their racial character, certain of the inhabitants "changed," too: *one is one's address.* When Mowbray, for example, became "White space only" in the mid-1960s, so did a number of its inhabitants become Whites, shedding—at least legally—their previous, rather indeterminate status.

Another parallel can be pointed out. Recall that Marais (1939) prefaced his remark about the lack of de jure residential segregation in the Cape by the rider "those of the Coloured people who could pay for it. . . ." The implication is clear: the market mechanism was instrumental in bringing about a degree of de facto racial segregation. And, in general terms, allowing for the topographical peculiarities of Cape Town and Durban and for the evident difference in degree of residential mixing, the social geography of Cape Town was similar to that of Durban, where, prior to the institution of the Group Areas Act, "The distribution of Europeans varies with income, the concentration of high-income groups, like that of the European population as a whole, being related to the desirability of the residential area." And "To a large extent the present ecological distribution of the races is a distribution of income groups. Race differences and economic differences tend to coincide" (Kuper, Watts, and R. J. Davies, 1958, pp. 136 and 213). Can we extend this "tendency to coincide" in Durban to the assertion that in Cape Town, with its Brazil-like phenotypic continuum, the most dark have been the most poor and the most light, the most rich?

Certainly the Black Africans in Cape Town (202 enumerated in 1875, 1,581 in 1911, 8,893 in 1921) have usually been the least wealthy, emigrating from the distant eastern Cape without urban skills. Without urban skills, many of the Coloureds also emigrated from the countryside, but at least they had a Europeanized culture and their now native Afrikaans language, which gave them some handle on survival in town. Also, of course, many of the Coloureds (and Malays) in Cape Town were of the artisan class, descended from skilled house slaves. Thus, Coloureds, with lighter complexions than Black Africans, in general have tended to hold a higher socioeconomic position than the Black Africans. "Even among the poorest coloured people one may hear remarks implying their superiority over the 'kaffirs' [pejorative name for Black Africans]. The common nickname given to dark children 'kaffertjie' is primarily a reference to the colour and hair texture of the child so named, but is not felt to be complimentary" (Whisson, 1971, p. 65).

Thus, *within* the Coloured group a darker skin has usually been associated with lower socioeconomic status. Unterhalter (1975), for example, found there to be a higher proportion of darker skinned Coloureds living in the public housing rental section of the Coloureds' Riverlea zone of Johannesburg and suspected that some of these Coloured persons were in fact "passed" Black Africans. Detailed examples of such passing in Cape Town are documented by Wilson and Mafeje (1963). Conversely, lighter, or fairer, skin among Coloureds has usually been associated with higher economic status: "Entry into the [Coloured] elite is eased considerably by the possession of a fair complexion and European features" (Watson, 1970, p. 17). Also, Unterhalter (1975) found that the lighter skinned residents of Riverlea were those living in the home-ownership zone, that is, the zone of the highest socioeconomic status. The lightest skinned Coloureds have frequently passed for White; both Dickie-Clark (1966) and Unterhalter (1975) found that their most common reason for so doing was gaining better economic opportunities. With the important exception of the "poor Whites" during the period between the two world wars, Whites have always been close to, or at the top of, the socioeconomic continuum in South African cities, and most have lived in the desirable zones as contemporaneously defined. In toto, then, race differences and economic differences *have* seemed to coincide.

Yet, especially since in Cape Town's case we are dealing with continua—of pigment, of economic status, and of space—we can anticipate that not *all* Whites lived in the most desirable residential zones: hence, the extensive integrated zones of Cape Town. The appropriateness of designating these zones as integrated is attested to by the fieldwork of Scott (1955) from the early 1950s. Given the overlapping socioeconomic levels of many Whites and Coloureds in much of the older working-class housing zone from the city center to Observatory, it is clear that the phenotypic continuum enabled some Coloured people to pass into the White group. Various neighborhoods such as Hopeville (Gardens),[5] lower Woodstock, a portion of Salt River, and the northern end of Observatory were enumerated by the government census of 1951 as having a predominance of Whites. Yet, Scott and his house-to-house surveyors, who were mostly Coloured teachers and postmen (who presumably possessed an intimate knowledge of many of the households on their beat), found just a few months after the census that Coloureds predominated in these same areas. A good number of persons, then, were apparently passing for White, at least in the census returns. Watson (1970) investigated this phenomenon in detail in Observatory during the 1960s. And Whisson noted the *gradients*—as opposed to discrete categorizations—of the space of these older areas: "Until the Group Areas Act . . . the class/colour continua in the inner city area tended to rise on two axes—altitude (the higher one lived the better) and distance from Cape Town station (the further the better)."[6]

Although the Group Areas Act was passed in 1950, it was not until the mid-1960s that it was actually *enforced* in the areas mentioned. Indeed, in some areas—for example, Salt River—it is only now about to be implemented (January 1980).

Throughout these older tracts the architecture of two- and three-story gabled tenements and bungalows with verandas and roofs of corrugated metal sheeting bears a striking and not coincidental resemblance to that of British India. The Cape was an important way station on the imperial route to India (especially before the construction of the Suez Canal); British administrators and soldiers from India frequently took furloughs at the Cape; and, as King (1976) noted, the forms of housing in colonial urban India, especially the bungalow,[7] were diffused to many parts of the British Empire, from Malaya to Uganda to northern Nigeria, and to South Africa. A photograph of District Six's main artery, Hanover Street, taken about 1970, shows the Indian colonial architecture of the area (Figure 3). The impression of India in the photograph would be heightened if the concentration of Indian shops on Hanover Street could be shown, a concentration unrivaled elsewhere in greater Cape Town until the Indians were expelled by the Group Areas Act.

Architectural evidence of the Indian connection can also be found in other areas of the city. The rail line to Sea Point (no longer extant) facilitated the beginnings of higher-status residential development on

Figure 3. Hanover Street, District Six, circa 1970. All of this area is bulldozed rubble in 1980. (Photograph used by permission of Human and Rousseau, publishers, and Chris Jansen, photographer.)

the Atlantic coast, and in that area today there are buildings of an imperial British Indian flavor, as on High Level Road above Three Anchor Bay. In addition, there was high-status Anglo-Indian[8] Wynberg, with its military camp. Wynberg eventually became a commuter suburb, for, as a branch railway extended southward toward Simonstown along the eastern flanks of Table Mountain during the early 1860s, the more affluent found that they could work in Cape Town and live in agricultural villages such as Mowbray, Rondebosch, Newlands, and Claremont or even farther south in Wynberg itself. Consequently, Cape Town began to sprawl outward along the line of this branch railway to form the southern suburbs. This brings us directly to the second type of residential pattern, another kind of mixing: interdigitation, or pockets.

Interdigitation

With the development of affluent, White, residential suburban tracts, the zones of Coloured laborers' and servants' homes in the villages were enveloped, forming "Coloured pockets." In the majority of cases, the socioeconomic levels of most Whites and Coloureds were different. Therefore, when population density built up inside the impacted pockets owing to differential growth rates, there was less likelihood of any outward spatial expansion by Coloureds. They could not afford the higher-quality housing that surrounded them, and generally Whites were not prepared to move out. Population pressure continued to rise inside the pockets, whose borders with surrounding White space became increasingly well defined. Under these circumstances, White/Coloured indeterminacy and passing were much less in evidence. There was little racially ambiguous space; it became clear who were Whites and who, in their constrained space, were not. "In the old 'coloured villages' (Mowbray, Rondebosch, Newlands, Protea, etc.) I get the *impression* of less ambivalence as the whites were *generally* a social class ahead. Hence, the coloured villagers were socially compact."[9] Scott (1955, p. 151) wrote of the Coloured pockets of Newlands, where

> obsolescent[10] terrace housing . . . , built nearly a century ago for Irish immigrants employed in the local brewery, is now almost wholly inhabited by Coloureds. It is noteworthy, however, that this Coloured quarter, like most ethnic quarters, is compact and well defined.

The families (over 100 of them) who provided much of the data for the case study described in Chapters 7, 8, and 9 came from three adjacent pockets in Mowbray-Rosebank. Map 2 is a detailed representation of one of these pockets, the Valley, as it looked just before its erasure by the enforcement of the Group Areas Act during the mid-1960s. Members of thirty-nine households that had been located there were interviewed, and it is from the information they provided that this reconstruction was made. From the map, it can be seen that the amount of space available to each household was generally greater for Whites than for the crowded Coloureds; and further, it should be borne in mind that the average White household was smaller than the average Coloured household. It can also be seen that there is indeed a generally clear-cut White/Coloured border. As one young person from this area said, in words that sum up the nature of preapartheid relationships:

> If they had really meant equality with us we wouldn't have been on our particular little streets. There were not too many places where White and Black households alternated along the street as neighbours. And although our relationships with the White people seemed quite friendly, we were hardly in and out of each other's arms all the time.[11]

Segregation

Mixing was least likely, naturally, in those areas where richer Whites could afford to buy their segregation, the third type of resi-

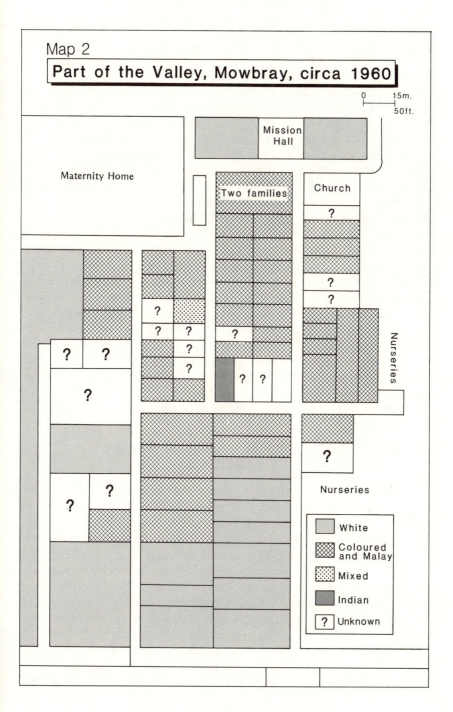

Map 2

Part of the Valley, Mowbray, circa 1960

0   15m.
⊢——⊣——⊣
50ft.

Mission Hall

Maternity Home

Two families

Church

?

?

?

?

?

?

?

?

?

?

?

?

?

?

?

?

?

?

?

Nurseries

?

Nurseries

| White |
| Coloured and Malay |
| Mixed |
| Indian |
| ? Unknown |

dential pattern in preapartheid Cape Town. These Whites firmly established residences in such suburbs as Fresnaye, Sea Point, Clifton, and Bishopscourt. The geographic factors involved were aloofness from industry and proximity to amenity, either to the Atlantic coast or (in Bishopscourt's case) to the grand views and semirural ambience available on the lower slopes of Table Mountain. There, the only black or brown faces were those of live-in domestic servants or gardeners.

In sum, the poorest neighborhoods, such as the insanitary and crowded working-class housing tracts of District Six, were markedly lacking White residents. The richest neighborhoods were wholly lacking in residents other than Whites (save retainers). Moderately affluent suburbs were usually almost wholly White, with perhaps some pockets of Coloured residents. The older neighborhoods of intermediate-to-lower status were mixed. Batson (1947), using 1936 census data and a 75/25 percent cut off point, found that 62 percent of the White Capetonians lived in European residential zones, 4 percent in non-European zones, and 32 percent in mixed zones; 51 percent of the non-Europeans lived in non-European residential zones, 11 percent in European zones, and 34 percent in mixed zones. (In addition, 2 percent of the Whites and 4 percent of the Blacks lived in what Batson called "nonresidential" zones of Cape Town in 1936.) Europeans and non-Europeans were virtually equal in number in Cape Town at that time, so it would seem that a third of all Capetonians in 1936 lived in mixed zones (as defined by Batson). Maps 3 and 4, based on Batson's work, show, respectively, the patterns of non-European and European settlement.

LEGISLATED SEGREGATION BEFORE APARTHEID

It might seem that after the emancipation of the slaves in 1834 White governments at the Cape were satisfied with allowing a more-or-less unhindered market system to produce a pattern of de facto residential segregation. The segregated pattern was not complete, however, because the threefold meshing of color, socioeconomic status, and space also manifested elements of overlapping and mixing, either by integration or interdigitation (pockets).

Still, the impression that such residential mixing was tolerated with equanimity by the White power structure in a *totally* laissez faire manner is misguided. Racially restricted covenants were, after all, not outlawed, and more important, the authorities had already—long before the word "apartheid" became current—imposed elements of active, de jure residential segregation. This flatly gives the lie to the

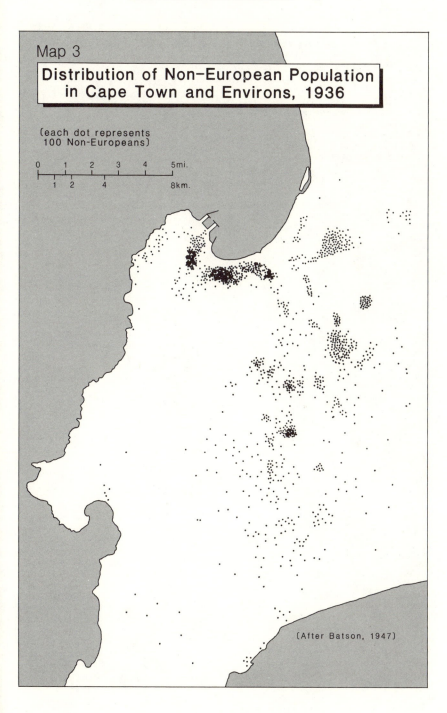

Map 3

Distribution of Non–European Population in Cape Town and Environs, 1936

(each dot represents
100 Non-Europeans)

(After Batson, 1947)

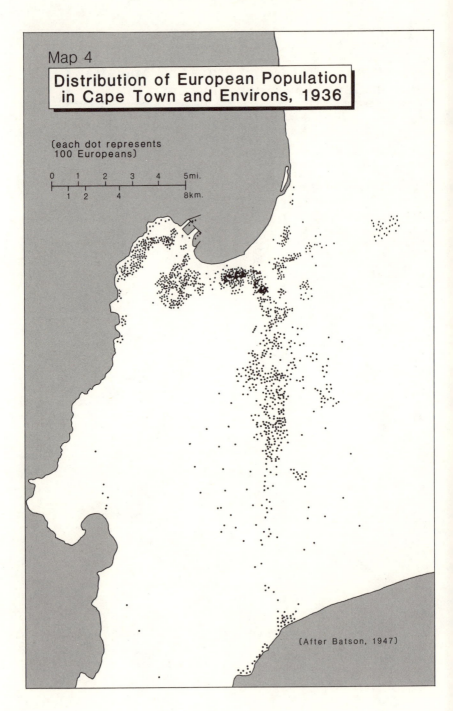

Map 4

Distribution of European Population in Cape Town and Environs, 1936

(each dot represents
100 Europeans)

0   1   2   3   4   5mi.

1   2   4   8km.

(After Batson, 1947)

statement made by Nel (1962)—a geographer-apologist for White
supremacy—that the "fact is that the races in South Africa's urban
areas have traditionally segregated themselves." Segregation is not
simply the working out of something "in the nature of things" that
just happens via the market mechanism, as if by an ordained (super-
naturally?) plan. Consider the fact that in Cape Town the *legal* enactment of residential segregation for Black Africans (then termed
"Natives") had already started in 1890.

It could be anticipated that, if a White power-holding minority
were to enact segregative laws for urban areas through a motive of
fear for its future security, it would first enact them against those
whom it perceived to be the greatest threat. These would be the
Black Africans—the *swart gevaar* (Black peril)—who are not only
those who greatly outnumber the Whites in the land, but are also
those who have seemed most culturally dissimilar and strange to the
Whites and whose material standards of living and of health have generally been the lowest in South African urban areas. And, thus, they
have been those whose social distance is greatest from the ruling
Whites.

Official colonial census figures are probably underestimates, but in
1865 274 Black Africans were enumerated in Cape Town proper,
with over 400 more in Papendorp (the future Woodstock), then on
the periphery of the city. "By 1881," reported Saunders (1978, p. 29),
"there was again a sizeable African population in Papendorp—*such
that Whites began to talk of the need to establish an official 'Kafir location' for it . . .*" [my emphasis]. It was in 1890 that, with Black
Africans being employed as laborers on Cape Town docks, the custom-
built Dock Native Location barracks began to provide accommodation in a segregated compound. Until then, most Black Africans had
been housed on their employers' premises or in rented rooms nearby.
The majority of Black Africans continued to live in this manner
throughout the city; by the end of the century, Saunders estimated,
some 10,000 Black Africans lived in greater Cape Town. When bubonic
plague broke out among them in 1902[12], a fearful public demanded
that they be segregated from the rest of Capetonians; thus, a "government reserve" was established at Ndabeni. In Port Elizabeth the same
sequence of events occurred that year: after the plague Black African
dwellings were burned and cleared and a new township was established
out at New Brighton. "Natives who were living under insanitary conditions in the slums of Cape Town were offered accommodation at a
low rental in Ndabeni" (Wilson and Mafeje, 1963, p. 3)—but some
5,000 to 6,000 remained in the city; they were not forced to move

out. The 1918 influenza epidemic[13] again drew attention to the slums, and in 1923 a model township for Black Africans was established at what was then a location distant from the city, Langa, on the sand dunes of Uitvlugt on the Cape Flats. During that same year, the Natives (Urban Areas) Act was passed, restricting Black Africans' entry into the cities of South Africa.

The law did not seem to have any watertight effect, however, despite amendments passed in 1930 and 1937, and the growth of the Black African population in greater Cape Town continued, especially during World War II. In 1921, 8,893 persons were (officially) enumerated; in 1936, 14,160; in 1946, 35,197. Yet, Langa's population in 1944-1945 was only 7,849. It is obvious that Black Africans still lived in the city, and in case histories of 19 persons who came to Cape Town during the 1925-1930 period[14] the following loci were mentioned as residences: Langa (8), Cape Town (central area)/District Six (7), Woodstock (2), Claremont (2), and Athlone, Salt River, Wynberg, Sea Point, and Lansdowne (1 each). (See Map 1.) In 1952 (as Wilson and Mafeje [1963] informed us) only one-third of the Black Africans in Cape Town were living in official "locations"; Scott (1955) considered the proportion for the same period to be even lower, under one-fifth. Black Africans in 1952 were scattered throughout the predominantly Coloured residential areas of the city and under conditions of extreme squalor in shantytown squatter camps on its periphery. The situation was similar in Port Elizabeth and in other areas. The intent to confine Black Africans to ghettos was evident, even though it had not been fully implemented because the surge of Black Africans to the urban areas during the World War II industrial spurt brought a demand for housing so enormous it could not be met quickly.

A sequence is clear. Each time Cape Town grew out and enveloped their previously distanced "locations," the Black Africans were moved. The location at the docks has been razed; so too has the next one established, Ndabeni. Then they were moved out to Langa, which today houses only a small proportion of the Black Africans in greater Cape Town. Today, most Black Africans live in the *presently* peripheral Nyanga and Guguletu townships, which have been established since the mid-1950s, and in peripheral shantytowns such as Crossroads. (See Chapter 10.) Recall the proposition made in the introduction in Chapter 1: the most effective plan for societal control by spatial manipulation in apartheid is that of *continual removal*. As an African National Congress leader expressed it in the 1950s, the experience of the Black African was "forever hamba," forever moved on.

The Black Africans represented a potential numerical and strategic threat, and so the Whites enacted laws in an attempt to contain them. Most of the Indians originally were brought to South Africa by the British as cheap indentured laborers for Natal's sugar plantations from 1860 onwards, but a good number of them subsequently became very successful shopkeepers. Hence, Indians were perceived by many Whites as an economic threat, and ordinances were enacted against them, too. For example, Indians were forbidden to settle in Bloemfontein or anywhere in the Orange Free State by an ordinance imposed in 1891, which is still in force. In 1885 the Transvaal government prohibited Asians from owning fixed property except in streets or areas that were especially allocated for their residence. These laws were passed by the Afrikaner republics before the Anglo-Boer War, but the British settlers in Natal—where by far the greatest majority of Indians lived and still live—were scarcely different. Nel's "traditionally segregated themselves" is once again false; Kuper, Watts, and R. J. Davies (1958, p. 158) wrote of pre-group areas Durban, Natal, that "economic factors and cultural affinity do not fully explain the segregation. In the last resort, it rested also on deliberate policy and indirect compulsion."[15]

For example, in 1922 an ordinance passed by the Durban City Council reserved certain areas of the city for Whites only. This restriction was aimed at the Indians, many of whom had already become highly adept traders. The term used by Durban Whites in reference to Indian residential expansion into formerly White areas was "penetration." Instituted at the White residents' insistence, a 1941 union government commission's investigation into such "penetration" found the main cause in, not surprisingly, the desire of the Indian community for good investments. If certain areas, such as Durban's alluvial flats, lost their attraction for White buyers, then Indians would be next in line to buy there. In Durban two years later, 1943, the "Pegging" Act was passed in order to maintain the status quo in property-ownership patterns; this legislation was followed in 1946 by the Asiatic Land Tenure and Indian Representation Act.

Before apartheid was instituted in 1948, then, de jure segregation containing Indians existed in three provinces of South Africa: the Orange Free State, the Transvaal, and Natal. In the fourth, the Cape, there was very little legislated segregation. The municipality of East London was, in 1895, empowered to segregate its Indian population, but in Cape Town there was no de jure segregation of Indians. With the number of Indians small in proportion to the total population of the city and with 94 percent of the Indians' residences attached to their shops, as Scott (1955, p. 155) found, the distribution of Indian shops appears to be influenced more by the standard of living in the areas served than by ethnic considerations. No less than 938 shops, or nearly 97%, were found in low grade[16] residential localities, but, only 824, or 85%, in non-European areas.

The shops also clustered in old (pre-1910) areas of the city. Thus, in Cape Town the threat the few Indians offered to the White property-owning power was limited, so laws against them were not deemed necessary.

COLOURED PENETRATION
AND INCREASED SEGREGATION

Fundamental to an understanding of past and present racial patterns in South African cities is an appreciation of numbers: the different population groups' varying numbers in the country in general and in the urban areas in particular. In Cape Town it is most pertinent to observe the differing growth of White and Coloured populations over the past 100 years or more, tabulated in Table 1.

Table 1
Cape Town Population Growth, by Race, 1865-1975

Year	White	Coloured and Asians	Black Africans	Total for Municipal Area
1865	15,118	13,065	274	28,457
1875	18,973	14,093	173	33,239
1891	25,393	25,235	623	51,251
1904	44,203	31,318	2,147	77,668
1911	86,239	80,449	1,569	168,257
1921	111,784	89,259	8,684	209,727
1930	134,680	121,670	est. 6,000	est. 262,350
1936	152,244	135,621	13,583	301,448
1946	180,805	171,767	31,258	383,830
1959	196,560	307,350	72,711	576,621
1975	253,570	488,470[a]	100,530	842,570

a. Includes 11,000 Asians (that is, Indians and Chinese).

It can be seen from Table 1 that Whites have outnumbered Nonwhites (predominantly Coloureds) in census returns at least since 1865. The Nonwhites' potential for faster population growth was being checked by their poverty and lack of sanitation, which resulted in high rates of infant mortality and susceptibility to tuberculosis and to epidemics (for example, the bubonic plague epidemic of 1902 and the influenza outbreak of 1918). But by 1938, according to Scott's 1955 estimate, Whites were outnumbered by Nonwhites in Cape Town. By 1948 Whites were outnumbered by Coloureds, that is, with Black Africans and Indians not included in the comparison. Despite a number of complicating municipal boundary changes, the overall situation is clear: from 1930 to the present day, Cape Town's White population has *doubled,* while the Coloured population has *quadrupled* through natural increase and rural-urban migration.

This rapid increase in population together with the inability of Coloureds—both through low income and through a measure of informal racial discrimination—to settle wherever they pleased, led to a buildup of population density in many Coloured residential areas. The primary settled area of Cape Town in 1937 skirted the mountain from Bantry Bay (southern Sea Point) via the city center and Observatory-Mowbray south to Plumstead (Map 1). Within this belt, Batson (1947, p. 410) found, "it is a general rule . . . that the higher Density Zones have a greater proportion of Non-Europeans than the lower Density Zones." For 1951 a similar relationship holds. The superposition of the tracts of over 100 persons per acre of residential land in 1936 (Map 5) upon Scott's map of "ethnic areas" for 1950-1952 (Map 6) shows that 98 percent of these tracts were classified by Scott as Nonwhite (that is, as Coloured, Malay, or Black African).

Note the small extent of the areas Batson showed as having at least 100 persons to the acre in 1936 (superimposed on Map 5 in white outline) compared with Scott's 1951 delineation. Even allowing for discrepancies resulting from the different methods used by the investigators, it should be appreciated that their source of raw data was the same—the official Union of South Africa census. Thus, the increase in population density during the fifteen years between 1936 and 1951 is striking, especially the rise to prominence of Langa, the wholly segregated Black African township. Coloured population densities rose during this period, too. What this meant in practical terms was graphically spelled out in 1950 by the housing supervisor of the municipality of Cape Town:

> Almost every house in the districts where the Coloured people live is packed tight. Children grow up and marry and in turn have children and are unable to find a place of their own. A family is turned out of an overcrowded house and finds shelter with friends for a few days—which grow into weeks, months, years. They sleep in living rooms, in kitchens, in passages, in garages . . . (*Cape Times*, 20 June 1950).

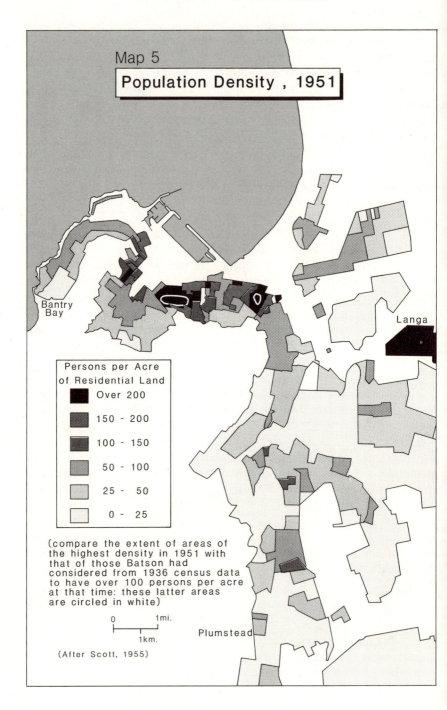

Map 5

Population Density , 1951

Bantry
Bay

Langa

Persons per Acre
of Residential Land

■ Over 200

150 - 200

100 - 150

50 - 100

25 - 50

0 - 25

(compare the extent of areas of
the highest density in 1951 with
that of those Batson had
considered from 1936 census data
to have over 100 persons per acre
at that time: these latter areas
are circled in white)

0   1mi.

1km.

Plumstead

(After Scott, 1955)

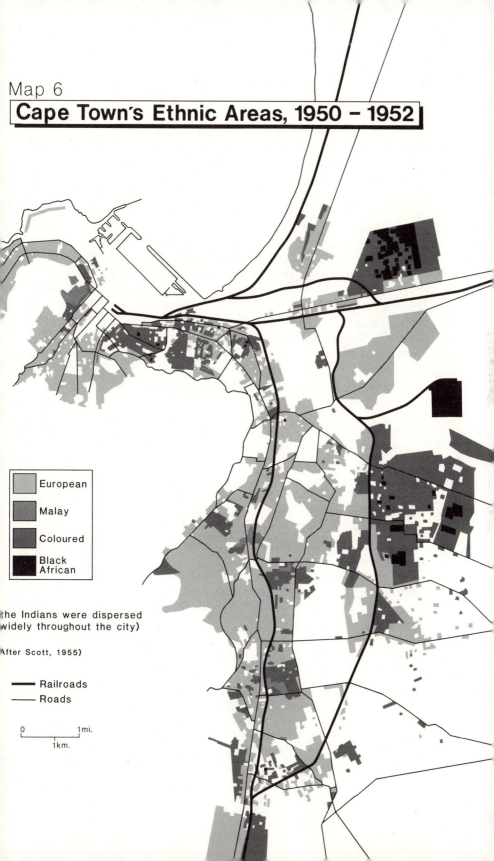

Map 6
Cape Town's Ethnic Areas, 1950 – 1952

European

Malay

Coloured

Black
African

(the Indians were dispersed
widely throughout the city)

(After Scott, 1955)

Railroads
Roads

0   1mi.
    1km.

The buildup of population pressure in the areas available to Coloureds had a number of effects. One was the alacrity with which expansion into proximate erstwhile White housing tracts occurred as *they* became available. That is, Whites were moving up the socio-economic ladder, aided in finding opportunities for jobs and apprenticeships by governmental intervention through its Civilised Labour policy, as Coloureds were hindered thereby. As the Whites moved up, many moved out. Crowded Nonwhites took their places in sort of "hand-me-down" spaces, as on Constitution Street (in upper District Six), in the Walmer Estate (upper Woodstock), in Salt River, and in Observatory. These areas are particularly in evidence in Map 7 as tracts where the intercensal decrease in White population was correlated with the increase in Nonwhite population. In Observatory, for instance, the White population fell by one-third from 1936 to 1960, while the Coloured population increased by almost half; during the same period, the Coloured portion of the total Observatory population rose from around 30 percent to 50 percent. Watson (1970, p. 23) noted that Observatory was attracting "better-class" Coloured residents (as his informants put it).[17] His informants also told him that the greatest single attraction of the district for Coloureds was probably that White and Coloured housing there were intermingled, thus facilitating Coloureds' passing for White. Scott (1955, p. 15) offered a description from Salt River (Map 8), "where decayed terraces, formerly occupied wholly by Europeans, have been invaded by small factories, neighbourhood shops, and Cape Coloureds [note the order of precedence] . . . . It would seem that as soon as Coloureds gain a foothold in a street, Europeans evacuate in the mass."

Whether this assertion can be substantiated by the map Scott offered as proof is a moot point. What Scott would have had to demonstrate would have been such maps showing the situations five years earlier and five years later and giving some indication of diachronic change. (I am reminded of Saul Alinsky's dictum that in America residential integration occurs during the period between the arrival of the first Black and the departure of the last White.) Neither can Scott, through the advancing of Map 8 as evidence, prove his point, nor can I disprove it through the map. Also observe Scott's use of the verb "invaded": as Whites moved out, Coloureds moved in; how should this be construed? Which causes which — or is it a chicken-and-egg problem? Scott seems to have decided that Coloured "invasion" *causes* White flight. If he had chosen to employ, say, the verb "supplant," no such implication would have been present. Scott's interpretation, like one commonly made by White Cape-

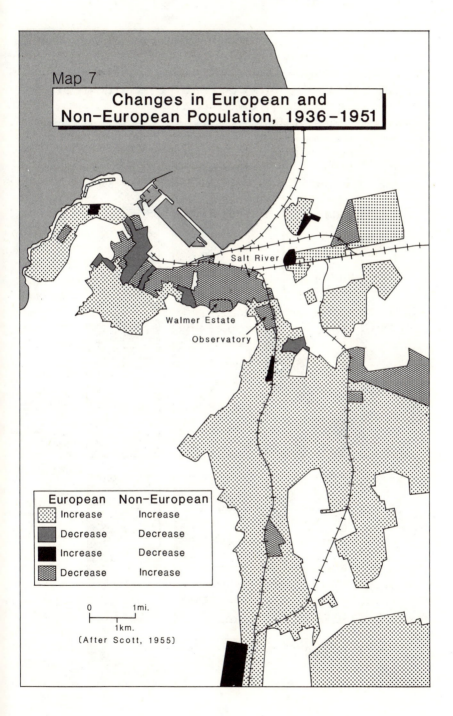

Map 7

Changes in European and Non-European Population, 1936–1951

Salt River

Walmer Estate

Observatory

European	Non-European
Increase	Increase
Decrease	Decrease
Increase	Decrease
Decrease	Increase

0   1mi.

1km.

(After Scott, 1955)

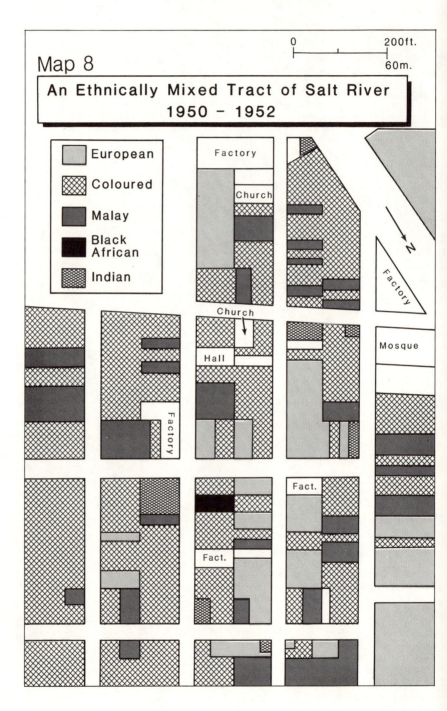

Map 8

An Ethnically Mixed Tract of Salt River
1950 – 1952

0   200ft.
                     60m.

European
Coloured
Malay
Black African
Indian

Factory
Church
Church
Hall
Factory
Factory
Mosque
Fact.
Fact.
Fact.
N

tonians at that time, was based on a belief in the threat posed by "invasion," "infiltration," and "penetration" by Nonwhites. Given the meaning of color for economic and social status, the motivating force underlying the fear of Nonwhite penetration into previously White residential areas is clearly the differential growths of the two populations. These White fears soon resulted in the manipulation of the space of Cape Town by the Group Areas Act, which was meant to ensure that they (the Whites) were not outnumbered within "their" cities and that the best locations remained theirs.

One other point concerning Cape Town prior to apartheid must be made: *residential segregation was increasing.* The ever-growing urban Coloured population had filled their older working-class tracts and pockets until they were bursting at the seams. Such penetration as occurred could not accommodate this population pressure, and areas of Coloured housing to jump surrounding White tracts. New Coloured housing grew beyond any intervening White areas, toward the Cape Flats, as at Athlone/Crawford. In this area Coloured people had been settling since 1900, clearing the Port Jackson scrub on the sand dunes in order to build their houses. These areas of settlement were already quite extensive by the 1936 census and were markedly "non-European" in residential character. (Compare Map 3 with Map 4.) Also, with their population growing unconstrained either by any surrounding White urban residential space or by any topographical barrier, their population densities were not great. Thus, they constituted the great exception to Batson's posited relationship between higher population densities and Nonwhite residential areas.

The "voluntary" expansion of the urban Nonwhite population into de facto segregated areas like Belgravia and Gleemoor in Athlone was complemented by "involuntary" segregation in the sense that municipal housing estates *for Coloureds only* were being established. Maitland Garden Village had been set up during the 1920s, and near Athlone a generation later came Bokmakierie, Silvertown, and the wide, windswept wastes of Kew Town (an unsuccessful attempt at transplanting the Welwyn Garden City-like avenued vistas then beloved of British town planners). We have seen that municipal housing for Black Africans (Ndabeni, Langa) had long been segregated. Good Hope Village in Brooklyn and Epping Garden Village, established by the Citizens' Housing League (a nonprofit organization), were for (poorer) Whites only. Also, numerous new private developments—as in Lansdowne, a very "exposed" salient of a White residential area vis-à-vis Nonwhite territory—continued to insert servitudes in the title deeds stipulating that the residences were to be inhabited exclusively by Whites.

Increasing segregation also arose from the manipulations of the Civilised Labour policy. Erstwhile poor Whites were, from the later 1920s onward, improving their socioeconomic status and buying segregation in newer all-White suburbs. The same legislation dampened the development of a Coloured middle class with the financial reserves needed to purchase property in more desirable areas. After World War II, Bergvliet and Meadowridge were rapidly developed as middle-income suburbs, but they were available to returning *White* servicemen only. Finally, at the bottom end of the scale, the city's peripheral squatter camps, such as Windermere and Cook's Bush, housed only negligible numbers of Whites, if any. In toto, then, Scott was quite correct when he referred to "the trend towards residential segregation that has been increasingly evident this century."

A glance at Map 1, where the places cataloged in the last paragraphs are underscored, indicates that they are *all* outside the main belt of 1936 settlement and therefore constitute the newer areas of the metropolis. The mixed areas, however, were predominantly in the older, main belt of settlement, especially in the docks-to-Observatory working-class tracts. As their populations fell (relative to the populations of the growing newer suburbs), it was clear that the metropolis *as a whole* was becoming more segregated, with both private and public sectors having a hand in the procedure.

Confirmation comes from Port Elizabeth, where W. J. Davies (1971) showed that White/Nonwhite residential segregation increased during the intercensal period between 1936 and 1951. This he demonstrated both by Lorenz-type segregation curves and by the provision of certain statistics. For example, enumeration districts having less than a 50 percent Nonwhite occupation housed 88.4 percent of the White population in 1936, 90.1 percent in 1946, and 92 percent in 1951. Similarly, in 1936, 54.1 percent of the city's Coloured population lived in enumeration districts that had less than a 50 percent Coloured occupation; by 1951, this proportion had fallen to 33.0 percent (from 54.1 percent). "This quantitative evidence," stated Davies (1971, p. 103) "clearly indicates the increasing prevalence of racial residential segregation in Port Elizabeth *before* the implementation of Group Areas legislation. *The same tendency can be applied to South African cities in general* . . ." (my emphasis).

In the light of such evidence for increasing segregation, why did the Whites perceive a need for the group areas legislation? First, the tracts of racially mixed housing would still have existed for the foreseeable future, if they had been left to themselves. Hence, the following excerpt from a White politician's speech.

And the first problem we had to face here was to prevent any further deterioration in the existing position. We had to see to it that the mixed areas which have grown, which have continued in the past years will not be allowed to continue further. . . . And as I say, in the Cape particularly —judging by the representations and petitions which have been brought in —there are a large number of areas in the Cape—in the Cape Peninsula, in Port Elizabeth and East London—which could immediately be declared as group areas, to give security for the inhabitants that their property will not be depreciated by the purchase—which is today free in the Cape Province—by a non-European next door to their property.[18]

These words were spoken in Parliament in 1950 by the Afrikaner Nationalist minister of the interior, Dr. Dönges, whose party had come to power in 1948. It seems clear, then, that even though the *overall* pattern may have been one of increasing segregation, many working-class poorer Whites—by whose votes the National party had, in part, been brought to power, to whom it was beholden, and whose loyalty it wished to cement further—still felt threatened by such Coloured penetration into lower-status residential tracts as continued. Note that the minister's phrase "to give security for the inhabitants" obviously referred to *White* inhabitants; no security whatsoever was being offered to Nonwhite inhabitants by the Group Areas Act.

Richer, mainly English-speaking, non-Nationalist Whites in Cape Town already had "security" (that is, money) with which to distance and so cushion themselves against Coloured penetration. However, there was political capital to be made during the depressed late 1930s out of the fears of the predominantly Afrikaans-speaking, lower-status Whites. Already in 1937, Karl Bremer, later to be a minister in the National party government in power after 1948, was reported as urging that group areas be established to combat the "infiltration" of Coloured people into Woodstock and Observatory.

National party strategists at this time were indeed deciding to make Coloured segregation a main plank in their platform for the 1938 parliamentary elections (since 95 percent of the electorate was White). They lost the election, but then they circulated their policy in the form of a petition that was so widely supported that it stimulated the victorious United party to propose a somewhat milder scheme of "complete and parallel" segregation in an attempt to outflank Nationalist propaganda. The Cape Provincial Council prepared a draft ordinance providing for the residential segregation of Coloureds in urban areas. The ordinance was opposed unanimously by the Cape Town City Council, which included Coloured members (for example, the Muslim Zainunissa "Cissy" Gool, elected in September 1938). It also provoked a large-scale demonstration in Cape Town, which was organized by the National Liberation League (founded by the Coloured radical James La Guma in 1935). To protest the United party's scheme, which was intended to "peg the present position" (like the legislation shortly to be enacted against alleged penetration by Indians in Natal), the Non-European United Front organized on 27 March 1939 another great demonstration in Cape Town. Mrs. Gool eloquently and powerfully harangued the crowd of 15,000 outside the Houses of Parliament. The police attacked the demonstrators, and the meeting turned into a riot. Eventually, the government vetoed the Cape Provincial Council's draft ordinance and dropped its own "voluntary colour segregation policy." The Nationalists did not drop theirs. As Dr. Dönges's speech (quoted earlier) indicates, they began implementing the policy nine years later, having won the 1948 election on the segregationist manifesto first put forward in 1938, a manifesto that had maintained its great appeal to the less affluent Whites. Apartheid is the implementation of that manifesto.

CHAPTER THREE

Apartheid: The Plan

But in whose image is space created?

David Harvey,
Social Justice and the City, 1973

A QUESTION OF NUMBERS

Apartheid attempts, through the group areas conception, to "deal with" the fact that Whites are being increasingly outnumbered by Nonwhites in urban areas. Before the urban milieu is considered in detail, it should be placed in the context of what is happening in South Africa as a whole. The institution of group areas is one scale — what Van den Berghe (1966) has termed the "mesosegregation" scale — of the apartheid plan for confronting the "problem" of the decreasing proportion of Whites in the South African population (Table 2).

Table 2
Population by Racial Group, South Africa, 1921-1977

Year	Total	Whites	Coloureds	Asians	Black Africans
Annual Populations:					
1921	6,928,580	1,519,488	545,548	165,731	4,697,813
1936	9,589,898	2,003,857	769,661	219,691	6,596,689
1951	12,671,452	2,641,689	1,103,016	366,664	8,560,083
1960	16,002,797	3,088,492	1,509,258	477,125	10,927,922
1977[a]	26,946,000	4,375,000	2,436,500	765,000	19,369,500
Percentage increase per Annum:					
1951-1960	3.10	1.88	4.10	3.30	3.00
1960-1970	2.75	2.24	3.29	3.04	2.80
1970-1977	2.51	1.91	2.35	2.54	2.67

a. Midyear estimate, including Transkei.

In 1921 South African Whites were outnumbered by Nonwhites in the ratio 1 to 3.6; in 1960, 1 to 4.2; in 1977, 1 to 5.2; and the White proportion continues to fall. In the cities, the same pattern of disproportional growth in the segments of the population is evident (Table 3). How does apartheid deal with this "problem"?

Table 3
Intercensal Percentage Increase by Racial Group
in Four Major Cities, 1921-1960

City	1921-1936			1936-1946			1946-1960		
	White	Black African	Coloured and Asian	White	Black African	Coloured and Asian	White	Black African	Coloured and Asian
Johannesburg	69	96	–	28	68	–	17	60	–
Cape Town	48	60	51	27	150	28	27	85	80
Durban	59	52	–	34	61	–	49	80	–
Port Elizabeth	104	145	–	17	68	–	53	136	–

SCALES OF SEGREGATION

The Interpersonal Scale

Apartheid does not represent segregation for its own sake; it is not a simple by-product of White racist attitudes. *Segregation means domination.* It is one tool by which the increasingly outnumbered White ruling group can maintain social distance from, and hegemony over, other groups in South African society. Yet, total segregation is clearly an impossibility; South Africa's sophisticated urban industrial economy requires both producers and consumers from *all* racial groups. All South African citizens, albeit to unequal degrees, have been integrated into the economy. So there is, inevitably, frequent face-to-face contact between the rulers and the ruled.

Robert Sommer (1969) made a distinction between "dominance" and "territoriality." Simply stated, both are mechanisms through which superordinates can maintain a higher status than their subordinates. When superordinate and subordinate share the same space, status is underscored by ritualized behavior, or etiquette, with the subordinates continually expressing their submission to their betters; thus, the desired "social distance" is maintained. Social distance can also be maintained by spatial segregation. Superordinates appropriate larger and/or more desirable territory as their own exclusive domain.

In an urbanized and industrialized South Africa, interracial face-to-face contact is made inevitable by the very nature of the economy, and an element of "dominance" in interracial social interaction can be anticipated. Petty apartheid—the microsegregation of public transportation, elevators, washrooms, beaches, restaurants, schools, hospitals, and even cemeteries—implements this system of social dominance. The legal reinforcement and extension of long-customary social distance on a personal level serves to remind all members of the society of *what* (more than *who*) they are. Petty apartheid attempts to provide psychological and emotional security for the ruling minority. Except in a very few specific cases, no White person may be subordinate in any official role to any Black person.

So extensive is this microscale apartheid that minor, cosmetic relaxations of regulations are hailed as great advances by those who wish to believe and to demonstrate that "the government is moving in the right direction." The Whites and Nonwhites notices came down at post offices in the Cape Peninsula, but the postmaster general, L. Rive, blandly informed the public (September 1976) that it was still policy for persons to be served, whenever possible, by members of their "own" racial group. Public buses in 1979 were desegregated in Cape Town. Benches were desegregated in Joubert Park, Johannesburg, as were the urinals (but not the tearoom) in the Gardens in Cape Town. The case of this tearoom is instructive.

> Almost a year ago the Government refused permission for all races to use the existing Gardens tea-room. Since the [Cape Town city] council approved a plan to convert The Bothy, a historical building in Queen Victoria Street, into a tea-room for non-Whites, the Government has: given permission for Whites to run the tea-room but not to use it; issued a permit only for Coloured people to use the tea-room; given permission for only Coloured waiters to be employed; by implication, barred Africans, Malays and Indian people from using the restaurant; through the office of the Bantu Affairs Commissioner, given permission for Africans to use the tea-room although they were still barred by the Department of Community Development's permit; subsequently said all races, except Whites, will be free to use it; and now turned down the council's request that anyone, without racial restrictions, be allowed to tender for the lease (*Argus*, 15 April 1976).

Another example underscores the contemporary confusion over petty apartheid in South Africa resulting from the government's efforts to relax some of the restrictions in an attempt to mitigate its unsavory image overseas. Certain of the more expensive hotels have, over the past five years, been accorded international status—"international" in the sense that Zulus, Coloureds, and Whites in the government's lexicon are defined as members of different "nations." The clientele of such hotels must be somewhat affluent, and, thus, economic segregation (with its implication of indirect racial segregation) is in these cases taking the place of overt racial segregation. However, if you are Black, once you have paid your money, you still may not be able to take your choice.

> Many hoteliers reported that contradictions and anomalies in the restrictions attached to international status could cause difficulties with guests. Only black visitors holding foreign passports could use all hotel facilities. Other blacks could not drink in men's only bars. They could not dance if the hotel was not in a suitable group area, unless by special permit, although they could eat at dine-and-dance restaurants. They could swim if resident at the hotel, and be served liquor at mixed sex bars if resident or a bona fide guest of a resident. Blacks who were not residents could be served liquor only if they were taking or about to take a meal on the premises, or attending a function, such as a conference. . . . There was a 10-15% limit on rooms occupied by blacks, and certain key posts like maitre d'hotel and chief chef had to be white (South African Institute of Race Relations, 1979, p. 364).

Such petty apartheid restrictions are easy targets of both the barbed racial humor of South Africans and the sensationalism of foreign journalists. Still, such situations are not mere examples of egregious illogicality. They represent the conscious efforts of the rulers to maintain their social distance from the ruled, backed by the law's sanctions.

The Urban Scale

On a second, citywide scale space becomes essential in the system, for, returning to Sommer's formulation (1969, p. 23) for a moment, "a society compensates for blurred social distinctions by clear spatial ones—physical barriers, keep-out signs, and property restrictions." Presumably, Sommer had the Black American experience in mind, that is, the often alluded to (for example, Schnore and Evenson, 1966) lack of residential racial segregation in "old" southern cities as opposed to the situation in northern industrial urban centers. On the mesosegregation scale in South Africa, this proposition also clearly has some validity. From Cape Town's three and a quarter centuries of developing social geography, it can be observed that during the slave owning period Whites did not need to underscore their evidently superior social rank with spatial segregation. Even after the emancipation of the slaves, when the Coloureds became servants (as in the Deep South of the United States), the British colonial government perceived no need to provide any legal means of territorial segregation in Cape Town, for Whites clearly dominated the subordinate Coloureds in all respects. At that time, the Whites were not outnumbered by the Coloureds in the city, and the latter "knew their place." This was "dominance."

However, with industrialization comes the possibility —although not the inevitability—that the demand for manual labor will not be based primarily on color, as it was on the agrarian slaveowning Cape. There is a potential for an equalization in status between White and Coloured as they become part of a single working class, that is, a potential for "blurred social distinctions." One of the ways in which this potential blurring can be countered is by the witting imposition of a more formal "territoriality," that is, by the deliberate policy of spatial segregation as exemplified by the group areas conception.

The Regional, National, and International Scales

The cities of South Africa have been remodeled over the last thirty years with a thoroughness that has seldom been equaled in the world. Berry (1973) decided that probably only Israel and the People's Republic of China (and I would add the Pol Pot regime's Democratic Kampuchea from 1975 to 1979) have attempted such drastic urban reorganization. Yet, there is an evident constraint upon the South African city planners: they did not have a tabula rasa upon which to begin after 1948. All of the preexisting urban fabric could not be pulled down, nor could a city be shifted en bloc to a new site more favorable for apartheid's particular purposes.

However, with the tremendous strides made by the South African economy from World War II until the recession of 1974-1980 it has been possible to establish new industrial areas and new cities under virtual tabula rasa conditions. Advanced transportation technology, such as the electrification of commuter rail services, and the increased number of private motor vehicles owned by Nonwhites have made it possible to put miles of open country between the various racial components of the work force. This has become particularly "desirable" as the proportion of Whites in the total population continues to fall and as the Coloureds and Black Africans continue to urbanize, despite stringent restrictions on the latter's urbanization.

Map 9 shows graphically the progression from the rather haphazardly segregated city of the preapartheid era (A), to the group areas city (B), to the ethno-city (C). The ethno-city approach allows "White South Africa" to use the artificially cheap Nonwhite labor necessary to maintaining its profitable industrial production while at the same time maintaining the security and privileges of segregation. New industry, if it is owned by Whites, as is likely, will probably be established on the edge of the White city so that the White workers can travel to work without inconvenience and so that the Nonwhite workers need not traverse or skirt any White residential areas whatever (this in order to avoid "friction"; see p. 85). Such established White-owned industry as remains near the center of the now-White city may be made accessible to Nonwhites through the construction of transportation corridors, which, if necessary, will have buffer zones on each side. New industry, if it is owned by Nonwhites, will be placed at the edge of the Nonwhite cities. The White government may even direct White-owned industry, especially that with a labor force overwhelmingly Nonwhite, to a location on the outskirts of a Nonwhite city.

Today, enjoying wide powers with its preexisting Group Areas Act and Community Development Act plus the more recent Environment Planning Act, the White government is in a masterful position to mold the space of South Africa. Map 9(C), using some basic geographical concepts, presents a pattern of racial segregation when it is seen as a structure of formal regions or it shows a pattern of economic integration when its structure is viewed as one functional region.

An example of such plans is the ethno-city of Atlantis, about 50 kilometers north of Cape Town. Unlike the Mitchell's Plain project, which is simply a rather distant new dormitory suburb of Cape Town for Coloureds only, Atlantis was clearly planned as an ethno-city with its own economic base. It is to function interdependently with other centers within the general greater Cape Town region.

> Opportunities available to Coloured entrepreneurs were almost unlimited, said the Minister of Economic Affairs, Mr. J. C. Heunis, when he recently opened (17 January 1977) the new industrial complex at the Coloured city of Atlantis, Cape Town.

> He said that at Atlantis there were no obstacles in the way of Coloureds establishing industries in the industrial area. Since 1974 assistance had been offered to 68 prospective industrialists, and at least 61 of these projects would go ahead.

> Present indications were that by 1980 there would be about 6,000 Coloured industrial workers and a further 6,000 workers attached to service industries at Atlantis.

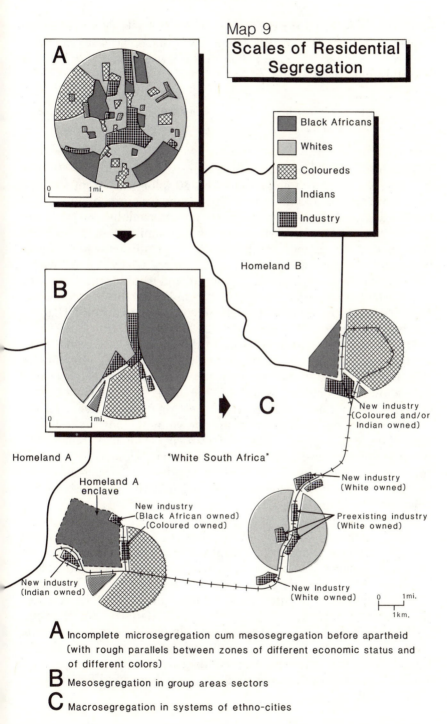

Map 9
Scales of Residential Segregation

Legend:
- Black Africans
- Whites
- Coloureds
- Indians
- Industry

Homeland B

A

B

Homeland A

"White South Africa"

C

Homeland A
enclave

New industry
(Black African owned)
(Coloured owned)

New industry
(Indian owned)

New industry
(Coloured and/or
Indian owned)

New industry
(White owned)

Preexisting industry
(White owned)

New Industry
(White owned)

0   1mi.
1km.

A Incomplete microsegregation cum mesosegregation before apartheid
(with rough parallels between zones of different economic status and
of different colors)

B Mesosegregation in group areas sectors

C Macrosegregation in systems of ethno-cities

The Minister added that the development of Atlantis should not be based only on supplying the local and Cape Town markets, but should also be directed to markets in the rest of South Africa and overseas (*South African Digest*, 4 February 1977).

It is envisaged that by the year 2010 Atlantis will house 500,000 people in six separate towns ranging in size between 60,000 and 150,000 people. For the next four years, 2,000 homes a year are planned (*South African Digest*, 21 January 1977).

Another example is Ennerdale (where work began in 1978), 30 kilometers south of Johannesburg and 30 kilometers from Vereeniging. It was planned as the future city for the Coloured population of the Witwatersrand, with both a fast commuter rail link to Johannesburg and an industrial park of its own. A similar case is the Black African city of Verena, which is to be built northeast of Witbank, planned for a population of nearly 1 million. It is situated "within easy reach of Pretoria and the East Rand, and would form part of the Black country it borders, although it would be established in a White territory, said Dr. Snyman (Chief director of the Highveld [Bantu] Administration Board)" (*South African Digest*, 27 October 1978).

Dr. Snyman's remarks bring us to the national-scale grand apartheid of the homelands or bantustan conception. His reference to "the Black country it borders" indicates that the South Ndebele and/ or Lebowa[1] homeland would be the area where inhabitants of Verena were to hold and exercise their rights of citizenship. The geographical aspects of this plan are shown by the borders of Homeland A on Map 9(C). The Black African city is (as in Verena's case) designated an enclave of nearby "independent" Homeland A, within the White territory of the Republic of South Africa. (Such a piece of territorial legerdemain has also been debated for Soweto, which is adjacent to Johannesburg.)

In terms of geographical fragmentation, a *slightly* less farfetched situation is that of Homeland B on Map 9(C). This homeland is not far from a White ethno-city. Thus, the Black African labor force for this city's industry can be placed in a dormitory Bantu ethno-city on the very edge of Homeland B's territory, from where Black Africans can commute into "White South Africa" for work. Such relationships exist at present, as can be seen from Map 10. For example, Mdantsane is not a Black African township on the outskirts of White East London; it is considered a homeland settlement within the bounds of the Ciskei. Similar bonds exist between Durban and Umlazi, Durban and KwaMashu, Pietermaritzburg and Edendale, and

Map 10

Homelands and Zones of High Economic Intensity

"Final" Consolidation Proposals, March 1975, with Selected "White Cities" and Their Tributary Black African Homeland Townships

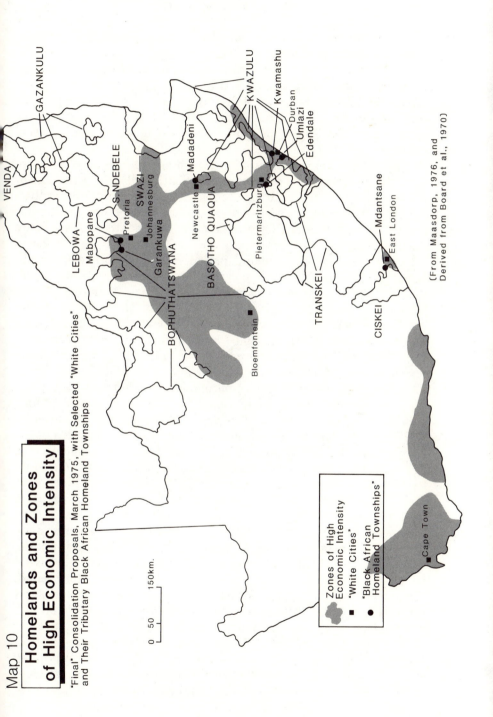

VENDA

GAZANKULU

LEBOWA

Mabopane

S. NDEBELE

Pretoria

SWAZI

Johannesburg

Garankuwa

BOPHUTHATSWANA

Newcastle

Madadeni

BASOTHO QUAQUA

Bloemfontein

Pietermaritzburg

KWAZULU

Kwamashu

Durban

Umlazi

Edendale

TRANSKEI

CISKEI

Mdantsane

East London

Cape Town

Zones of High
Economic Intensity

"White Cities"

"Black African
Homeland Townships"

0   50   150 km.

(From Maasdorp, 1976, and
Derived from Board et al., 1970)

Newcastle and Madadeni; all four Black African cities are in the Kwa-Zulu homeland. Pretoria also is near the Bophuthatswana homeland; workers from the dormitory ethno-cities of Garankuwa and Mabopane commute daily to their jobs. Although Johannesburg is approximately 50 kilometers south of Pretoria, it is now considered possible that Johannesburg could draw more of its Black African labor force from within the Bophuthatswana homeland if a new rail line were constructed.[2]

Why all this territorial juggling with homeland borders? Why are they so important to the White government? And what is the role of the homelands in the political economy of South Africa? Basically, I consider Dr. Verwoerd's plan of grand apartheid to be an attempt made by the Whites to have their cake and eat it, too. Nonwhite labor is essential to the functioning of South African industry. Hence, a permanent Nonwhite presence in cities originally established as "the white man's creation"[3] is inevitable. However, although Whites may want Nonwhite labor, they definitely do not want its concomitant: urban Nonwhite political clout. Thus, the scheme to accord political rights to the majority Black Africans in some peripheral "homeland" even though Black Africans may work forty-nine of fifty-two weeks of the year in the cities of "White South Africa." ("Homelands" do not appear feasible for Coloureds or Indians, who together do not outnumber the Whites anyway.)

These homelands (formerly called "native reserves") have long played a dependent role as reserves of labor for the industries of "White South Africa." Today, however, they may be accorded political "independence" by the White South African government, as in the case of Transkei (26 October 1976), Bophuthatswana (6 December 1977), and Venda (13 September 1979). Thus urban Black Africans whose ethnic roots (maybe as long as four generations ago) go back to, say, the Tembu tribe in the Transkei are liable—even when they were born in a "White South African" city—to be unilaterally declared "foreign" Transkei citizens. By this imposed legal fiction, they may lose all claim to a more equitable participation in the material wealth of South Africa to which their labors have contributed. They also lose any right to stay in the city beyond their usefulness for White industry, having become supposedly "migrant," contract *gastarbeiter*. The basis upon which Black Africans were allowed in "White South Africa," said Minister of Bantu Administration M. C. Botha on 20 August 1976, was "to sell their labour and for nothing else." By contrast, *within* their "own" territory—as defined for them by the White government—Black Africans have the same legal citizenship rights as the Whites enjoy in *their* "own" territory.

From this concept flow euphemisms like "separate development" and even "plural democracy," the original term "apartheid" having attracted to itself too much opprobrium. Hence, the Afrikaans-language newspaper *Die Vaderland* (28 January 1977) trumpeted, "It [National party policy toward separate development] is honest and dynamic, . . .

> it is a cornerstone of National Party policy that what it demands for the Whites it will also grant the Blacks. This, in fact, is the basis of the home-land policy. . . . This shows the sincerity of the Government—and the great majority of the White voters who support it—that it has no wish or desire to suppress the Black man. On the contrary just as it demands sovereignty for itself, so does it not only grant it to the Black man but also makes it dynamically possible. This is a development that should satisfy everyone, except, of course, those who are so beset with integration as an ideology, and desire White extinction that nothing else will satisfy them. The Government and the Black man, too, has come a long way with his (the Black man's) political development. The time has now come to tackle equally dynamically the economic development of the Black states of South Africa.

And ex-Prime Minister Vorster once asserted,[4] "If I were to wake up one morning and find myself a Black man, the only major differ-ence would be geographical" (*Star* [Johannesburg], 3 April 1973). Black Africans do not accept this interpretation, nor does the world diplomatic community. *No* state—not even Rhodesia during the last phases of White minority rule—has recognized any of the three "independent" homelands.

Compared to the industrial core of South Africa, in whose urban areas over half the country's Black Africans are living and working, the outlying, economically eviscerate homelands are but peripheral dependencies. On Map 10, the disposition of the homelands, with their obverse, the "zones of high economic intensity," is striking. The economic role of the unrecognized "independent" Transkei is fundamentally the same as that of a number of similarly peripheral states that *are* recognized as "independent," such as Lesotho and Swaziland. The functioning of the southern African economic system until now has clearly relegated such states to the status of "South Africa's hostages" (Halpern, 1965). Selwyn (1973a; 1973b), Maas-dorp (1976), and Smith (1977) represent just three scholars who have applied the core-periphery conception to the interdependencies in the southern African economy.

On a final, general scale, we can note that the Republic of South

Africa, although it still relies on its export of primary materials, is no mere neocolonial peripheral dependency of the First World; it is in many ways a member of the First World isolated at the southern tip of a Third World continent. However, as is frequently pointed out, within the republic's borders the Third and First Worlds (the Black and the White worlds) coexist uneasily. They do not coexist passively; they are bound together, interdependent in a common economy, while assiduously being put asunder by law in the social and political spheres.

THE GROUP AREAS ACT

Although there is at present a trend toward guarded "liberalization" of some aspects of apartheid under Prime Minister P. W. Botha, who assumed office in September 1978, there remain certain areas of policy that apparently are considered nonnegotiable. One of these areas is the homelands policy; another is the inhibition of racially mixed residential zones in urban areas, which is one of the central functions of the Group Areas Act. "It is the essence of the apartheid policy which is embodied in the Bill," stated the Prime Minister D. F. Malan when the group areas bill was introduced to Parliament in 1950 (less than two years after the National party took office). Minister of the Interior T. E. Dönges said during the same debate, "We believe that this Bill will be one of the cornerstones for preserving a White South Africa." Clearly, the Group Areas Act is still considered to be just that.

The Group Areas Act was originally passed in 1950 and since then has been amended continually (usually to close loopholes). It is complemented by the Group Areas Development Act, now renamed the Community Development Act, whose function is putting into practice group areas decisions. Over the last twenty years, the expulsion of over 150,000 Capetonians from their homes has been effected through "community development" legislation—a striking example of Orwellian doublespeak.[5]

The Group Areas Act Number 41 of 1950 imposed control throughout the Union of South Africa[6] upon all interracial sales of property and interracial changes in occupation of properties. The Group Areas Board was established to plan group areas for the various racial groups in settlements throughout the country, its aim being to achieve total racial homogeneity in each residential zone and a "satisfactory" disposition of such zones in any given settlement. When, after public hearings, whose recommendations are purely advisory, the government approves a plan, it is brought into force by proclamation. (See Chapter 5.) Group areas may be proclaimed for occupation, for ownership, or for both by a specified racial group. Generally, a proclamation refers to both occupation and ownership and gives the government full right of eminent domain. Persons of any other group become "disqualified" persons and must move out within a certain amount of time after they receive official notice to do so. By law, they must be given at least a year's grace period from the date of the proclamation and at least three month's notice before having to leave dwellings and twelve month's notice (after the initial year) before having to leave business premises. Disqualified owners of businesses can continue to *own* their properties for the rest of their lives, but their heirs must sell them within a year of the owner's death to a person qualified to own property in the area. In cases of extreme hardship, the minister of the Interior may grant permits for continued occupation and ownership by disqualified persons. Companies other than banks, mines, and large factories—almost all of which are owned by Whites—are given a group character according to the race of the persons holding the controlling interest. Among the very few exceptions to the act regarding "disqualified" persons are live-in domestic servants and caretakers.

Apart from these exceptions, the act overrides any previously existing property owning or renting rights. From its lengthy and comprehensive provisions, two sections from the amended Group Areas Act Number 36 of 1966 can be used as examples.

Section 23 is entitled Establishment of Group Areas, for both occupation and ownership. Paragraph 4 of section 23 reads:

> Notwithstanding anything to the contrary contained in any law, any contract in terms of which any disqualified person occupies land or premises to which any such notice or permit relates, shall lapse with effect from the date determined. . . .

Section 43 is entitled Powers of Members of the South African Police. This section describes the all-encompassing powers of any police officer in the matter of group areas, as in many other matters in the republic.

> When [investigating] . . . an offence or alleged or suspected offence under the provisions of this Act . . . he may without warrant—a) at any time during the day or night without previous notice enter upon any premises whatsoever and make such examination and enquiry as may be necessary; b) at any time and at any place require from any person who has in his possession or custody or under his control any book, document,

or thing, the production to him of that book, document or thing then and there or at a time and place fixed by him; c) . . . .

The unequivocal assertion of eminent domain in section 23(4) is reiterated in sections 26(1), 26(4), and 27(1)(d). Kuper, Watts, and R. J. Davies (1958, p. 160) sagely pointed out the conclusion that must surely be drawn from the enactment by a White parliament of such draconian provisions: "The acceptance by Europeans of such revolutionary changes in the traditionally sacred rights of ownership indicates their conviction that the provisions of the Group Areas Act would be applied against Non-Europeans, and for the benefit of Europeans." Nel (1962, p. 207), on the other hand, attempted to convey the impression that the law deals with both White and Non-white alike and also attempted to minimize the extent of its impact: "A relatively small number of people, both White and non-White, do become the 'victims' of this law." What are the facts? In the House of Assembly[7] on 9 March 1976 the minister of community development, Marais Steyn, provided the following figures (Table 4), which had been requested by Helen Suzman, a member of Parliament who opposes apartheid.

Table 4
Group Areas Removees, by Population Group

Group	Removed	Awaiting Removal
Coloureds	305,739	93,929
Indians	153,230	44,590
Whites	5,898	733

When the sum of both those removed and those waiting to be removed is expressed as a percentage of the total population in each's racial group, the proportions are 16.2 percent of Coloureds, 25.6 percent of Indians, and 0.15 percent of Whites.

These figures indicate that the act, in pursuing the goal of achieving racially homogeneous residential areas in South African cities, was not aimed at the Black Africans. Legislation had already been passed in 1923 (and indeed earlier) to provide for their segregation, although these laws had not always been vigorously enforced. The Group Areas Act does, nevertheless, facilitate the meshing of Black African segregation into a citywide spatial plan for total segregation; the previously existing laws (the Natives [Urban Areas] Acts of 1923, 1930, and 1937) provided for Black African segregation only in an ad hoc manner in overall spatial planning. That is, prior to the Group Areas Act the prime concern was segregating the Black Africans, usually on the periphery of the city. Little attention was consciously paid to their disposition relative to Indians or Coloureds nor to the long-term likelihood of their peripheral locations being eventually overtaken by the expanding White urban residential tracts. They (the Black Africans) could always be moved again. Group areas planning, however, tries to create racial *sectors* within cities (with room for centrifugal sprawl), rather than enclaves, actual or potential. (See below Chapter 4.) So, when tens of thousands of Black Africans have been moved from one part of a South African city to another, as in Johannesburg's Western Areas, it has not been under the provisions of the Group Areas Act *itself*,[8] although they were being moved to fit a group areas ideal. This fact is demonstrated by their absence in Steyn's figures. The act was not directly aimed at Black Africans, nor was it aimed at White South Africans. It was aimed at those "in the middle": the Coloureds and the Indians. By 1950 the Indians' freedom to purchase property in any area from a person of any race was already somewhat circumscribed; but, for the 90 percent of all the Coloureds who lived in the Cape Province in 1950, the act was the first legal restraint placed upon their property rights, their first experience of de jure disqualification. Because of the act, 1 Coloured in 6 is removed, as is 1 Indian in 4—but only 1 White in 666.

In an attempt to explain these figures to Parliament, Marais Steyn (9 March 1976) said, "Ninety percent of the families which had to be moved came from depressed and/or slum areas. . . . [It is only] in the exceptional cases where housing which was still habitable has had to be vacated." Thus, slum clearance and the concomitant "health hazard" argument are frequently employed as official justifications for group areas removal of persons (almost always Nonwhites) from one part of a city to another. The act, however, was attacked in Parliament by Helen Suzman in 1961 (23 February): "You do not need a Group Areas Act to clear slums; there is a Slum Clearance Act under which one can quite readily clear slums; and . . . to put up great housing schemes [in which those removed have been resettled] . . . also has nothing whatever to do with the operation of the Group Areas Act." Indeed, the point is not the establishment of great schemes but rather the place *where* they have been established: at the periphery of Whites-only central cities. The *location* chosen for resettlement reveals an intent quite different from that of the government's pronouncements; the intention is the execution of social distancing and not a concern for health hazards.

The Strategic Motive

There are, then, more profound reasons for group areas than the minister of community development chose to advance. The outnumbering of Whites by Nonwhites in the country as a whole and in the cities in particular continues to grow more marked. A parallel can be drawn with the fears of the upper, ruling classes of Britain when they were confronted with that totally novel and therefore unpredictable phenomenon, the great industrial city as epitomized by Manchester. Of this city in 1842 W. Cooke Taylor wrote (p. 6):

> [One] cannot contemplate those "crowded hives" without feelings of anxiety and apprehension almost amounting to dismay. The population is hourly increasing in breadth and strength. It is an aggregate of masses, our conceptions of which clothe themselves in terms that express something portentous and fearful. We speak of them . . . as of the slow rising and gradual swelling of an ocean which must, at some future and no distant time, bear all the elements of society aloft upon its bosom, and float them — Heaven knows whither. There are mighty energies slumbering in those masses.

As a description of the White South Africans' widespread fear of the urban *swart gevaar*, this passage can hardly be bettered. Ten years earlier, another commentator viewing Manchester had warned of "the evils of poverty and pestilence among the working classes of the close alleys, . . . where pauperism and disease congregate round the source of social discontent and political disorder in the centre of our large towns." Here is the strategic motive, which is indeed one of the two primary underpinnings for the group areas conception.

What did nineteenth-century rulers do to defuse the situation—how did they deal with the "crowded hives," the slums close to their city centers? Engels in 1844 (p. 74) wrote:

> In reality the bourgeoisie has only one method of solving the housing question after *its* fashion. . . . This method is called "Haussmann." . . . By "Haussmann" I mean the practice which has now become general of making breaches in the working-class quarters of our big towns, and particularly in areas which are centrally situated . . . [the laying down of] streets (which sometimes appear to have the strategic aim of making barricade fighting more difficult).

Of twentieth-century South Africa, van den Berghe (1966, p. 411) is firm in his agreement:

> The older non-white shanty towns with their maze of narrow, tortuous alleys were often located close to White residential or business districts;

they are now systematically being razed as a major military hazard. . . .
The new ghettos are typically situated several miles from the White towns,
with a buffer zone between.

Adam (1971, p. 123) also considered that,

> since the widespread unrest of the early sixties, white rule is efficiently
> prepared for internal conflicts. The design and location of the African town-
> ships has been planned on the basis of strategic considerations. Within a
> short time such a location could be cordoned off, and in its open streets
> any resistance could be easily smashed.

Such statements are not searching for ideological-conspiratorial or
Machiavellian motives where none exist in fact. Slum clearance and
(usually) improved Nonwhite segregated housing is not merely the result of a managerial and meliorative planning concern for health hazards. Surely no more striking proof of this can be found than the
expressed opinions of the government minister in charge of the security
system within South Africa. Jimmy Kruger, minister of justice, when
interviewed by the *Financial Gazette* on the possibilities of urban
guerrilla warfare,

> said he did not think an organised campaign would get off the ground. One
> of the big advantages of South Africa was that the residential areas were
> segregated. Overseas, urban terrorism was largely sparked off by a mixture
> of mutually antagonistic groups within a limited geographical area, and
> this was often accentuated by overcrowding. "We have fortunately managed
> to avoid this here," said Mr. Kruger (*South African Digest*, 2 September
> 1977).

Whether or not we agree with his analysis of the causes of urban
guerrilla warfare, which predictably leans on the so-called "friction
theory," (see p. 85), the strategic motive for group areas segregation
has been made crystal clear. It is in this light that we can understand
the wholesale clearance of Cape Town's District Six, for example.
Certainly, there were sections of deteriorating housing, but equally
important was its status as an area with a 95 percent Coloured population immediately adjacent to the White city center. Generations of
Coloured occupancy had made it a cultural symbol for the Coloured
people; but, with its proclamation as a group area for Whites only,
the Coloured homes were demolished.

Another observer who would seem to see this strategic situation in
a similar light was Arthur Keppel-Jones in his astonishingly prescient
tour de force *When Smuts Goes* (1947). He imagined an abortive
Black uprising in 1972: "There were two other theatres of rebellion

[in addition to the Zulu and Xhosa homelands] which, though small, were dangerous because of their proximity to the nerve-centres of the Republic. One lay on the western fringe of Johannesburg [i.e., Soweto] ; *the other, stretching from District Six to Maitland and Langa, isolated central Capetown . . .*" (p. 121; my italics). To read Keppel-Jones's book thirty-three years after its first publication—before, it should be remembered, the Nationalists came to power—is to be both chilled by his prophecies and impressed by his foresight.

The importance of the strategic motive was underscored again during the urban unrest during the Cape winter of 1976. After a number of weeks of rioting in the Black African and Coloured ghetto townships outside the city on the Cape Flats, violence flared in the city center itself. An editorial in the city's Afrikaans-language daily is illuminating.

> This is the work of cunning people. . . . It was also a cunning, calculated move to get [school] children to come to the center of the city and make it the scene of their rioting. Obviously it was intended to involve the general public [an interesting euphemism for Whites] in what had up till then been confined to Black and Brown residential areas, helping to create a crisis psychosis and thereby ensuring much more publicity (*Die Burger,* 3 September 1976).

Clearly, according to *Die Burger*, violence and riot in the Nonwhite townships was not as intolerable as violence and riot in the White city.

In addition to the wholesale clearance of inner-city Nonwhites, there is another strategic method whereby the rulers may attempt to lessen the "problem." Again, there is a parallel with urban England during the Victorian era.

> The necessity of coping with the dangerous masses of working people accumulating in the centres of the cities is a theme which is constantly repeated. T. Chalmers [1821-1826] insists on the principle of "locality" as an instrument of both religious and civic administration in towns. [Whereby] . . . the unmanageable mass which would otherwise form into one impetuous and overwhelming surge against the reigning authority could be split up into fragments. (Dennis, 1958, p. 203).

Glass (1955, p. 16) also noted that a decline in the upper classes' fear of the British laboring masses during the last two decades of the nineteenth century was attributable in part to the fact that "the heterogeneity of the British working class was discovered *and encouraged*" (emphasis mine). The policy of divide and rule was espoused.

In contemporary South Africa, subsumed under the strategic functions of group areas legislation are definitional elements. Those persons who are termed Nonwhites by the apartheid laws do not constitute one solid and undifferentiated mass. There are objectively existing and subjectively experienced differences among them. Thus, although Black Africans on the Rand may express a preference for tribally mixed housing (as Patricios [1975] found), Soweto is internally segregated into numerous ethnolinguistic sections. (See Holzner, 1971). Similarly, the overall category "Coloured" has, through the Population Registration Act of 1950, seven legislated subcategories. Three are generally considered "Asiatics": "the Indian group" (99 percent of the "Asiatics"), comprising those whose original home was in the British Indian empire; "the Chinese group"; and "the other Asiatic group." The other four subcategories are generally considered "Coloureds": "the Cape Coloured group," Coloureds in the strictest sense, constituting in 1970 over 93 percent of those in these four subcategories; "the Cape Malay group," (5.9 percent); "the Griqua group" (0.65 percent); and "the other Coloured group" (0.06 percent).

Among White South Africans there exist similar ethnolinguistic divisions. By precisely the same governmental logic, the Whites could be legally divided and spatially segregated into Afrikaners, English-speaking Christians, Jews, Portuguese, et cetera. However, this is not done. Leo Kuper (1956) commented:

> The danger is in the numerical preponderance of the non-whites. It is a threat, however, only if the non-whites are united. . . . The Group Areas Act (1950) gives the Governor-General [now the state president] the necessary power to subdivide Coloureds and Natives but not whites. . . . If my interpretation is rejected, then we must assume that it is sheer accident that the government has . . . discriminated against the Whites by withholding from [them] the privilege of communal living.

Adam's (1971, p. 72) reaction was a little different.

> Whether the Afrikaner past with its former progressive nationalism is projected on to the other groups, or whether Apartheid is merely a witting device of *divide et impera*, is hardly significant compared with the fact that obviously a widespread ethnic narcissism in all groups responds to such offers.

Promoting consciousness of ethnic differentiation rather than allowing the formation of a unified Black bloc is clearly in the White government's interest. It should be noted here that in the lexicon of the South African government the adjective "racial" refers to either the threefold White/Coloured/Black (Bantu) differentiation or in a general usage to the fourfold White/Coloured/Asiatic/Black (Bantu) categorization. The adjective "ethnic" refers to the distinctions *within* these categories, such as Indians versus Chinese among Asiatics or Sotho versus Shangaan among Black Africans—or the instructive case of Cape Malays among Coloureds.

In terms of subsection 12(2) of the (revised) Group Areas Act Number 36 of 1966, the state president has the power to "create" a group for the purposes of the act; that is, the act states that there is (a) a White group, (b) a Bantu group, (c) a Coloured group, and (d) "any group of persons which is under sub-section (2) declared to be a group." Under this act, then, Cape Malays are recognized as such only in the places where they are numerous enough to warrant (in the government's eyes) their own group areas. Therefore, in East London no attempt was made to separate the Malays from the general Coloured group among whom they were living. In Port Elizabeth the Group Areas Board decided there should be a separate Malay group area, but the city council opposed this action. Eventually, the board agreed with the city council on the grounds that there were, in fact, too few Malays to warrant establishing a group area for them.

In Cape Town the situation is uniquely complex. There are clearly enough Malays to warrant the provision for separate, specified Malay group areas according to the criteria of the act, for the Malays make up approximately 20 percent of the Coloured population of the Cape Peninsula. Thus only Malays are allowed to inhabit their historic territory, Schotsche's Kloof, the Malay Quarter. However, the residents of Schotsche's Kloof make up only a small portion of the Malays living in Cape Town, and attempts to establish other segregated Malay group areas in the Surrey Estate and in Wynberg were vociferously opposed and eventually dropped. (See Chapter 5.) Therefore, all Malays who do not live in Schotsche's Kloof are free to live anywhere in the Coloured group areas of Cape Town. This is a self-contradiction in terms of the act. In any given urban area (in this case, the city of Cape Town), there are either enough or not enough members of any subgroup to warrant their having a separate group area. But in Cape Town the Malays seem to have been permitted (or rather obliged) to have the best of both worlds: they are segregated where some might wish to be so (in "their" quarter) and not segregated among the Coloureds in general, elsewhere. Legal opinion has pronounced that in relation to land outside those areas, they [the Malays] will fall in the general "Coloured" group and they will shed their character of belonging to a sub-group. Outside the specified districts [that is, the Malay group areas], a genuine Malay can freely sell to or acquire from a coloured because they fall in the same group, but in relation to land inside the specified districts, this identical Malay may not enter into the same kind of transaction with a coloured, because there they belong to different groups (Hiemstra, 1953, p. 3).

At this point, it begins to seem as though the whole legalistic exercise of subsection 12 (2) is merely a demonstration of the government's power of definition. When, according to the Group Areas Act, is a Malay not a Malay? " 'The question is,' said Alice, 'whether you can make words mean so many different things.' 'The question is,' said Humpty Dumpty, 'who is to be master, that's all.' "

The Alice-in-Wonderland quality of the law masks a real issue. It is in fact perfectly logical and generally appropriate that, when a particular minority group is relatively very small, the mainstream society, with its power to define the group's members externally, tends to subsume them into a more general minority group, which includes persons with allegedly related characteristics; but, when the group is larger and more visible, its members may be allowed a more specific identity. For example, Guatemalans in the United States general society probably would be considered, at least at first, to be members of a larger Spanish-speaking group; in the East Los Angeles barrio, however, with a sufficient concentration they might well be defined distinctively as Guatemalans, as opposed to Mexicans and other Spanish speakers. The difference is that the South African apartheid policy demands that this kind of societal convention be codified legally. However, the truth of Humpty Dumpty's statement regarding mastery is well understood by the advocates of "Black consciousness," who clearly perceive and oppose the White government's manipulation of differences among its subdivided Coloured, Asiatic, and Black African subjects. As a South African Students' Organisation leader proclaimed in 1977, "It's *our* turn to define now." This is the essence of Leo Kuper's remark: Blacks are divided, Whites are not. Unity is to be challenged for the Nonwhites at all costs and by all means fostered for the Whites.

Not only does the Group Areas Act define categories of persons within the Nonwhites, it also helps distinguish Whites from Nonwhites. In section 12 of the Group Areas Act, Groups for the Purposes of This Act, it is stated that a White is ". . . any person who in appearance, obviously is, or who is generally accepted as a white person, other than a person who although in appearance obviously a white person, is generally accepted as a coloured person" or who is married to or cohabits with any person who is not White. The emphasis on social acceptance means that it is in fact possible for citizens of South Africa actually to have their official "race" changed by the courts of the Race Classification Board—a Kafka-esque notion to anyone unfamiliar with the republic. In 1977, for example, nine Whites were reclassified as Cape Coloureds, as was one Black African; but forty-four Cape Coloureds became Whites, as in 1975 did two Chinese. During the process of legal reclassification to White status, the board investigates such questions as whether the would-be Whites' closest friends are White, whether at work they are employed as Whites for the appropriate rates of pay, whether they attended and their children attend White schools, whether they attend a White church and participate in White voluntary associa-tions, whether they habitually use without challenge Whites-only amenities (as defined by the Separate Amenities Act of 1953), and whether *they live and are accepted in a White residential neighbor-hood.*

When in pre-group areas cities in South Africa working-class Whites and Coloureds lived in integrated areas, as in inner-city Cape Town, in many instances social distinction could not be made among them. Fair-skinned Coloureds passed for Whites because they could straightforwardly claim social acceptance by some of their White neighbors. Poor Whites, who migrated in tens of thousands to the cities to escape the rural depression between the world wars, may have been poorer than many artisan Coloureds and as such were liable to absorption into the latter's ranks. Whites, already a minority in South Africa—and a decreasing minority because of differential reproduction—could not afford to "lose" so many of "their own." Hence, the great (overt) aversion to miscegenation among White South Africans.[9] Among the very first laws the Afrikaner Nationalist government enacted were those preventing interracial marriage and sexual relations; these were designed to combat infiltration into the White group by Coloureds or vice versa. Also, in order to bolster this ambiguous *who's who,* the group areas conception offers a definite *who's where;* that is, if such a person lives in such a suburb (segre-gated), whatever his or her appearance, then he or she can *only* be Coloured: one is one's address. In this way can group areas aid in racial definition. Such bolstering of fuzzy social distinctions by spatial means is a clear example of what Sommer called "territoriality."

The Economic Motive

The Group Areas Act has been borne most heavily by the Indians, with one in four of them having been resettled. Yet, of the four major population groups in South Africa, the Indians are by far the smallest, being only about 750,000 in number. There are almost six times as many Whites as Indians. Strategic motives seem unlikely, except locally in Durban. Why, then, should the *nationwide* Group Areas Act assault Indians so heavily? The motive is not so much strategic, as it is economic.

Kuper, Watts, and R. J. Davies (1958, p. 220) saw their work on Durban, where by far the greatest number of South African Indians live, as an illumination of a situation in which "the opportunity for material gain is linked with the monopoly of power. . . . [For the Whites] the Group Areas Act converted political power to material gain." In this regard, the act is just one instance of the rise to economic power of Afrikanerdom subsequent to its taking over the government of the South African state. Fatima Meer (1976) did not doubt that the act's main target was the Indians. Leo Kuper[10] agreed: "There was a convergence of interest—English getting rid of competitors, Afrikaners gaining entry, more particularly in the rural areas." And of Durban: "In general, the Technical Sub-Committee's plan involves the redistribution of resources in favour of Europeans. . . . The value of European investments in the city [thereby] . . . would rise by £6,000,000 to £120,000,000, while Indian investment would fall to about £18,500,000" (Kuper et al., 1958, p. 192).

The business and trading success of a number of Indians rendered their economic status higher than that of many Whites. This made them visible and therefore vulnerable to attacks by those whose constituency included poorer Whites; that is, the Afrikaner nationalists. In 1838 the *Voortrekkers* defeated the Zulus at the Battle of Blood River, a sacred place indeed for the Afrikaners. On the centennial of the battle, National party leader D. F. Malan warned of "meeting the Non-European defenceless on the open plains of economic competition." The poorer Whites' fear and envy of the Indians was a powerful source of support for the group areas legislation, whereby wealth was obligatorily redistributed from the Indians to the Whites. This support did not come only from the poorer Afrikaans-speaking Whites. Solidly English-speaking Durban was, as we have seen, devising its own strategy before group areas to redirect investment from Indian business to English-dominated commerce, even though the English sector was already the most economically privileged in South African society.

Consider the racial breakdown of those who had been moved from business premises by the Group Areas Act by the end of 1975 (Table 5). The same pattern appears in data on those who were still, in 1975, waiting to be moved (Table 6). Before the Group Areas Act

Table 5
Business Displacements by Race and Province

Race	Cape	Transvaal	Natal	Total
White	3	8	10	21
Coloured	38	33	11	82
Indian	139	668	470	1,277
Chinese	3	—	—	3

Table 6
Planned Business Displacements by Race and Province

Race	Cape	Transvaal	Natal	Total
White	48	—	12	60
Coloured	195	48	4	247
Indian	897	2,332	552	3,781
Chinese	617	—	—	617

was enacted, the distribution of Indian residences frequently mirrored the distribution of economic activity, rather than any ethnic distributions, as Scott (1955) found in Cape Town. For Indians it was necessary as part of their trading occupations that they be widely dispersed throughout the city, accessible to their multiracial market. To require Indians to live and trade in their own group areas (except by a ministerial permit, which is easily revocable) is to destroy their businesses. Yet, the location of the two small Indian group areas in Cape Town—Rylands and Cravenby—is very restricted.[11] There are moves afoot at this time (1979-1980) that may minimize any further removals of Indian businesses, that is, further than those removals already carried out. (See Chapter 11.)

One final way in which the group areas conception has worked to the economic advantage of Whites and to the detriment of Nonwhites has been through the renovation of housing, or "gentrification." This I consider to be property-market opportunism on the part of White realtors, rather than a conscious aim of the act. Indeed, there are provisions in the act that were inserted ostensibly to prevent such profiteering. The financial gain has accrued to the Whites through their purchase and then resale or rental, after renovation, of the homes previously owned by Nonwhites ejected by the act. In Cape Town this has mainly concerned Coloured people; and their small houses, into which were once crowded nuclear and even extended families, are now remodeled bijou Chelsea cottages occupied by middle-class Whites at a much lower density. Specific data on this trend will be provided in Chapter 7.

CHAPTER FOUR

Social Engineering through Spatial Manipulation: The Ideal Apartheid City in Theory and in Practice

You go to bed, you dream about it—and I am not exaggerating at all. I stayed just beyond the railway line, and the railway line in South Africa is very often and most always an indication of the whole thing there, because you know a railway line, or a river, or something like that, is a line of demarcation between Whites on the one hand and Coloureds on the other hand in a very physical sense. In any case, for me it was the railway line, and I see this thing over there all the time.

> Adam Small, interviewed at
> the California Institute of Technology,
> Pasadena, in 1971

DOMINANCE AND TERRITORIALITY

Sociospatial planning in the Republic of South Africa aims toward a goal opposite to what in the United States and in the United Kingdom are almost unconsciously professed basic ideals. Although the ideal is not achieved, public figures in the American and British societies continually stress the conventional wisdom that somehow a "mix" of social strata in a given area is societally wholesome: whether of classes in British new towns or of races in American cities, whether the voice is a White United States senator's[1] or the Afro-Americans' National Urban Coalition's.[2] The publicly expressed opinions of the National party in South Africa are the very opposite:

that a "mix" is undesirable and that racially/ethnically homogeneous neighborhoods are for *everyone's* good, Whites'[3] and Nonwhites'. Accordingly, in the South African Parliament in 1977 Senator P. Z. T. van Vuuren claimed:

> We make no apologies for the Group Areas Act and for its application. And if 600,000 Indians and Coloureds are affected by the implementation of that Act, we do not apologise for that either. I think the world must simply accept it. The Nationalist Party came to power in 1948 and said it would implement residential segregation in South Africa. . . . And we shall implement that policy. We put that Act on the Statute Book and as a result we have in South Africa, out of the chaos which prevailed when we came to power, created order and established decent, separate residential areas for our people.

A central justification for this viewpoint, that segregation is in the interest of all, is enshrined in the "friction theory." The belief is simply that any contact between the races inevitably produces conflict. Thus, the minister of the interior, introducing the group areas bill to Parliament on 14 June 1950, stated:

> Now this, as I say, is designed to eliminate friction between the races in the Union because we believe, and believe strongly, that points of contact —all unnecessary points of contact—between the races must be avoided. If you reduce the number of points of contact to the minimum, you reduce the possibility of friction. . . . The result of putting people of different races together is to cause racial trouble.

This assertion is very simplistic and has caused Kuper, Watts, and R. J. Davies (1958) in their study of Durban to devote some time to evaluating its truth. Basically, they correctly observed that the *conditions* under which contact occurs—that is, either equality or asymmetry of social relations—are what influence any potential for interracial friction. Still, the friction theory has some measure of sense to it, as may be illustrated by once again returning to the work of Robert Sommer (1969, pp. 12, 14, and 15), who wrote:

> [Animal studies] show that both territoriality and dominance behavior are ways of maintaining a social order, and when one system cannot function, the other takes over. . . . Group territories keep individual groups apart and thereby preserve the integrity of the troop, whereas dominance is the basis for intragroup relationships. . . . Group territoriality is expressed in national and local boundaries, a segregation into defined areas that reduces conflict.

Now compare Sommer's formulation with Dr. Dönges's speech advocating the group areas bill in Parliament on 31 May 1950.

> Hon. members will realise what it must mean to those groups, always to have to adopt an inferior attitude, an attitude of inferiority towards the Europeans, to stand back for the Europeans, where they live alongside the Europeans, but if we place them in separate residential areas, they will be able to give expression to their full cultural and soul life, and that is why we say that separate residential areas must be established.

The first half of this long sentence is a precise definition of "dominance," and the second half is about "territoriality." Dr. Dönges would doubtless assert that in his statement both Nonwhites and Whites are being offered the advantages, through the good offices of the government, of nonthreatening, snug communal living, secure from "friction," with law and order firmly and justly established. Negative overtones of the word "apartheid" are, therefore, misleading, unfortunate, and indeed undeserved. The phrase "separate development" should be used to indicate — just as with the homelands policy — that Whites and Nonwhites get fair shares of the urban pie in a separate-but-equal dispensation: "The [segregative and property] restrictions imposed on one group are also imposed on the other groups. Each group surrenders certain of its rights for the common good of all groups." These are the words used by Dr. Dönges during the same debate.

According to this concept, if we were to imagine (as I am about to do) what an ideally segregated apartheid city would look like, we would simply plan four quadrants of a circle, one for each of the four major racial groups, and ascertain which group was allocated which quadrant by a roll of the dice. Or we would work out how large each group's sector of the circular city should be, using a direct ratio of space to that group's proportion of the total population of the city; that is, if Black Africans made up five-sixths of the city's population, then the Black African sector would account for (360 × 5)/6 degrees, or 300 degrees, of the circle. But, if we did either of these things, we would not end up with anything that approached the present reality in group areas cities in South Africa.

However, we might choose to take government statements about "self-determination in their own areas" for all racial groups as being, at least partially, evasive verbiage. We might choose to consider Dr. Dönges's words about Nonwhites' "giving expression to their full cultural and soul life" as, at least partially, a politician's hyperbolical hypocrisy. And, if we did so and constructed an imaginary ideal apartheid city upon the supposition that segregation was not the aim but that *domination* through segregation was, then our city would end up being suspiciously like the group areas reality. Every time in the planning of this city that there was a choice to be made as to who would be out where, the Whites would get first choice. Every time there was any advantage to be extracted from the nature of the terrain, as from the disposition of a gully for a barrier or heights for domination, that physiographic advantage would go to the Whites. If we did this, we would find that what started off like a rather chilling and even perverse conceptual exercise in spatial planning eventually became a tellingly accurate replica of Cape Town's segregated reality today.

THE GROUP AREAS CITY IN THEORY

Basically, there is a common economy in South African cities, and it is in the workplace that members of all racial groups cannot avoid mixing. Industrial areas, therefore, are in a sense "common ground," for no person of any racial group lives there, although clearly they are *White* spaces in that Black African, Coloured, and Indian business people especially are not permitted equal access and are not able to establish concerns in these areas. Racial interaction proceeds in these areas, but on the Whites' terms. (In fact, the situation concerning industrial zones is a little more complicated than I have sketched here, and it is also an area of some uncertainty at present. See Chapter 11.)

Residential areas, however, can be systematically and unambiguously segregated. Such segregation is publicly espoused by the government as a conflict-management mechanism; that is, it is used for the minimization of friction. This being so, a concentric-zones-type city, with industry and commerce in large measure at its center, makes a poor candidate for the basis of an ideal apartheid city. Its annular form means that persons of different races would be continually crossing each other's spaces as they commuted to and from work downtown, thus giving rise to friction. (Incidents of this nature in American cities occurred a decade ago when a Black child being struck by a White commuter's car could spark off civil unrest if the citywide situation were already tense.) A better basis for an apartheid city—though not, of course, as effective as having totally separate ethno-cities—is the sectoral plan. W. J. Davies (1971) noted that this fact was appreciated, for example, by the group areas planners in Port Elizabeth. The sectoral plan minimizes a group's need to crisscross other racial groups' zones.

First in the field with such a well-thought-out race-space plan was Durban. In this city (which was a stronghold of British colonial sentiment not characterized by Afrikaner Nationalist politics) segregation plans were being conceived before the introduction of the group areas bill. In response to White fears of Indian "penetration," a city ordinance providing for Whites-only residential areas had been enacted in 1922, followed by the "Pegging Act" of 1943 and by another act in 1946. When the Group Areas Act became law in 1950, the members of the Durban City Council's Technical (city-planning) Subcommittee cooperated fully with the central government and presented their first report in November 1951. In it they offered seven principles, cool and logical derivatives of the British-style town planning of the time, whereby a segregated pattern might be achieved.

1. A residential race zone should:
   (a) have boundaries which should as far as possible constitute barriers of a kind preventing or discouraging contact between races in neighbouring residential zones;
   (b) have direct access to working areas and to such amenities as are used by all races, so that its residents do not have to traverse the residential areas of another race, or do so only by rail or by way of a common highway segregated from the residential areas abutting it;
   (c) be large enough to develop into an area of full or partial self-government or be substantially contiguous to such an area;
   (d) provide appropriate land for all economic and social classes which are present in the race group concerned, or may be expected to emerge in the course of time; and for group institutions, suburban shopping, minor industry and recreation;
   (e) be so sited that the means of transport most suitable for the group concerned is or can be made available.
2. The number of race zones not contiguous to zones occupied by the same race must be kept as low as possible; accordingly large areas offering scope for urban expansion not too remote from the group's places of employment are to be preferred to areas that cannot be expanded.
3. In order to give the maximum length of common boundary between working areas and residential zone, and thus reduce transport costs and difficulties, dispersal of industry in ribbon formation where practicable is preferable to the massing of industry in great blocks.
4. In planning areas for each race group, the present and future requirements of the group, in relation to other groups, must be determining

factors; the extent of situation of land presently owned, occupied or otherwise allocated to that group is not a material consideration.

5. Settled racially homogeneous communities should not be disturbed except in so far as it is necessary to give effect to the postulates set out above. . . .

6. Different race groups may have differing needs in respect of building and site development. In allocating zones to each race, due account must be taken of the topographical suitability of the land and of the extent to which the race group concerned can effectively utilize existing sites and building development.

7. The central business area and the existing or potential industrial areas should not, in the initial stages, be earmarked for the exclusive use of any [one] race.

These seven principles can be applied to our deduced apartheid city under the assumption that the Durban principles were applied to group areas planning in all South African cities. Whether this was so or not cannot be definitely known.[4] Although public hearings are held on group areas zoning in the localities concerned, the final decisions are made in the administrative headquarters in Pretoria and then ex cathedra proclamations are issued. Nevertheless, W. J. Davies (1971), in his painstaking study of the designing of Port Elizabeth's group areas, took as given the validity of the principles as a basis for the segregative planning. Kuper, Watts, and R. J. Davies's work (1958, p. 34), the most authoritative to date on group areas, stated unambiguously that "of all the major cities in the Union, Durban, through its city council, has shown the greatest enthusiasm for compulsory segregation, *and has indeed contributed to the planning of Group Areas legislation for the country as a whole*" (my emphasis). Finally, if these seven principles are accepted for the moment, it can be seen that what seems to begin as a purely theoretical exercise may turn out to have some applicability to the real world.

Following these seven "rules of the game," consider the likely appearance of an "ideal" group areas city built on previously unoccupied land and planned from its beginning. As a starting point, a few physiographic features of the projected city's site can be assumed (Map 11[A]).

Existing physical features should be used by the superordinate planning group; that is, Whites should get first choice. Thus (Map 11[B]), (1) the asymmetrical hill is used for the civic center and central business district for the whole city, although many of the facilities there may be for Whites only. The gentle western slopes of the

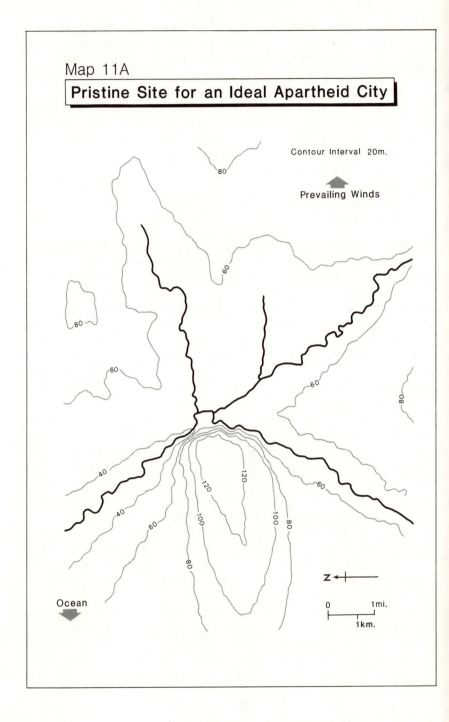

Map 11A

Pristine Site for an Ideal Apartheid City

Contour Interval 20m.

Prevailing Winds

Ocean

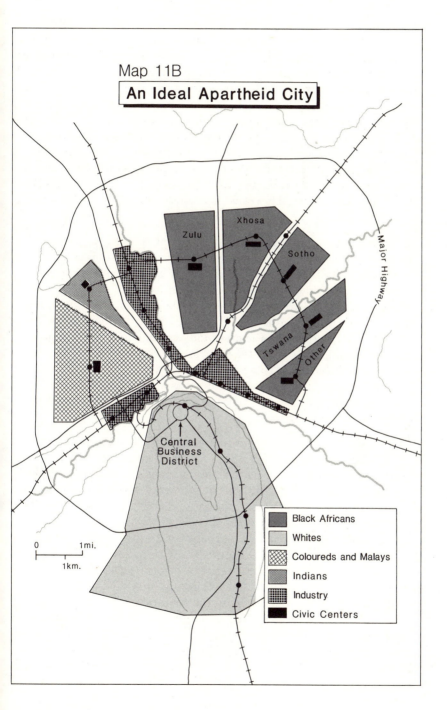

Map 11B

An Ideal Apartheid City

Zulu

Xhosa

Sotho

Tswana

Other

Major Highway

Central
Business
District

0   1mi.

1km.

Black Africans

Whites

Coloureds and Malays

Indians

Industry

Civic Centers

hill are reserved for White residential areas (principle 6). The Whites' possession of relief has a threefold function: (a) strategic physical defensibility, (b) psychological domination from an overlooking height, and (c) residential amenity. Were this a littoral area, the coast would be monopolized by the Whites for reasons (a) and (c).

(2) The rivers may also be used, according to principle 1(a), as (a) a barrier separating White residential areas from both industry and residential zones of other races and as (b) recreational space. The planners must take care, however, that the rivers are not used as racially mixed recreational space; that is, they could plan for the Whites to use the park on the west bank of the river and the Nonwhites, the east bank. However, W. J. Davies (1971, p. 129) noted this of Port Elizabeth:

> An interesting proposal put forward by the Joint Town Planning Committee was the provision for extensive "Green Belt" developments in the city, in all cases associated in one way or another with buffer strips between White and non-White Group Areas. A difficulty arises in this respect, though, since green belt development usually implies parkland. Which group, then, would have the use of the parks? Clearly freedom of use by all races was unacceptable in terms of the Act, and division of such parkland would be impracticable. The *reductio ad absurdum* conclusion is that such parkland should not be used by anyone—clearly an untenable situation. It would seem, then, that provision for parkland should rather be made inside each Group Area, since such use as border strips would inevitably lead to discord.

(From this last sentence it is apparent that W. J. Davies is a firm believer in the friction theory.) Rivers may also be used as (c) providers of water for industrial use. Other things being equal, the land along the river would be reasonably flat and would provide a preferred path for routeways, especially railroads, thereby increasing the likelihood of industrial establishment there.

(3) Industry is located in accordance with principles 1(b) and 3. The industrial zone separates Whites from Nonwhites and is located downwind from White residential areas. It also separates Black Africans from Coloureds and Indians. The absence of any buffer zone greater than a border strip or a minor roadway between Indians and Coloureds is not a great source of concern. It is common practice in apartheid planning to treat the Coloureds and the Indians for some purposes as one entity,[5] made up of people "in the middle," between the Whites and the Black Africans. What is important is that they are well separated not from each other so much as from Whites and Black Africans.

(4) For transportation, as in principle 1(e), (a) owing to the greater dependence upon the private car in White areas, there is less rail passenger service in these areas; (b) the converse is true in Coloured, Indian, and Black African areas. The rail routes, according to principles 1(a) and 1(b), carry the Nonwhite members of the labor force to their places of work without passing near White residential areas; and, whenever possible, rail lines and roads run the length of buffer strips in order to separate more effectively the different racial and ethnic zones. (c) Within the industrial zones all groups travel the same roads and rails (but in separate capsules—buses and railway coaches are racially segregated), symbolizing the integrative limits of the common economy. (d) The circumferential freeway runs through White residential areas for the convenience of the motorized White population. However, it rings Nonwhite residential areas for strategic considerations. During the early 1950s, such concerns prompted the Race Zoning Commission of the Durban branch of the National party to recommend that the greatest part of the seacoast, to a distance of 3 miles inland, should be held in White hands and that all important roads, railway lines, and water pipes should be situated in White areas. (During the October 1976 unrest in Cape Town, one of the two freeways out of the city, Settler's Way, was stoned, and the highway was closed for a time; this happened where it passed wholly through Coloured and Black African townships. The same thing happened during the June 1980 unrest, when the city was cut off from D. F. Malan Airport, which is reached via Settler's Way.) The circumferential freeway in the ideal plan of Map 11(B) was placed some distance out from the edge of the Nonwhite housing areas in order to leave room for sectorial centrifugal expansion, as dictated by principle 1(d). In Cape Town's group area planning, both military airfields, Youngsfield (near Ottery, now disused) and Ysterplaat (near Brooklyn), are in White zones. Let me emphasize my point again: all these strategic considerations indicate that group areas planning is not planning for segregation per se, but for domination through segregation.

(5) The basis for planning the residential areas in Map 11(B) has been the proportions of the various groups in the total South African population. This assumes the use of the present system of racial and ethnic categorization by which Whites are not subdivided ethnically by law while Nonwhites are. To assume such a system here is *not* to accept its validity as an analysis of the society's structure; rather, it is the legislated existential reality with which one is obliged to deal when making designs according to apartheid's canons. According to

the government's categorization, approximately 16.5 percent of the population is White; 9.5 percent, Coloured; 3.0 percent, Indian; 18.8 percent, Zulu; 18.5 percent, Xhosa; 14.0 percent, Sotho; 8.0 percent, Tswana; and 11 percent, other Black Africans. Since Malays account for only 0.6 percent of the total population of the republic, there is no Cape Malay group area in this plan; instead, they are subsumed under Coloureds. These percentages should not imply that—with allowances for the sectors of industry, commerce, transportation, and open space—it would be in these proportions that the remaining angles of sectorial spread are to be assigned. It is expected that Whites will live in more comfort and at lower densities than Nonwhites.

White households also include (as do the households of a few well-off members in other racial groups) the one Nonwhite domestic servant allowed by law to live on the premises in servants' quarters (which are structurally separate by law).[6] This allowance immediately imparts a basic unreality to the watertight residential segregation aimed for by the group areas legislation. Clearly, however, the desirability of total segregation is outweighed by the unwillingness of Whites to forego the South African Way of Life's Nonwhite domestic servants. "White by night" may be strategically desirable for the White cities, but it would not be practical politics for the National party to pursue it. Especially because it appreciated that there is frequently *more* than one Nonwhite person who regularly sleeps in the servants' quarters overnight, *Die Vaderland* (21 November 1968) noted its regret that

> people who call aloud for a solution of the race question continue to keep a small army of non-Whites in their homes or on their farms. They even shut their eyes to the fact that Bantu stay overnight on their property. It simply does not enter their heads to investigate who is sleeping on their property. Early in the morning it is not only Lyttleton that looks like a "black ant-heap." Let every Johannesburger, for example, take the trouble to stroll through the streets of his suburb between five and six in the morning. He will then see how potential thieves, thugs, robbers and so forth are exuded in their dozens from the backyards.

Whites, then, living at lower densities and with domestic servants on the premises, have an extraproportionately large space assigned to them in the ideal plan; this according to principle 6. In Map 11(B) the Whites and the Black Africans are allocated approximately equal areas, but their respective proportions of the total population are 16.5 percent and 70.3 percent. Confirmation of this pattern comes from present residential densities for the Johannesburg metropolitan area, whose planners proceed from a rule-of-thumb ratio of $1:3:3:4$ for, respectively, Whites, Coloureds, Indians, and Black Africans (the numbers in the ratio refer to the number of persons per unit of area).

The design of each residential area for each group accords with principle 1(c)'s size/compactness requirements, supporting a local civic center, small-scale suburban shopping areas, and recreational amenities. These tangible facets of "separate development" are, however, separate but unequal. Extensive suburban shopping centers in the Nonwhite townships are not permitted since they would offer too much competition to downtown stores. Outside of the homelands, Black African townships were until 1978 officially considered "temporary" settlements, their inhabitants merely sojourners in "White South Africa." Thus, the argument ran, there was no need to provide commercial or social facilities there. In this way, the "primate" civic center and central business district, attached to the White group area, dominates the whole city from its hilltop site, and the focal point of the metropolis is White.

With the White zone having first choice for placement, the positions of all the other groups' residential zones vis-à-vis the White zone accord to their various statuses as viewed by the Whites, who have total planning power. As Popenoe (1973, p. 40) wrote, "The extent to which a minority group of a particular ethnic status is segregated physically from other groups depends, in part, on its 'social distance' from the majority group. The broad principle here is that social distance is reflected in physical distance." It must be appreciated that, in the sense of this quotation, the Whites in South Africa are the "majority group." They have a majority of power although they are a numerical minority.

W. J. Davies (1971, p. 119) reported that in the group areas planning of Port Elizabeth "the Chinese were placed in closest proximity to the Whites because of the higher standard of living that this group had achieved in Port Elizabeth." The Chinese also represented less than 2 percent of the total population of Port Elizabeth at that time, and thus they constituted not only an insignificant threat to the status of adjacent Whites but also little strategic threat through their numbers. It is the strategic threat implicit in their numerical majority, as well as their great social distance, that has led to the spatial distancing of Black Africans from Whites. And it is this interplay of numbers, fears, and statuses that in my model apartheid city places the Coloureds' residential areas closest to the Whites, with the Indians'[7] areas next closest and the Black Africans' townships farthest away.

THE GROUP AREAS OF CAPE TOWN IN THEORY

How close is my hypothetical model of an apartheid city to the actual plan carried out for Cape Town? Let us assume as given as few characteristics as possible. (1) The physical site of Cape Town is unalterable in all but a few rather minor respects (for example, the "made ground" of the docks and city center foreshore where what was Roggebaai (*baai* is "bay") has been filled in (Map 12)). (2) The basic function of the city remains the same: it is a port and an industrial center that has South Africa's main communications artery running slightly north and east from the city toward the coastal mountain passes and eventually to the economic core of the country on the Rand. (3) The general proportions of the various racial and ethnic population groups will remain representative of the mix that has characterized Cape Town in the past. That is to say, the proportions of these groups in the *total* South African population do not apply in this case. At which juncture, however, should "the norm" for Capetonian population proportions be chosen? Clearly, the proportions are not set but are continually changing. During this century, there has been, as in other South African cities, a decline in the White proportion of the population, which has fueled White demands for the perceived security of group areas. But, since *some* date must be chosen as a baseline for this plan, let it be 1948, when the Nationalists acceded to power and group areas "development" became a certainty. At that time, the approximate proportions of groups in Cape Town's population were 44 percent White, 44 percent Coloured, 11 percent Black African, and 1 percent Indian. (4) The preexisting social geography and racial ecology of Cape Town in 1948 (Map 6) will not in any way deter the planners or cause them to deviate from their projected ideal spatial arrangements. People, whoever they are, may be moved about with impunity, like checkers on a board. However, (5) because of the symbolic value of the Mother City of South Africa situated beneath the towering backdrop of the face of Table Mountain, no attempt will be made to change the location of the city center; rather, it will be cherished on its familiar site.[8] The planners of this ideal apartheid city are White South Africans, and to them the Mother City's central precincts, where van Riebeeck first set foot in 1652, partake of elements of "sacred space." Based on these five characteristics, the pattern would be like that shown in Map 13.

White settlement must command the higher ground and also most

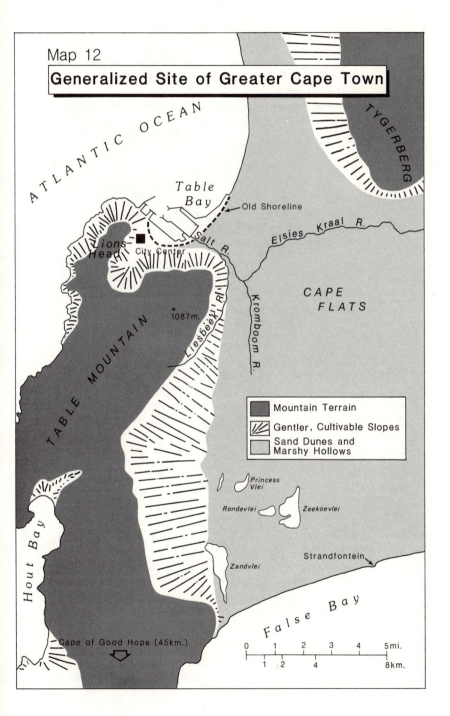

Map 12

Generalized Site of Greater Cape Town

ATLANTIC OCEAN

TYGERBERG

Table Bay

Old Shoreline

Salt R.

Elsies Kraal R.

Lions Head

City Center

CAPE FLATS

1087m.

Liesbeek R.

Kromboom R.

TABLE MOUNTAIN

Mountain Terrain

Gentler, Cultivable Slopes

Sand Dunes and Marshy Hollows

Princess Vlei

Rondevlei

Zeekoevlei

Hout Bay

Zandvlei

Strandfontein

False Bay

Cape of Good Hope (45km.)

0   1   2   3   4   5mi.

1   2   4   8km.

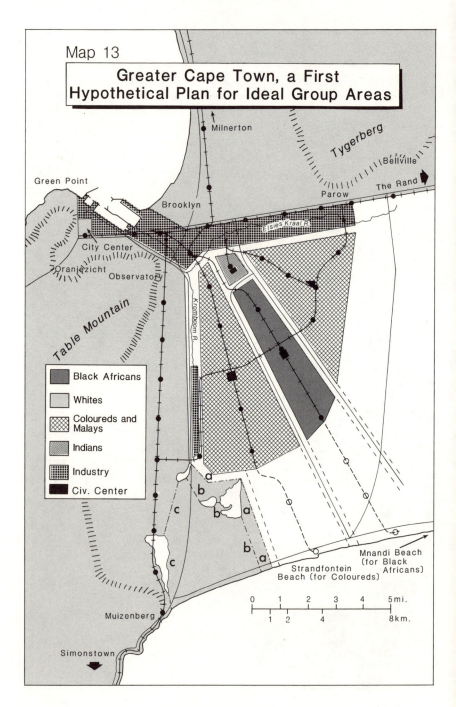

Map 13

Greater Cape Town, a First Hypothetical Plan for Ideal Group Areas

Milnerton

Tygerberg

Bellville

Green Point

Parow   The Rand

Brooklyn

Elsies Kraal R.

City Center

Oranjezicht   Observatory

Kromboom R.

Table Mountain

Black Africans

Whites

Coloureds and Malays

Indians

Industry

Civ. Center

a

b

c

b

a

c

b

a

Mnandi Beach (for Black Africans)

Strandfontein Beach (for Coloureds)

0   1   2   3   4   5mi.

1   2   4   8km.

Muizenberg

Simonstown

of the coast, for the purposes of defense, domination, and amenity. Thus, the Whites settle the flanks of Table Mountain along the western, Atlantic coast south from Green Point, and east from Oranjezicht to Observatory and south to Muizenberg (the southern suburbs). The eastern boundary of the White suburbs is fixed to the north by the Kromboom River. Southwards from its source, where there are no usable physical barriers, a strip of industry is placed, with the barrier emphasized by a major arterial highway.

Still farther south, there are the lakes, or *vleis*, large water-filled hollows among the Cape Flats sanddunes. What use could the Whites make of Princess Vlei, Rondevlei, and Zeekoevlei? There are three options: (a) to monopolize them, (b) to share them (with the Coloureds), or (c) to forego their use. Let us assume that the Whites choose option a and extend their areas out from the flanks of the southern peninsula mountains on to the Cape Flats in order to make use of the amenity value of the vleis. Since there are no topographical barriers, buffer strips will have to be created between White and Coloured areas and between White and future Coloured areas (observe the provision for eventual centrifugal expansion of Coloured and Black African areas toward their False Bay beaches, respectively, Strandfontein and Mnandi). Whites might choose option b, which combines the amenity and barrier functions of the vleis. However, according to the principles of apartheid, there can be no option b, for it would mean, if Whites occupied the southern and western banks and Coloureds the northern and eastern banks, that the groups would be *sharing* the vleis. The planners' reaction to this eventuality can be anticipated. Referring to Port Elizabeth's parks, museums, et cetera, W. J. Davies (1971, p. 210) wrote, "The inevitable *swamping* of such amenities by non-Whites that would result must be seen in the light of current race relations attitudes and would inevitably result in friction" (italics added). Such a conclusion is similar to those surrounding the "green belt" proposals in Port Elizabeth. If the Whites choose option c, they remain encamped on the gentle Pollsmoor-Tokai slopes of the mountain, west of the north-south freeway, with Zandvlei as an extra buffer extending toward Muizenberg to the south. But then they forego the amenity value of Rondevlei and Zeekoevlei. Since option b is no option, the choice is between a and c. Since, once again (as with live-in domestics), it can be assumed that the Whites want segregation but not at a price that denies them amenities, I can posit that the Whites would choose option a and take the vleis. Especially since their fear of the Coloureds is not so great, Whites would be prepared to live on the flat and not only on the higher land. This is in fact what has happened for the most part. Whites engage in sailboating, sculling, and water-skiing and occupy waterfront homes on Zeekoevlei, which is separated from the Coloured group area of Grassy Park by an official no-man's-land at least 100 meters wide (it was proclaimed as such on 8 November 1965; nothing has been built upon it).

The flanks of the other area of high ground, the Tygerberg, are also reserved for Whites, south to the northern suburbs of Parow and Bellville. In addition, the coast north of the port and its associated industrial area, from Brooklyn to Milnerton, is for Whites. This being so, it would immediately seem desirable to make a link from the coast there, eastward to Parow, to create a continuous tract of White settlement; the actual gap (as on Map 15) is under 10 kilometers. It should be noted that W. J. Davies has accepted the creation of such continuity as a prerequisite in group areas planning in an analogous situation, that of the Port Elizabeth-Despatch-Uitenhage "White corridor," although the gap in the Port Elizabeth area is at least twice as great as that from Brooklyn to Parow. If such a continuous Brooklyn-Parow-Bellville White residential zone is created, it can with facility be separated from Nonwhite areas to the south by an industrial strip along the primary communications artery. Finally, although residential use there is extremely implausible, the *whole* of the commanding Table Mountain is zoned as a White group area.

Always, then, the Whites choose the advantageous sites. Such was perceived to be a likely future by the liberal politician Dr. Edgar Brookes when he attacked the group areas bill in Parliament in June 1950.

He [the minister of the interior] wants to divide it [the land] and to have the first pick too. We know what we are talking about on these benches . . . and we know what every honest member of this House will admit —hon. members who have been on the Native Affairs Commission in this House will admit—that what you get for a Native location in an urban area is a bit of land which nobody else wants. Just what is left. They know that. They know that that is so all over the country. Do you suppose, Mr. President, that if there is any allocation of land between Europeans and Coloured in the Cape Peninsula, that the Coloured people would get Newlands or Kenilworth? [These are high-status White southern suburbs of Cape Town, with at that time some Coloured pockets.] . . . The Hon. Minister knows they will not. . . . This is the nature of this Bill: compulsory segregation administered by one race. And I do not trust the Hon. Minister to hold the scales equally between the races; I do not trust him in the least, to do so.

Brookes's mistrust was to be wholly substantiated.

According to my model, the Whites can be expected to claim an extraproportional amount of the space available for their low-density residential use. Both they and the Coloureds are numerous enough to be divided into two sections without doing violence to principles 1(d) and 1(e). Congruent with social distance, the Black Africans are placed as far away from the Whites as possible and beyond industry, and then they are further concealed by flanking Coloured zones, whose position is also congruent with social distance. There is no residential segregation *within* the Black African group because the proportion of those whose ascribed ethnic affiliation is other than Xhosa has always been minimal in Cape Town, currently amounting to only 4 percent.

Provision for rail lines and arterial roads fulfills their anticipated functions as buffer zones, and the transportation lines move Nonwhite workers through segregated facilities to their jobs and their beaches, with minimal crossing of each others' allotted zones. The main national road freeway to Johannesburg runs along the northern edge of the major industrial strip, thereby being retained within White territory. The circumferential freeway is also a good distance out from the present edge of the Nonwhite townships for similar strategic reasons, and it allows for future sectorial township expansion. The Whites, the most affluent group, are as car owners those who make the greatest demand for freeways, another reason for having the national road run close by the edge of the White northern suburbs. The Whites can, therefore, also live farthest from the city center, since travel is less of an imposition to them, especially if they move by freeway. Thus, it can be anticipated that, if the primary work area of the metropolis remains central- and inner-city Cape Town, then the White suburbs will outdistance and outflank the Nonwhite suburbs along both the east-west and north-south axes (that is, the northern and southern suburbs, respectively).

Finally, a minor revision to the general pattern may be made in the area covered by the Black African residential space. Since a high proportion of Black Africans in Cape Town are male Transkeian migrants living in dormitory barracks and since it is the government's policy to decrease the proportion of Black African families in the Cape Town population still further, it can be assumed that Black African residential densities will be higher than at first supposed for

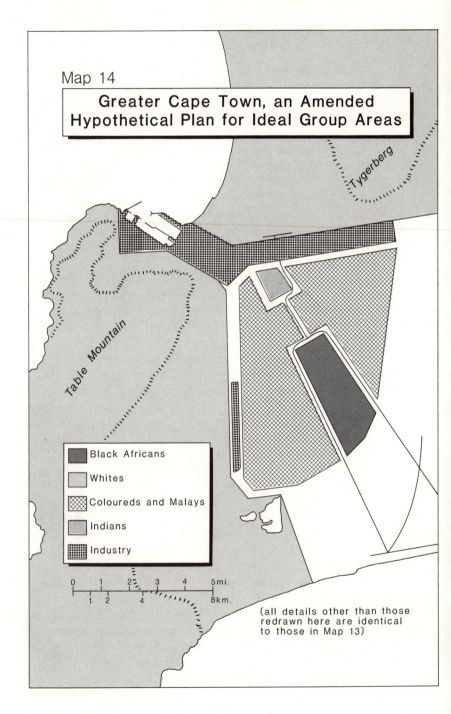

Map 14

**Greater Cape Town, an Amended
Hypothetical Plan for Ideal Group Areas**

Tygerberg

Table Mountain

- Black Africans
- Whites
- Coloureds and Malays
- Indians
- Industry

0   1   2   3   4   5mi.

1   2   4   8km.

(all details other than those
redrawn here are identical
to those in Map 13)

the purposes of the ideal model, and so their space requirement is lessened. If the shape of the Black African zone is made thinner, however, it will approach a sliverlike shape, and this is contrary to the compactness requirement. Instead, why not take away the northernmost portion of their zone as delineated in Map 13? The northernmost section is that which was city-centerwards, that most close to White residential neighborhoods. To remove it enhances, concomitant with the aim of maintaining social distance, the buffering of the Whites from the Black Africans by the Coloureds. The Coloureds find that their two residential tracts then approach each other over the land not allocated to the Black Africans, and the Coloured tracts thereby form an unbroken barrier between the Whites and the Black Africans. The resultant pattern is like that shown in Map 14. Already it is a disposition approximating the post-group areas reality of Cape Town, shown in Map 15.

GROUP AREAS OF CAPE TOWN IN PRACTICE

The introduction of just one more real-world constraint will greatly enhance the fit between the ideal model and reality. Clearly, group areas have been imposed for the benefit of the Whites.[9] There were tracts on the Cape Flats where Whites had settled before the Group Areas Act became law—such as Pinelands and Lansdowne—where, according to the model, they should not have been (Map 16). However, it is just not practical politics in South Africa's "Herrenvolk democracy" to attempt to uproot White voters for the sake of some model plan (or to take away their live-in Nonwhite domestics or their access to the amenities of the vleis). Especially when it came to power with the slightest of majorities and began to implement its apartheid program, the Nationalist government needed to garner all the White support and enthusiasm for its cause that it could. It could not afford to alienate White voters. Furthermore, it was and is most solicitous of White solidarity, and the forced removals of too many Whites would have been a very emotionally divisive issue. Whites are much more difficult, then, to move about than Nonwhites. In fact, trade-offs take place between the desire to achieve the ideal apartheid plan and the desire to move as few Whites as possible.

This is another example of the group areas plan imposing segregation not for segregation's sake but for the Whites' advantage. If the cost to Whites (who hold a monopoly on political power) is too high, then the ideal segregative plan cannot be implemented. The minister of the interior may have said in the debate on the group areas bill in

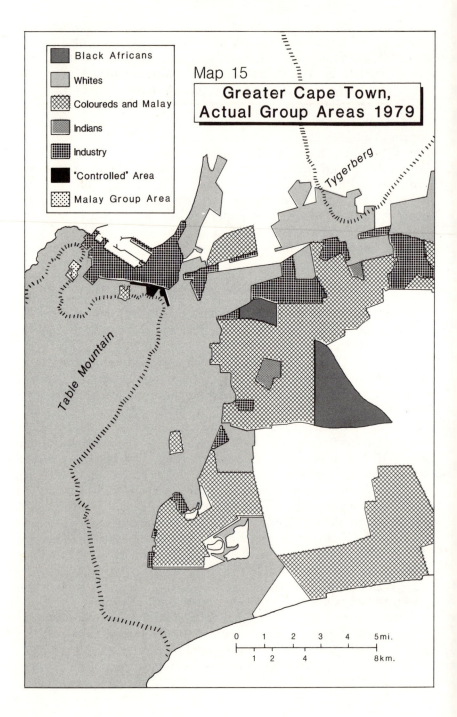

Map 15

Greater Cape Town,
Actual Group Areas 1979

Black Africans
Whites
Coloureds and Malay
Indians
Industry
"Controlled" Area
Malay Group Area

Tygerberg

Table Mountain

0 1 2 3 4 5mi.

1 2   4   8km.

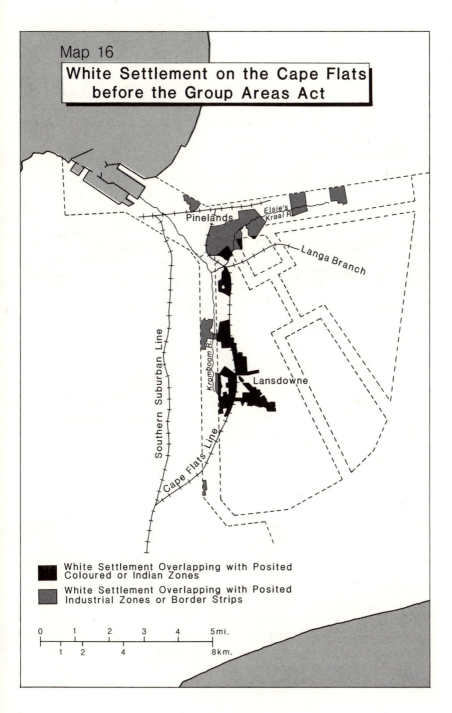

Map 16

White Settlement on the Cape Flats before the Group Areas Act

Pinelands

Elsie's Kraal R

Langa Branch

Southern Suburban Line

Kromboom R.

Lansdowne

Cape Flats Line

White Settlement Overlapping with Posited Coloured or Indian Zones

White Settlement Overlapping with Posited Industrial Zones or Border Strips

0   1   2   3   4   5mi.

1   2   4   8km.

1950 that "we must find living-room for the Non-Europeans, the Europeans will have to make sacrifices." But when (as Kuper, Watts, and R. J. Davies [1958] have documented) Durban's technical sub-committee tried to place some small burden of removal upon the city's Whites, there was a furor. One city councillor complained that "the human element" had been overlooked. The plans were redrawn, and the Whites were not moved—but more Nonwhites were. The relevant equation is thus "White equals human."

Similarly, in Port Elizabeth, as W. J. Davies (1971, p. 125) said,

the [Reference and Planning] Committee felt that it had little choice in allocating it [the area in question] to White development, since it already contained over eight hundred dwelling units housing almost 2,000 Whites. It was pointed out, though, that the area was unfavourably situated with respect to proper Group Areas planning, and would have been much more suitable for Coloured development in a natural consolidation of areas C1 and C2. . . . Unfortunately, it is also relevant that the majority of Whites already living in the area, which later became known as Algoa Park, were government supporters. A desire not to antagonise government supporters was thus apparently also influential in the decision to zone area W3 as a White Group Area.

The case could not be put more plainly: Whites are not to be moved. Nonwhites, however, can be moved as ideal planning requires, especially since in Cape Town most of them are Coloureds, whom the Whites have (at least before the 1976 riots) discounted as any active threat compared with the Black Africans.

Thus, the barriers constituted by rivers and industrial strips in the ideal (Map 14) cannot wholly be used, because Whites cannot be moved back behind them. What, then, is the next best barrier to the east on the Cape Flats for the preexisting White settlement? The answer is clearly the railway lines. The Langa branch almost wholly seals off Pinelands from approach from the southeast, the townships' direction. The potential barrier functions of the Cape Flats line's electrified double tracks and barbed-wire and chain-link fences on both sides are striking, also (Figure 4). More than half of the White settlement to the east of the Kromboom River is safely to the west of the Cape Flats line. Recall Adam Small's words in the quotation at the beginning of this chapter.

If this one modification, the railway barriers, is incorporated into the model, then a superposition of the resultant Map 17 upon the 1976 group areas reality reveals two things. First, there is in terms of the total metropolitan Cape Town population a congruence of about

Figure 4. The Cape Flats Rail Line as a Group Areas Barrier. Broadly comparable in socioeconomic status, Sybrand Park (left, city-centerward) is middle-class White, separated from Hazendal (right), which is upper-class Coloured. These areas were mixed residential tracts before the Group Areas Act. Today, the formerly blurred social distinctions between White and Coloured have been bolstered by spatial segregation—an example of Robert Sommer's dictum on territoriality.

75 percent between minimally constrained deductive model areas and actual group areas. This fact I consider suggestive. (Later, I will raise the congruence level to about 82 percent after a little further scrutiny.) Second, a map of "residuals" is produced by this superposition (Map 18). For some of these continuing, residual "anomalous areas" (those shaded), there is apparently no logic; for the continuing existence of others (those unshaded), some explanations can be offered.

It should be borne in mind that areas where various racial residential zones conflict with what ideally should have been border strips are not considered a conflict of any intractability in my analysis and so are not investigated here. Areas where various residential zones conflict with what ideally would have been nonresidential industrial tracts (those areas stippled) are not considered to represent as severe a conflict as those areas where two or more racial residential zones are confounded. Areas of solid black shading are small areas of in-

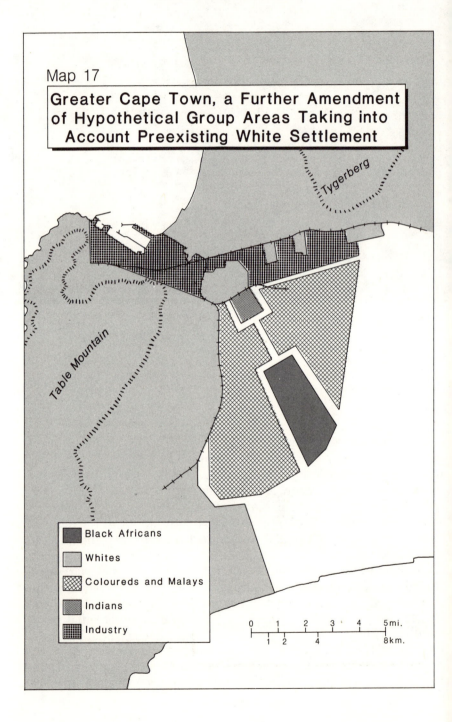

Map 17

Greater Cape Town, a Further Amendment of Hypothetical Group Areas Taking into Account Preexisting White Settlement

Tygerberg

Table Mountain

- Black Africans
- Whites
- Coloureds and Malays
- Indians
- Industry

0   1   2   3   4   5mi.
1   2   4   8km.

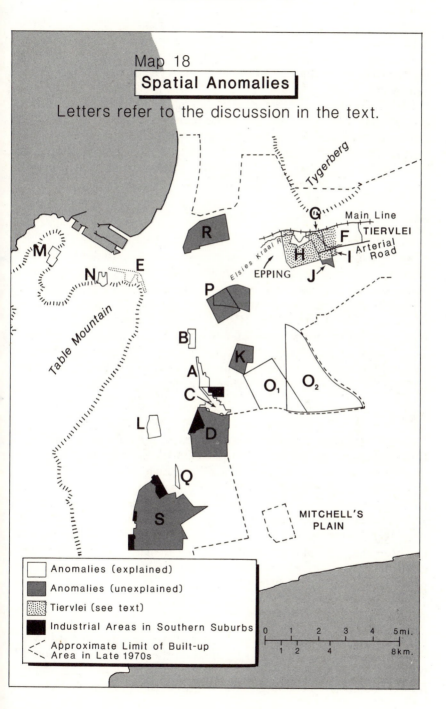

Map 18

Spatial Anomalies

Letters refer to the discussion in the text.

Tygerberg

Main Line

TIERVLEI

Elsies Kraal R.

EPPING

Arterial Road

Table Mountain

MITCHELL'S PLAIN

☐ Anomalies (explained)

■ Anomalies (unexplained)

▦ Tiervlei (see text)

■ Industrial Areas in Southern Suburbs

⌇ Approximate Limit of Built-up Area in Late 1970s

0 1 2 3 4 5mi.

1 2 4 8km.

dustry in the southern suburbs that do not mesh with the posited small areas of industry of Map 14. Nevertheless, it should be noted that all these industrial areas are at locations where White and Coloured group areas abut, and thus the industry is (in topological terms, as it were) in the *relational* position it was predicted to occupy, although it is not very effective in fulfilling the function of a continuous border. The same is true of the main industrial strip. Compare again Maps 15 and 17. Although more fragmented, its general position is satisfyingly close to what the model anticipated. Having made these prefatory remarks, I will now investigate each of these nineteen residual "anomalous areas," A through S, in turn.

Area A

Although area A lies beyond (that is, east of) the Cape Flats line, it was a White housing development before the Group Areas Act was legislated and has been retained as White by the Group Areas Board. Many of those living there were government supporters, and on its consecrated ground there stands the Afrikaans Dutch Reformed Church of Die Vlakte (the [Cape] Flats). To move this piece of White sacred space because of Coloured residential considerations would have gone very much against the grain. This area was much discussed at the public hearings for the determination of group areas in Cape Town in August 1956. (See p. 127).

Area B

North of area A, less than 2 kilometers up the rail line, a small section of Athlone to the *west* of the tracks (area B) has been declared Coloured. It is a very well established and high status area, and there was vociferous protest during the hearings in Cape Town after it was first advertised for White *or* Coloured. Many other Coloured people also protested vociferously on behalf of *their* tracts, but to no avail. Area B, however, was inhabited by an extraproportionate number[10] of the educated Coloured leaders. In particular, a Cape Town city councillor lived there, and his voice could be heard in important places.

Area C

A salient of preexisting White settlement, outer Lansdowne-Wetton, area C is perhaps too far beyond the pale,[11] too "exposed" to posited Coloured territory, to be retained as White, and indeed it has been declared Coloured. The Whites have had to move out.

Area D

The logic applied to area C, however, breaks down over area D. This area was undeveloped as residential land at the time of the group areas deliberations during the first half of the fifties (thus, there were *no* Whites to move out), and it seems clearly, in terms of group areas criteria of contiguity and compactness, to be a "natural" Coloured area. Yet, in January 1955, it was advertised as a White group area and was proclaimed such in 1961. It is separated from the body of White settlement in the southern suburbs by a military air-field and a golf course, by the double-track railway, and partially by industry and Coloured residential zones. Among the many specula-tions that might explain this anomaly, perhaps a likely one is the question of who owned the land in this area prior to its development and of what were their relationships with government. Certainly, negotiations over the purchase of Mitchell's Plain for Coloured resi-dential development, farther to the south, were delicate because cer-tain landowners were government supporters.[12] Such suppositions are hardly any explanation, however, so area D—unlike areas A, B, and C—is shaded in on Map 18.

Area E

Irregularly shaped area E is next to the railway in the old inner-city industrial tract and has until very recently been undeclared or "con-trolled." It consists of a narrow strip of lower Woodstock and lower Observatory, plus much of Salt River. This erstwhile controlled area's population is racially mixed but predominantly Coloured. In terms of the ideal plan, it should be White space. The Theron Commission recommended in June 1976 that it be declared Coloured. In July 1978 the Department of Planning advertised an investigation into converting it to a Coloured group area and deproclaiming a part of Salt River that was an industrial area from White to uncontrolled. The city councillor, the member of the Provincial Council, and the member of Parliament for the area organized a meeting at which over 400 White and Coloured residents unanimously resolved that the area should be open to both White and Coloured people. A survey re-vealed that of 332 householders visited in the entire area, 292 held this opinion (33 households could not be reached). The Cape Town City Council supported the residents' opinion and stated its opposi-tion to the Group Areas Act, saying it had contributed to the deteri-oration in race relations in the city. Eventually, in November 1979, it was announced that two of five sections of area E were to be proclaimed Coloured, after twenty-nine years of utter uncertainty—over half the average lifetime of the Coloured inhabitants. The three other zones were to *remain* controlled, that is, still uncertain. The significance of this decision, along with that made on area N, will become clearer in Chapter 6.

Areas F, G, H, I, J, K

In these northern suburban areas, as can be appreciated from Maps 16 and 14, the "problem" of preexisting White settlement on the ideally Nonwhite territory of the Cape Flats is not so great as in the southern suburbs. Un the northern suburbs, Whites are only spilling onto areas ideally industrial tracts or a little onto areas ideally border strips. Therefore, it will not be necessary, doubtless to the government's content, to remove White people (predominantly Afrikaans speaking and of [for Whites] moderate to low income) from Maitland, Thornton, and Epping Garden Village or from tracts of Elsies River and Tiervlei. Industry, however, could be extended a little to the south of them in order to buffer them more securely against Coloured space. This, in turn, propels the northern boundary of Coloured and Indian proposed group areas a little farther south. This minor modification has also been introduced into Map 17, as has the similarly minor modification of the main railway line to the interior not running dead straight as in the ideal plan, but a little flexed thereabouts. The ideal plan had assumed that all White residential areas would be north of the main railway line and all Nonwhite zones to the south; this is indeed the case eastward from Tiervlei out to the far side of Bellville, which marks the farthest edge of the built-up area of greater Cape Town. It was also assumed that a band of industry would complement the railway's barrier function here, and it does partially.

Area F was mainly White housing before group areas development, and under the ideal plan it should be an industrial zone. It has been accounted for in Map 17, and therefore it does not represent an anomaly. Area G is an anomaly in a minor sense, for it was undeveloped at the time of group areas planning and should ideally have become industrial, but in fact it has become White residential. Its position adjacent to area F, however, means that it could easily be consolidated with F to create a larger White area south of the main railway line. This area is somewhat isolated from the main body of northern suburban White territory across the line. Since neither industry nor railway is usable here as a barrier between Whites and Nonwhites, the use of the Elsies Kraal River might have been anticipated. However, White housing had already grown up south of the river before group areas; also, the river is very narrow at this point in its course. Thus, it cannot be used as a barrier to the south, as Map 18 demonstrates. Instead, a new arterial road fulfills this function somewhat imperfectly, for it is neither very broad nor is it a limited-access highway with nonstop traffic.

Areas H and I are Coloured group areas where industry was posited, therefore presenting no major anomaly. Area J is a small Indian group area, Cravenby, half where industry was expected, half where Coloureds were expected. Indians make up so small a group (with a little over 1 percent) of Cape Town's population that the bureaucracy could place them almost anywhere in the Nonwhite areas. I am ignorant of any explanation for the location of area J as an Indian group area or, similarly, for the location of Indian Rylands (area K).

This whole area (including areas F, G, H, I, and J) is broadly known as Tiervlei. The border between Whites and Nonwhites is partially maintained by an industrial area, but elsewhere Tiervlei lacks impermeable barriers. Attempts to bolster the separation of Whites and Nonwhites there have been made through the renaming of the various portions of Tiervlei according to their racial status. The White northern areas, F and G, are now officially called Parow Valley; the Coloured southern areas, area I and southward, are now officially called Ravensmead. Less than 2 kilometers to the east there is a similar ill-defined frontier between Coloured Elsies River (area H) and White Epping (indicated on Map 18). There the border runs down First Street, a minor street that does not even rate a bridge over the little Elsies Kraal River. Most instructive, then, is the following aggressively defensive letter published in the *Argus* (7 April 1976), headed "It Didn't Happen in Epping."

I refer to the report in The Argus on March 27 headed "Stabbing in Epping: 3 arrested."

As a resident of Epping I wish to point out that this report is misleading. It says the body of the victim of a stabbing was found off Second Avenue, Epping. There is no such address in Epping. It is in fact in Elsies River.

The report further says that Mr. Strydom and two friends went to a shebeen — an illicit liquor outlet — in the Coloured area of Epping. There is no Coloured area in Epping, which is a European housing scheme.

You will no doubt understand the embarrassment caused to inhabitants of Epping by this incorrect publication.

J. J. LEIBBRANDT[13]

Epping

In toto, my analysis of these areas (F, G, H, I, and J) shows that the first four and part of the fifth overlap only onto an expected industrial zone. This is hardly a serious fault in the ideal segregative plan.

Area L

Coloured area B, where Whites are expected, is similar to the anomaly of area L, lower Wynberg, a high-status (for Nonwhites) Coloured enclave surrounded by White territory. It is bordered on its west side by the suburban railway and on its north and east sides by major roads. It has always been a substantial Coloured and Malay area, but this, of course, is not a sufficient reason for its survival as such. The Battswood Training College for Teachers (for Coloureds, Indians, and Malays) was established there in 1891. The college was operated by the Dutch Reformed Mission Church, which is the racially segregated daughter church (for the Nonwhites) of the Dutch Reformed Church (for the Whites). The mission church has many White clergy, and it should be stressed that at the group areas public hearings in 1956 the Wynberg Mission Church, strongly committed to "missionary" social work in its area, utterly opposed any removals. It conducted at least two surveys of its own in order to place evidence before the Group Areas Planning Board to support the Nonwhites' claim to remaining where they were. One of the ministers, an Afrikaner, was D. P. Botha, who later (1960) wrote a much-discussed book advocating the inclusion of the Coloured people with the Whites, *Die Opkoms van Ons Derde Stand* (*The Rise of Our Third Estate*). He has been moderator of the Mission Church from 1947 to the present. Championed by such Whites, Nonwhite Wynberg can be assumed to have had friends with access to power who were able to defend it. Interviews with Reverend Botha in April 1975 and August 1978 wholly confirmed this supposition. Area L was proclaimed Coloured on 10 February 1961, and yet a number of the home owners I met there in 1975 and 1976 still expressed their uncertainty about the area's future security. Their uncertainty had a basis—they had *no* legal grounds for security; the act continues to prescribe eminent domain. Thus, after the proclamation of February 1961, whereby nearly all of Cape Town's southern suburbs were declared White, Dr. R. E. van der Ross in "Coloured Viewpoint" in the *Cape Times* (23 February 1961) wrote, "What perturbs those who are going to 'safe' areas [for example, lower Wynberg] is the strong and justifiable feeling that there is really no safe area. If a man can be uprooted once he can be uprooted again, just when someone else needs his home." And *The Theron Commission Report* in 1976 (van der Horst, p. 64) noted the insecurity felt by some of its Coloured informants in this regard: "As soon as the houses of the white people appear on the horizon then we wonder if we shall have to shift once more."

Area M

This area constitutes perhaps the most striking anomaly in all greater Cape Town. It includes Schotsche's Kloof (the Malay Quarter), proclaimed for Malays on 5 July 1957, plus a minute area, Schoonekloof, abutting mainly on the southwest, proclaimed for Coloureds on 25 May 1962. It is a unique case. Not only is it adjacent to the city center of Cape Town, it actually *overlooks* it from higher ground. Schotsche's Kloof is itself overlooked by yet higher ground proclaimed for Whites on Signal Hill, but there is no White residential development there. The Malay Quarter has great historical value, and indeed it is being renovated, in part in order to play more effectively its role as one of the tourist attractions of Cape Town — to the distaste of some of the residents of Schotsche's Kloof. It is a small area, and its population is under 2,000 persons.[14] Therefore, it represents no real strategic threat, especially since its people, Cape Malays, are part of a tiny minority in the South African population. The Cape Malays also had an Afrikaner champion, I suspect, in Isak D. Du Plessis, who in 1944 published his historical-ethnographical book *The Cape Malays.* In fact, he was appointed head of the (then) subdepartment of Coloured Affairs on 5 March 1951, under the Department of the Interior (one of the department's functions was to plan group areas). He is also a respected senior figure in the Afrikaans academic establishment and was for eight years the honorary chancellor of the Coloureds' University of the Western Cape in Bellville-South. From such appointments it is clear that he would have been in a position to influence the proclamation of Schotsche's Kloof as a Malay group area.

Area N

Anomalous area N is a portion of upper Woodstock called Walmer Estate. After twenty-four years of uncertain controlled status, it was proclaimed Coloured, although it is flanked by White areas, in June 1975. Once again, it is rather a small area and so cannot be considered a major strategic threat. But District Six, the historic focus of Coloured sentiment, borders area N on its immediate west. Declared White in 1966, District Six is being razed to the ground, thus engendering much bitterness among the Coloureds. When area N was declared Coloured, therefore, its publicity value was enormous: "District Six Reprieve" was the banner headline in the *Cape Times* (26 May 1975). "For the first time now they will really own it," stated *Die Burger* (27 May 1975) ("they" were the Coloureds; "it" was District Six). The publicity was misleading; area N is not District Six, which is still being bulldozed. This matter will be further considered in Chapter 6.

Area O

The situation with regard to areas O_1 and O_2 is simple. O_1 represents the expected positioning, based on almost geometric ideal apartheid, of Black African space; O_2 represents its actual positioning. Given the extensive range of Nonwhite space available for Black African township establishment, the partial overlap of O_1 and O_2 is satisfying support for the spatial logic of my model. The shape of O_2 represents the preexisting land division in the area—what was available for acquisition as an African township during the 1950s—as opposed to the ideal radial-sectorial shape of O_1. With this in mind, it will be appreciated that a lateral shift of only 3 kilometers will bring it into congruence with O_2. Such a piece of spatial juggling is, I submit, quite defensible, because the relationship of this Black African space to all other spaces remains the same. It is still the farthest from the Whites, partially beyond industry, and wholly sealed off by Coloured space on its west and north sides (that is, city-centerwards). The shift has in no way altered the contiguities.

Area P

Area P is an expected Indian space—again by little more than a geometric criterion—but in fact it is the Black African space of Langa. When Langa was established in 1923, it was far out of the city on the Cape Flats dunes. Since that time, the city has grown out to meet and surround it. It is now separated in its western portion from White Pinelands by only Jan Smuts Drive (an arterial road) and the railway. This is the most precipitous social gradient in Cape Town,[15] were people physically able to traverse it. In terms of apartheid's spatial logic, Langa is today too close to White space. I predict its eventual expunction—it happened before with the Dock Native Location and Ndabeni—when and if the government feels secure enough in its hold on civil peace to do so and when it has the means and the

will to provide alternative accommodation for Langans out at Ny-
anga-Guguletu (area O_2).

Area Q

Area Q is a sliver of Southfield, a White area where a Coloured one
was expected (and to the west of this sliver, not drawn in on Map 18,
another thin slice of Southfield where a border strip was expected).
There was already *some* White settlement in Southfield before group
areas planning, but it is beyond (that is, east of) the Cape Flats railway line. Although its eastern border is the busy arterial Prince
George Drive, it is still in an exposed position vis-à-vis Nonwhite
space: Parkwood council rental township, a housing project for poor
Coloureds, is very close by. Indeed, the most exposed White space of
all would be on the west side of Prince George Drive itself. There is
a telling spatial logic, then, to the report in the *Argus* of 9 September
1976 concerning "the first time houses belonging to White residents
have been attacked" during the greater Cape Town unrest, which was
then into its second month.

> Mrs. Rosemary Wheeler . . . [was in her] house on the corner of Banier
> Road and Prince George Drive late yesterday when half-bricks and stones
> were hurled through the windows. . . . About 9:45 p.m. the front win-
> dows were smashed . . . a crowd of about 300 surrounded the house.
> The police were called, but when they arrived the crowd dispersed and
> disappeared into Parkwood Estate, which is across the road from the
> Wheeler's house.

Figure 5 shows Mrs. Wheeler's house. Note the defended space of
this house, its solid, white, concrete surrounding wall, its tiny slit
windows facing Prince George Drive and the Parkwood project, and
the "burglar bars" (iron grilles) on the side windows of the house
next door. [16] Are the residents prepared for a siege?

Area R

Area R is a Coloured group area where a White one was expected.
This area formerly included the notoriously squalid shantytown of
Windermere, where both Coloureds and Black Africans lived in tin
pondoks, of which there still remain a considerable number. The area
adjoins White space only for a one-and-a-half block stretch at its extreme southwest corner, and even there a small border strip has been
carefully inserted. Elsewhere, it is separated from White areas to the
northwest and the north by a new suburban railway line, a freeway

Figure 5. Prince George Drive, the Boundary between Parkwood, a public housing project for Coloureds, and Southfield, a White Group Area. The Coloured people face Table Mountain as they cross the road. Southfield is an exposed salient of White space on the Cape Flats. The house on the right was the first White one to be attacked during the Cape riots of 1976 and is visibly an example of defended space in 1978.

and beyond that a military airfield; to the east by open ground (the unused Wingfield airfield) and then by an arterial road; to the south by industry, the main railway line, a major highway, and cemeteries: an effective battery of spatial barriers. Having said all that, I can offer no explanation why the model and the reality should be so discordant or why area R should remain a Coloured area.

Area S

Area S is the enormous new housing area of Retreat-Steenberg, a Coloured group area where Whites were expected according to the model. Again, as is true partially for area Q and certainly for area R, it is difficult to explain area S's anomalous position. However, it is worth noting that although anomalous in terms of the geometry of the ideal plan, in *relational* terms area S is less anomalous, especially since it can be seen to be lying on the Cape Flats side of that effective racial barrier, the railway.

Summary

The areas shaded in on Map 18 are those where I feel there is no adequate explanation for their existence on what ideally should have been the territory of a different racial group. The areas stippled are those where no adequate explanation is felt to have been given for the existence of a residential area on what ideally should have been an industrial zone. Area E, still in part controlled, is difficult to evaluate. For areas B, L, M, N, O_1 and O_2, and Q, some surmised partial explanations have been advanced. What we are left with is a pattern demonstrating that well under 5 percent of the Whites living in greater Cape Town are situated where ideally they should not be, with about 20 percent of the Coloureds,[17] 100 percent of the Indians, and perhaps 30 percent of the Black Africans so situated. This works out to about 18 percent of the total population of Cape Town not living where it should be according to a highly ideal geometrical plan, subsequently tinkered with but not in any fundamental way modified.

Is this approximately 82 percent congruence suggestive? Is the reasoning process circular (using a model constructed after the fact) and invalid? Or does it, as I would claim, have some heuristic validity? If one is prepared for the moment to go along with the latter supposition, it will be appreciated that there are two possible ways of accounting for the 82 percent congruence. The first is that the percentage is so high because the main lineaments of Cape Town prior to apartheid were already cast in a race-class mold not so different from apartheid aims anyway; all the present government has done is to clean up most of the race-space anomalies. The second way is to see the government as one strong willed, implacable, and not to be turned aside from its decided goals since it came to power in 1948. The present look of Cape Town, then, is due more to the Nationalist government than to what it received as a legacy from a British imperial laissez faire past.

This second interpretation is doubtless that which the government and its supporters would favor; and, especially, how the government would like its Nonwhite subjects to see it: as omnipotent—a psychological consummation devoutly to be wished. The government cannot be deterred or deflected; it has its plans laid out, and it does not change its mind; it does not bow to the pressure of the mass of public opinion (that is, of the Nonwhites); and any questioning of it that oversteps the mark that the government has already decided upon will be met undeviatingly and utterly predictably with force—the government holding nearly all the instruments for imposing its will and not being hesitant to use them. If the government can persuade its Nonwhite subjects that this is the case and, further, if as in Cape Town the mass of its Nonwhite subjects are members of the Coloured group (who are a "privileged" minority among the South African Nonwhite population anyway and therefore are unsure about the value of radical societal change), *then* it is possible to account in part for the lack of overt physical resistance to the forced removals of so many Cape Town citizens from their homes.

To compare Map 15 (present group areas) with Map 6 (ethnic areas in 1950-1952) is indeed to be struck by the simplification of the social geographic pattern and to be induced to think in terms of the second interpretation offered earlier. However, the government is *not* omnipotent and it is constrained to act pragmatically, certainly with regard to preexisting White settlement and to the economy. It cannot change the functions (or the history or the site) of Cape Town overnight, nor can it tear down the accreted fabric of the city everywhere and begin over anew. In this sense, District Six is the exception.

Perhaps one could combine these two evaluations and find a middle position. That is, the first interpretation above, that apartheid is merely an extrapolation of the socioeconomic-cum-racial segregation that had gone before, I believe misses a real shift to more draconian spatial control. T. J. D. Fair (1969), having observed the redrawing of Cape Town's space by group areas, considered the resultant pattern to be one of "fragmented nuclei." This is a somewhat unilluminating conclusion. I suspect, rather, that there is a good deal of underlying coherence to the pattern, for the reasons that have been inherent in the spatial model discussed in this chapter. Group areas is a design for domination; therefore, the second interpretation is valid. Yet, to see the present group areas of Cape Town as the perfect working out of a total, implacable blueprint for segregation is also a limited view. The existence of anomalous areas indicates this limitation, as does the very nature of the explanations offered for certain of these areas (such as areas B, L, and M). In fact, some of the details of the present group areas were arrived at in a rather ad hoc manner, being partially susceptible to the efforts of pressure groups while the precise disposition of group areas for Cape Town was under deliberation.

CHAPTER FIVE

Putting the Plan into Practice: Cape Town since 1950

The Institute has examined [official] proposals . . . for group areas in Cape Town . . . and it calls upon the Minister of the Interior to reject them as incompatible with the justice which he states will guide his decisions.

South African Institute of Race Relations,
press release, 1956

THE MECHANICS OF IMPLEMENTATION

After the Group Areas Act became law in 1950, interracial transfers of property were frozen. In the Cape Province the freeze began on 30 March 1951. Each municipality was requested by the Group Areas Board to provide proposals for the establishment of group areas. Port Elizabeth did so without significant protest. The Cape Town municipality, having some Coloured city councillors and espousing historically a liberal attitude on segregation compared with the White political sentiments elsewhere in the union, refused to provide proposals. The Cape Town City Council maintained that instituting group areas would cause great hardship for vast numbers of ratepaying citizens (that is, those who paid city taxes). It refused to cooperate with the board in any way.

W. J. Davies (1971, pp. 25-26) has expressed his regrets about such an attitude of boycott. Because of its familiarity with local conditions and because of the necessity

to arrive at a workable plan for future development . . . the local authority, in fact, is the only body really qualified or able to provide the kind of information required prior to any proclamation further than the Controlled Area stage. . . . By cooperating with the Group Areas Board in this respect, the local authority could at least have some say in what is to become of its area. The alternative is to have a completely arbitrary and probably unsuitable zoning plan imposed. It would appear that any competent and realistic local authority has little choice but to cooperate fully, whether it agrees with the policy or not.

The Cape Town City Council maintained its boycott, however, refusing to provide detailed survey data on racial patterns of occupation and ownership, unless the information was subpoenaed. Nevertheless, the northern suburban municipalities of Goodwood, Bellville, and Parow—Afrikaner Nationalist strongholds—cooperated readily with the board. The Western Province Land Tenure Advisory Board (as it was titled) drew up its own proposals and advertised them at the beginning of 1953. The board's proposals were then, as mandated by the act, opened for comment and criticism through written depositions from interested parties and communities.

Eventually, a public hearing had to be held, at which a committee of the Group Areas Board, appointed under the act's provisions, heard submissions and countersubmissions from those whose interests were involved. No one, however, had the *right* to appear before the committee to argue his or her case; the committee could exercise its discretion as to whom it would hear. When the public hearings were completed—in Cape Town they lasted for three weeks, August 2 through 23, in 1956—the committee made recommendations to the central Group Areas Board in Pretoria. The final plan, which went to the minister of the interior (today such plans go to the minister of planning), was the decision of the whole Group Areas Board, not just of the commissioners (of whom there were two in Cape Town). The minister then had the power to accept, reject, or amend the plan as he saw fit. When he had approved of the plan, it was proclaimed in the *Government Gazette* that from the date announced the areas in question were to be for the use of the designated racial and ethnic groups only. The law provided for no further protest.

In most cities, the actual removals do not begin until at least a year after the announcements, and the whole process can take many years. Probably partially due to the Cape Town City Council's boycott, it was seven years after the passage of the act in 1950 and four years after the relevant proposals had been debated initially that the first group areas proclamations were made for Cape Town, on 5 July 1957. Most of the metropolis had been proclaimed after another five years. However, District Six was only proclaimed White in 1966, and parts of Salt River are still unproclaimed some thirty years after the act became law.

The board's first proposals for particular group areas in Cape Town were published just three years after the passage of the act. Most of them were for areas that were already de facto segregated residential zones; hence, the board termed them "noncontentious." Suburbs situated above the city in Table Valley—Oranjezicht, Gardens, and Tamboers Kloof—and those beneath the mountain on the Atlantic coast—Green Point, Sea Point, and areas south to Bakoven— were zoned for Whites, as were Pinelands, Thornton, Epping, and the Boston Estate in Bellville. (Here I might mention, by the way, the matter of Sea Point's being zoned for Whites only. It may have been "noncontentious," but two Coloured persons who lived in the small Coloured enclave of Tramways Road in Sea Point committed suicide when they were told that they would have to leave their homes.) Athlone, Kew Town, and other northern Cape Flats areas, all predominantly occupied by Coloureds, were advertised for Cape Coloureds; Schotsche's Kloof was advertised for Malays, as was the Surrey Estate; and Rylands was advertised for Indians. The last two areas especially excited debate and could hardly have qualified for the label "noncontentious." No proposals were offered for the central city, District Six, or the central industrial areas.

In August 1954 proposals for Woodstock, Maitland, Milnerton, and Brooklyn (northern suburbs *within* the municipality of Cape Town), plus schemes prepared by the municipalities of Goodwood, Parow, and Bellville, were advertised; they were debated at sessions of the board in April and May 1955. In a précis of the group areas situation as it was unfolding in greater Cape Town in 1955, Horrell (1956, p.75) reported that the (White) town council of Bellville "made the drastic proposal that all Non-White residents should move out of the present developed suburbs to an area across the railway line, in Bellville South." Although Horrell used the adjective "drastic," this is what has in fact happened: *all* of Bellville north of the railway is now a Whites-only group area, and Bellville-South is wholly Coloured.

Some of the northern suburban areas, for example the Acres in Goodwood, were mixed residential zones at the time of group areas development. Another area of greater Cape Town that was even *more* mixed was the southern suburbs, which were almost exactly half White and half Nonwhite: in 1936, 60,400 and 62,100 persons, respectively.

The zoning proposals for the southern suburbs were advertised in

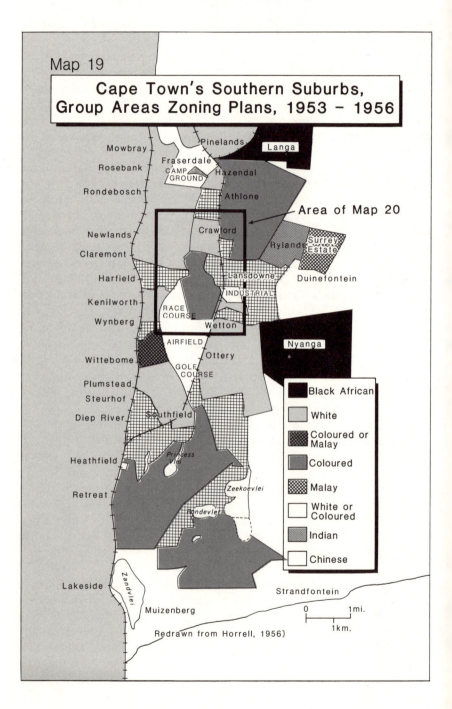

Map 19

Cape Town's Southern Suburbs, Group Areas Zoning Plans, 1953 – 1956

Mowbray
Pinelands
Langa
Fraserdale
Rosebank
CAMP GROUND
Hazendal
Rondebosch
Athlone
Area of Map 20
Newlands
Crawford
Claremont
Rylands
Surrey Estate
Harfield
Lansdowne
Duinefontein
INDUSTRIAL
Kenilworth
Wynberg
RACE COURSE
Wetton
AIRFIELD
Ottery
Nyanga
Wittebome
GOLF COURSE
Plumstead
Steurhof
Diep River
Southfield
Heathfield
Princess Vlei
Zeekoevlei
Retreat
Rondevlei

Legend:
- Black African
- White
- Coloured or Malay
- Coloured
- Malay
- White or Coloured
- Indian
- Chinese

Lakeside
Zandvlei
Strandfontein

Muizenberg

0   1mi.
1km.

Redrawn from Horrell, 1956)

January 1955, and Horrell's (1956) adjective was again "drastic." She also noted (p. 77) that, with the Cape Town City Council boycotting the process of zone planning, "it was not made clear from whom [the proposals] originated." The proposals (Map 19) envisaged the removal of all Nonwhites, except domestic servants, from the area to the west of the suburban railway line. According to the 1951 census, this area was half White and half Nonwhite: 19,811 Whites, 18,278 Coloureds and Asiatics, and 507 Black Africans. Extensive removals of Nonwhites were planned east of this railway line, too, between it and the Cape Flats line south from Pinelands.

A storm of protest arose, especially from Nonwhite organizations. It seems clear that Cape Town as a whole was generally unwilling to have group areas thrust upon it. In parliamentary elections—in which a universal White suffrage heavily outweighed a then still-existent limited Coloured franchise—it was predominantly United party candidates who were returned to Parliament by the city's constituencies. This party, then that of Smuts, opposed the National party. Today, the United party is extinct, but after the Whites-only parliamentary elections in 1977 the liberal-reformist Progressive Federal party opposition holds 7 of the 8 parliamentary seats within the city of Cape Town, the National party just 1. Yet, in the country as a whole, the Whites in 1977 voted in 134 National party members of Parliament and only 17 Progressive Federal party members. This information is interposed here, not to imply that Cape Town Whites were actively voting against segregation, but rather to point out that most of them were satisfied with the de facto partial segregation already in force and wanted the situation left alone, as, of course, did the majority of Coloured Capetonians.

To return to my account of the group areas debate, the furor generated by the board's January 1955 proposals was not lessened by alternative proposals advanced later that year in July.[1] Muriel Horrell (1956, p. 77) has stated that these alternative proposals appeared "presumably as a result of written representations submitted to the Board by many individuals and groups, including the Institute of Race Relations."[2] Note once again the cloaked nature of the workings of the Group Areas Act, through a government bureaucracy in distant Pretoria, evident in Horrell's phrase, *"presumably as a result of . . . ."* Also, earlier, we saw that "it was not made clear from whom [the proposals] originated." Also, there is Prof. R. J. Davies's expressed uncertainty (see footnote 4, Chapter 4) about just how the plans were arrived at, despite his long familiarity with group areas planning and his work on the benchmark Durban study with Leo Kuper and Hilstan Watts. Also, when in 1976-1977 I attempted to gain access to the records of Cape Town group areas planning from the 1950s, I was told by a Department of Community Development official that the planning recommendations were confidential, that they and the notes taken at the 1956 public hearings had been sent to the minister of the interior in Pretoria, and that that was where they were kept, if indeed they still existed.

THE COMMISSION OF INQUIRY OF AUGUST 1956

Since, however, the hearings held by the August 1956 Commission of Inquiry were public, it was possible for me to go back through the reports in the Cape Town newspapers. The Afrikaans-language *Die Burger*'s editorial line on group areas could have been anticipated: it was supportive of the government, and it tried to play down any possible racial injustice by taking a supposedly neutral managerial attitude. The Cape Town City Council's boycott was considered by *Die Burger* to be irresponsible, because "its duty is to assist the Group Areas Board—in the interests of all the inhabitants of Cape Town—to demarcate the Group Areas in such a manner that inconvenience is kept to the minimum that is consonant with a thorough job" (7 August 1956).

The *Argus* was somewhat less dogmatic but similarly managerial in its attitude. Its editorial on 2 August 1956 stated that the city council was in a dilemma. Since the Group Areas Act was law, the city had an obligation to obey it, although the act was "quite impracticable." But, since the city council was responsible to all its ratepayers, a large section of whom wished to have nothing to do with the act, the council also had an obligation to take that view into consideration: "It is all very well for Nationalists to assume that the views of these people can be airily brushed aside because they are not White . . . ." The *Argus*'s conclusion was that the real crux of the matter was the severe shortage of homes for Coloured Capetonians: "If it is really desired to get Coloured people to move from a particular region, the only fair and effective way is to give them homes elsewhere. Give them houses and they will occupy them. That is the answer to the problem, and the council should insist on it." Promising new homes was cold comfort indeed for any Coloured Capetonians who wanted to stay where they were, say in a Newlands or Mowbray pocket, because they liked it there. The *Argus* was in fact supporting semiinduced segregation, as had already been partially implemented before group areas legislation with the establishment of

Coloureds-only public housing schemes in Cape Flats locales such as Kew Town.

A number of examples of the conduct of the public inquiry illuminate the *zeitgeist* in Cape Town during the 1950s. I found it an indefinably curious thing to open old newspapers and to turn quickly from headlines concerned with a world crisis to very provincial ones: from the Suez crisis to the arguments, counterarguments, and quibbles of individuals going on before Dr. J. F. van Rensburg's commission of inquiry held in the Old Supreme Court in Cape Town's city center.

A. H. Broeksma, Q.C., represented the Group Areas Coordinating Committee (representing twenty-four mainly Nonwhite organizations in the Cape Peninsula), two Malay community organizations, and a Coloured teachers' association. Testifying before the commission, he proposed that the Group Areas Act was unworkable and that the situation should be allowed to "rest where it is." Dr. van Rensburg, the chairman, replied, "My duty is to see that this task that cannot be carried out, is carried out" (*Argus*, 2 August 1956). On 7 August, Mr. Broeksma informed the chairman that Coloured organizations in Lansdowne had decided—as had a large and influential sector of Coloured Capetonians—to boycott the proceedings, an attitude he (Mr. Broeksma) described as "unfortunate but understandably human." Dr. van Rensburg responded, "Please tell your clients that this committee notes their decision with deep regret, because we are sincerely anxious to do justice to all sides."

Despite the attitude of boycott taken by the city council and many Coloured Capetonians, Whites were well represented at the hearings, usually having engaged counsel to put forward detailed facts supporting of their claims. Reports of their appearances before the commission were also published by the *Argus*. For example:

> Mr. P. Schaap (representing the European property owners of Lotus River Estate) said that whether people agreed with the Group Areas Act or not, it had been known for three years that the inquiry would be held.

> The people whom he represented had worked hard to give the committee a good insight into European properties in the particular area (*Argus*, 2 August 1956).

On 8 August, an area proposed for either Whites or Coloureds in the Southern Suburbs was discussed. This area straddled the Cape Flats railway line and was a zone of mixed White and Coloured housing (Map 20). Anomalous area A (which was discussed in Chapter 4) today forms part of it, and it was referred to in the hearings as area

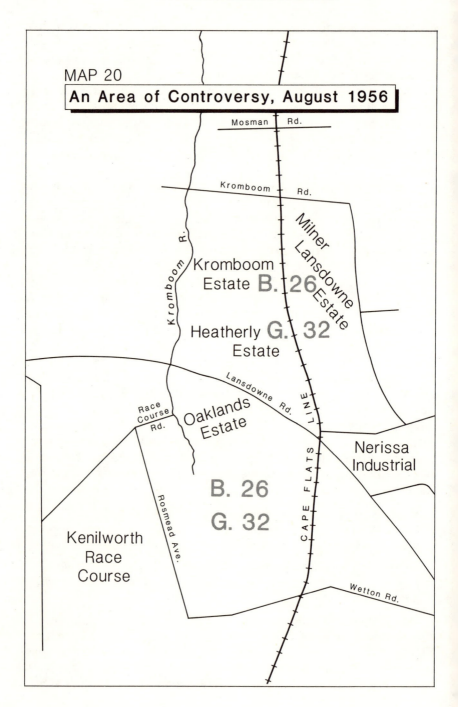

MAP 20

An Area of Controversy, August 1956

Mosman Rd.

Kromboom Rd.

Kromboom R.

Milner Lansdowne Estate

Kromboom Estate B. 26

Heatherly G. 32 Estate

Lansdowne Rd.

Race Course Rd.

Oaklands Estate

CAPE FLATS LINE

Nerissa Industrial

B. 26
G. 32

Rosmead Ave.

Kenilworth Race Course

Wetton Rd.

B.26 or G.32. Dr. van Rensburg questioned M. M. Kritzinger, former principal of the Lansdowne primary school, who was White, about the area:

"You have said there are White people in this area who cannot find buyers. Is this because of the uncertainty about racial zoning?"—Yes.

. . . Cross-examined by Mr. Ben Pienaar [counsel for the Wynberg Ring of the Dutch Reformed Mission Church], Mr. Kritzinger admitted that if it were not for the Group Areas Act there would be a natural tendency for B.26 or G.32 to become a Coloured area.

Mr. Pienaar: Would it be prejudicial to the Whites in the upper part of B.26 if Heatherly Estate and the north side of Race Course Road become Coloured? [see Map 26] — [K] Yes. [P] Why? — [K] Because there would be Coloured areas inside White areas and the Whites would be afraid of penetration.

[P] In other words, if such a recognition of the Coloured people's rights were made, the Europeans would move from the whole of B.26? — [K] Yes.

[P] Then it would be a natural sifting out process, not so? — [K] Where would the White people go?

[P] I am not asking you where the Coloured people would go, so why should you ask me where the White people must go?

Mr. Kritzinger said the better class of Coloured people also wanted to be segregated from their own "weaker class."

Mr. Pienaar: If they were given the opportunity, do you not think the better class of Coloured people would buy up houses in this area and between Mosman and Kromboom Roads? — [K] Naturally.

[P] Do you not think that would be a good thing? — [K] No.

In reply to further questions by Mr. Pienaar, Mr. Kritzinger said it would be undesirable to have a European group area on the east of the Cape Flats railway line in B.26 [this is anomalous area A] with Coloured areas in the rest of the zone.

He added: It would be better to leave it as it is.

Mr. Pienaar: What would happen if it was left as it is? — [K] All the Europeans would leave. Mr. Kritzinger said that as it was all his friends had left the area where he was. He was the only one who had stuck it out (*Argus*, 23 August 1956).

The upshot of these exchanges was that *the whole area* was proclaimed White, over 90 percent of it on 10 February 1961 and the remaining northernmost portion, between Kromboom and Mosman

Road, on 5 June 1964. Coloured people were still being moved out of the area in 1975.

At the end of August 1956, a very contentious issue was discussed before the commission. This was the proposal to zone a small portion of lower Wynberg for either Whites or Coloureds, plus a large portion to its immediate south for either Malays or Coloureds. These two portions together comprise today's anomalous area M. Both the head Muslim priest in Cape Town, Sheikh Behardien, and the Dutch Reformed Mission Church's Reverend D. P. Botha opposed the proposal vehemently.

> He [Rev. Botha] gave detailed figures of the owners and occupiers of properties in the Battswood area. He said that the racial division of the Coloured population into two sections—Malay and Coloured—on racial grounds, was not justified.
>
> "The only justification for such a division is on a religious basis," he said.
>
> The Malay group are different—if one can call it so—because they practise the Mohammedan religion in contrast to the majority of the Coloured people, who profess Christianity. . . .
>
> [It is my church's] sacred duty to register its protest with a Christian Government against the establishment and proclamation of religious groups and their entrenchment against one another.
>
> This, indeed, is the nucleus of the ghetto system and the death-knell of all missionary action. . . .
>
> . . . The blood-relationship between the Christian Coloured and the Mohammedan Coloured (Malay) is such that the proposed division would mean large-scale family disruption—and I mean, literally—on a great scale (*Cape Times*, 15 August 1956).

Dr. van Rensburg said that Reverend Botha's evidence was very important (*Cape Times* 15 August 1956).

The whole area in question was proclaimed Coloured on 10 February 1961. Many Malay people continue to be home owners there, however. This ethnic admixture is impermissible in terms of the act when within the same jurisdiction (in this case, the municipality of Cape Town) there is also a Malay-only group area (as in Schotsche's Kloof). The reason this contradiction has been winked at and the reason for this Coloured/Malay area's continuing anomalous existence as an enclave in White territory must surely be the forcefulness of the Mission Church's stand.

An example of a White community association's attempt to bend the facts a little in their favor occurred later on 14 August. The area concerned was another mixed neighborhood, located in the *V* formed by the junction of the southern suburban and Cape Flats railway lines at Diep River, shown on Map 19. The area was generally known as Steurhof, or Meyerhof Estate, the northern portion of which was predominantly White at that time, the southern portion predominantly Coloured.

> Mr. Leonard M. Rowen, chairman of the Northern Districts Ratepayers' Association, said he had been given a mandate by the White section of Meyerhof Estate to ask for the whole area to be declared White. [And referring to the possibility of the southern portion being declared Coloured:] It is impossible for you, as a committee of the Land Tenure Board, trying to implement the Government's policy of apartheid, to have a small pocket of Coloured people in a White area, he said. [However, Dr. van Rensburg then pointed out] . . . that the 1951 census figures showed that in the southern part, which Mr. Rowen wanted declared European, there were 402 Europeans, 12 Indians, six Malays and 1,054 Coloured people. [To counter this, Mr. Rowen said that now, five years after the census] the Europeans outnumbered Coloured people by half as many again (*Cape Times,* 15 August 1956).

But this contention was disproven by Ben Pienaar, counsel for the Wynberg Dutch Reformed Mission Church, which had made a detailed survey of the area, believing that, if it put the facts before the commission, the board would in good faith take cognizance of them.

> Mr. Pienaar put detailed statistics to Mr. Rowen, showing a block-by-block analysis of the population in the southern section, with a preponderance of non-Europeans. . . . The area presented by Mr. Rowen as a "non-European pocket", might be regarded better as an extension of a heavy non-European concentration on the other side of the suburban railway line, between Steurhof and Diep River stations [claimed Mr. Pienaar] (*Cape Times,* 15 August 1956).

Still, it was Mr. Rowen's interpretation that was favored. The whole area was on 10 February 1961 proclaimed a White group area.

At the conclusion of the inquiry, A. H. Broeksma (speaking for the Group Areas Coordinating Committee and other groups) told the commission that Cape Town was "a multi-racial city with a well-established sociological set-up" that should not be disturbed and that "we are utterly dependent on our multi-racial labour-force, and they are utterly dependent on us." Should such an "upset" be perpetrated by the government against "the non-Europeans. . . . The feelings of resentment will develop into a feeling of hatred. The writing is on the wall. . . . In the name of justice and human decency, I ask that you leave things as they are" (*Argus*, 25 August 1956).

Ben Pienaar, for the Mission Church, reiterated this appeal: "We [Nonwhite and White Capetonians] complement each other and build each other up. And these are the things that make for our greater maturity. . . . Human beings were not made to fit laws: the laws must be made to fit the people. . . . We are not conditioned to it [the concept of group areas]." He also added that it was especially important, particularly in semi-rural areas like the Cape Flats, that Europeans retain some form of contact with, and influence on, the Coloured community. For all its laudable and doubtless sincere championing of Nonwhite interests, the Mission Church was using a paternalistic argument; perhaps it is using it because it thought it was the kind of argument that would appeal to the board, like the Coloured teacher who said before the board that, because of laws that seemed to be directed against Coloureds, youths were losing respect for those of their leaders who held moderate views and were beginning to feel that they could not trust White people. Most tellingly indicative of the attitude of the Mission Church toward its Coloured flock—as opposed to its attitude toward Black Africans—was Mr. Pienaar's statement of mixed astonishment and consternation that "we cannot think of our Coloured people as being pushed aside into —I do not know how else to express it—*locations*!" (*Argus*, 23 August 1956).

In his closing remarks, Dr. van Rensburg claimed that it was apparent that the property market had been very adversely affected by the uncertainty caused by the Group Areas Act.[3] He also verbally chastised the Cape Town City Council for boycotting the proceedings and refusing to cooperate with the board and thus prolonging the uncertainty. Finally, he said that, since the information elicited at the hearings had not been enough to fill the commission's needs, it would still have to collect many facts and statistics, work that might take many months.

THE EQUITABILITY OF THE IMPLEMENTATION OF THE GROUP AREAS ACT

After discussing the parallel preproclamation deliberations in Port Elizabeth during the 1950s, W. J. Davies (1971, p. 136) insisted that

the weight of evidence presented in this work clearly indicates the care taken over race zoning . . . and it is hoped that this will assist in dispelling any pre-conceived notion that the Group Areas Act is in itself a discriminatory piece of legislation. Although instances can certainly be cited of hardships caused to non-Whites by Group Areas decisions, it remains the contention of the writer that these stem from the injudicious *application* of the Act, and not from shortcomings within the Act itself.

In view of the statistics on removals of various groups we have already considered (pp. 72, 82), Davies surely could only have been making an attempt at mystification. "No amount of amending legislation," argued Helen Suzman in the House of Assembly in Cape Town on 23 February 1961, "can make the Group Areas Act an equitable measure because its very nature is discriminatory and therefore it cannot be administered with equity. It is a rankly discriminatory measure."

Suzman's accusation is borne out by the facts in Cape Town. The mixed areas discussed during the public hearings were all from Cape Town's half-White, half-Nonwhite southern suburbs. Four-and-a-half years after the public inquiry, virtually all the southern suburbs—with the minor exception of lower Wynberg—were proclaimed White. On the same day as Helen Suzman assailed the act in Parliament, Dr. R. E. van der Ross wrote in the *Cape Times* (23 February 1961):

> For the Coloured, the Sandy Wastes [of the Cape Flats]. . . . The first thing that strikes one about the proclamation is its extreme arrogance. . . . The matter of the inequity of practical provision, of facilities, of distance from work, of schools, hospitals, police protection, roads, lighting, sewerage, to mention but a few of the many respects in which the displaced Coloured persons will find discrimination, serve only to emphasize the unfairness of the entire conception of the proclamations.

Van der Ross then expended a lot of energy in questioning the validity of the proclamations that might have been, as he implied, the result of an unfair inquiry that did not pay due regard to all interests. But this is mere sciamachy—to question the sincerity of the mode of imposition of the act is futile indeed. Even the government-appointed Theron Commission (van der Horst, 1976, p. 9) was prepared to state that "in the Group Areas Act, only the whites have been fully protected from the presence of other groups, while the approval of coloured people has not been sought in making proclamations."

The reaction of Cape Town's *Argus* to the draconian southern suburbs proclamation was, once again, very much a managerial one, as exemplified in the headlines, "Cape Group Areas a Prickly Problem" (11 February 1961) and "Doubt and Uncertainty over Coloured 'Pockets' [that is, Claremont and Newlands] " (16 February 1961).

Slightly different from the *Argus*'s reaction was another from a White source, which is perhaps rather typical of "liberal" Cape Town. It was apparently a more "sympathetic" reaction, but it was very close to being oriented toward maintaining the status quo. David Bloomberg, when he was mayor of Cape Town in the mid-1970s, wished his motto to be "For all the people" (the government excluded Coloured city councillors in Cape Town in 1972). Bloomberg was interviewed by three Coloured students for their Spes Bona High School (Athlone) decennial yearbook (1975).

> Schoolboy: Can you tell me your views about the uprooting of people from the areas in which they have been living for years?

> Mayor: You are obviously referring to the Group Areas Act. I know because I was born and brought up in Cape Town. I refer to the White and non-White community, which have historically always got on extremely well together. I was brought up in an area in Sea Point where I lived adjacent to a voluntary Coloured area. There was never any trouble, there was not, in my opinion, any need to move the people. All I can say is that I am totally opposed to it and this has been the attitude of my council at all times. But the Group Areas Act is now the law and I do also believe in upholding of the law and the Group Areas Act being the law, we as the Council must implement it. One cannot, in our society or any other society, choose which laws you are going to obey and which laws you are going to disobey. Unfortunately, for the survival of this country one has to obey all the laws. At the moment Group Areas is one of the laws.

Such cleaving to the rule of law in essence lends support to the institutionalized violence of apartheid laws that violate the civil rights of peaceable citizens. It also makes it easier for those who profess to be liberal in sentiment to absolve themselves of responsibility for such laws, to indulge in (as Patterson [1953, p. 128], in reference to the South African Art Gallery in the Gardens in 1951, sniped) "a somewhat typical Capetonian tendency to evade the issue rather than proceed to open segregation or the reverse."

Even if most Capetonians did not wish to proceed to open segregation, that is what has been imposed upon Cape Town. The imposition of de jure segregation has affected the *meaning* of space in the metropolis, as the group areas changes in the city center, District Six, and Mowbray exemplify.

PART III
PEOPLE

CHAPTER SIX

Group Areas and the Meaning of Places: Whose Mother City?

Where, then, ah! Where shall poverty reside,
To 'scape the pressure of contiguous pride?

Oliver Goldsmith,
"The Deserted Village," 1769

You can take the people out of the heart of District Six, ou pellie, but you'll never take District Six out of the heart of the people.

Coloured resident of District Six
at the time of its proclamation as a White Group Area

THE MEANING OF CAPE TOWN

If there is one quality that Cape Town does not lack, it is what Kevin Lynch in 1960 (p. 9) called "imageability," "that quality in a physical object which gives it a high probability of evoking a strong image in any given observer." Cape Town must be located on one of the most splendidly and dramatically compelling sites of any city in the world, the very antithesis of the bland placelessness of, say, a Columbus, Ohio. If one is unsure of one's bearings in the Cape Town metropolis, one looks to Table Mountain, the lodestone. Figure 6 gives an impression of its presence from the railway at Salt River, looking across upper Woodstock; its top is over 1,000 meters (3,500 feet) above the photographer's vantage point. Beneath this mountain "White South Africa" and the Cape Coloured people had their origin over three and a quarter centuries ago: hence, the name the Mother City.

Figure 6. Table Mountain Looms over Inner-city Cape Town.
(Photograph used by permission of Mark Povall.)

This very intimacy leads to an ambiguity at the heart of "Colouredness." The Coloureds owe their place above the Black Africans in the present structure of South African society to their close ties with the Whites. Yet, this very closeness has the potential of great trauma should the Whites decide to separate themselves, to distance and reject the Coloureds (as they have since union in 1910 and especially since World War II). And in the structure of space there exists a parallel: for in the central city space mirrors society, and the Coloureds have been distanced geographically as the Whites have repudiated them societally.

Coloured space in Cape Town is in a sense as old as that of the Whites; Cape Town is as much, if not more, the mother city for Cape Coloureds (and Cape Malays) as it is for South African Whites. District Six and the Malay Quarter on the one hand and Cape Town city center itself on the other are but two sides of the same coin. The effect of the group areas apartheid upon this bond is striking. The city center has been retained and cherished as a symbol of White history. The small Malay Quarter is being preserved in a somewhat sanitized fashion, and up to 2,000 Cape Malays continue to live there on a Malays-only life raft in an otherwise Whites-only center city. A square kilometer or more of District Six has been obliterated, its tens of thousands of Coloured occupants ejected to the Cape Flats, with only a bulldozed wasteland left behind. And the Loader Street area, above the docks and adjacent to the city center and the Malay Quarter, has had all its Coloured, Malay, and Indian inhabitants expelled. Upon their removal, the area has become a classic example of renovation. Middle- and upper-income Whites have moved in, their Porsches and Mercedeses (and pleasure boats on trailers) standing at the curbs where the bicycles of previous occupants once leaned. I intend to delineate in detail three examples of how group areas development has affected the meanings of Cape Town places: two in this chapter, the third in Chapter 7.

THE CHERISHING OF WHITE ROOTS

Cape Town as it lies beneath its mountain is a symbol, a focal point of values and sentiment: what could be termed "affective space." When an ideal group areas plan for Cape Town was being conceptualized (Chapter 4), one of the few prerequisites that had to be accommodated was that the city center must remain where it was and in White hands. In molding the space of Cape Town, Afrikaner Nationalist group areas planners could not possibly have waived the city center as White space. It is a place sacred to the White South African nation. Consider Figure 7, the Gardens, which once were kept by the Dutch East India Company in the area next to their fort. The impeccably tended and watered lawns surround two statues. The one in the center of the photograph is of Field-Marshal Jan Smuts (1870-1950), the most world-renowned statesman of South Africa during the first half of this century. He was accepted by the Western powers at that time, as his successors in the office of prime minister have not been (publicly) since then because of their apartheid policies. The statue to the right is of Bartholomew Diaz, the Portuguese navigator who first rounded the Cape in 1488. In the background are the South African Art Museum and the Great Synagogue and Jewish museum; as a backdrop to it all, the exquisite "tablecloth" cloud tumbles over Table Mountain's front face, which looks north out to sea and to the Whites' origins in Europe. Smuts loved Table Mountain passionately and wrote of it shortly before his death in 1950: "It is indeed the greatest natural monument of South Africa. . . . Our national temple, our Holy of Holies."[1] A few yards away (although not shown in the photograph) is Cecil Rhodes's statue, which faces northeast, toward Cairo. "Your hinterland is there"; his gesture is decisive. The shaded walk leads to the old campus of the University of Cape Town and to the South African Museum, next to which are the headquarters of the Dutch Reformed Church. In the other direction 200 paces, the path passes the Houses of Parliament, the South African Library, and St. George's (Anglican) Cathedral to the top of Cape Town's main street, Adderley Street. Here there is another statue of Smuts, and then at the foot of Adderley Street one of Jan van Riebeeck, close to where it is assumed his feet first touched South African soil; beyond lie the ships in Table Bay harbor. The area symbolizes the history of South Africa; nearby is what was once the British colonial government house, and another 200 yards away is cobbled Greenmarket Square, where the slave market was held. The concentration in this small area of so many of the public institutions of the country is remarkable.

A perceptive journalist for the Johannesburg *Star* suggested (21 January 1977) that it might be dangerous that the South African Parliament[2] was then deliberating in such an atmosphere of unflustered calm, in an ambience of palpable history. During that time of urgency immediately after the Soweto and Cape riots, how far away did the peace of the Gardens feel from the center of crisis and dynamism in the republic: Soweto and the Rand. How far away did the Gardens seem from the Cape Flats and Langa, too, where there had been rioting and burning of government schools only eleven days earlier.

Figure 7. Sacred Space: The Gardens in Cape Town City Center.

The distance in spirit was immeasurably greater than the mere 11 kilometers of physical distance that separated the ornamental alleys, walks, and fish ponds of the Gardens from the Nonwhite townships on the Cape Flats.

In 1950-1952, there existed Coloured population concentrations immediately adjacent to this White sacred space: to the west in Schotsche's Kloof and off Long Street; to the south in an area of lower Gardens (Hopeville), such as Wandel Street and Glynville Terrace; to the east in inner District Six; and to the northwest in the Loader Street area. (See Map 1.) Scott's (1955) researchers found at that time that significant passing for White was occurring in Hopeville and off Kloof Street (an extension of Long Street). Tuan (1977) told us that sacred is holy and holiness means separation, definition, and, indeed, *apartness*—the precise English translation of "apartheid." To uphold the sacredness of White inner Cape Town space, a distancing of the Nonwhites is necessary, for the Coloureds especially remind the Whites of what some of the Whites irrationally fear they might become, if distance and separation are not maintained by institutionalization. Thus, all Nonwhite and mixed space near the city center—with the small (but striking) exception of the Malay Quarter —has been expunged. The Whites now have a monopoly of inner-city space. The very act of guarding and cherishing this place as White *requires* the expulsion of all who are not White. This brings us to the subject of District Six, which is adjacent to the center city.

OBLITERATION: THE DERACINATION
OF COLOUREDS FROM DISTRICT SIX

The razing of District Six has been variously explained. One White view is that it simply constitutes slum clearance. Cape Town's *Die Burger* (27 May 1975) editorialized about District Six: "One wonders whether this name will be retained in the days to come. Perhaps. Many a despised name has afterwards become a title of honour. . . . It was a disgrace to the Mother City. . . . South Africa's best-known slum." This is an apparently businesslike approach that has nothing to do with racial matters. If there is a slum next to the city center, then naturally it should be cleared. There are examples from other countries: as Nigeria approached independence (1960), questions began to be asked by Nigerians about the appearance of their federal capital of Lagos—could they be proud of it? It too had a slum adjacent to its center. Marris (1961, p. 117) reported on the attitude of the Lagos Executive Development Board to their appointed task:

> They were carrying out a Government policy for which there was widespread support, and they believed that even at the cost of some hardship, slum clearance was right. The working out of a fair housing policy depends not only on the hardship that may result, but on how far national interests may in justice override the interests of a few.

And as the impressive façade of Nigeria's new Central Bank has risen next to where slums once stood in Lagos, so it was with slum clearance in Delhi in 1976, and earlier in both Manila and Kuala Lumpur, too: "It would appear that national prestige, more than concern for the social welfare of squatters has been the most active force leading to their shift in these two cases" (McGee, 1967, p. 169).

Such a managerial planning philosophy purports to be both practical and clear mindedly nonideological; it becomes a question of the national interest. The question that must in the South African case be addressed is—in a society so fundamentally cleaved—*whose* national interest? It is assuredly not that of *all* South Africans taken as a whole, nor in part or in whole that of the Black Africans, nor of the Coloureds, nor of the Indians. Consider W. J. Davies's account of "slum clearance" through group areas development in Port Elizabeth. His words sound objective, but they mask a total acceptance of White supremacy. Of this city's South End, overwhelmingly Nonwhite but zoned for Whites only under group areas, W. J. Davies (1971, p. 75) wrote:

> [It] played a useful part in the economic development of the city. Trade was conducted freely with all races, and the proximity of South End to the Central Business District seemed to assure the area of continued economic prosperity. However, most of the buildings, both residential and commercial, were old, even in 1946, and much of South End was in a stage of incipient decay. Neither the Coloured and Asiatic nor the White population in South End were in a position to rehabilitate the area on the scale that would have been necessary. Consequently, since 1946, the process of urban decay set in, and the area adopted what can only be described as an unwholesome character. Quite clearly, such an area could not have been tolerated so close to the Central Business District of one of South Africa's major cities, especially in view of the fact that access from the city *to the main tourist attraction, the beaches,* lay through South End (my emphasis).

First, this "main tourist attraction" is *for Whites only!* Second, note the subtle shifting of ground as the excerpt proceeds: at first we are informed that the South End may be about to start "decaying"; a couple of sentences later it is stated as a *fact* that decay had set in. Third, there is the general suggestion that the apartheid planners were obliged to decide, even regretfully, that the South End had to be made White, hoping that excessive hardship for removees would be avoided.[3] This same line was taken by a high-ranking Afrikaner bureaucrat in the Department of Community Development who granted me an interview on 4 June 1976. With his map of the group areas of the Cape Peninsula on the wall behind his desk, he explained to me how his job was a difficult one—surely I was reasonable enough to appreciate that?—and that he had to work very hard at keeping his emotions from getting involved in what he had to do. Slum clearance, however, had to be seen through.

It is an indisputable fact that many parts of District Six *were* a slum, although it might be asked who can define a slum, and by what criteria. Professional urban planners of a predominantly middle-class background usually make the definitions. And "slum," according to Zorbaugh's (1929, p. 128) celebrated *The Gold Coast and the Slum*, can be defined as "an area marked by the extreme physical deterioration of the buildings and by the equally severe social disorganization of the inhabitants." Or a slum is, as Graves and Fletcher defined it in 1941 (p. 70), "a residential area occupied predominantly by poverty-stricken people living in housing which is so deteriorated, so sub-standard or so unwholesome as to be a menace to the health, safety, or welfare of the occupants and the adjacent community."

From these definitions we should note two things—first, the interests of "adjacent communities." Regarding urban renewal in the United States, Glazer (1965, p. 200) wrote:

> Experience so far shows that almost invariably the despair in areas slated for demolition is not channelled into meaningful political opposition; it is outweighed by the arguments for renewal presented by planners to the city fathers and *the prejudice among middle-class citizens against allowing what they consider slums to remain standing near them* (my emphasis).

Second, observe the automatically assumed connection between visible physical dilapidation and supposed social dysfunction, a connection that is not necessarily proven. Marris (1974, pp. 53-54) puts this nicely:

> Physical squalor is an affront to the order of society, which readily becomes associated with other signs of disorder in the public image. Crime, drunkenness, prostitution, feckless poverty, mental pathology do indeed cluster where housing is poorest—though not there only. Once this association has been taken for granted, any anomalous pattern of life embodied in shabby surroundings is easily assumed to be pathological, without much regard for the evidence. Bad housing thus becomes a symbol of complex discordances in the structure of society and so to be treated as if it were a cause of them.

For such reasons, the anticipation of social dislocation in shanty squatter settlements may be even greater than in other slums. It is precisely this supposition that will be discussed in Chapter 10, which deals with the present peripheral shantytowns of Cape Town. In their case, I will attack the image of criminality as in large degree misleading. In the case of District Six, it is less easy to dismiss such allegations. Gangs such as the Killers, Jesters, and especially the Globe (with, it is thought, at least 300 street fighters in 1948) were ever present and powerful. Pinnock (1980, p. 11) claimed that some parts of the Globe's turf in District Six were "no-go" areas for the police and that "one of the state's reasons for the destruction of District Six was to smash the lawlessness of the gangs—the armies of the unemployed." Certainly, the perceived lawlessness of District Six was such that all of it was declared a "no-go" area to visiting Allied servicemen during World War II.

Another concomitant argument regarding both the demolition of shanties and slum clearance through group areas removals of housing tracts like District Six is the anticipated health hazard argument. Scott (1955, p. 154) made much of this in Cape Town, especially noting mortality from tuberculosis there. His explanation hinged only on racial factors rather than on evidently plausible economic factors (that is, the state of development in the country as a whole and the rich-poor variations among its inhabitants).

> Even the European death rate, low as it is by comparison with the non-European, would be considered as epidemic for a comparable income-group in Europe or North America; it is undoubtedly due to contact between white and nonwhite. The European rate ranges from 176 [per 100,000] and 160 in the ethnically mixed areas of Woodstock and Salt River respectively to 47 and 46 in the favoured residential districts of Fresnaye and Rondebosch.

It is logical to infer two things from Scott's statement: (1) that Whites do not make "contact" with their Nonwhite domestic servants in Fresnaye or Rondebosch, both areas with large numbers of live-in servants, and (2) that it is reasonable that Whites should wish to separate themselves from Nonwhites in order to protect their health. No mention was made of attempts to improve the standards of health in the Nonwhite areas. Is the poor health of Nonwhites to be taken for granted, or does it not matter as long as they are separated by a veritable *cordon sanitaire* from the Whites? [4]

These attitudes can be contrasted with the second major White attitude toward the slums, what *Die Burger* of 27 May 1975 assailed (with some justice) saying "The sentimentality uttered in recent years over South Africa's best-known slum is enough to make one choke." Richard Rive—who should know, for he is a Capetonian writer classified as Coloured and brought up in District Six—also attacked the retrospective romanticization of such slums as his now-demolished tenement home (Rive, 1980). A sanitized District Six has become an adjunct of the coffee tables and wall-hung prints of many White Capetonians, a "quaint" memento of Olde Cape Town. This image has even on occasion permeated scholarly writing.

> In Cape Town they [the Cape Coloured people] dwell amid poverty, disease, and crime in a slum of singular character near the center of the busy

white [White!] Parliamentary capital of the Republic. . . . Here, narrow streets wind up the foot of Table Mountain leading tortuously back on themselves past one- and two-story houses and shops with painted tin roofs, false fronts, gables and balconies, scrolls and intricate lattice-work, domes, gargoyles, and Doric, Corinthian, and Ionic capitals in haphazard combination—all giving on some sordid square or unkempt garden. The Oriental blends and clashes with the Victorian, a peeling and crumbling return to the colonial past. Former respectability has now faded to squalor with all the charm of a doomed anachronism (O'Toole, 1973, pp. 1-2).

Just the place for a Sunday afternoon tour for Whites in their motorized capsules, one would think, rather like what the partially "restored" Malay Quarter seems to be becoming. In a picture guidebook of Cape Town (Baker and Katzen, 1972, p. 81), Stanley Baker, then a student at the University of Cape Town's law school, wrote of District Six in the following terms:

All kinds of odours hit the nostrils—the salty smell of freshly-caught Cape Salmon; varied curry powders, conjuring exotic visions of the erotic East and many others, combined with the not inconsiderable tang of B.O., more especially on a hot Saturday morning when the area is thronged with shoppers. . . . Not that, aesthetically speaking, District Six has much to commend it. It is ugly, slum-ridden, bleak. A survey done in 1969 showed that 43% of the households were overcrowded. Prostitutes, drug-runners, "skollies" (thugs), violence have all plagued the area. No sane person is proud of District Six. Yet Capetonians feel an affection for it, a paternalism, much like a parent does for a child that is ugly.

The meaning of District Six for Coloured persons is very different from "no sane person is proud of District Six." Cape Town is the mother city for both White and Coloured South Africans. Within less than a year of van Riebeeck's arrival, "proto-Coloured" "half-caste" children were certainly born there. They are equally the founders of Cape Town. The Whites can trace their roots back *beyond* South Africa to Europe and they have been able to appropriate territory for themselves that they now call "White South Africa": two fundamental bases of pride and group solidarity. The Coloureds—separated from the White portion of their heritage, especially since apartheid's institution—can as yet claim neither.[5] And yet, if there *has* been any place, any space that Coloureds have looked upon as "our territory," it is—or *was*—District Six.

The New Year's Day Coon Carnival has been one of the few *specifically* Coloured aspects of Cape Town cultural life. Stompie, the

pseudonym[6] of a Coloured humorist, explained why January 1 should
be declared an official holiday for Cape Coloured people:

> Now, Jan van Riebeeck did mos [in fact] land here early in April, hey?
> According [therefore] van Riebeeck Day. So de firs' t'ing dose Hollanders
> does when dey lands are to pallie up to de Hottentot girlies in de super-
> miniskirtjies. Dose girlies had minis and topless an' whole boksemdice
> [kit]. An' you know mos dose Hollanders been on de watter a blerrie
> [bloody] long time. . . .
>
> So okay, you count nine months from de beginning of April, an' see where
> you comes out. Right! Beginning of Jannewarre. Nuwejaar. Tweede Nuwe-
> jaar [second of January]. Dere was so many dat dey did somma' call de
> ouens [fellows] according de calendar. Dat's why dere is so many Janne-
> warries and Febbewaries among de Coloured people.
>
> So dat de special meaning of Nuwejaar are dat it are really de time of de
> birth of de Coloured People. Dat's why de Coloured People did always
> have a special feast time dose days.
>
> . . . We got to start a campaign. Like de Afrikaner. He are always starting
> campaigns. Now we start a birthday campaign.
>
> We collecks money to build a monument. Somma here, byre Castle Bridge,
> byre start of District Six. An' we puts a plate on which read:
>
> "Here (or very nearby) de firs' Coloured Person were born on Nuwejaar
> (or very near) in 1653."

A number of things can be observed in Stompie's humor. There is
his mocking of the Afrikaners' penchant for organizing and mobiliz-
ing themselves on a cultural-nationalistic *volk* basis, which helped
Afrikaner-specific bodies and campaigns in their struggle to be rid of
British imperial control. Another point is the importance of place
—District Six. A third point concerns the dialect of the piece. Stompie is trying to mirror by his style of writing Gamtaal, the lower-class
Cape Town Coloured speech, a mixture of English and Afrikaans.
"Taal" is Afrikaans for *language,* "Gam" (the *g* pronounded as a gut-
teral *h*) Afrikaans for *Ham,* in the Bible the son of Noah who was
destined to be the hewer of wood and the drawer of water. Stone
(1972) reported that lower-class Coloureds, when another of their
number lets them down, use the fatalistic saying "Gam is mos so":
"That's the way it goes with Ham"; it seems that they have internalized their subordinate role in the unalterable scheme of things. (See
also van der Ross, 1979, pp. 2, 36-37, and 74.) My experience in this
regard is extremely limited. Few of the Coloureds from Mowbray, an

inner suburb of Cape Town, whom I interviewed were truly lower-class people; and if they had been it would have been very difficult for me, as a middle-class, English-speaking White foreigner, to have had any real appreciation of what they might have been trying to express. Nearly all those Coloureds whom I met were "respectable." Some "respectable" Coloureds would object strongly to Stompie's style of writing, considering it unworthy, a perpetuation of the Whites' image of Coloured people as unlettered clowns, just as the Coon Carnival is.

However, Gamtaal is not necessarily "unworthy"; it can be a tremendously effective vehicle of communication. Adam Small wrote a fine poem in Gamtaal about District Sixers.

Ons't gewag vi de Hanoverstraat
    se bus
soggens assie plekke noganie oepe is
Ons't gewag vi die Hanoverstraat
    se bus
Saans assie plekke al toe is.
	We waited for the Hanover Street bus
	In the morning when the shops
	    weren't yet open
	We waited for the Hanover Street bus
	In the evening when the shops were
	    already closed.

Hoe call djulle vi ons?
—die city se commuters
die labour force
die labour potential
die labour source
en gits!
djulle punch tikkits
en djulle figure vi ons uit in djulle
    computers in
net so
kant en klaar
    (anners riekent weer ons is die
      workers of de land
    dja
    en hulle riekent fight, dja
    kôs hulle riekent workers of de
      world, unite!
    dja)
	What do you call us?
	—the city's commuters
	the labor force
	the labor potential
	the labor source
	and shit!
	you punch cards
	and you work us out in your
	    computers
	just so
	nice and neat
	    (Others reckon, again, we're the
	      workers of the land,
	    yeah
	    and they reckon fight, yeah
	    'cos they reckon workers of the
	      world, unite!
	    Right on.)

Nou daai's alles well en good en grand
ma eintlik issie lot van djulle
    laat
Why?
simply kôs 'n mens figure nie mense
	Now that's all well and good and grand
	But actually the lot of you are
	    way off the beam.
	Why?
	Simply because a person doesn't

daai ways yt	work people out
kôs vi daai ways praat oor mense	in those ways. Life's too big
issie lewe far te great	a thing for
simply kôs oor mense moet 'n mens	people to be talked about in those
praat	ways. Simply because a person's
net soes 'n mens moet praat oor mense	got to talk about people in the way
dja net so	you've got to talk about people.
	That's just it
en daa's niks annerste om te glo nie	And there's nothing else to believe
why?	Why?
—kôs very simply mense is mense	— 'cos very simply people are people
dja, kôs very simply	Yeah, 'cos very simply
net daai:	just that:
mense is mense	people are people.[7]

Alluded to in Small's poem is the working-class nature of District Six, and, although it was 95 percent Coloured/Malay in composition, there were in addition persons from other South African population groups living there: Whites, Black Africans, Indians, and Chinese. In considering this, Davids (1974, p. 4), a Malay, wrote in a positive spirit that

> it was the affinity of the working-class culture that binded the settlers into a community. There was a consciousness of kind bred by poverty. There was a life-style common to all. There was the economic hardship experienced by all. There was mixing across the colour line, inter-marriages in this community in which the only leveler was the common poverty. This refuted the myth that contact leads to racial friction.

At this point, is is appropriate to augment more explicitly the discussion of District Six by assessing its pervasive spatial *meaning* for the Coloured people of the Cape. We have already seen in Chapter 1 how common it has been in Cape Town for Coloured people to be put in their place, to be told just who they are by Whites. They have been told that they can have no pride in their "bastardy"—"the *honour* of a half-caste!" Even some of the subordinate Black Africans, upon whom the brunt of apartheid has fallen, assert that Coloureds are *amalawu*: a pejorative term implying that they are people without customs and traditions, without pride in themselves (Wilson and Mafeje, 1963). Some Coloureds may take no pride in their Colouredness, but many with whom I talked took pride in being respectable Capetonians; many were certainly proud of being South African. *Place* of origin—home—has become an essential element of self-definition for Coloured people. Edelstein[8] found, as did *The Theron Commission Report* in 1976, that the majority of the Coloured people in his survey "do not look for integration with Whites any more than with Africans. They regard themselves as neither White nor Black but as South African, and they yearn to be accepted as such. They have, incidentally, a better claim to that title than anyone" (*Star*, 15 September 1973). On numerous occasions interviewees told me that Cape Town was the best place in the world: "The only thing wrong with this place is the government—all that apartheid nonsense."

When we consider the "Cape Coloured" appellation, one affixed by the defining Whites, we can see that it has two constituents. One is pejorative, and it is rejected by some, as we have seen. As late as 1919, some members of the African Political Organisation (APO), the primary political voice of the Coloured people at that time,[9] wished to change the name "Coloured" to "Eurafrican." Even more interestingly, in 1911 use of the name "Cape Afrikaners" had been mooted in the *APO Journal* of January that year (M. Simons, 1976). In this second suggestion we note that "Cape" has been retained. Indeed, although in the name "Cape Coloured" the second portion has negative connotations, the first portion, "Cape," is a source of pride. The most common nonpejorative nickname for "a Coloured person" in South Africa is "a Capey"—a locational rather than a racial designation.

By removing Coloureds from District Six, the Whites are doing more than clearing slums or underpinning their exclusive claim to central Cape Town's sacred space. *They are also destroying one of the symbols of whatever Coloured identity may exist, a space in parts at least seven generations deep and one with associations with the emancipation of the slaves.* The Zulus may have been vanquished, but there remains Ulundi, site of the royal kraal, and Isandhlwana, where they defeated the British in 1879 at South Africa's equivalent of the Little Big Horn. For the Afrikaners there is the center of the Mother City, the Voortrekker monument in Pretoria, the Battle of Blood River monument in Zululand (surrounded by an 8-foot-high chain-link fence to prevent Zulu cattle from trespassing on such a place), and perhaps the new monument to the Afrikaans language on the hillside above Paarl in the Boland, about 60 kilometers inland from Cape Town. For the English-speaking White South Africans, whose identity has always been more indistinct, there are today the conscious attempts of the "1820 Settlers" organization at Grahamstown. But what do the Cape Coloureds have?

"In the case of the 'Cape Coloured group,'" Whisson (1973, p. 221) wrote, ". . . people so classified include many whose values reflect their immediate ancestry, who have no relationship of any sort and no common residential [that is, inherent] economic, social or physical features with many others so classified." Furthermore, apart from the Islamic religion of the Cape Malays, Coloured people possess very few indubitably Coloured cultural attributes that they do not share with South African Whites. But, despite this hetero-geneity and lack of an exclusively Coloured culture, one of the co-hesive elements among those persons today legally classified as Cape Coloureds has been their home territory, their "Cape-ness." This is a profound illustration of the dialectic of place and identity, of the dictum of Georges Matoré (1966, p. 5) that, indeed, "A man is his place."

Patterson (1953) maintained that persons with the same ethnic mix as Cape Coloured but living outside the Cape *cannot* claim the designation of "Cape Coloured," but only "Coloured." Branford (1978) implied the same. This fact can be taken too far—I am not really prepared to assert, for instance, that those classified as Cape Coloured who are Johannesburg-born and who live on the Rand are any less "truly" Cape Coloured by virtue of their backgrounds. How-ever, this tends to become a rather futile discussion, because almost nine of every ten persons so classified live in Cape Province, and it has been a very stable proportion, as *The Theron Commission Report* observed. In 1951, 89.5 percent of all Coloured[10] persons lived there; in 1970, 87.3 percent. Furthermore, about one third of all Coloured people in South Africa live in the Cape Peninsula. Not only is this residential pattern a distributional focal point, it is an affective symbol: Cape Town is where the Coloured people began. And where precisely was this beginning, according to Stompie's tongue-in-cheek history?—"Byre start of District Six."

To this emotional attachment can be added a still greater burden of spatial meaning. The Coloureds' distinctive Coon Carnival on New Year's Day traditionally traced its raucous, flashy, and high-spirited circumambulations through the streets of the city center, Woodstock, and District Six. On 11 February 1966, District Six was proclaimed a White group area.[11] The next year, the government claimed that the Coon Carnival processions constituted a "traffic hazard" and confined the carnival troupes to the Hartleyvale soccer stadium (in Observatory), where the carnival has since been celebrated. I suspect, however, that the real reason for the introduction of the restriction at that particular time was to inhibit the symbolic assertion of Coloured ownership of, and identity with, inner-city Cape Town, particularly the place called District Six. It was no longer "theirs"; therefore, if they frolicked their noisy and music-making way through it, then their activity might easily be construed as an expression of resistance to government plans. Adolph "Dollar" Brand is a Cape Muslim jazz musician who has achieved fame both inside and outside South Africa's borders. He attended Trafalgar High School in District Six, from the second story of which Figure 8 was taken in 1976. His lament is entitled "Blues for District Six" (Pieterse, 1971, p. 5) and tells of the Coons.

> early one new year's morning
> when the emerald bay waved its clear waters against the noisy dockyard
> a restless south easter skipped over slumbering lion's head
> danced up hanover street
> tenored a bawdy banjo
> strung an ancient cello
> bridged a host of guitars
> tambourined through a dingy alley
> into a scented cobwebbed room
> and crackled the sixth sensed district
> into a blazing swamp fire of satin sound
>
> early one new year's morning
> when the moaning bay mourned its murky waters against the deserted
>   dockyard
> a bloodthirsty south easter roared over hungry lion's head
> and ghosted its way up hanover street
> empty
> forlorn
> and cobwebbed with gloom

To remove, by group areas planning, District Six's inhabitants (save the small number of Whites) is to remove Cape Coloureds, Cape Malays, Indians, Black Africans, and Chinese. The last three groups possess a certain cultural pride in their own ethnic identity, I assume, and the Malays, too (although their past includes slavery and involuntary miscegenation), still possess their spatial focal point—Schotsche's Kloof—and their spiritual focal point—Islam—with their religion rendering them proud members of a powerful world community. However, there remains the overwhelming majority of the removees from District Six, the Cape Coloureds. I would assert that the trauma of mass removal for them is proportionately greater because their space at the foot of the mountain in Cape Town was one

Figure 8. District Six in 1976.

true source of pride in themselves as a distinguishable ethnic entity. Thus, for them the obliteration of District Six is a humiliation that leaves an aching lacuna in self-concept and self-esteem and a profound and bitter resentment.

Conversely, from the White government's viewpoint, there are other symbols involved. As well as the simple strategic reasons for expelling the large numbers of Nonwhites from "crowded hives" next to the city center, there is the bolstering of the sacred space of the city center itself as a White place and the further symbolism in the very act of destroying District Six. Hilda Kuper (1972, p. 422) has stated a general proposition concerning "a single politically defined territory. When one group is dominant it may express its domination by ignoring, neglecting, and even obliterating the established sites of the subordinated people." By victorious Rome, Carthage was razed and *plowed with salt.* And what of one of the few things that the Cape Coloureds could really feel was theirs? Figure 8 shows Cape Town city center from across what was inner District Six. And by a photograph of a Cape Coloured workman stepping across the rubble of demolished homes in District Six (in Small and

Jansen, 1973), the first portion of a poem by Adam Small reads:

Die bulldozers, hulle't gakom	The bulldozers, they came
romtomtom	rumble rumble
dóm	Stupefied
was ons mos	We really were
stóm mos	Just dumb
al die djare	all the years
Klaar gakom het hulle	They came right on in
en plat gadonner	and knocked it all down flat
alles hieso	all of it here
alles, alles,	all, all,
hyse, harte	houses, hearts,
die lot,	the lot,
alles,	all of it,
God!	God!
—so pêllie,	—So, old chum,
Klim yt die klippe yt	Climb out from the rubble
op,	up,
óp!	up!
Djy dink sieker ek is cynical?	You probably think I'm cynical, eh?
God, pêllie, ek is serious	God, old pal, I'm serious

There is yet another symbolism in District Six. Its construction during the incipient industrialization of British imperial rule from the second half of the nineteenth century, especially during the score of years between 1885 and 1905, meant that for Afrikaner Nationalists it also stood in part as a reminder of their forcible colonial subordination to the British. For example, *Die Burger* asserted on 27 May 1975:

> District Six is one of those legacies from other days, with other rulers and authorities, which a Nationalist government had to take over willy-nilly and then decided to clear it up. . . . And then, as in other cases, the real guilty ones deftly placed the whole caboodle on the head of the Afrikaner nationalist as a reproach and yet another injustice to the Brown people.

The occasion that give rise to this editorial was the announcement on 23 May 1975 that inner-city anomalous area O was to be pro-proclaimed Coloured after many years of indefinite status. (The actual proclamation occurred on June 13.) Adjoining areas to the east had been proclaimed White in 1958, and those immediately to the west (District Six), White in 1966. The area in question was a portion of lower Woodstock and the Walmer Estate. This being so, certain remarks later in this same editorial are worthy of comment. "Everybody professes now to be happy that a part of District Six will be 'given back' to the Coloured people. When and in how far did it ever belong to them? For the first time now they will really own it." *Die Burger's* "For the first time now they will really own it," referring to District Six, is culpably misleading. The area in question is *not* a part of District Six, nor do Cape Coloured people consider it to be so. Furthermore, *strictly* speaking, *Die Burger* may indeed be totally correct when it claims that District Six "did . . . [not] . . . ever belong to them ['the Brown people']." District Six may have been occupied almost entirely by Nonwhites but the majority of the properties were owned by White absentee landlords. O'Toole (1973, p. 99) stated that "in District Six, the unofficial Coloured 'capital,' estimated value of properties in 1966 [the year it was proclaimed White] was 17 million rand for those owned by whites and only 6 million rand for those held by Coloured, even though only 1.3 per cent of the population there was white." However, the distinction that is relevant is between perceived ownership in terms of sentiment flowing from generations of occupancy (to Cape Coloureds, District Six was "theirs") and legal ownership in terms of property deeds (to White absentee land owners, District Six was in monetary value almost three-quarters "theirs").

Yet, it was not possible for *Die Burger,* pursuing this strict legal-ownership tack, to ignore the claims of Coloured sentiment. Every Capetonian is aware of these claims; they are too powerful to be waved aside as having no legal or practical importance. Thus, the editorial was concluded in a self-justifying tone:

> The Government, which removed a blot from the face of Cape Town and received more kicks than halfpence from it—also from pale Afrikaans intellectuals—will have to keep its hand on this development, in full consultation with the Brown people themselves rather than with the kind of White people whose bad conscience over their high living standard bedevils so many good things in our country.

The "liberal" *Cape Times's* reaction to this same proclamation was predictably a little different, although in part it also was misleading. Its banner headline across the front page declaring a "District Six Reprieve" was factually incorrect. *Cape Times* cartoonist Grogan depicted a Coloured man struggling to carry an enormous rock, labeled apartheid, on his back, bent almost double. The figure was glancing backward, smiling hopefully at three chunks of the main rock fallen to the ground. One was labeled Nico Malan, the new Cape

Town opera house at which, after a successful White boycott, Coloureds were eventually permitted to attend cultural events. (One of the more famous news photos in Cape Town during my two initial years there was a smiling Adam Small mounting the steps into the Nico Malan complex, newly opened for all races, to view the production of *his own play, Kanna hy kô huistoe.* Until that time, Small, a Coloured, was barred from entering the Nico Malan complex by apartheid legislation. Among other things, the play deals with Cape Town slum life and the group areas.) A second fallen chunk was labeled Blue Train, the luxury express from Cape Town to Pretoria, today no longer reserved for Whites only. The third piece was labeled Hotels and Restaurants, for then a few were being opened to all racial groups and hence dubbed "international" by the government. (See p. 62.) A fourth chunk of rock in the act of falling was labeled District Six.

Such headlines and cartoons were probably a result of wishful thinking in the *Cape Times*'s editorial office. The newspaper did note correctly in its text (26 May 1975), however, that

> Mr. Loots' [the government minister responsible] decision is no more than a step in the right direction. The heartland of District Six remains zoned as an area for Whites only. . . . The zoning of District Six as a White area was a flagrant injustice, even if considered within the framework of the ideology of separate development. Few actions of the Nationalist Government have caused more bitterness and resentment in the Coloured community of the Cape. A complete reversal of the District Six zoning would be a symbolic act of great meaning, a gesture of reconciliation which would be universally acclaimed.

Some Whites, then, had an inkling of the symbolism of District Six for Coloured people. The Cape Town City Council (especially, the *Cape Times* hinted, through the behind-the-scenes effort of the mayor at that time, David Bloomberg), the Cape Town Chamber of Commerce, the Cape Ring of the Dutch Reformed Church, and the (English-speaking) Churches' Urban Planning Commission were all in favor of District Six's being reproclaimed for Coloureds. The next day (May 27), the same newspaper reported some Coloured reaction, for example, that of David Curry, deputy leader of the Labour party, who said that the proclamation was "political fraud . . . trying to bluff the people, . . . the Government is expert in rocking-chair politics. It gives the impression it is moving, but stays in the same spot."

Even in the report (van der Horst, 1976, p. 70) of the government-appointed Theron Commission (a minority of the commissioners were Coloured), recommendation 115 (which was not accepted by the government) read:

> District Six, together with the areas known as Woodstock (now White) and Salt River (now controlled), be declared coloured group areas.

> Voting: 11 for; 5 against; 2 abstentions; 1 minority recommendation. Minority recommendation [as van der Horst abbreviated it]:

> A committee representative of the National Monuments Commission [12] and the University of the Western Cape be appointed to preserve a small area of District Six, where old traditional living patterns [13] and possibly former crafts be demonstrated. This block should be declared a coloured area "purely for conservation purposes." Supported by 4 members.

The historic association between the Coloured people and District Six thus was clearly recognized. Such recognition is also found in the city council's naming of new Cape Flats Coloured townships after District Six locales. (See Chapter 9.) And in reviewing four books about the Theron Commission, the South African Institute of Race Relations' *News* (April 1977) chose one keynote photograph to tell the readers that the pages they are looking at are concerned with the place of the Coloured people in South Africa. The thematic photograph showed children playing in District Six. Although it has been proclaimed White space for fifteen years and though it is now mostly bulldozed waste, District Six's associations remain indelible — this despite such ploys as the government officially renaming the area Zonnebloem in 1979.

The properties acquired by the Department of Community Development through the removals from District Six have not yet been resold at prices acceptable to the government. The minister of community development said on 23 March 1976 in the House of Assembly that none of the District Six properties acquired by his department at a total cost of more than 22 million rand had been sold but that attention was being given to "positive steps for the sale of properties." After two more years of "positive steps," the minister announced in 1978 that *one* property had been sold, for R56,880, while the amount disbursed on acquisition had risen to R24,383,953 (since 1966). By January 1980, only seven properties had been sold, for a total of R233,000. Hoping to inject some life into this tract of real estate, the minister of community development had announced in May 1978 a 9-million-rand rehabilitation scheme for District Six. Later in 1978, phase one of the plan was unveiled: a 2.5-million-rand apartment complex for White police and armed services personnel, a 1.5-million-rand allotment for roads and services, and a 0.5-million-rand White housing complex of twenty-five apartments. In addition, the Afrikaanse Christelike Vroue Vereniging (Women's Institute) announced plans for a 2-million-rand high-rise building to house crèches, a home for the aged, and a hostel for working women (for Whites only).[14] In 1979, another proposal to build a new 44-million-rand technikon (technical college) in District Six stirred up a great deal of controversy, since it required the demolition of 348 houses still standing and inhabited by 354 families (that is, about 2,500 persons, not yet removed, almost all of whom were Coloured). It is noteworthy that, along with the Good Hope Centre (for trade and conventions) completed near the castle at the foot of District Six, these projects are all institutional and/or financed by public capital. Holders of private capital have seemed very loth to invest in the "new" District Six. No such residential development for Whites, who are the only people qualified to live in this group area, has occurred. This is due in part to the oversupply of White housing plots in the metropolis, in part to the fact that the area is from an urban planning point of view probably suited to less-profitable low-income housing, and in part due to the lingering "slum" stigma attached to the area. There is, however, another reason, too.

In an editorial on District Six entitled "A White Elephant," the *Cape Times* (1 August 1974) chose to draw a moral from the marked lack of buoyancy in this particular land market:

> There was so little interest in the public auction of the first three stands that the Department [of Community Development] refused to accept the highest offer. It is too early to expect the government to recognise the real reasons: that Cape Town people are reluctant to become associated with the redevelopment of an area that was taken from the Coloured community, the most notorious example of such action.

Even though the *Cape Times* may be overplaying the moral sensitivity of some of its mainly English-speaking White readers, there is some truth to its assertion. For example, a "Friends of District Six" association —with prominent members who are White academics and priests and at whose meetings at least once in 1979 the mayor and deputy mayor of Cape Town participated in a semiofficial capacity— has been very visible in its attempts to dissuade White private investment in the "tainted land" of District Six.[15] This group annoyed the powers that be enough to excite government spokespersons to make a charge of what was termed "economic terrorism"! The group also reacted most guardedly to the November 1979 announcement that parts of Salt River and lower Woodstock (anomalous area E) were going to be proclaimed Coloured, considering it to be in part a propagandistic move to deflect criticism from the continuing White status of District Six. Indeed, during 1979 the secretary for community development said that in District Six a point of no return had been reached and that the government would not alter its plans; in December the prime minister announced that the area's status would not be changed.

The measure of sensitivity over District Six demonstrated by some White Capetonians is not matched, however, by White behavior in the "liberal" city as a whole. An identical "redevelopment"/Coloured dispossession issue exists in another part of Cape Town, the inner suburb of Mowbray. There fewer qualms have been felt by White Capetonians over private investment in "tainted" properties. In what were once Coloured pockets, gentrification has occurred, the profitable purchase and resale by Whites of the homes of Coloureds ejected by the Group Areas Act.

CHAPTER SEVEN

Mowbray: From Community to Gentrification

In Mowbray everybody knew everybody else—you could see strangers.

Group areas removee
now living on the Cape Flats

The term "community" is frequently invoked in tones of profundity by ideologues (social scientists as well as "laypersons") from the far left to the far right. Like motherhood and apple pie, it is considered synonymous with virtue and desirability.

Marcia Effrat,
"Approaches to Community:
Conflicts and Complementarities,"
1973

A BRIEF HISTORY OF MOWBRAY

There is no doubt that Khoikhoi herdsmen once pastured their stock by the Liesbeek River on the land that is now Mowbray, but the first recorded history dates from 1657. In that year, Dutch *vrijburghers* established South Africa's first White farms. The dovecote of Coornhoop Farm, Mowbray, was constructed in 1657 and still stands. The following year, the first slaves were imported, and so as early as the seventeenth century slaves—with their White masters, the ancestors of the Coloured people—worked on the farms of what was to be named Mowbray. Later, in 1724, three runaway slaves from Welgelegen Farm were executed near a crossroads tavern and their heads impaled for public display. The tavern immediately became known as Driekoppen ("three heads"); it formed the nucleus of a hamlet that gradually grew into a village, which was called Mowbray after 1850. After the emancipation of the slaves in 1834, some Coloured ex-slaves lived a little apart from the Whites in their humble dwellings, continuing to work as servants and gardeners for the White families. These Coloured residential zones, and indeed the whole *dorp* (village) of Mowbray, were later enveloped by the spread of Cape Town's built-up area, but they retained their identity to an extent. From these origins came the three Coloured pockets that made up Non-white Mowbray (Map 21).

One of the three pockets grew up next to Hare's brickyard, which apparently began operations after 1830 (Simcox, 1975). Known as the Bo-Dorp (upper village), or the Malay Camp, it was established to house the brickyard workers. Many Malays, apparently, worked as foremen and draymen, delivering the bricks around Cape Town by horse and cart; Black Africans did the dirtier "kaffir work"—as two old Muslim brickyard workers called it—in the brickyard itself.

The second pocket, the Dorp (or, simply, Mowbray), was certainly an area of Coloured/Malay settlement by the mid-nineteenth century. In 1854, St. Peter's Parish Church (Anglican) was founded, and the church school next to it in the 1860s, which was attended by Mowbray's Nonwhite children in the primary grades. (This practice became de facto educational segregation.) During the 1860s, also, the mosque was established in Mowbray and has been continually used since then for worship and the Islamic madressa school.[1] The Methodist church also established a primary school in Mowbray, which many Coloured children attended.

By the end of the nineteenth century, the third pocket, the Valley, clearly existed as a zone of Coloured settlement, muddy and ill drained in parts, low lying and susceptible to inundation from the Liesbeek River. Many ex-residents of the area told me about the floods, which presumably accounted for the unattractiveness and low value of this land to the Whites—hence, Coloured settlement there, and also a few hundred yards to the south on Alma Road-North Street in Rosebank. Other indications of the growing Nonwhite population of Mowbray were the founding of the Pirates cricket club by 1888, named after Mowbray's "coon troupe" of that time (recall that the activities of the "coons" are reported to have begun after Queen Victoria's Jubilee in 1887), and Perseverance, Mowbray's Coloured rugby club founded in 1889.

These three areas were separate entities up to a point, but all were Mowbray. In the words of Mr. Koopmans, a young man in his thirties in 1975, remembering some childhood activities:

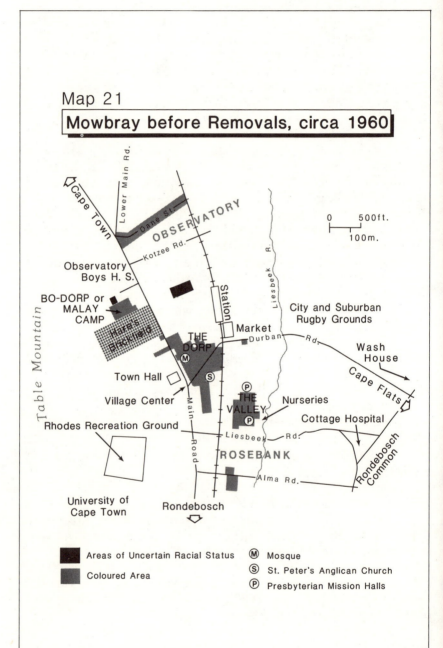

Map 21

Mowbray before Removals, circa 1960

Areas of Uncertain Racial Status

Coloured Area

Ⓜ Mosque

Ⓢ St. Peter's Anglican Church

Ⓟ Presbyterian Mission Halls

We would get together in a bunch and have fights with the Mowbray European boys. We would get up a cricket team from the Valley to play the
Dorp or the Bo-Dorp—the brickfields—and we'd have fights with them,
too—in a sort of boys' gang, not criminal, a bunch of us rather. We were ri-
vals, like houses in a school,[2] you know. But if it was a question of people
from outside, then we were all Mowbray, no doubt about that.

This quotation not only underscores the fact that it was *Nonwhite*
Mowbray that was considered the focal point of loyalty, it also pro-
vides a choice example of various levels of in-group and out-group
combinations in a "segmentary system" as outlined by Evans-
Pritchard (1940) and, especially, by Suttles (1968, pp. 31-35).

THE NATURE OF COMMUNITY

Suttles (1972, p. 76), commenting on many earlier community
studies, rather acidly wrote:

> Only the local grass-roots community, self-governing and self-initiated,
> deserved to be called a community. Everything else was an artifact and,
> lacking the magic touch of the invisible hand, considered unreal or inau-
> thentic. The model of such "natural" communities may have been a myth
> more often than not.

The term "community" has seemed not only value laden but also
incapable of definition. Hillery (1955), in an exhaustive review of the
literature, found that seventy-three of the ninety-four definitions he
gleaned from it included area as a charateristic. The second most
common characteristic of "community" was common ties; the third,
social interaction. Apart from these general points of overlap, the
term appears to be a morass of indefinition. At one pole some commentators, such as Webber (1964; 1968), have considered common
ties to be the nexus and physical place per se to be irrelevant; thus
Webber's "non-place urban realm." Others, such as Tilly (1973, p.
212), gathered at the other pole. ". . . [Webber] chooses to make
solidarity define communities and to leave the extent of territoriality
problematic; we choose to make territoriality define communities
and to leave the extent of solidarity problematic." Still others, such
as Hillery himself (1968), seem to have lost themselves in a semantic
maze: "No satisfactory order could be discovered. After seven years
of trying to make theoretical sense of the field, I decided to begin at
the other end: to study community by investigating the things that
had been called community. This approach (which took another

seven years). . . ." For all the energy he expended over fourteen years, Hillery was not able to provide a firm definition of the term.

Although searching for a definition does not seem fruitful, *some* construct must be adopted. For the time being, then, let us use that of Marris (1977), for it seems to illuminate some of the characteristics of Mowbray. Marris posited that "community" (whatever it may be) has two salient qualities: (1) the notion of community as acknowledgment — living in an area where people accept responsibility for one another, almost "a microcosm of human experience"; and (2) the notion of community as territory — appropriating the familiar places that have become comfortable. They become a resident's stamping ground, his or her space, where he or she can say, "I am known and can find my way about." The combination of these two qualities results in what Wild (1963) has called "fields of care."

Marris considered Bethnal Green in London's East End to have been an example of "community" as he perceived it. It was here that Young and Willmott conducted their celebrated 1957 study (revised in 1962, p. 115). In their search for the essentials of community, they concluded that "the interaction between length of residence and kinship is therefore the crux of our interpretation. Neither is by itself a sufficient explanation." This definition binds *particular* kinds of common ties (kinship) to area/territory (as inevitable in length of residence in one place).

Another factor in the genesis of community that is frequently mentioned is common work and work place (and common vulnerability), as is evident in company towns. Such a shared experience, however, did not play a prominent role for the Mowbray residents I interviewed. True, there were Hare's brickyard in the Bo-Dorp and Starke and Ayres's nurseries in the Valley as places of employment for a number of the local men. Also, some of the women worked at similar tasks, as domestics in White Mowbray and Rosebank or as machinists in the clothing factories of Woodstock and Salt River. However, these work places account for only a few of the residents, and they also were not work places where the labor force had had an exclusively or even a primarily "Mowbray" character. Most ex-Mowbrayite principal wage earners, both males and females, held jobs outside of Mowbray in many different work places, which were mainly in the Salt River to Cape Town inner-city tract.

Any of these factors can engender strong feelings for community in a locale — as in Mowbray. Constituents they may be, but of themselves these factors are not sufficient to have *caused* the Mowbray community. The references to Mowbray have, in fact (usually without it being spelled out), been concerned wholly with *Nonwhite* Mowbray: Mr. Koopman's childhood antagonists were "the Mowbray European boys." Therefore, I did not simply encounter some welling up of a "natural" community, with all its undertones of the nostalgic half-look backward to an imagined (idealized?) rural past of village solidarity. As opposed to "sentimental ties . . . accounting for the progressive development of a localized web of interpersonal relations and intimacy," Suttles (1972, pp. 12-13) proposed that "most likely, local communities and neighborhoods, like other groups . . . come into existence . . . [through] . . . their 'foreign relations' . . . and have to settle on an identity and a set of boundaries which over-simplify their reality." Indeed, the *sufficient* condition for the crea-tion of the Mowbray Nonwhite community was "foreign relations": relations with Cape Town's Whites. Out definition as *Non*white, as a result of White political and property-holding power, is the single most important factor in the genesis of the Mowbray pockets' com-munity.

To this indisputable causative condition, one qualifying. factor must be added. Apparently, as in feeling a sense of "Colouredness," being treated as an out-group *in its turn* and by its very nature stimu-lates the reactive growth of some measure of solidarity, some measure of shared understandings among "us." About Coloured people other than those trying to pass for White, Whisson[3] asked:

> . . . are there not "avoidance rules" and preferences for "we coloured people" to live together and associate together—expressed by the unwill-ingness to incorporate whites into the groupings?—whites make "us" feel uncomfortable, remind us of what we are not, etc. Exclusiveness is not wholly one-sided.

It is surely a commonsensical notion that, very frequently, "antagon-ism from without breeds association within." This is so whether the antagonism is based mainly on color, as in Mowbray or in Washing-ton, D.C. (see Hannerz, 1969, p. 153), or on class, as Durant (1939) found in the London suburbs during the 1930s (and whose dictum I just quoted).

This last factor leads to a paradox concerning the community of Nonwhite Mowbray. An individual (as a *Non*white) was excluded, and yet on a citywide scale his or her status partially arose from that from which he or she was excluded—reputable White Mowbray-Rosebank (Figure 9). The Mowbray Nonwhite pockets were low-income areas in a reasonably high-income sector. Naturally, then, the inhabitants of these pockets, although poor, emphasized their pride

Figure 9. A House in Mowbray-Rosebank, near the Cottage Hospital. The White matrix in which the Nonwhite pocket of the Valley was set is exemplified in this home.

and respectability —*by association*—in being from Mowbray. A Malay bricklayer, in 1975 living in a well-established council tenantry scheme in Silvertown, near Athlone, told me that "around here there's not so good a class of people, from Cape Town [that is, the inner city: District Six]. They're not like Mowbray people, who were very respectable; living with the Europeans we were a better class of Coloured people."

Of the 100 people I interviewed, 13 specifically volunteered (there was no question in the interview schedule on the subject) that in Mowbray they had gotten on well or had been friends with "the Europeans." One person, a septuagenarian, complained: "The government treats all Coloured people alike, both the respectable and the working-class; but I was brought up like the Whites. . . . My friends were White [and so were his first cousins]. We would go hunting for buck on the Flats in June. We didn't worry about colour." (Of this person, another much younger person opined "Oh, he's been a play-white for years!"[4]) Being close (both spatially and socially) to Whites was for some of the people interviewed part of the pride that nearly all ex-Mowbrayites showed in being *Mowbray se mense*: Mowbray people.

THE REPRESENTATIVENESS
OF THE MOWBRAY SAMPLE

Pride in being from Mowbray also stemmed, more straightforwardly, from the socioeconomic and cultural characteristics of Coloured and Malay Mowbrayites themselves. Poor the ex-Mowbrayites may have been vis-à-vis their White neighbors, but in relation to other Coloured Capetonians they were generally of middle (a few even upper) income. Less qualitative than the claims of some regarding their coziness with the Mowbray Whites are the objective data that demonstrate Nonwhite Mowbray's above-average status.

The nature of "community" in the Nonwhite pockets of Mowbray before group areas development, as Effrat (1973, p. 2) warned, should not be idealized. Although the informal segregation that existed prior to apartheid may have been less unpleasant than today's legislated segregation, I have tried to avoid sentimental portrayals of a past golden age in Mowbray, which could so easily be constructed from the frequently sentimental words of the people expelled. Various factors rendered Nonwhite Mowbray a *partial* community. But, even though it was not "whole," the lost community is a source of regret for most of the people I interviewed and it is entirely appropriate that their expressions of "grieving for a lost home"[5] be included here. As the first quotation at the beginning of the chapter suggests, they felt it to be *their* place.

Most of the raw data for this and the next two chapters were collected through interviews I conducted with members of 100 households who had been expelled from Mowbray by the Group Areas Act during the mid-1960s. These 100 households represent approximately half of all Nonwhite households expelled from Mowbray. Through meeting a number of strategic informants, I was introduced to others via friendship and family networks. The interviews took place over the period between April 1975 and February 1976 and were carried out with a 130-item questionnaire.[6] The smallness of the original Mowbray community facilitated the cross-checking of information: many ex-Mowbrayites knew a great deal about their ex-neighbors. Further verification came from interviewing a number of long-term White Mowbrayites and from various written records, such as those of the local churches and the city of Cape Town. Despite my informants' initial suspicion, the fact that I contacted people through their social networks made a 99 percent response rate possible. Only one person refused to have anything to do with me, although three or four others were rather uncooperative. Nearly everyone I met eventually warmed to the idea of helping me in my "study of the history of Mowbray" (as I put it). The interviews lasted at least an hour, many much longer. To some friendly households I returned for help again and again.

By using both the data I gathered personally and those from various other sources, a clear delineation of the better-than-average status can be drawn. For example, first consider occupational status. A 1964 University of South Africa survey found that in the Cape Peninsula 12.6 percent of Coloured household heads were in professional and white-collar occupations. The 1960 union census for Coloureds in Tract 74 (Mowbray) gave the figure as 13.6 percent; in my sample it was 15 percent.[7] For skilled laborers, the same three sources, respectively, found for the entire Cape Peninsula, 11.5 percent; for Mowbray itself, the percentages were 48.3 percent and 44 percent. For the combined categories of semiskilled and unskilled workers, the comparable figures were 56.4 percent (Cape Peninsula) and (for Mowbray only) 38.1 percent and 39 percent. Of this last, only 5 percent were unskilled. The socioeconomic level of Coloured people generally is, of course, higher in the urban areas than in the rural areas, so comparisons with the urbanized Cape Peninsula are particularly telling. A comparison of Mowbray with *national* averages for

Coloured persons shows a much greater discrepancy. It is clear that Nonwhite Mowbray was an area lived in by persons of above-average job status.

Second, as a category, Coloureds who speak English, and not Afrikaans, as their native language are of higher socioeconomic status than other Coloureds, at least in Cape Town and in Natal. Nationally, only about 10 percent of Coloureds have English as their mother tongue. In Nonwhite Mowbray, the 1960 union census found that 25.6 percent were native speakers of English; my survey, 31 percent.

A third indicator of status among those in the Coloured category is religious affiliation. As groups, Muslims are of higher status and adherents to the Afrikaans-speaking Dutch Reformed Mission Church (NGSK) are of lower status. Nationwide, in 1960, approximately 6 percent of Coloureds were Muslim, whereas about 28.5 percent belonged to the NGSK. In Mowbray the 1960 census found 39.1 percent to be Muslim and only 8.7 percent NGSK; 45.1 percent attended English-speaking Protestant churches. In my sample, 35 percent of the ex-Mowbray households were Muslim; this was not only a higher proportion of Muslims than among the Coloureds of the country at large, but this proportion was also higher than that in the Cape Peninsula Coloured population, which is generally estimated to be approximately 20 percent.

A number of indexes underscore the higher average status of Muslims (Cape Malays) among the Coloured population. Malays are, as a group, more likely to be home owners than Christian Coloureds.

Table 7
Religious Affiliation and Residential
Status of Mowbray Sample

Religion	Home Owner	Council Renter	Private Renter	Total
Muslim	18	14	2	34
Christian	23	37	4	64
Total	41	51	6	98

Whisson[8] found this to be so in various locales on the Cape Peninsula, and I found it so in Mowbray, as Table 7 indicates. The same disproportion is true for occupational status: Malays are more likely to have higher job status as Table 8 indicates. In addition, eleven out of thirty-four Muslim households in my survey had a telephone, but only fourteen out of sixty-four Christian households did. The same was true about car ownership: only one-quarter of the Malay people I interviewed had no car or access to one in the same household, whereas over one-half of the Christian people I interviewed were in this situation.

Table 8
Religious Affiliation and Occupational Status
(controlled for sex, males only)

Religion	Occupation						Total
	1	2	3	4	5	6	
	(High Status)				(Low Status)		
Muslim	5	3	4	16	6	0	34
Christian	4	2	4	17	23	2	52
Total	9	5	8	33	29	2	86

Note: There was also one Hindu household, whose male head's job status was high, category 1.

A fourth indicator of status is housing. When they lived in Mowbray, 28 of the 100 heads of household interviewed were home owners (there were a number of co-owners in extended families); 42 of the 100 were home owners by 1975-1976. For the Coloured category, this is far above both the Cape Town metropolitan proportion and that of the country at large, where, according to Doman (1975), about 30 percent of Coloureds are home owners. Another perhaps more likely figure for the 1970 countrywide home-ownership proportion is smaller, only 23.1 percent.[9] Even the poorest people in the Mowbray pockets were less poor than a general Coloured Capetonian sample. Of those thirty-six ex-Mowbray households that moved to Bonteheuwel and Heideveld council rental schemes, thirty-two (the poor) were originally housed "economically," and only four (the still poorer) were housed "subeconomically."[10] By 1976, none was housed "subeconomically." Therefore, my sample was not representative of *all* council renters, because both "economic" and "subeconomic" sectors continue to exist within the housing projects. Also, only one interviewee removed to a *pondok* (shanty); yet, 20 percent of all the Coloureds living in greater Cape Town in 1976-1977 were housed in shanties. (See Chapter 10.)

A fifth indirect, and possibly unreliable, indicator of the higher-than-average status of Mowbray removees is that about four-fifths of the housing that they occupied is still standing; that is, it was not irredeemable slum housing, but it was renovated and made profitable for resale to the Whites who replaced the removees.

Whatever the value of this last indicator, the preceding data have clearly demonstrated that Mowbray was a better-than-average Coloured Cape Town community. And if, as a Bureau of Market Research report showed in 1975, over one-quarter of all Coloured persons in South Africa were then living below the "minimum living level," [11] we can be sure that few, if any, of them were ex-Mowbrayites. One last minor consideration: some of the people whom many of the removees might have been inclined to included among "us" became members of "them," that is, they were Pass-Whites. Clearly, their socioeconomic status (putting aside for the moment their racial classification) was higher than any Coloured average.

The preceding discussion has shown to what degree Coloured Mowbrayites differed from Coloureds both in Cape Town and in South Africa as a whole. Although Mowbrayites did deviate from the norm, this does not mean that their consistently higher indexes somehow cushioned them against the trauma of group areas removals. Much of the remainder of this study will show that their experience was very representative of that of Coloured South Africans in general. In some ways, indeed, their experiences may have been *more* unpleasant than those of many removees, for they had more to lose.

There is one final point to be made before coming to grips with the data that are to follow. That is the question of the representativeness of the sample with regard to sex and age. These were South African households being interviewed during the mid-1970s, and much of the interview questionnaire dealt with community life during the first half of the 1960s. That being so, "normal" household structure was definitely perceived by them to be the nuclear family, the husband being viewed as the "head of the household" and the "primary" wage earner, with the wife, when she was employed, a "secondary" wage earner. (There were two Muslim households in which the husband was—quite legally—a polygamist; one of the men told me so, the other did not.) So the "normal" interview pattern was usually an evening, weekend, or Christmas vacation visit; both husband and wife were interviewed together, and I tried to be sensitive to any differences of opinion or emphasis that arose between them; grown children sometimes participated, too. Only thirteen "heads of household" were female: four had never married, four were widowed, four were divorced or separated, and one had a common-law marriage with a "husband" whose participation in the household was clearly marginal and very unpredictable. This skewing of the data toward older, married, male "heads of household" probably makes little difference for the purely objective questions that made up 90 percent of the questionnaire (for example, "Where did you use to go to the hospital, when you lived in Mowbray?"). For the last three questions in the interviews, the open-ended and affective ones, however, some important differences among age- and sex-groups probably arose. Women who worked as housewives at home, for example, could be expected to feel the loss of "community" more than men who were away from home every workday and whose jobs did not change after their forced removal from Mowbray. In these matters, which are especially important for the material discussed in Chapter 9, I have frequently pointed out the differences in viewpoint of male and female and of old and young interviewees.

COMMUNITY IN NONWHITE MOWBRAY

Some Objective Data

Mowbray was only a part-time community for many of its inhabitants, particularly for men of working age. In only twelve of seventy-two cases[12] (16.6 percent) did the head of the household work in Mowbray at the time of group areas removals (Map 22). Nevertheless, it was the place to which the breadwinners came *home* in the evening. There were others who had the opportunity to participate more fully in the community: those who worked in Mowbray (for example, a number of Muslim tailors), those who were retired and spent their days in their homes or more likely on the stoop or at some street corner or perhaps at a bar, the home-tied housewives, the young children going to primary schools in Mowbray, and the adolescents, some who had left school and some who were home from high school by midafternoon and all the time during the school holidays. Whether they were in Mowbray most of the time or not, however, for all the Coloured inhabitants their three pockets signified the comfortably familiar context of their lives.

Their familiarity came from long residence. Although only 36 of 100 household heads, and only 18 of 82 spouses, had been born in Mowbray itself, the average length of residence in Mowbray for the heads of households interviewed was thirty-three years. This is a long time—it represented up to two-thirds of the average Coloured life span during the mid-1960s, when the removals occurred.[13] It is clear that there were certain anchor families—Mowbray families—and that these were mostly Muslim. At the same time, other families and in-

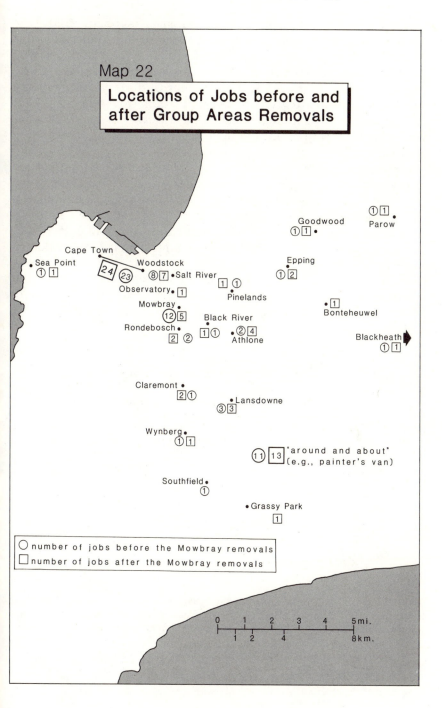

Map 22

Locations of Jobs before and after Group Areas Removals

○ number of jobs before the Mowbray removals
□ number of jobs after the Mowbray removals

dividuals were continually moving in and, especially, out. The marked outward movement was greatly due to the children of large families who could not find housing for themselves nearby and who upon marriage moved out to Athlone or wherever. There was, therefore, a continual turnover, and to attempt to portray Mowbray as a *purely* before-and-after group areas situation would be somewhat misleading (almost akin to assuming that African society was static at and until the arrival of Europeans from the seventeenth century onwards).

Nevertheless, there was sufficient underlying stability for *70 of the 100 households interviewed to have had kin at another address in the village, 49 of these at two or more other addresses.* Ten households, 9 of them Muslim, were related to 8 or more separate households in Mowbray. Thus, the relationship that Young and Willmott (1962) considered particularly crucial to community—that between length of residence and kinship—was readily discernible in Nonwhite Mowbray. Table 9 was constructed from the interview data. If the categories are collapsed as indicated on the table, then, with four degrees of freedom, chi square equals 16.3142, which is significant at the .05 confidence level.

Table 9
Cross-Tabulation of Length of Residence and Number of Kin Households

Years in Mowbray	Number of Related Families										Total
	0	1	2	3	4	5	6	7	8	9 or More	
0-4		2	1	1							7
5-9	2										0
10-19	10	1	2		2	1					18
20-29	5	7	3	1		2		1	1		41
30-39	8	8	6	2	1					3	51+
40-49	2	2	2	2	1	1		1		3	55+
50-59		3	1	3		2				1	33+
60-69			1	1						1	44+
70 or More	1					1				1	14+

Note: The years in Mowbray are how long the interviewee (the head of the household) lived in Mowbray. The number of related families is the number of family groups related to the interviewee that lived in separate households in Mowbray at the same time.

From the chi-square statistic, a number of further relationships concerning kinship were calculated to be significant at the .05 level. For example, to be a Mowbray Muslim (as opposed to being a Christian) was to be demonstrably more likely, and that not through chance, to have a greater number of kin in Mowbray[14] (Table 10). Consider also the six other relationships shown by Table 11, each of which links the number of kin households to some other variable. Each of them seems to be plausible at first sight—such as linking presence of kin to whether the parents of the head of the household were born in Mowbray or not—and each is, indeed, found to be significant at the .05 level.

Table 10
Religious Affiliation and Number of Kin Households

Religion	Number of Kin Households									
	0	1	2	3	4	5	6	7	8	9 or More
Christian	24	19	12	5	—	3	—	—	—	1
Muslim	5	2	4	5	4	4	—	2	1	8

Kinship represents a very basic "support system" relied upon particularly by poorer people like the people I interviewed and also, in the case of the Muslims, relied upon even more so because of cultural predilection. My questionnaire, in addition, sought out further information indicating the supportive and familiar context of the former lifeworld of Mowbrayites. To questions such as "Where did you use to go, when living in Mowbray, for your place of worship, or your doctor, or your food shopping?" the preponderance of the reply "in Mowbray only" is noteworthy (Table 12).

Table 11
Relationships between the Number of Physically Separate
Related Households in Mowbray and Other Factors

Other Factors	x^2	x^2 for .05	Degrees of Freedom	N
The birthplace of the head of the household	10.17	9.48	4	100
Whether the head of the household had or had not ever lived outside Mowbray prior to group areas removals	18.23	9.48	4	99
Where the wife (in male-headed households) had lived prior to marriage (in Mowbray or not)	7.14	5.99	2	84

Table 11 — *Continued*

Other Factors	χ^2	χ^2 for .05	Degrees of Freedom	N
How long the parents of the head of the household had lived in Mowbray, or if they had not	25.43	12.59	6	97
Birthplace of the parents of the head of the household	23.83	5.99	2	96
How long the grandparents of the head of the household had lived in Mowbray, or if they had not	18.39	5.99	2	89

Table 12

Accessibility of Interviewed Households to Various Services When They Lived in Mowbray

Service	In Mowbray Only	Not in Mowbray	Both in and Not in Mowbray	No Answer
Place of Worship	91	7	2	—
Doctor	80	14	5	1
Hospital	Mowbray and Rondebosch Cottage Hospital: 60	Groote Schuur: 65	High degree of overlap between Cottage Hospital and Groote Schuur	—
	Mowbray Town Hall (Clinic): 4	Other: 5		
Plumber	70 (19 self)	14	1	15
Electrician	66 (14 self)	8	1	25[a]
Meat[b]	29	1	2	—
Sporting Events	34	16	37	13
Bar	27	0	1	72[c]

a. Fourteen households had no electricity in Mowbray.

b. An oversight in interviewing means that there are only thirty-two cases here; but the trend is quite unmistakable.

c. By far the most unsuccessful question in the interview! (See Chapter 1, p. 18.)

Related to the replies to questions about accessibility of services is the fact that most Mowbrayites were able to use walking as a common means of transportation. Walking costs nothing and is a very versatile mode of access—by which I mean a pedestrian is not necessarily constrained to any particular route, to particular boarding and alighting points, or to any timetable established by other people; walking also facilitates meetings with friends and neighbors encountered en route. Accessibility to friends by walking when the interviewees were living in Mowbray was very great: for 60 percent of them, *all* their five best friends lived in Mowbray. For the remaining 39 percent (there was one inapplicable answer), all had *some* of their five best friends in Mowbray.

The households in Mowbray were under 1 kilometer from Rondebosch and Mowbray Cottage Hospital and under 2 kilometers from Groote Schuur Hospital. (See Map 21.) Thus, 45 of 100 households I interviewed said that they walked to the hospital; another 26 both walked and took the bus; and 21 traveled by bus alone (to Groote Schuur). The replies to questions about trips to the doctor were similar.

For sporting events, people went outside of Mowbray somewhat more often. Mowbray was within walking distance of the attractive Camp Ground, or Rondebosch Common (Map 21), where sport could be almost spontaneously organized; cricket, baseball, tennis, and soccer were mentioned. Mowbrayites also had the use of the Rhodes Recreation Ground close by, were not far from Hartleyvale soccer stadium in Observatory; and, most important (for Christian Coloureds only),[15] the City and Suburban rugby league had its ground at Mowbray just across the Liesbeek River until 1959. Rugby is very much South Africa's national sport and Perseverance, Mowbray's team, was a target of Coloured Mowbray's sentiment. However, an important source for sport *outside* of Mowbray was three stations down the line (2.5 kilometers): Newlands. There (White) cricket and rugby were played, including international games against the British, French, Australians, and New Zealanders, games to which numerous Coloured Mowbrayites used to go.[16]

To a question concerning schools for Nonwhites, "within Mowbray" answers—apart from replies about the youngest children— were fewer. In the primary standards (through approximately the sixth grade in the United States), forty-eight of the seventy-two households responding to this question reported that their children attended St. Peter's Church Mission School in the village. Since another nine of the seventy-two reported the Mowbray Methodist Church School, then 80 percent of Mowbray's younger children went to school within walking distance of their homes. However, because Mowbray's Nonwhite population was so small, there was no high school for the children of the village, so, for sixty-four households, high school children had to travel out of Mowbray by public transportation. Most high school students (from seventeen of the households) went to the Wesley Training College in Salt River, 2.15 kilometers distant; others went to Claremont, District Six, and Athlone.

The answers concerning high schools direct attention to Mowbray's accessibility to other Coloured population centers. From Mowbray there are important routes, with very good public transportation, to the south, north, and east. (Table Mountain blocks the west.) North-south through Mowbray run Main Road and the southern suburbs railway line. These are joined at Mowbray by what was once the main access road to the Cape Flats (until the freeway, Settler's Way, was built during the 1960s), the still-important, axial Klipfontein Road. Mowbray is a prominent transportation node, especially since it is where the Athlone-area labor force changes from bus to train during its morning journey to Cape Town and vice versa during the evening.[17]

Mowbray's superior accessibility facilitated traveling outside of the area for shopping for things other than the everyday milk, bread, and groceries. For clothes, thirty-three percent of my sample reported that they shopped "in Mowbray only"; thirty-four, "outside of Mowbray"; and thirty-three, "both." They mentioned places such as Cape Town city center, Claremont, and, most frequently, Salt River (where the prices, reputedly, were lower). These three areas are easily accessible from Mowbray; the average distance of 2.27 kilometers traveled for buying clothes did not represent a significant hardship for the shoppers. Efficient public transportation was also important for Mowbrayites when they wanted to go to the bioscope (the movies). Unless a Coloured Mowbrayite was "fair enough to pass for White" at the Savoy in Mowbray or, more often, at the Lyceum in Observatory, he or she went by bus (as 72 percent of the interviewees reported) to Salt River, Woodstock, Athlone, or Claremont.

Some Subjective Responses

The outlines of the Mowbray pockets—the social bonds within them and their external connections—should by now be clear enough for the reader to appreciate some of the meanings of the "free responses" that my interviewees offered. Most of the questions on the questionnaire were purely objective. As I administered it, I tried (not always successfully, I admit) to elicit factual, rather than emotional or "slanted," replies. The last three questions, however, were attitudinal and more open-ended. When any rapport between the subject and myself had been generated, it was in replies to the last three questions that it came through. The last question of all usually drew out the most revealing responses: "What's life like here—for example, is the house as good? What things strike you most, how different is it here compared with the way it was in Mowbray?" The quotations that follow report the interviewee's experiences; the quotations are arranged *in the same order of frequency* with which various facets of Mowbray life were mentioned. The words represent *their* perception of their lost home.

"Mowbray Was Safe"

Of the households 48 percent indicated that they felt that "Mowbray was safe." A Coloured salesman of thirty-two said, "My friends all lived in Mowbray, we all grew up together, like a community. It was quiet, you could leave a bicycle on the stoop, it'd be there the next morning. We didn't lock houses." In Kew Town, I was told, "You can't walk back here at night like we used to at eleven o'clock down Lower Main Road Observatory, home to Mowbray." Of the households 15 percent mentioned walking at night in Mowbray as a specific example of its safety. A question of some importance here is whether the change in security was due to a change in place or a change in time; was it due to the loss of Mowbray or to societywide changes. For the majority of the ex-Mowbrayites I interviewed, it is both. (See Chapter 9). A number of people, other than the 48 percent, did not say in so many words that Mowbray was safe, but they *implied* that, usually by contrasting the past with the present (1975-1976). That is to say, if the question were "How different is it here compared with the way it was in Mowbray?" and the response were "Here we wouldn't dream of going out at night," then something would definitely have been said about Mowbray's relative safety. Such replies, however, were not included in the 48 percent cited.

"Mowbray Was One Big Family"/"You Knew Everybody"

Since 37 percent of the households expressed such sentiments, clearly, the physical safety of Mowbray was complemented by its psychological safety, which is expressed in this quotation from one ex-Mowbrayite: "There was no delinquency among the youngsters there. Every grown-up person acted as a father. Here [Kew Town] you rectify a child and the parents say, 'Hey you, leave my child alone.' " A Muslim living in Bonteheuwel remembered that as a child, thirty years earlier, "We were more scared of the old people than of the police." Another Muslim, a tailor in his forties, recalled:

When I was fifteen or sixteen, if we did anything rude, offhanded in the street—like going to bars or smoking or taking a dame out—you'd get a

pak [a good clip on the ear] at night at home, they [parents] knew about
it right away. . . . It was the old men who used to stand at the corners
chatting or sit on the stoops. They'd pretend to be reading the Koran or a
comic or playing kerem[18] or whatever, but out of the corner of their eye
they were really watching you.

The quality of local surveillance is here superbly captured. However,
before we become too lyrical about the autonomous social control
and the "authentic" sense of "community" inherent in these quotations, we should look at the other side of the matter, which was
exemplified by a handful of responses. One woman contradicted
herself in consecutive sentences, first by extolling Mowbray and then
by remarking upon the lack of privacy there.

My husband say, "If this Group must fall, we'll go back to Mowbray
tomorrow." I said, "It'll never fall, and we'll be dead one day." . . .
Everyone knew everyone there: all classes — and the Europeans — mixed in.
People knew too much . . . but there was good feeling, not skindering
[gossiping].[19]

If this woman unintentionally revealed her ambivalence, there was
little in the views of a highly educated fortyish professional woman:
"Mowbray's village atmosphere was claustrophobic. . . . Squarehill
[a home-ownership scheme in Retreat, where she lived at the time of
the interview] is absolutely dead; no music society, nothing. Not
that there was in Mowbray, but you could get to it." For this
woman, Mowbray was clearly not the center of affective space; Mowbray was at least in part negative, "claustrophobic."

The most formally educated person of all the ex-Mowbrayites I
encountered, who held a degree from the University of Cape Town
and once had been a politically active figure "banned" under the
Suppression of Communism Act, exhibited a certain impatience with
Mowbray's character. It was too sheltered, too nice a village, and
too "smug"; it had no political awareness as lower Claremont had.
He asked, "Why don't you study it [that is, Claremont]? — the APO
[African Political Organisation] was active very long ago there." He
almost seemed to be saying that Mowbray deserved its fate.

The Muslim tailor already quoted told me how the strong Muslim
family structure in Mowbray clipped his wings.

Now Mr. Cohen [owner of a large clothing store on Main Road, Mowbray]
saw I was good at styling clothes — just making them up[20] bores me — and
he offered to sponsor me to go up to Windhoek, South-West. He offered
four times, but the old man, my grandfather, said I had to stay here with
the shop because I was my father's eldest son.

This man was carrying on the family tailoring business, no longer in Mowbray but in lower Woodstock. He was very dissatisfied with Heideveld, to which he was removed, and he was intent on bettering his status. He had applied to the Cape Town City Council for a loan to buy a house at the new Coloured satellite city of Mitchell's Plain.

Mowbray Was Centrally Located

The nodality and accessibility of Mowbray was mentioned by 37 percent of the households. Interviewees said, "Mowbray was very convenient; it was right on the spot; buses, trains, good shops. Everything was near." The contrast with their present situation is marked. (See Chapter 8.)

To Return to Mowbray . . . ?

Of the households 36 percent expressed a desire to return to Mowbray. As a Muslim businessman in his thirties put it, "For all the tea in China, I'd go back to Mowbray." The remarkable fact is that there was *no* question in the interview asking whether the subjects wished to return to Mowbray. Certainly, after responding to the fact-seeking part of the questionnaire and then being given the invitation at the end to say what he wished, one interviewee looked at me and said, "I suppose you're going to ask us if we'd like to go back." The question was not directly posed, however.

A Coloured bus driver in Silvertown, who was a driver in the (Coloureds-only) Cape Corps during World War II and went up Africa to the western desert with the South African forces, said spontaneously, "Of course we'd like to go back. Everybody knew you in Mowbray, what day you were born, exactly who you were married to, and where that one came from, and who you were related to." The tenor of this last quotation shows that it was a *past* Mowbray to which the removees wished to return. The problems involved in a real return were not considered, because the thought of return was utterly hypothetical, a wistful unreality. The exigencies of the post-Mowbray experience have colored the perception of the lost Mowbray. Many of those living in the council rental townships looked back to the golden age of Mowbray, and for three concrete reasons—their overall situation may well have been more happy then. (In a study of parallel group areas expulsions from Simonstown, Whisson [1972] offered a deft dissection of the image of a past golden age held by removees.)

. . . Or Not to Return to Mowbray?

Nearly all of the ex-Mowbrayites who had become home owners, however, were better off materially than they were when they lived in Mowbray, and a much lower proportion of them expressed a desire to return. In fact, 21 percent of the households stated that "here [away from Mowbray] the house is better"; a partly over-lapping 13 percent recalled that in Mowbray the quality of housing had been poor. Focusing on the nature of the interviewees' post-Mowbray housing, we find that a good proportion of home owners and private renters (who rent in home-ownership areas) felt that things had been tangibly improved; council renters were less san-guine. (See Chapter 9.)

Apart from the physical qualities of the housing, there were other factors at work. One was overcrowding. A young teacher, Mr. Koopmans, a home owner, said:

> We've got a nice house here . . . [however] I'd like to go back—but that's hypothetical. And even if there was no group areas apartheid, it's still hypothetical because Mowbray was already segregated and it wasn't possible to find more housing for Coloureds. If I was newly married and wanted to start my own home, we couldn't have stayed anyway.

A concomitant of overcrowding was intrafamily tension. In Silver-town a well-established Coloured family man, in his fifties and a clerk in a big city-center office, said, "We were reasonably happy in Mowbray, but we are very happy here. . . . You see, after our marriage we lived thirteen years in my mother-in-law's house in the Valley. She's very strong willed. There was a lot of strife in the home." This man was not a home owner but a renter in what is one of the best-established city council schemes. Even though he was a renter in more raw Bonteheuwel (a place he did not like), Mr. van der Walt noted, "*But*—it's what you make of it. The house is better here than the leaky old house we shared in Mowbray, the wife, me, and three kids all in one room."

One of the two private renters living in Rylands who talked of the disadvantages of the Mowbray housing caught some of the ambiguity of the removals: "There were certain aspects where people benefited, from ten to a room to two to a room. But in the majority most peo-ple felt uprooted, especially the old people." This same businessman said, "For all the tea in China, I'd go back to Mowbray."

Ambiguity is evident in the replies of another couple in their thirties, who live in Bonteheuwel.

> It's a long way to the shops, it's a long way to friends. . . . The house *is* better here: the Mowbray house had damp walls, rotten floors, we had to rewire the electricity, the landlord didn't care. . . . [Yet] Mowbray was a nicer place, we'd like to go back. Mowbray was safe.

This couple, in order to escape "the poor quality of the schools here" sent their eldest daughter to Harold Cressy High School, which had a good reputation, in Cape Town city center. The distance one way was 12 kilometers; the time she spent traveling *one way* to school was between seventy-five and ninety minutes, and so she spent almost three hours traveling every school day. For this family, the housing may have been better, but the overall milieu was definitely perceived as worse.

Street Life

Of households 14 percent viewed with approval the former activity on the stoop and street life in Mowbray. A young white-collar worker, Mr. Delport, in his thirties and living in home-ownership Crawford, said:

> People didn't live *in* their houses, they came out at night to chat on street corners. People met at certain shops or at the [itinerant] vegetable man and would talk about their problems. Kids don't play on the streets here. People're more worried about individual status.

As well as chatting in groups or playing kerem, some men also waited at certain corners for the Chinese-numbers runner to come up from District Six with the winning number. There were two "banks" for this illegal gambling—*fafi* was another name for the game—at three o'clock and at seven o'clock.

Three households disliked this "running in and out of other people's houses"—it was not "respectable"—and they were glad that it did not go on in their new neighborhoods.

In an Athlone home-ownership estate, an ex-Mowbray couple, both born in St. Helena,[21] differed in their opinions on their removal. The wife "would go back tomorrow. But my husband far prefers here. . . . *We* don't go in for going round visiting people's houses for cups of tea [that is, in casual fashion, which is 'not done' in their new neighborhood]." And the husband said, "In the Valley there were always noisy children on the street. That Gammy Harris was always breaking my windows playing cricket on the street there, and every year I'd give the house a new coat of paint and before it was dry a ball would have hit it."

Socializing with Whites

Of households 13 percent claimed that "in Mowbray we were friends with the Europeans." One private renter (out of six) and eight home owners (out of forty-two) but only four council renters (out of fifty-one) made this claim. Perhaps present home owners were likely to have been among the most affluent Mowbray Non-whites and therefore the most likely to have had contact with the Whites. Yet, for all the protestations, the social distance between Coloureds and Whites almost certainly was there, as the following example indicates.

A Malay foreman worked at Hare's brickyard for fifty years. In his youth he was a fine spin bowler at cricket, as a number of other sports-conscious removees told me while trying to support their contention that Mowbray was always a good nursery of athletes. He did in fact play for the (Nonwhite) Western Province team in national tournaments in Johannesburg and Port Elizabeth. When I talked to the foreman's White employer of all those years, he was interested to hear of Suleiman's cricketing prowess, for he claimed never to have known of it! Indeed, why should he have? The employer said, "You mustn't get the idea that apartheid started with the Nats, young man. We had always kept apart socially before that."

A Blot on the Mowbray Landscape

Finally, 5 percent of households told me that in Mowbray, "the Buildings" 'weren't a good place.' "The Buildings" constituted one area the ex-Mowbrayites, at least the majority of them who were conventionally respectable, were rather shamefaced about: "Oh, you've heard of them, have you . . . ?" Two-story tenements either side of a stubby cul-de-sac by the railway line in the Dorp, "the Buildings" were the scene of a certain amount of riotous behavior and within their dilapidated walls were illicit liquor outlets, or *smokkelhuisies*; they have since been torn down. A White priest who had lived in Mowbray for a long time was wholly delighted by this and felt that it was a fine example of slum clearance made possible by the Group Areas Act. The members of the seven households I interviewed who had lived in the Bruce Street cul-de-sac certainly did not attempt to eulogize it. The youngest of the heads of households interviewed, a clerk in his twenties, told me that "it's a relief to be in a house of your own—[after] all that fighting in Bruce Street." When I interviewed him, he was living in an "economic" cottage in Bonteheuwel and found the house to be superior to what he had experienced as a youngster on Bruce Street in Mowbray.

An old Malay sign painter told me, "In Mowbray there was no trouble except for Saturday afternoons when the crowds used to come for City and Suburban, and afterwards to the Buildings, where they got rowdy." Although the Buildings have been obliterated (like District Six), four-fifths of the physical fabric of Nonwhite Mowbray remains intact, having undergone, instead, a metamorphosis of renovation: "gentrification."

GENTRIFICATION

Mowbray was cleared of its Coloured inhabitants during the mid-1960s. To gain an impression of what it was like during that period, we can observe what is happening in a similar southern Cape Town suburb today. Since the mid-1970s, lower Claremont—Harfield Village—has been in the process of being cleared of its mainly Coloured inhabitants. The ambience of the area is palpable. After being proclaimed for Whites, an Indian shop is "disqualified" by its owner's legal race and holds a closing-down sale (Figure 10). Figure 11 shows a street on which one house and a corner shop have been purchased and spruced up by incoming Whites, while the remainder of the street has a run-down look. Why bother to paint your facade when you are a Coloured person about to be removed from your home? The newly established corner business is devoted to selling shiny copper warming pans, carriage lamps, and other internal and external decorative paraphernalia to the anticipated (indeed, inevitable) influx of Whites, who will want to give some "character" to their new homes. Around the corner, the process of Chelseafication (as the renovation done to create what Cape Town realtors list as Chelsea cottages might be called) can be observed. The previous Coloured inhabitants have moved from their homes to the Cape Flats. Now a pergola, over which vines will soon trail, several little alcoves set into walls by new Grecian pillars, and new wooden shutters for the windows are being added, as are a new, higher enclosing wall and electric burglar alarm systems (Figures 12 and 13).

A glance at the real estate sections of the newspapers is also informative. From the *Cape Times*, 8 March 1976: Durr Estates were proud to announce that

> at last we have a plot for sale in Harfield Village: 441 sq. m.; R9,000. Newly, tastefully restored cottage with 3 bedrooms (main-en-suite), 2nd bathroom, lounge with fireplace, separate dining room, french windows to n/f patio and secluded garden, studio and kitchen. R31,000 o.n.o.
>
> We have a selection of houses in this appreciating area from R19,500.

The phrase "this appreciating area" is a euphemism for "this area where skin complexion is becoming lighter because of group areas removals." The facilities offered in this house to adventitious Whites

Figure 10. Harfield, 24 March 1976. The removals continue as another business closes down.

Figure 11. Transformation of a Corner Shop, Harfield, 1976. It is probably just coincidence that the only two cars in the photograph are standing outside the house owned by Whites.

Figure 12. Transformation of a Chelsea Cottage in Progress, Harfield, 1976.

Figure 13. Transformation of a Chelsea Cottage, Interior Completed, Newlands, 1976.

must put it far above the means and the standard of living of those Coloured people who previously inhabited it.

Mowbray went through the process of gentrification approximately fifteen years ago. The interplay of group areas proclamations and profits from property deals is a recurring piece of Cape Town gossip; especially common are the unsubstantiated rumors that plague prominent White political personalities. Such was the case in Mowbray. A careful investigation at the deeds office in Cape Town and of the records of the city of Cape Town's department of building survey provided definite facts about the prices paid for the houses of removees—first by the renovators and then by the new owners. Before discussing the enormous profits sometimes made by White renovators and buyers for resale, I should make a number of qualifications.

First, there was not a completely free, or laissez faire, market in Mowbray, because the Group Areas Board provided information freely on what they considered the "basic value" of all property, once any area had been proclaimed for a certain population group. The official procedures whereby such a valuation was to be arrived at were spelled out in section 33 of the Community Development Act of 1966, which supersedes the Group Areas Act for such purposes; provision was made in the legislation for objections to the basic valuation.

Second, disqualified owners—in Mowbray's case, Coloureds in an area proclaimed for Whites—were not *directly* forced to sell, although certain clauses in section 34 of the Community Development ment Act made it disadvantageous not to have done so once eleven years had passed after the date of valuation. Most important in section 34 was the provision in subsection 2: *the board had a preemptive right on any sale*. Thus, any disqualified owner who had advertised widely and had received an acceptable offer *first* had to offer the property to the board. If the board waived its right, sale was made to a qualified person.

> The snag was that if you sold . . . above the Basic Value, the Board took 50% of the difference ["appreciation contribution"] and if you sold below, they made up 80% of the loss ["depreciation allowance"]. . . . The reaction of Coloured owners was that of outrage. . . . They sold out at the Basic Value or a bit above [but see Chapter 11, p. 317]. They did not *have* to sell; they could have moved out and let the house, but no white would have moved in without extensive renovations which none of them could afford."[22]

Such conditions obviously favored a buyer's market.

Third, when a Coloured area is being obligatorily dissolved to become a White zone, property prices in the vicinity rise "in this appreciating area." How could that be controlled for? Finally, of course, real estate is an area of entrepreneurship where profits are meant to be well made; for some speculators, "excessive" is a word that has no meaning.

These advertisements published in the *Property Argus* in early 1976 concerning Harfield Village were the manifestations of exactly what happened in Mowbray.

Argus 14 February
CLAREMONT/HARFIELD: R18 750 buys pair adjacent semis, easily convertible into Chelsea cottages; very early occupation, close Kenilworth Centre; jump at this true bargain. Security Estates, telephone 61-5000/1, ev. 61-7710.

6 March HOUSES FOR SALE
CLAREMONT/HARFIELD: R24 850, Victorian cottage completely renovated by experts; new roof and plumbing, rewired; no parking problems within high walls surrounding property. Lounge, interleading dining room, playroom. 2 bedrooms. (doubles), bic. Best value in Harfield. Security Estates, Ph. 61-5000/1, eve 61-7710.

CLAREMONT (Harfield): Terrace of 3 cottages, ideal for the renovator. R15 000 the lot, bond available. Paramount Auctioneers 2-3566, 52-4157 after hours.

The Mowbray figures are listed in Table 13. It is important to note in the remarks column how the first (necessarily White) purchasers renovated the property, if at all. *Then* look at the prices the first purchasers received for the Chelseafied cottages when they subsequently resold them to other Whites. It should also be remembered that the city's department of building survey, from which I gained this information, does not consider any alterations to have been carried out—and, therefore, it does not record them—when a house has only been repainted, replastered, or reroofed with the same material as the old one. This provision may be pertinent for the house in case 5, for example.

Even with all these qualifications in mind, it is meaningful to attempt *some* comparison of the Mowbray real estate market with the Cape Town-wide market during the period between 1963 and 1972. Figure 14 is a graph of this information.

In 1963-1964, there was a 34 percent increase in the average price per sale, from R5,677 to R7,630. From 1964 to 1967, price increases slowed, from R7,630 to R8,329, only a 9 percent increase

Table 13

House Prices Subsequent to Group Areas Removals, Renovated Chelsea Cottages

Case	Seller	Buyer	Date (of Deed of Transfer)	Price	Price Increase as % per Annum	Remarks
1	A	Stable Associates	12.20.65	8,400		Stable made internal alterations, new bathroom, drainage, etc.
	Stable	Peredur Investments	10.23.68	26,167.92	74.36	
2	B C	C	12.18.65	4,000		No alterations
		D	12.8.69	6,250	14.15	
3	E F	F	1.29.65	2,640		F put in internal alterations, new bathroom, and drainage
		G	1.18.66	7,000	170.40	
4	H Annbar	Annbar Properties	11.28.63	1,800		Annbar made substantial internal alterations (it made three houses into one)
		I	8.18.68	13,500	137.55	
5	J K	K	7.22.64	2,200		No alterations
		L	4.21.71	10,000 }	133.36	{ (22,000: property divided into two by K)
		M	4.21.71	12,000		
6	N Stable	Stable Associates	4.4.66	2,780		No alterations
		O	8.9.66	3,700	94.43	
7	P	Community Development Board	2.28.67	1,400		
	Community Development Board	Carbrook Investments	11.9.67	1,800	41.08	Carbrook made internal alterations and additions to bedrooms and bathrooms, etc.; new windows and drainage were added
	Carbrook	Q	4.24.68	8,500	809.00	
	Q	R	3.11.69	10,750	30.00	

	Buyer	Seller	Date of Transfer	Price	as % per Annum	Alterations
8	<u>S</u>	T	10.21.63	1,600		No alterations
	T	U	9.24.65	2,900	41.66	
	U	V	4.20.66	4,150	75.69	
9	<u>W</u>	Community Development Board	11.30.65	1,700		Stable made internal alterations to kitchen and bathroom and added new drainage
	CDB	Stable Associates	10.13.66	1,800	6.76	
	Stable	X*	10.23.68	5,000	86.46	
	X	Mowbray Cottage Homes	5.10.72	10,000	28.18	
10	<u>Y</u>	Z	11.24.64 (7.1.64)	2,800		No alterations
	Z	AA	11.24.64 (7.21.64)	4,000	745.30	
	AA	BB	4.28.65	5,400	45.34	
11	<u>CC</u>	Annbar Properties	11.8.63	2,050		Annbar added extensions to kitchen, a new yard wall, and drainage (these alterations were incomplete at time of sale)
	Annbar	TJBurke Trust	11.25.67	13,200	134.40	
12	<u>DD</u>	Annbar Properties	11.11.63	1,000		Annbar made a new extension to house (living room and kitchen) and internal alterations and added new bathroom and drainage; the valuation was then set at R3, 590
	Annbar	EE	2.6.67	9,000	224.77	
13	<u>FF</u>	Cottesloe Cumulative Holdings	8.31.64	1,300		Cottesloe made internal alterations, added new windows, new doors, new bathroom, new steps and stoops, and new roof, and took walls down inside
	Cottesloe	GG	12.17.65	2,400	65.20	
14	<u>HH</u>	K	2.14.64	2,100		No alterations
	K	II	8.4.68	8,300	66.00	

NOTE: Nonwhite sellers are underlined.
*Peredur Investments and X above are one and the same person.

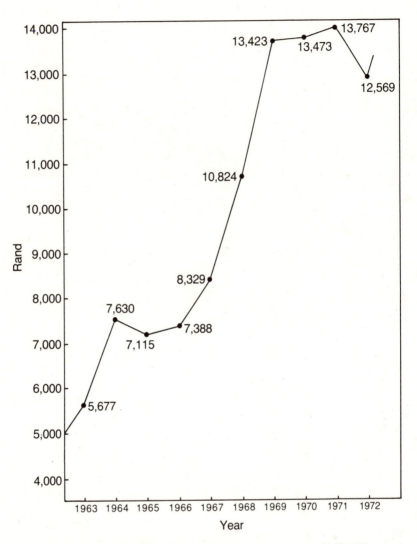

Figure 14. Average Selling Price of Properties in Cape Town, 1963-1972.

over three years. The period between 1967 and 1969 saw another spurt, from R8,329 to R13,423, a 61 percent rise in two years. Then, prices held steady for two years before falling somewhat, to R12,569 in 1972. Thus, average property values throughout the city rose by 121.4 percent over the nine years from 1963 to 1972.[23]

It can be computed that, with the exception[24] of case 2 in Table 13, *all* the transactions shown registered profits *above* the mean Cape Town increase for the time period involved. Some transactions, of course, involved renovations. But, of those that did not, case 8 is noteworthy; T made an 81 percent profit in slightly less than two years; the Cape Town average was a 25 percent increase for this time period. In case 14, K cleared a 295 percent profit over a period when the comparable Cape Town average increase was 76 percent. In case 10, Z made a R1,200 profit on a R2,800 house in one day! (This according to the date of transfer for the deeds; in fact, it took him three weeks, from 1 July to 21 July 1964.) Could he have repainted or replastered in that time? If so, the transaction would have fallen under a "no alterations" designation. Nevertheless, he cleared a lot of money. In case 7, it was *not* the Community Development Board that profited financially from a Coloured family's removal; it was Carbrook Investments, who, in less than six months, disbursing on quite substantial alterations to yield a presentable Chelsea Cottage, resold at a 372 percent profit; this is a rate of *809 percent* per annum. (The figures for profits in percentages per annum have been inserted into Table 13 to facilitate comparisons between cases.)

Who were Carbrook Investments, Stable Associates, and Annbar Properties? A (White) lawyer made it possible for me, via the registrar of companies office in Pretoria, to discover who the directors of these companies were at the time of the sales. As it turned out, the directors were local (White) realtors, auctioneers, and architects, living nearby in Rondebosch, upper Newlands, Kenilworth, Wynberg, and Claremont.

One of the auctioneers, from an extremely well known and long-established Cape Town family firm, granted me a lengthy and informative interview. Indeed, his firm had not infrequently held auctions on behalf of the Community Development Board. Of course, when a particularly "hot" piece of property was coming up for resale through the board, he heard about it very quickly (what else would I have expected?). And one of the architects involved in these profitable property speculations, who lived in a cottage in Newlands once occupied by Coloureds, was then busying himself without self-effacement in liberal-reformist Progressive Federal party politics and with problems of low-cost housing, being concerned about the severe housing shortage for Coloured people on the Cape Flats . . . to which he had in a sense contributed.

This was what Coloured owners of property in Mowbray experienced, but most ex-Mowbrayites had been renters living on property owned by absentee White landlords. It is extremely difficult to gain access to figures on rents before and after group areas development, for these are kept by the Community Development Board and may only be released to owners and current tenants. Nevertheless, an Afrikaans-speaking senior academic helped me by persuading the Department of Community Development to search out some pertinent figures on two Mowbray streets. One of the streets had been completely renumbered, with the low numbers starting at the opposite end of the street, so extra care was required to make sure of the comparisons.

The qualifications that apply to the home-sale figures apply also to rental properties. A lot of money must have been spent on some of the renovations, particularly the last one listed (Table 14), which made two homes into one and added a swimming pool. Also, in these cases, sale was from White to White, and it was the new White tenants who were paying the enormously high rents (up to 1,000 percent) compared to those paid by the Coloured renters ten years earlier. It was reassuring to discover that in these eight cases (for which I had interviewed the ex-tenants on the Cape Flats and asked them their monthly rent for their Mowbray housing) the ex-tenants' replies tallied with the official records. Thirty-nine of the sixty-three households interviewed (that is, 62 percent) who had provided estimates of their Mowbray rent said that, at the time of removal, the rent was between R5 and R9 per month; this estimate was confirmed by the board's records. The *Argus's* report of 16 February 1961 also confirmed that the average monthly rent in the comparable Coloured Claremont and Newlands pockets in 1961 was about R10.75. In addition, Whisson and Kahn (1969) confirmed these estimates; furthermore, they noted the addition in Newlands of swimming pools (Figure 13 shows a typical example) and rent increases of around 1,000 percent in ten years.

The data in Table 14 cover terraced (row) cottages owned by Town and Country House Properties, of which the directors are three women, one from Paarl, one from Bishopscourt, and one, the mother of the first woman mentioned, from high on the flanks of Lion's Head above Sea Point. The last woman, one of Cape Town's noted personalities, has been the object of malicious innuendo concerning her property dealings because her husband was a minister (and the first English-speaking one since 1948) in the Nationalist government; he had been a United party member of Parliament for many years before switching to the National party. Rents are controlled in Cape Town, but, when it can be proven that a building is over 100 years old, its rents may be decontrolled, and may go as high as the market permits. This these women were able to prove in a well-remembered court action for six of the eight cases, despite the great amount of renovation and alteration that had been done on the properties. The properties thus were exempted from rent control (except numbers 16 and 18,

Table 14
Renovated House Rents Subsequent to Group Areas Removals

Address	Occupant (Date)	Rent (R per month)
John Street:		
#3	Expelled Coloured (1965)	5.00-9.00
	Subsequent White (3.4.69)	53.58
	Subsequent White (1.12.72)	68.00
#15	Expelled Coloured (1965)	5.00-9.00
	Subsequent White (3.4.69)	38.58
	Subsequent White (5.13.76)	64.00
#16	Expelled Malay (owner) (1965?)	—
	Subsequent White (9.24.68)	36.22
	Subsequent White (4.30.69)	37.58
#18	Expelled Malay (1965)	5.00-9.00
	Subsequent White (9.24.68)	56.50
	Subsequent White (4.30.69)	58.61
Queen Street:		
#13	About-to-be-expelled Malay (3.13.64)	9.00
	Subsequent White (2.28.69)	77.00
	Subsequent White (1.12.72)	77.00
	Subsequent White (4.10.76)	c. 100.00
#17	About-to-be-expelled Malay (3.13.64)	9.00
	Subsequent White (2.28.69)	77.00
	Subsequent White (1.12.72)	80.00
	Subsequent White (4.10.76)	c. 100.00
#19	About-to-be-expelled Coloured (3.13.64)	8.50
	Subsequent White (2.28.69)	70.00
#21	About-to-be-expelled Coloured (3.13.64)	9.00
#19/21*	*Combined rents* of about-to-be-expelled	
	Coloureds (3.13.64)	17.50
	Subsequent White (1.12.72)	159.00
	Subsequent White (4.10.76)	210.00
	Continuing White (5.10.76)	231.00

*Two units combined into one, with extensive renovations (e.g., swimming pool added).

John Street) on either 31 October 1970 or 12 November 1970. Presumably, it is partly their business success—plus, evidently, their political connections—that accounts for most of the insinuations about them, particularly about the minister's wife. Careful checking has established that her husband was *neither* in the government *nor* a member of Parliament at the time when Mowbray, on 10 February 1961, was declared White. Thus, although the adage "there's no smoke without fire" has been true in a number of political/property scandals unearthed in South Africa during recent years, it cannot in the least be demonstrated that in this case inside information was given before group areas proclamation for Whites, so that purchase at the low prices then obtaining might be made. Town and Country House Properties was only registered as a company on 25 May 1964. At that date, however, the woman's husband was a minister in the government and remained so until 1972, and it was this fact that occasioned comment. Certainly, it can be said—but not more than this—that these three ladies did well because of Coloured removals from Mowbray, as did many other White property dealers, as well.

POSTSCRIPT: WHAT REMAINS?

It seems appropriate to record what some ex-Mowbrayites thought on returning and seeing their Chelseafied former homes. The homes after group areas removals are inhabited at a much lower density mainly by younger Whites, many of them professionals, many of them students drawn by these attractive bijou cottages close to the University of Cape Town and Groote Schuur Teaching Hospital, and many of them very liberal politically.[25]

Mrs. Carelse, after coming in from Heideveld council rental township to pick up her pension at the Mowbray post office, talked sentimentally about her old home.

> And I meet all the old Mowbray people there. Old Mr. Gelderbloem said to me he comes and has a look at his house when he gets his pension. I went down to Ayres Street, looking at my old house [where she had lived for thirty-two years] and my loquat tree, and the English lady who lives there now came out asked me what I was standing there for and I said I was looking at the tree I'd planted. And she said "Shame! Come in and pick from it and fill a bag."

On the surface seeming to be more matter-of-fact, a St. Helena-born Crawford home owner in his late fifties told me:

> I was there one day off from work going by where we lived and one of our vans was outside moving furniture and as I pulled up behind, the European man living there now came out. So I said, "This is my house for over thirty years." He was very surprised. Then he said, "Come in and see"—and I was astounded at the changes; they'd put in oak floors and knocked walls

down to join up with the cottage next door and made a nice big living room and modernized the kitchen and put in tiles and things. . . . When we were leaving, the roof was almost coming down inside—bulging down, you know—but now that was all done up. . . . It felt a bit strange.

It is sentiment too that brings ex-Mowbrayites back to their places of worship, especially for the big religious festivals. Figure 15 shows a Friday midday at the Mowbray mosque; two of the three worshippers are ex-Mowbrayites. The man washing his feet and arms to the elbow preparatory to worship is standing in front of a toilet that was for a while a center of controversy. The toilet stands on that part of the original Muslim plot that was the imam's house. (See note 1.) Before prayer the men used to use it to empty their bodies of waste so as to be "clean" for prayer. When group areas development demanded that the Muslims sell the imam's house (but not the mosque itself[26]), the toilet also was sold. In 1975, there was a legal fight taking place between the new White owner of the imam's house—and thus of the toilet—and the Mowbray Muslim congregation, who wished to use the toilet on Fridays.

In addition to the renovation, there have been other changes in Mowbray. The stores in the village center that once catered to the local Coloured and Malay clientele took on a more Black African character during the 1968-1975 period (the center is the transfer point for riders changing from the Cape Flats buses to the trains going into Cape Town.) By the bus terminal, standing on the site of "the Buildings" and some Coloured and Malay houses, can be found everyday ex-Mowbray costers hawking fruit and vegetables from their barrows. At least one of them frequently sleeps over in Mowbray. He used to live on Hare Street, a hundred yards from his barrow's pitch; in 1976 he officially lived in Bonteheuwel.

Of the City and Suburban League rugby ground nothing remains but a rusting turnstile; the rest has become the playing field of the Afrikaans-medium White high school, Hoërskool Nassau. Perseverance was started as the Mowbray Coloured rugby club; seven of its eight founding members were Mowbray men. In 1957, the team photo showed six out of fifteen players, plus the chairman, treasurer, and selector, all born in Mowbray. In 1959—*just before the group areas proclamation*—Persies moved out to Athlone. It has now been more than twenty years since the team played in Mowbray, and the Mowbray character of the club is weakening. The concentration of Mowbrayites in the club is today in the upper echelons, not at the player level; thus, the chairman, four of seven "union life members," one of three "delegates to the union," four of five "stalwarts," and one of

Figure 15. Mowbray Mosque, Friday at Noon, in the Dorp, 1976. Note the muezzin on the balcony calling the faithful to prayer.

four "honourable members" were in 1974 ex-Mowbrayites. However, only thirteen of sixty-nine playing members (less than one in five) were ex-Mowbrayites. The proportion must continue to fall.

Many of the ex-Mowbrayites were not aware of some of the more recent changes in their old neighborhoods. This fact was vividly brought home when a fire destroyed some *pondoks* in the Vanguard Estate in May 1975. One of the nearest neighbors with a car was an ex-Valley person. She recounted how they rushed some of the injured to the hospital, avoiding Groote Schuur because of its crowdedness and slow service. Instead, they raced to the Valley's hospital: Rondebosch and Mowbray Cottage Hospital. When they arrived, they found that the Cottage Hospital had not been taking emergency cases for two years, but out on the Cape Flats the women had not heard of the change. It was not for sentimental but for practical reasons that a Mowbray facility was chosen. Similarly, Mrs. Carelse told me:

> I still go to Mowbray by bus to get my pension in the post office. "We can transfer it out there," they said. "Oh no, " I said, "I was born in Mowbray. It doesn't look as if I shall die in Mowbray,[27] but I'll get my pension here, thank you very much."

Figure 16. Indian Corner Business, Allowed in the Valley by Ministerial Permit, 1975. The owner of the shop, who was also the owner of the Mercedes, had to move out in 1977.

She neglected to mention what she told me on a subsequent occasion—that the Athlone post office was crowded but the Mowbray post office was not.

In the Valley, the Indian corner shop stayed on by ministerial permit until 1977 (Figure 16); today it has gone, and the building itself has been renovated. There are only Coloured domestic servants (Figure 17) among the Whites' carriage-lamped Chelsea cottages on Spin Street. Brought up on this very street, a Silvertown man in his thirties told me, "Always if I'm round there I drive round. It looks the same, except they've taken off the veranda, and painted it black and white and called it a Chelsea cottage." Figure 18 gives an excellent impression of the transformation. One of the few original households remaining (because its owners gained White racial classification) is a contrast to its immaculately spruced up neighbors. Continuing the quotation: ". . . and Kasiem, a friend of mine there, I don't know where they've gone, I never saw them again."

Figure 17. From Resident to Retainer, the Valley, 1976.

Figure 18. Before and after Gentrification, the Dorp, 1976.

CHAPTER EIGHT

Ex-Mowbrayites: The Geographies of Apprehensiveness, Distress, and Disadvantage

We have a wonderful band of non-Europeans . . . oh, they're very happy where they are now.

> Mowbray Presbyterian Church worker (White),
> 10 February 1975

If I heard I could go back, I'd take a helicopter tomorrow.

> Group areas removee (Coloured),
> 6 June 1975

SPACE, UNITY, AND HETEROGENEITY
IN NONWHITE MOWBRAY

Since the breakup of the Nonwhite Mowbray community, the community's people have adjusted to their new neighborhoods with varying levels of success. Like the young man whose regretful words closed the previous chapter, many ex-Mowbrayites lost contact with their old neighbors, and they had to build again in a new place a society of friends and acquaintances. For some, this process was easier than for others; for a few, it proved impossible.

It is clear that *the* causative factor behind the existence of the Mowbray Nonwhite community was the external *force majeure* of White power. And, as Suttles (1968) has informed us, through such "foreign relations" members of a community are forced to tolerate an identity in the eyes of the wider society that oversimplifies their reality. Despite there being within the Mowbray Nonwhite pockets a degree of heterogeneity, White power did not recognize it as significant.

Yet, White external power in one sense may have contributed to the Nonwhite people's perceptions of heterogeneity within their community, for a plausible consequence of imposing a single Nonwhite label on underlings is a tendency, as was written in 1963 of Black African Capetonians, "towards an emphasis on stratification within the subordinate castes. . . . In Langa there is a lively consciousness of differentiation within the African group" (Wilson and Mafeje, 1963, p. 142). Or as Patterson wrote of Coloured Capetonians ten years earlier: "Some Coloured informants have claimed, almost with pride, that their group recognises more class-distinctions than do South African whites amongst themselves" (Patterson, 1953, p. 163).

Paradoxically, I am about to propose the opposite. The preceding two quotations are from works by, respectively, two social anthropologists and one sociologist. I understand their points, but I also claim that they have overlooked space as a variable and that they have missed another point: that White external power can not only enhance preexisting internal heterogeneity, it can also induce internal solidarity. As a geographer, I assume that it was partially the *spatial* component of White power in the wider society that catalyzed the growth of elements of community within the Mowbray Nonwhite pockets, imposing from without the "unity" of a community of exclusion, of common stigma, and of common Nonwhiteness. This imposition was expressed in a direct form by the constricted space in which Nonwhite Mowbray was held: space is the mirror of society. At the same time, a contrary reactive force among Nonwhite Mowbray grew up: the (albeit limited) defensive quality of reciprocity and community among those experiencing the common stigma. A major concomitant of this sentiment of community was territory, turf. The pockets of space of Nonwhite Mowbray, leftovers, almost, from the Whites and, hence, "negative," became endowed through the years with "positive" meaning for those who lived there.

This space, then, was not merely reflective of social relations, of Coloureds receiving hand-me-down space. It also *in its own right* affected social relations, it provided a sense of affective focus and solidarity for the people there, and it contributed to what cohesion the Mowbray village had: "We were *Mowbray se mense*"; "In Mowbray, people were together, we were a knitted community. Now we're all scattered." The previous chapter amply demonstrated the strength and extent of the spatially bound community within the pockets. It was White "walls" that contributed greatly to such localized social congress. These White walls were abolished by group areas development, almost inevitably leading to the disintegration of the community. This is not a statement of spatial determinism; the ex-Mowbray Muslims still have a sense of community, many still coming to the Queen Street masjid (mosque) on Fridays (Figure 15). To a lesser extent also, St. Peter's Church and the Presbyterian church still attract their ex-Mowbrayite parishioners. *But the essential spontaneity afforded by physical propinquity is gone.* "We only see them at Eid[1] now, when we go back." "You should see us all back at St. Peter's at Christmas and Easter." "We went to a funeral back there, some of us hadn't seen each other for ten years. We were going around crying and kissing each other. Oh, you should've been there to see us."

The Whites' power has changed from a centripetal, or holding, pressure to a centrifugal pressure; from containment to abolition. A diagram can summarize the situation simply (Figure 19). The Mowbray Nonwhite community was like a wooden wheel: remove the wheelwright's metal band around the rim and there is still some cohesion among the dowel-jointed wooden parts, which have been knocked together and rubbed against each other for so long. But that bond is not enough, and, as soon as something is demanded of the wheel, it falls apart, out come the spokes, the center cannot hold. The different parts of the wheel represent the different social constituents internal to the Mowbray pockets. To the heterogeneity of Nonwhite ex-Mowbrayites, once masked by externally induced common residence, spatial expression has been given by the removals. The various elements of heterogeneity (categories that overlap each other to some degree) can be seen in Figure 19: the older and the younger; the better-off and the poorer; the homeowners and the renters; the Indians, the Cape Coloureds (Christians), and the Cape Malays (Muslims).

It is the last two categories that constituted the most notable internal source of differentiation of the Mowbray pockets, there being very few Indian and, I believe, no Chinese or Black African households. Four interviewees mentioned the good relations in Mowbray between the Malays and the Coloureds. Why did they feel it necessary to mention this? The response of Adam Small to questions about the Cape asked of him in 1971 (p. 18) is very revealing.

> I do not think that there are any basic antagonisms between the Coloureds who are not Malays and the Malays. There is a very nice relationship existing on the whole. I think what keeps them apart is more their individual cultural-religious backgrounds than anything else. One crowd of people goes to church on a Sunday and the other, *I don't know when,* goes to the mosque (my emphasis).

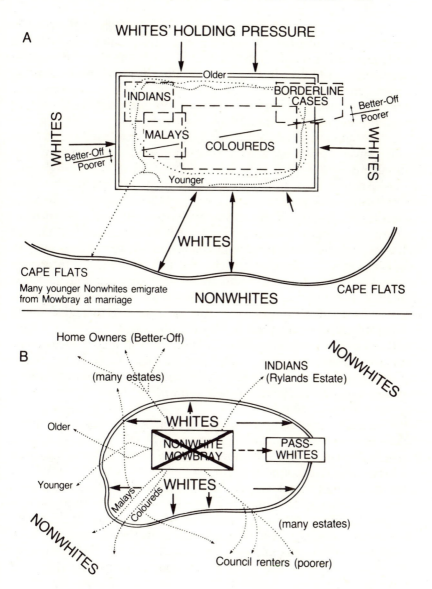

Figure 19. Centripetal and Centrifugal White Pressure on Nonwhite Mowbray.
A. Containment.   B. Abolition.

Even more remarkable than Small's professed ignorance of Muslim observance was the occasion upon which an old Coloured lady, removed to Salt River, who had lived in Mowbray for over fifty

years, said to me: "There were no other Frederickses in Mowbray."
"Yes there were," I said, "I've met some." "No, there was just that
family on Durban Road." "But there were two lots on John Street,"
I countered, "Abdul, Mansur . . . ." "Oh . . . you mean *Malays*!
. . . yes, there were."

While they were living in Mowbray, no Malays ever played, it
seems, in the City and Suburban Rugby League—which was the
active discriminator I am not sure; I suspect it was the league. Conversely, Muslim pride of an exclusive tenor was evident on a number
of occasions.

For example, one interviewee said, "In 99 percent of the cases
when Muslim marries Christian, whatever the sex, it's the Christian
who converts to us." Intermarriage was certainly not unheard of in
Mowbray. A young Muslim wife named Rashida was brought up
as Rosemary, and some of her old friends do not seem in any way to
resent her; in fact, one of them referred me to her for an interview.
Much more rare, it seems, is the converse, which occurred in Mowbray in a celebrated case. A Muslim man converted to Christianity
when he married a Coloured Christian woman and thereafter acted
as treasurer of the Perseverance rugby club—in the City and Suburban League—for fifty-one years. He died just before the group areas
removals in Mowbray. His younger brother—a diligently practicing
Muslim who was one of my most helpful informants and who had
encyclopedic knowledge of Mowbray, which he was keen to give
me—*never* mentioned him.

We have seen that being a Muslim is generally correlated with higher socioeconomic status, both generally in South Africa, and specifically in Mowbray. Table 8 showed this to be so and also indicated
the range of socioeconomic status among Nonwhites in Mowbray,
given its general "respectability." At the lower end of the scale were
a few casual unskilled laborers, a fisherman, some laborers for the
municipality, a groundsman for a nearby exclusive and private
White boys' school, some housewives, a washerwoman for local
Whites and for "the young gentlemen up at UCT" (White students
at the University of Cape Town), and some domestic servants. At
the other end of the scale, above the Muslim tailors, plasterers,
builders, and contractors who had their own small businesses, were
a number of successful Indian and Coloured business people (one
of whom passed for White) and schoolteachers, one a deputy principal.

Despite such heterogeneity, all the Nonwhite residents of Mowbray were dealt with in the same way; they were expelled. The

Group Areas Act is no respecter of Nonwhite persons. However, there *is* one category of persons who were members of the Mowbray Nonwhite community and yet who were not expelled. Their ambivalent status is expressed in Figure 19; they were the Pass-Whites.

THE GEOGRAPHY OF APPREHENSIVENESS

Passing for White

Throughout the history of the Cape since 1652, among those who might have come to be called Coloured have been many who in fact came to be called White.[2] Successful passing into the self-evidently advantageous status of White requires cultural parity, economic parity, and parity of pigmentation and physical appearance. Cultural parity is almost a given, but there are, nevertheless, numerous subcultural traits (for example, certain idiosyncrasies of vocabulary and grammar) by which some Coloured people claim they can always recognize one of their number who has passed for White. A most illuminating example of the importance of subcultural traits was the experience of the Carnegie "Poor White" Commission in the northwest Cape during the economically depressed 1920s. The commission's investigators found it impossible, on grounds of economic status and physical appearance, to distinguish impoverished Whites from Coloured Basters. They eventually realized that the distinction was to be found in the Basters' speech: they always addressed the investigators as "baas" (boss). Such habits, even those not so obviously a reflection of social subordination, must be expunged by Coloureds trying to pass for White.

Economic parity is necessary to support a material life-style that can be accepted as that of a White. The fact that many of the Cape slaves were skilled artisans has meant that throughout Cape Town's history there have been at least some Coloured people whose abilities to earn have been as great or greater than those of some Whites. Watson (1970, pp.1—2), who studied the phenomenon of passing in working-class Observatory, just north of Mowbray, described the interior of a typical dwelling in Observatory.

> Most of the space in the neat but drab sitting-cum-dining room is taken up by a large and highly-polished table, surmounted by a posy of artificial flowers. Bordering the wall are heavy Victorian armchairs, grease-stained and inconspicuously patched. There are no side-boards or ornaments, but on the wall are more pre-Raphaelite prints, and some wedding photographs. In a prominent position is a florid radiogram, tuned to the

commercial radio. This is the visitors' room, scarcely used: the social centre of the home is the kitchen.

Watson's description, with the addition of doilies on the polished table and a tinted family portrait photograph on the wall by a plaque with the motto "Home Sweet Home," fits exactly the interior of an "economic rental" cottage in Heideveld Coloured township to which an elderly Mowbray lady had been removed. She had lived only a kilometer and a half from the street Watson was describing, to which her economic status was comparable, and she was fair skinned. Her "respectability" and house proudness took the same form as those of working-class Whites in Observatory. There was one indubitable clue to her Colouredness, of the same kind that the Carnegie commissioners had noted fifty years earlier: "Some of my friends said, 'Go on, Jennie, why don't you give it a try [that is, passing]?' You know, I don't go for all that nonsense, Mr. John." After an acquaintanceship of many months, I was still, and was always until my departure, addressed by her as *Mister* John.[3]

The similarity in appearance of Coloureds and Whites is a source of continual wry comment in Cape Town. A celebrated story about the Parliament concerns a rather dark National party member who furiously appealed to the Speaker after he sensed a racial barb in an opposition United party member's comment. Called upon to apologize, the United party member began, "I see the honourable member for Rooifontein has turned white with anger . . ."! Conversely, I frequently met fair-skinned Coloured people who told of incidents such as waiting to be served in the Nonwhite line at post offices and then being directed by the postal clerk to the White side. These are such commonplaces of life in Cape Town that a visitor may quickly learn to overlook them. In the *Cape Times* (19 September 1974), for example, there was this report: "A Coloured father searching for his seventeen-year-old son, who had threatened to commit suicide, was turned away from the police mortuary because the body of his fair-skinned son had been placed in the section reserved for Whites." One of the Mowbray Coloured removees I interviewed, an ambulance driver, told me about two incidents.

One man rigid with sciatica or something, couldn't move, lying on a stretcher. We were taking him to the Coloured side. He looks up as he's carried in, sees the Nonwhite signs, gets up and walks across to the White side. I let him go; I didn't help him.

And there was a woman, we took her from an accident to the Coloured side of Groote Schuur. She looks up as she's taken out of the back of the ambulance and sees it's the Coloured side, takes out her identity card and thrusts it at me, doesn't say a word. I can see it's a European one. She gives me a dirty look. I just stare at her, poker-faced, though beneath I'm laughing at her, and take her to the White side.

Of the 100 households I interviewed, 18 admitted that they had close relatives of the same generation[4] who were classified as White. One fair-skinned ex-Mowbray woman of high socioeconomic status, when asked by me where she went to the bioscope (movie theater), replied:

All over. . . . I don't feel bad about passing for White for an evening out; I'm not a play-White. I'll squeeze everything out of this society that I can. Now the way I look I've been in both sides of Groote Schuur, and then it's like night and day, you really see it all clearly.

After the emancipation of the slaves in the Cape, the White-Coloured distinction was a flexible and customary one that fluctuated along the phenotypic and parallel socioeconomic continuum. A comparison can be made with urban Brazil: "The Brazilian outlook assumes that everyone would like to be White and the Whiter a person is the higher he is likely to be in the social status scale" (Banton, 1967, p.280). The lack of formal segregation in the Cape before 1948 and the extensive zone of fuzziness between the races resulted in a situation whereby Findlay in 1936 estimated that the number of escapees into the White group was at least equal to the number of persons then officially deemed to be Coloureds.

A favorite method of escape into the White group was leaving the Cape and heading for the northern provinces—"the Kimberley Train"—where the uncompromising boundary between Whites and Black Africans appeared to overshadow the concern over who was truly White among the almost White. A number of interviewees referred to "those Transvaal *boere* [that is, Boers, Afrikaners] . . . [who are] not Whites at all." An old woman said to me, on being asked whether she was a widow, "My husband left me in 1950 to go to Durban to become a European." It may have been a coincidence that 1950 was the year of the Population Registration Act. This act is one of the present South African government's draconian attempts to determine once and for all who is and who is not White through the issuing of identity cards. Yet, despite this act and the uncompromising residential segregation imposed by the Group Areas Act of the same year, passing continues, although on a reduced scale.

In the past Cape Town officialdom tried to be flexible in its dealings with "these children that we try to pretend didn't exist," as a senior official of the Cape School Board expressed it to Watson during the 1960s. (Watson's work emphasized educational passing.) For example, in January 1938 the Department of Education— *not* a separate department of *Coloured* education like the one established by the Nationalist government in 1963—wrote to the Cape School Board in these terms:

> Once it is clear that a child is not European it is illegal to admit it to a school for Europeans. It is a matter for policy whether the eyes should be closed to any such cases. If and when application is made for admission of a second or third child, own brother or sister of a child already admitted, it becomes clear that one or other parents is not of unmixed European parentage or extraction, then legally all the children must be excluded. However, if it is a borderline case and one or more children have already attended school for a considerable time it would be more equitable to leave them.

This quotation nicely describes the preapartheid situation in Cape Town, where an official equivocation was a realistic response to the impalpable but undisputably existent zone of overlap. It also serves to indicate once more the tone of preapartheid Cape Town's "liberalism": in both social and spatial spheres, the (White) powers that be of the city were prepared to abide by directives imposing a half-hearted brand of segregation.

Watson unearthed borderline cases of unbelievable complexity. His diagram of a Pass-White's family tree demonstrates the situation clearly (Figure 20): there are persons in the family who were both White and Coloured at one and the same time. In upper Woodstock, Whisson is currently pursuing research in this field, believing that some people depend on race-classification ambiguity as a coping mechanism. Whisson also feels that Watson, seeing the phenomenon from a White point of view, missed the fear and anguish such situations bring the families concerned.[5] Sometimes, the psychological stress becomes intolerable, and tragedy results. I had not been in Cape Town two months before an almost incredible horror story of this kind came to light; it is included at the beginning of this book. Perhaps more typical of the conditions under which Pass-Whites live are some Mowbray examples. In order to protect the informants' anonymity, I have changed some of the specific details of their histories.

One of the major points being made in this and in the following

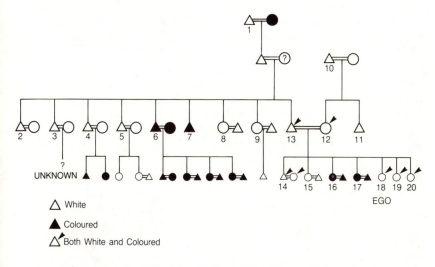

Figure 20. A Pass-White's Family Tree. (From Watson, 1970, p. 21.)

chapter is how, after group areas expulsions, the preexisting social heterogeneity in Nonwhite Mowbray has been given spatial expression by the various areas to which people were removed. A striking spatial expression of this heterogeneity can be found in the fact that some erstwhile Nonwhites were not removed. That is to say, there are a number of Pass-Whites still living in Mowbray, although others have moved into different White group areas where they were not known, allegedly to cover their tracks. I found two cases of this course during my work on the Cape.

One of the persons whom I sought out on the Cape Flats was the Muslim man who had been Mowbray's barber for Nonwhites (by custom, not by law). He told me:

> When the Group started coming, I noticed that Jack Edwards stopped coming to me for his haircut and went up to the White barber up on Main Road. "Hello," I said to myself, "I know what he's up to." And he went for White and did get a White [identity] card.

An old woman in Kew Town, who had close relatives who *are* classified as White, told me, "When we had to leave they said 'Why don't you reclassify White?' Many did, like on Uitsig Close, but it's only for the money and I don't want to split up from my children." Only one household that lived on the quiet cul-de-sac of Uitsig Close was not able to pass for White and remain there. According to a member of that household, Mr. van Wyk, "All the rest got White tickets. But we were unlucky. Though my White friends can come and visit me here, whereas if I'd stayed there we might have worried. There's more White in me than Coloured, from my father, you see, he's a Hollander."

Mr. van Wyk is indeed extremely fair, and after removal he moved to an exclusive Coloured home-ownership area where "there's the same class of people as there in Mowbray." His house was in the Fairways Estate, so named because it is across the tracks of the Cape Flats line from the Whites' Royal Cape Golf Course in Ottery (although some less affluent Coloureds tartly claim there is another reason for its name). Mr. van Wyk sold his Mowbray house to the Community Development Board. In 1976, it was still owned by them, and it housed a White inspector for the board (one of those officers who oversees the ejection of racially disqualified persons from their homes).

Even more telling was something that emerged in an interview with Mr. and Mrs. Brown and their two daughters, who were among van Wyk's ex-neighbors who were able to stay in Mowbray. Mrs. Brown was darker than many Coloured people, and her husband and daughters were quite European in appearance. The family was extremely suspicious of me at first, but I was able to say truthfully that I had been referred to them by a trustworthy local White source. I mentioned everyone (except Mr. van Wyk) from whom I had learned the history of Mowbray. The interview with the Browns lasted for over two hours. Mrs. Brown had been a member of a women's volunteer ambulance corps, along with a number of the ex-Mowbrayite women I interviewed, and she told me much of the area's past. Mr. Brown unbent less easily and said, "You won't go telling tales on us [that is, South Africa] overseas, will you—like that young fellow Hain?[6] . . . We're all Nationalists here." It then came out that one of the daughters was married to an inspector for the Community Development Board. When a person is on the White/Coloured borderline, clearly it is safest to have intimate connections to those who draw the borderline. Most certainly the Browns are all Nationalists.

Another family I knew was split apart by apartheid. Some full siblings were classified as White and others as Coloured. A Coloured one, a mother living in Manenberg rental township who was far fairer than Mrs. Brown, told me:

I'd like to be out of here before Johnny [aged two years] grows up with all these ruffians. That's why I go out with them so much; we'd rather go to Mowbray than stay here. I'd do anything to get out of here. We go to Mowbray every Saturday and Sunday.

Indeed they did, and they spent all of those two days visiting their grandmother who still lived there, an old woman who befriended me and told me a great deal about Mowbray. On one of the many occasions I dropped by for a cup of tea and a chat, she told me of the following incident.

> Last year now the group areas man [an inspector for the Community Development Board] came along and asked to see my card, and my husband's, too, though he was dead. So I showed him, and then he said there'd been a report that a lot of Coloured people came to the house. So I took him to the door and said, "Look up and down the street. You see all these houses? Well, all Coloured people used to live here, and they were my friends, and if they come in from Manenberg or Bonteheuwel or those places to do their shopping, well, sometimes I'm leaning out over my stoop looking up the street and I see them, and I say 'Come in and have a cup of tea.' Now there's no harm in giving a Coloured person a cup of tea, is there?" And you know, John, he just smiled, and went away, and I've never seen him again.

Those members of the family who are classified as White had a strong disinclination to use racially segregated public transportation. The reason, for those of them whose appearance was racially ambivalent, is very plain: they were risking their White status when they did. In Capetonian folklore there is the unfortunate character who, while waiting at a bus stop (White and Nonwhite using the same ones) is passed by *both* Nonwhite *and* White buses, because the drivers have to make instant racial assessments as they drive by. This happened to at least one of the people I interviewed, and he told me about it mirthfully. But it no longer happens in Cape Town, because in 1979 the city's buses were desegregated.

Passing for White is not only a question of tiny points like ambivalence over buses, which after all are situations that can be laughed off by some people. Recall Mr. van Wyk's saying "if I'd stayed there we might have worried." Like Vichy France, where personal motives occasioned denunciations of Jews, communists, and Maquisards, the world of many Pass-Whites is painfully insecure. This consideration restrained me from going to visit another Mowbray Pass-White, who, as I was told (by an ex-Mowbrayite friend of hers), had a nervous personality and would have been very frightened of my questions.

A few expelled interviewees mentioned those who had passed with a measure of disfavor, but most who said anything about the subject seemed to think that, well, it was *their* (the Pass-Whites') business. Only two ex-Mowbrayites ever allowed themselves to express bitterness over their ex-neighbors' successful passing. One was Mrs. Smith, who told of her expulsion from Mowbray in this way:

> When we knew we were going to have to go, we left. My father was an Englishman, but you see with this [she tweaked the skin of her cheek ironically, rancorously] that group areas man came round and said we would have to go. I don't want mud thrown in my face, so we left before they actually chucked us out.

Having said this, Mrs. Smith then started to denounce the Pass-Whites still living in the Mowbray of which she had been deprived.

The other person who expressed anger on this score was a man who told me of a Mr. Pasquali (whose mother still lived in Mowbray) who moved out of Mowbray, got into real estate in the northern suburbs, made a lot of money, and eventually became mayor of one of the staunchly Afrikaner Nationalist municipalities there! When the man I was interviewing angrily began this story, he was chided by his wife, who tried to stop him by saying, "Ag, come on Aaron man, it's no good tale-telling."

Passing for Coloured/Malay

Owing in part to the generally high socioeconomic status (in Coloured terms) of the ex-Mowbray people I interviewed, I do not believe I encountered any ex-Black African Pass-Coloureds in my research. There is an interesting question, though: would I as a White foreigner have recognized them as such, if I had encountered Pass-Coloureds? A Coloured friend told me that one way in which Coloureds recognize an ex-Black African among their number is when he or she cannot pronounce the Afrikaans word *jakkals* (jackals) correctly, erroneously separating the two consonants *l* and *s* with an epenthetic vowel. This is an old saw rather like passing a pencil through a Coloured person's hair to see whether they pass for White or qualify for membership in a sports club.

A borderline that I did encounter, though, was that between Indian and Coloured. The Muslim Cape Malays can be subsumed under the general Coloured label for the purposes of the Group Areas Act[7] and, as it was explained in Chapter 3, they may live anywhere in Coloured Cape Town. A Muslim classified as Indian may live, unless exempted by special permit from the minister of community development, only in two small Indian group areas, Rylands and Cravenby. Also, until 1976,[8] an Indian's right to operate certain businesses only held in the Indian group areas. Therefore, it is greatly to his or her advantage to be classified as a Malay rather than an

Indian, for he or she then can legally trade in a much wider area of the metropolis. There have been a number of court cases, presumably based on business jealousy, in which certain traders have accused others of not being Malay Muslims but Indian ones.[9] It was even suggested by the minimally supported and highly conservative National Coloured People's party leader (Dr. Clifford Smith) that all Muslims be reclassifed as Indians: "This will immediately prevent the Indian from using the Malay as a bridge to exploit our people" (*Post* [Johannesburg], 2 November 1969). In this way, the Indians are being scapegoated as the Jews of Africa, the corner shopkeepers (*babbies*) in the poorer areas whose inhabitants may perceive them to be avaricious and foreign.

At the time I interviewed them, one ex-Mowbray Muslim family renting in Indian Rylands was preparing to move to a home-ownership plot in the Coloured group area Surrey Estate. Since Moosa was not changing his official ethnic group affiliation through the Race Classification Court, it was apparent that the family was or would be living in one or the other group area illegally, and they did not wish to be found out. In accordance with the race classification law, in 1978, by the way, six Indians became Malays, while two Malays became Indians.

THE GEOGRAPHY OF DISTRESS

For many of those Mowbrayites who did not pass for White, the day of their quitting was one of the most important of their lives. A number of the people I interviewed told me the precise date; one family even showed me black-and-white photographs of their belongings being piled onto a *bakkie* (pickup truck) while their neighbors were milling around.

> The facts are always less than what really happens. . . . If you get a law, like group areas, under which various population groups are . . . uprooted from their homes and so on, well, somebody may give you the figures, how many people are moved, how many jobs were lost. But, to me it doesn't tell you nearly as much as the story of one individual who lived through that (Nadine Gordimer, *The Listener*, 21 October 1976).

On 10 February 1961, Nonwhite Mowbray was given three years' notice, the Valley, five years. Of the 100 households I contacted, 17 had moved out before they actually received their letters and the community development inspector came around to enforce them. "It really hurt at the time," said one person; "I've never seen my husband cry, but I did when we got the letter saying we had to go to Bonteheuwel," said another. And a Heideveld man said, "We were the last people out, we *battled* to stay there." In fact, Mr. and Mrs. Hermans were not the last to leave, for another person I interviewed had this story to tell.

> But they were hard. I remember going down to the city [to the offices of the Department of Community Development] to plead for more time, and I was praying "Please God give me some help," and you'd go in and they wouldn't even look up or say anything to you. And they came round to my house to tell us to get out and looked at it—I'd done it up nice and had a bathroom put on and things—and one said, "D'you know, I wouldn't mind living in one like this." Then they said they'd got a place for me in Bonteheuwel, and now they'd got that, we'd *have* to go. But I was scared of that place, especially for my daughters, who I'd brought up nice and who were then teenagers, and I knew we were getting this place [home-ownership plot] ready but not in time for them—so we would have to move twice, you see, and all the business it is. So I sat down and wrote a really sad letter, telling them everything—oh, it was a shame—and you know it must've touched one of them because they came and said I could stay for a while. Now all the others were moved out, but we stayed on for a year until this place was ready, thank God for His goodness to us! You know, I'd like to find that man who was so kind to us, to say thank you; they weren't generally like that at all.

Some other people, a group of Malay men who were in the process of negotiating for home-ownership plots, defied the community development officer, went to court, and got a six-month stay of their eviction orders. Another woman, although she recognized her lack of choice in the matter of removal, exploited what little room for maneuvering she had: "We left when we knew we were going to have to go. The longer you wait, the further in [to the Cape Flats] you'll have to go—now they're building out at Mitchell's Plain."

The community development inspector in Mowbray, an ex-policeman to whom the pseudonym Mr. Burger will be given, was remembered for his bullying abruptness by not a few of the people I talked with.

> He came round to chuck us out, he was very rude. "Now look here," I said, "you'll be polite. You call me *Mrs.* Carelse and I'll call you *Mr.* Burger. Do you have children?" "Yes, two," he said. "All right," I said, "I have two daughters. They were born, confirmed, and married out of here. This is their home. You'd better watch out, the mills of God grind slow, but they grind very, very small. You've got an education, haven't

you?" "Yes," he said. "Well," I said, "why do you go and choose to do this rotten job? The stream will surely sweep you off one day, too." "Oh no, not us," he said. "Oh yes, you," I said.

"Are you a relation to Mrs. Abrams up on the other street?" he [then] asked me. "Yes," I said. "I thought so, because she's just thrown me out of *her* house. 'I pay my rent,' she says."

These people were taking a chance by mentioning "Mr. Burger" by name, as were those seventeen percent who were prepared quite openly to articulate anti-group areas sentiments, usually the most overtly political remarks that came out of the interviews. Said one, "This group areas was the most vicious law they ever did."

Another story concerning Mr. Burger bears an authentic Cape Town stamp. A very respectable Malay tailor in his fifties said to me: "I told that group areas inspector where to get off—I didn't invite him to sit down or anything. I kept him standing while I told him off." Not inviting the man to sit down was the height of bad manners. A great many Cape Town people, especially the Malays perhaps, pride themselves on their hospitality, and not to invite somebody in for a cup of tea when they come to talk is very bad form. To continue the tailor's story, "Well, he must've written it all down in the car when he went, because when I went down to see them [in their city-center headquarters offices] they looked me up in a file, told me all that I'd said, and they got me out *very* quick!" Another removee described his experience with Mr. Burger this way.

> He came and said we had to move. We didn't want to. He said the council have got a new place for you down in Heideveld. We came down here, didn't like it at all, went back, and told them so. Well, it's that or nothing, he said. And we had to go, and that was that.

And another said, "After all those years it wasn't easy to leave, but we had to go, we had to obey. That man said, 'If you don't want what we have to give you, you can sit in the street.'"

There was no physical resistance in the Nonwhite Mowbray community to this Hobson's choice. Everyone there knew who held the instruments of force that could be used "if necessary." A young man in his thirties said, "It was so humiliating to be chucked out." A successful Athlone businessman in his forties, a home owner when he lived in Mowbray said, "They didn't give us a fair price for the houses; they gave us a penny-ha'penny." An old Malay Camp resident who served in both world wars—pursuing von Lettow-Vorbeck under Smuts in German East Africa during World War I, and acting as a driver up Africa during World War II—had this to say:

You make a place of your own, you make it comfortable for your old age, then they come and tell you you've got to go. And you can't start again, time's against you—you remember those people who committed suicide in Tramways Road, Sea Point? They gave me a month's grace, to build by my son-in-law's land, but it wasn't finished, and they were there on the last day of that month, saying there was a 240-rand fine if I wasn't out. I don't think they gave us a true value for our house, and all the rates we paid.

A young home-owning teacher (quoted on pp. 40 and 163) said:

It was *humiliation.* And the whole thing's a vicious circle, a trap within a trap: if you want to speak out, you have to leave [South Africa]; if you want to stay, you've got to keep quiet. . . . Yes, I'll help you, but this is a very negative study; it won't get us back.

In Bonteheuwel Mr. Abraamse said:

I was very unhappy coming out here to the wilderness. Coming out on the bus I was thinking where is he riding me to, out all this way? I felt so degraded, so low to have to leave our house in Mowbray. One night soon after the group areas put us out here, I'd had a couple of tots and I got off the last bus, couldn't find my way to this house; some children had to bring me to the house.

Two separate sources not in his family told me how this man used to go back to the house after he had been moved out; it was standing empty, and he would just sit there and weep sometimes.

Such distress is not unique to the people who have been moved by group areas proclamations. There are endless examples from many areas "redeveloped": from Boston (Fried, 1963; Gans, 1972), Philadelphia (Levy, 1978), Lagos (Marris, 1961), and Yorkshire (Jackson, 1972, p. 1). Jackson quoted an informant:

I'll tell you what, I've noticed this with the old folk that's been moved away—they don't seem to have reigned long. It's too bad rehousing old people, they should leave them alone . . . do you know they were both dead within twelve month. Somehow it seemed to knock all t'stuffing out of them.

Many people simply lack the resilience necessary to construct anew a social world around themselves, and they give up. Here are some examples of this kind of grief over moving from Mowbray. "My mother was born in Mowbray and was sixty-nine years old when they moved her out. She couldn't overcome it. She went to stay with her sister in Salt River and went to bed and never got up again, for four years, and died at seventy-three." (The minister of community development is empowered to prevent the removal of disqualified persons when he is convinced that "severe hardship" would result.) Another example: "He was very poorly and went delirious from time to time and would talk on about going home to Mowbray." Instead, he died in Belgravia Estate, Athlone, in March 1975. And again:

> A lot of people died after they left Mowbray. It was heartbreaking for the old people. My husband was poorly, and he used to just sit and look out of the window. Then before he died he said, "You must dress me and take me to Mowbray. My mum and dad are looking for me, and they can't find me in Mowbray." Yes, a lot of old people died of broken hearts.

It seems coolly insensitive to ask whether there is any evidence of this impression being statistically valid. Old people are always dying, and the fact that younger people notice it might tell more about the living than about the dead. There was no way to compute comparative death rates before and after the removals. Only lamenting assertions by survivors testify to the suffering of so many of Mowbray's old people.

THE GEOGRAPHY OF DISADVANTAGE

Map 23 shows where the 100 households I studied lived in 1975 (44 at that time had moved once more after their removals from Mowbray). By far the most common destinations were Bonteheuwel and Heideveld, with 18 removed households each (less than they once had, due to subsequent moves out). These two council rental schemes were being developed at the time Mowbray removals occurred. No other one residential area has even half that number of ex-Mowbray households in it, as Map 23 demonstrates. Ex-Mowbrayites have been quite widely scattered, with 95 percent of them living farther from the city center than they did when they lived in Mowbray. These facts permit a number of basic comparisons.

Work Places

Map 22 shows the places where Mowbray heads of households worked both before and after group areas development. Clearly, the basic pattern did not change. Five-sixths (of applicable cases) kept the same job locations. The only noteworthy changes are that Mowbray, predictably, lost seven jobs and Athlone gained two. The

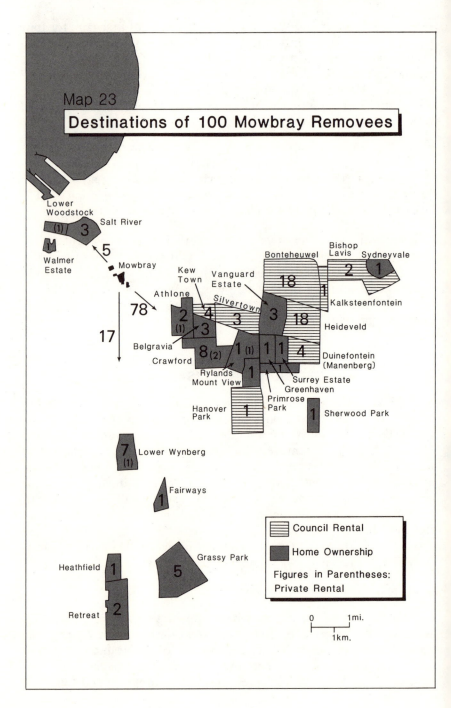

Map 23

Destinations of 100 Mowbray Removees

"around and about" response introduced some complications for measurement, and so only sixty-three cases provided comparative data. Of these, 16 percent changed their job locations since Mowbray days; 8 percent of these people said they were actually *forced* to change by group areas rulings. The daily, inevitable journey to work and back is probably the most important statistic in all the comparative data that are to follow; it is the largest tangible imposition stemming from group areas removals from Mowbray. Basically, the poorer are now farther from their work than before; this same change has also occurred in other cities, for example, in Detroit and Philadelphia (Deskins, 1973; Muller, Meyer, and Cybriwsky, 1976). However, in these North American metropolises, it is the jobs that have been suburbanized while the Black poor have remained trapped in their ghettos. In Cape Town, the Coloureds have been involuntarily moved to suburban ghettos and, for the present at least, their jobs have remained in the inner city.

These jobs, it must be stated, are those of the heads of the household. Unfortunately, I did not ask these specific questions on the location of jobs of any secondary wage earners in the family, for example, women working as machinists in clothing factories and as domestic servants. Cilliers informed me that from his research he has found that group areas removals have frequently disrupted the secondary wage-earning pattern.[10] For example, a woman removed to Bonteheuwel was much farther from madam in Rosebank, and it did not seem worth the time and effort and bus fare to go there anymore. Cilliers has found, as I did with ex-Mowbrayites, that primary wage-earning patterns remain essentially undisturbed.

"Undisturbed," however, means only that the place of work was unchanged but not the nature of the journey that must be made to get there. A lower Wynberg ex-Mowbrayite lived 6.5 kilometers farther south on the southern suburbs line: "The job in Salt River is further, but I've managed it quite well. I wanted to battle my way through, though it took a lot out of me—but I wanted the overtime." Of the sixty-three measurable cases, five remained the same distance from their jobs. Ten were closer, with an average decrease of 5.4 kilometers.[11] (There were also three more who were closer, but by an amount that could not be precisely measured.) Forty-eight were farther away, by an average (one-way) increase of 7.9 kilometers (Figure 21). The average distance to the job when these people lived in Mowbray was 5.36 kilometers. This reflects the fact that the primary area of employment remains the Salt River-Woodstock-Cape Town tract. The average distance traveled increased to 10.51 kilometers.

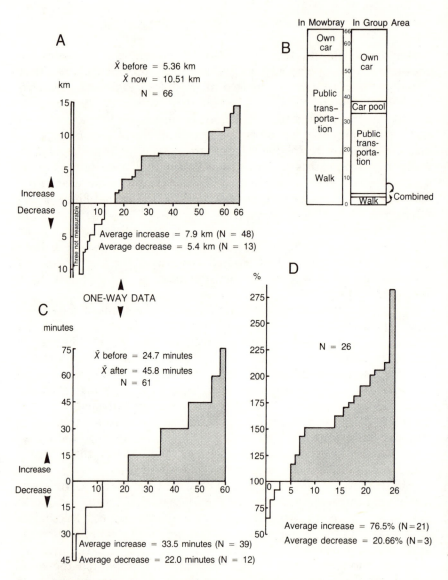

Figure 21. Diagrammed Data Relating to Jobs before and after Removal from Mowbray. A. Distance. B. Mode of Travel. C. Time. D. Costs (for public transportation only).

There are similar statistics on the time required for traveling to work. Before removal the average overall travel time was 24.7 minutes; after removals it was 45.8 minutes. The newer averages are based on twelve workers whose time decreased an average of 22.0 minutes; on ten whose travel time remained the same; and on thirty-nine (two-thirds of cases) who traveled on the average 33.5 minutes longer *one way*. For this two-thirds of the principal wage earners of the households, the average journey time each day was (24.7 + 33.5) × 2, which was 1 hour and 56.4 minutes. Of this, *1 hour and 7 minutes of the journey extra each day was thanks to the Group Areas Act*. Common sense surely tells us that such erosion of otherwise discretionary time will likely have a negative effect on the worker's family relationships. Chombart de Lauwe's studies on the time budgets of manual workers in Paris indicate clearly that those who took longer to work returned home more tired, were less able to help their wives, and played with their children less. I cannot immediately think of any reason why what Chombart found to be the case for urban France in 1960 should not be applicable to Cape Town in the 1970s.

The mode of travel to work used by removees also changed. In Mowbray, nine traveled by private car; after removals, thirty-one did (four in a carpool). Eighteen walked to work in Mowbray; by 1976 only three walked. This marked shift away from walking (free) and toward the private car (costs per kilometer variable and problematical) makes the reliable evaluation of comparative travel costs difficult. However, comparison is possible for public transportation (bus and train). Thirty-nine traveled by public transportation in Mowbray; thirty-one did by 1976. Very simply, we can compare what it would cost the traveler to get to the job were he or she (of those who did *not* change their work places) still living in Mowbray with what he or she actually did pay living where they were living after removals, by the same mode of transportation. Only twenty-six cases are strictly comparable; of these, in two instances costs were precisely the same; three on the average 20.66 percent less; and twenty-one (81 percent) on average 76.5 percent more. [12] Figure 21 shows all these data in detail; compare the area of increase (shaded) with the area of decrease (blank) in the diagrams.

Health Services

In many ways Nonwhite Mowbray was a pocket more fortunate than most. One of the most remarkable advantages it had was its proximity to health care—as opposed to, for example, District Six, which had only one maternity hospital. Nevertheless, this does not detract from the imposition suffered by the ex-Mowbrayites consequent upon their removal; it means rather that it is probably relatively greater than what might be representative of removed Capetonians as a whole. When located in Mowbray, the households interviewed were about a kilometer from Rondebosch and Mowbray Cottage Hospital and under 2 kilometers from Groote Schuur.

In computing the figures that follow, the indispensable Day Hospital system used on the Cape Flats has been included. These clinics mainly function diagnostically; doctors (and frequently medical school students) refer nontrivial cases to Groote Schuur and other fullfledged hospitals. For many of the people I interviewed, these nearby Day Hospitals are of great service. But even when these are treated as if they were full-service hospitals (as Groote Schuur and the Cottage were in Mowbray), distances to care were much higher. The average distance to a hospital in Mowbray was 1.42 kilometers; after expulsion from Mowbray, it was 5.29 kilometers. Of ninety-six comparable cases, seven were the same distance away from a hospital; fifteen were closer, by an average of 0.9 kilometers; and seventy-four (over three-quarters) were farther away, by an average increase of 5.21 kilometers (Figure 22 [A]).

In addition, doctors were close by in Mowbray: seventy-nine of the ninety-eight who replied said that their doctor was then less than half a kilometer from their homes. The average distance to the doctor in Mowbray is computed to have been 0.78 kilometers; in 1976 it was 2.44 kilometers. The situation in 1976 (Figure 22 [B]) was that in ninety-one cases in which comparison was possible, twenty-one households were the same distance from a doctor as then; eight were closer; but sixty-two (two-thirds) were farther away, by an average increase of 2.75 kilometers. That, of course, as for the hospitals, is only a one-way distance.

Places of Worship

Of the 100 households I interviewed, 33 percent still walked to their places of worship and 30 percent reported them to be the same distance away as in Mowbray. (See Figure 23.) These high percentages reflect the fact that many people, unwillingly at first (and perhaps still) changed their allegiance from one of the Mowbray churches or from the Mowbray mosque to places of worship closer to their new homes—for example, from St. Peter's to the (Anglican) Church of the Resurrection in Bonteheuwel. Others continued to go back to Mowbray every Friday or Sunday, but, when they did not own cars or have access to them, the journey was tiring. Eventually, people will come back less frequently than they once did until their attendance becomes only a ritual assertion of Mowbrayness at Eid, Christmas, and Easter. Mr. Petersen, a successful businessman, who owned a car and was a very keen churchman—a sidesman at St. Peter's—talked in his Crawford home of

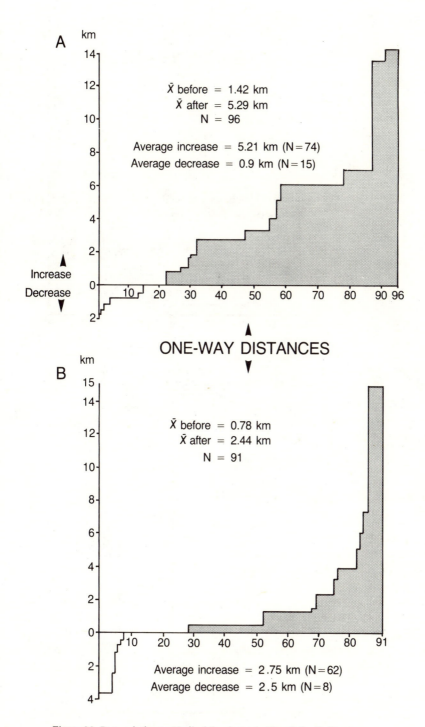

Figure 22. Data relating to Medical Services. A. Hospitals. B. Doctors.

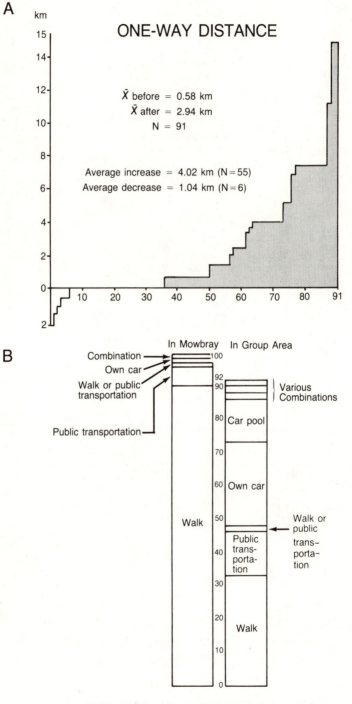

Figure 23. Data for Place of Worship. A. Distance traveled. B. Mode of travel.

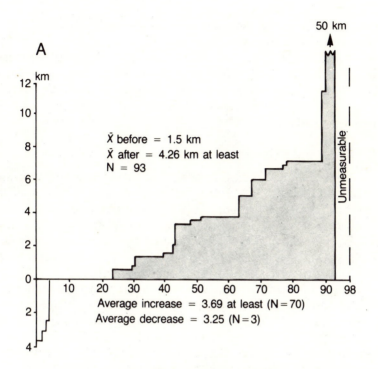

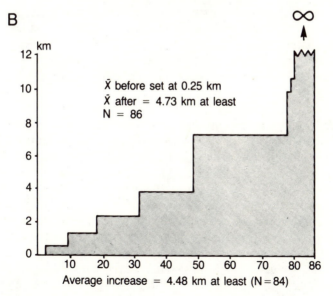

Figure 24. Data for Best Friends. A. All best friends. B. Ex-Mowbrayite best friends.

the whole business of belonging to a church there in Mowbray. . . . Without a car most non-Europeans can't go, so most are in churches out here [on the Cape Flats]. So we don't know any church people here, and we can go to St. Peter's [twice every Sunday], but of course the Europeans wouldn't come out here; they're scared like we were when we first came here. . . . Mowbray's our home, where we belong; we'd go back there if we could.

Best Friends and Relations

As well as the distinction between "*all* best friends when living in Mowbray" (Figure 24[A]) and "those best friends who were also Mowbray coresidents" (Figure 24[B]), there are a number of complications in these data. Some interviewees mentioned as a "best friend today" a person living very distant, for example, in Johannesburg. To include such a distance would greatly distort the averages because such a move was clearly not due to the workings of the Group Areas Act. In fact, this brings us to a more general point: we cannot *automatically* impute *all* the increases in distances to changes resulting from group areas removals. It is a sociogeographical platitude to refer to the ever-increasing ease of spatial mobility. If one has a car, it might seem to be as little effort (though more costly) to drive 8 kilometers to see a friend as it did to walk from the Valley to his home in Dane Street, Observatory, during the early 1960s. There have been societywide changes, and there have been changes due to group areas removals, and there have been changes on both levels combined. I believe distances would have increased anyway over the last fifteen years. But would they have increased *this much*? This is a difficult question; I would need a wholly comparable control group to answer it adequately.

A very interesting table (Table 15) can be drawn up to contrast present (1976) social visiting patterns with relatives and patterns with friends. The visits circled were the most common ones made by my informants; those boxed were the next most common. Relatives visited were clustered between 3 and 10 kilometers distant; those relatives visiting, between 2 and 10 kilometers distant. Compare this finding with the fact that 70 of the 100 households who furnished this information had, when living in Mowbray, at least one set of relatives living *within half a kilometer* from them (whom we may fairly assume they visited and received visits from).

᾽ Friends, however, fell consistently into two categories. The most common visits occurred with persons living under half a kilometer distant. This finding is strong evidence for the growth of ties with

Table 15
Visits Reported to and from Relatives and Friends

One-way Distance Involved (kms)	⟨0.5	0.5-1	1-2	2-3	3-5	5-10	10-20	20-50	⟩50	Not Appli-cable
To relations	1	2	10	6	14	24	11	2	2	28
From relations	0	1	7	18	16	29	9	8	4	8
From friends	30	8	4	10	10	15	4	0	4	15
To friends	28	4	5	4	15	15	4	2	1	22

new people during the period since removal to the new residential area. Mowbrayites were to a significant extent scattered by group areas removals (Map 23), and so many of the proximate friends must have been new neighbors. Only half as frequent were the second most common friendship visiting distances, but their distribution was consistent. Most of them were between 3 and 10, especially between 5 and 10, kilometers. I would hypothesize that these visits were in large part to ex-Mowbray friends scattered across the Cape Flats. Only six of ninety-five ex-Mowbrayite interviewees responding said they had kept up with none of their old Mowbray friends; and only twenty-four, with few. Two-thirds of respondents, then, were trying and succeeding to some degree to maintain contact with their dispersed friends (recall that 55 percent of all the people interviewed had a car in the household in which they lived). From Figure 24 (B), we see the average distance to the home of a best friend who once lived in Mowbray was *at least* 4.73 kilometers. This agrees with the explanation of the bimodal friendship distance pattern indicated by Table 15.

School

Distances to primary schools were essentially unchanged by the removals from Mowbray. As in Mowbray, most Coloured households, wherever they were living, were within half a kilometer of a primary school. (See Figure 25.)

Access to high schools was slightly *better* than in Mowbray, where all students had to leave the village. No child then attended a high school less than 1 kilometer from home; in 1976, 35.8 percent did. For the majority of homes, a high school had become closer. However, some Coloured parents, in their search for good schools and in order to avoid "township schools," sent their children long distances to such institutions as Harold Cressy (in Cape Town), Livingstone (in lower Claremont), and Athlone High. Thus, the costs for travel and the average distances eventually were about the same as if the students were still living in Mowbray.

Shopping

For Coloured people shopping for clothing (Figure 26[A]), Mowbray had its own stores as well as being easily accessible to large shopping centers in Cape Town, Claremont, and Salt River. There is

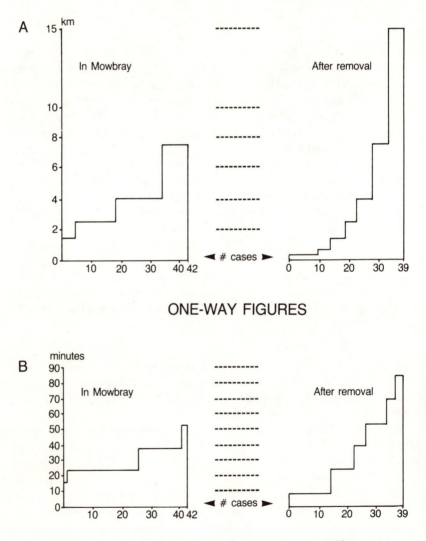

Figure 25. Data for High School Attendance. A. Distance. B. Time.

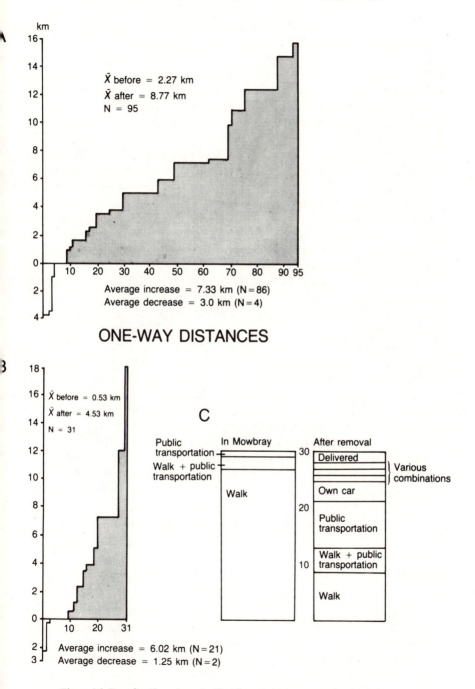

Figure 26. Data for Shopping. A. Clothing. B. Meat. C. Mode of travel.

an almost total lack of established, competitively priced shopping areas on the present-day Cape Flats. This is no accident. Just as I predicted such a situation when I modeled my ideal apartheid city (Chapter 4), so W. J. Davies (1971, p. 158) noted (in explaining Port Elizabeth's group areas patterns) that in Durban the city's apartheid planners "further indicated that the provision of such group amenities [suburban township shopping centers] should not be allowed to affect the status of the [White-owned] Central Business District." Patricios confirmed that this is the general pattern for South Africa's larger urban areas;[13] again, this entails the poorer (having been expelled from the inner cities) having to travel farther. For 90 percent of the measurable cases in my survey, the average increase in distance to clothing stores was 7.33 kilometers. This average journey to the stores and back of 14.65 kilometers was traveled by public transportation by 53 percent of the people interviewed, and they paid the increased fares in addition to losing time and suffering inconvenience.

For meat shopping (Figure 26[B]), Mowbray's Coloured residents had both *halal* (Muslim) and regular butchers, and they had fish shops. The average distance to meat shops for the thirty-two households providing this information was only 0.525 kilometers in Mowbray. For twenty-one of these households, the average increase in distance was 6 kilometers. This is not to say that these people were living over 6 kilometers away from a butcher's shop. Township prices are simply too high (for example, see "Blacks Pay Twice Price," *Cape Times*, 25 March 1974), and a once-weekly trek to the supermarkets of Kenilworth, Rondebosch, Athlone (sometimes), Salt River, or Cape Town was more economical. The change in mode of travel followed naturally from this. In Mowbray, twenty-seven of thirty walked to buy their meat; in 1976, fourteen of thirty went by public transportation—and they paid the fares. Information of a predictably similar nature was also gathered on shopping for consumer durables, such as saucepans, versus everyday shopping for bread.

Movie Theaters

Since there was no Nonwhite bioscope in Mowbray, the average distance traveled by Nonwhites living there was 3.36 kilometers. Of my sample, 14.75 percent were still the same distance away, and 36 percent were closer, by an average of 2.93 kilometers. (See Figure 27[A]). This last is a figure influenced by the opening of the Oasis Cinema in Bonteheuwel in 1972, over ten years after the establishment of the estate. Until then, accessibility was much lower, and indeed in 1976 a higher proportion, 49 percent, were *still* farther away

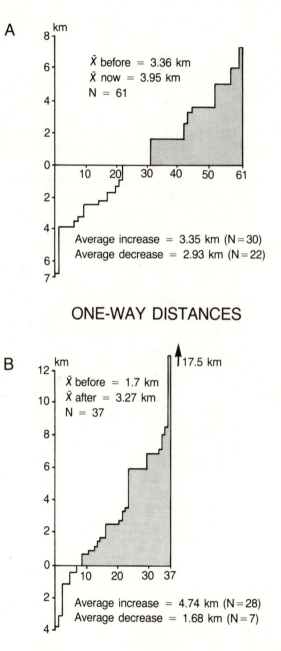

ONE-WAY DISTANCES

Figure 27. Data for Entertainment. A. Bioscopes. B. Sporting events.

and by a greater average distance, 3.35 kilometers. In toto, somewhat greater inconvenience has resulted from group areas removals for ex-Mowbrayites attending bioscopes. *The Theron Commission Report* (1976) confirmed this situation to be general in South Africa; it found that provision for entertainment for Nonwhites had deteriorated in the Cape Peninsula since 1965 especially, because a number of Coloured cinemas in areas that were declared White had to be closed. This resulted in a reduction by 21 percent of cinema seats for Coloured persons (van der Horst, 1976, p. 87). Another point: A number of the people I interviewed were afraid to go out to the bioscope at night. As a result, the popularity of home movies among the interviewees, and among the Coloured Capetonians I knew, had become more widespread.

Sporting Events

In Mowbray, sport could be enjoyed nearby and could be quickly organized. (See Figure 27[B].) Prior to their removal, only 13 percent of my sample never went to sporting events; in 1976, that figure was 59 percent, partly, perhaps, due to the by then older-than-average age distribution of removees. Also, in Mowbray, those who were not devoted aficionados were liable to go from time to time, especially when the Mowbray teams were playing an important match, for there was little effort involved in going. When they lived in Mowbray, forty-three percent could walk to sporting events; in 1976, only seven percent could. The changes in comparable distances can be gauged from Figure 27 (B); in sum, the removees found that they had less access to this element of social life than they had before.

The last of the tangible comparisons concerns the Nonwhite people's access to plumbers and electricians. Because such a high proportion of their answers could not be precisely measured (for example, "The plumber comes to the house" and "In Mowbray I used to phone the landlord in Sea Point when I got in to work [Cape Town city center] in the morning"), providing diagrams would give a misleading impression of precision. Nevertheless, the comparative figures indicate that there has also been an overall increase in the average distance to both these services since expulsion.

Summary

All the information provided in this section documents the hard, quantifiable impositions that have been the lot of removed Nonwhite ex-Mowbrayites. I consider this evidence to be indisputable. It reveals the Group Areas Act for what it is: an instrument for institutionalizing the disadvantage of those not in power.

CHAPTER NINE

Ex-Mowbrayites: The Geographies of Status and Fear

The name "Athlone" had a question mark by it when we were forced out here.

Home-owning removee,
21 July 1975

LIFE ON THE CAPE FLATS

The intangible effects of the group areas removals upon ex-Mowbrayites were no less real than the tangible ones. The most common response freely offered to a question about life in the new Cape Flats group areas was not one pertaining to tangible impositions—increased distances to jobs and health care facilities or whatever—but pertaining to an intangible imposition: increased fear for physical safety.

The postremoval experiences of those who were resettled in private housing and those in public housing show a significant contrast. The people I interviewed were well aware of the differences in the quality of life in the various Coloured group areas of Cape Town. The inhabitants of the different housing zones are inescapably characterized, also: one is one's address. Nevertheless, fear is a reality for *all removees*, whatever their status, whatever their housing, and whatever the gradual improvements on the Cape Flats through time. And, indeed, as I will show later in the chapter, *all Capetonians*, whatever their color and class, sometimes experience fear for their physical safety.

"Here It's Unsafe"

Removees had a lot to say about their milieus. The most common quality they ascribed to Cape Flats life, volunteered by 52 percent of the households interviewed, concerned the lack of physical security there. Furthermore, 48 percent of the removees extolled the lost Mowbray's safety and in so doing implied the lack of safety they felt in their new homes. Since this 48 percent partially overlaps with the 52 percent being considered here, it is probably fair to say that about two-thirds to three-quarters of all the people interviewed expressed some concern for their safety.

In Bonteheuwel I was told, "The nearest police station's in Bishop Lavis, a half-hour's walk. There's no telephone in any emergency, the public phones are vandalized. The people opposite have a phone, but you can't knock [wake] them up in the middle of the night."

A resident of Belgravia (a home-ownership area), who lived next to a large stretch of open ground, said:

> If our phone rings and it's for the neighbour, one [of us] walks across the street to tell them, while the other goes to the edge of the garden to watch her. And when 'Tifa comes home in the evening and it's dark, then we go [by car] to pick her up at the bus stop, wouldn't dream of letting her walk down.

In Bonteheuwel one evening, Mr. Gierdien came in late from visiting his mother by car in Heideveld; his wife and we had already started eating the Malay curry dinner she had prepared.

> "As I came by the corner back there there's a gang of skollies [ruffians] surrounding a man, about a dozen of them, backing him off the road into the shadows [onto a plot of waste ground]. He was pleading with them." "What did you do?" we asked urgently. He shrugged. "Why didn't you drive and tell the police station?" "Man, by the time they got there . . . you can't do nothing."

Among all the people interviewed who expressed concern over the lack of safety were 34.90 percent of the home owners ($N = 43$) and 72.55 percent ($N = 51$) of the council renters (over twice as many). Twenty-one people specifically mentioned not feeling free to walk at night as an example of what they meant by feeling "unsafe." Six said that they felt almost like prisoners in their houses, staying indoors during the evenings just listening to the radio. An elderly woman in Kew Town told me, "It's not so safe these days, especially *these* quarters. At night time about seven o'clock we're all in bed, except Sundays. After church we go to bed about nine o'clock." And in Bonteheuwel, an informant said, "I don't see these neighbors too much. There's too much boozing and carrying on, running from one house to the other. Once in my house, I stay in and scratch around." Four households, two council renters and two home owners, claimed that it was not merely unsafe on the Cape Flats but that it was unsafe everywhere, "even in Mowbray" and "even in Sea Point, these days." But a man in Heideveld expressed what most seemed to feel: "I'm not a communist; I like fair play, that's all. . . . Times do change, but it's the moving that did it."

This statement is no empty assertion. Computation of an overall index[1] for crimes against the person for the present urban environment, weighted accordingly for the 100 interviewees (18 in Bonteheuwel, 8 in Wynberg, et cetera), yields a figure in 1977 of 15.35 crimes per 1,000 people in the population, compared with Mowbray's 1977 rate of only 7.5. Map 24, which was prepared originally by the Cape Town city engineer's office and which bears a note pointing out that the map should not stand on its own since it has an incomplete or possibly incorrect information base, nevertheless shows a clear and instructive general pattern. As far as crimes against the person are concerned, the Cape Flats are *not* as safe as Mowbray or Sea Point these days.

"The Neighbors Are Quiet/Nice/Good"

Exactly half of the removees I interviewed expressed some satisfaction with their neighbors. However, the greater proportion of satisfied home owners (58.1 percent of whom were satisfied; $N = 43$) and private renters (50 percent; $N = 6$) in comparison with council renters (43.1 percent of whom were satisfied; $N = 51$) should be noted. A good number of the satisfied households also said that even so, their new neighbors were not as good as the ones they had in Mowbray.

"Here Everyone Minds Their Own Business/We Just Greet"

Such a description of one's neighbors offered by 31 percent of the households, is not necessarily negative. A person interviewed in the Sydneyvale home-ownership scheme said, in reply to my question, "What are the neighbors like?": "They will help if we need a screwdriver or a jack. . . . We're rather distant but relations are good. I greet them, in the garden, then go inside." In my interviews, 39.5 percent of the home owners ($N = 43$) and 50 percent of the pri-

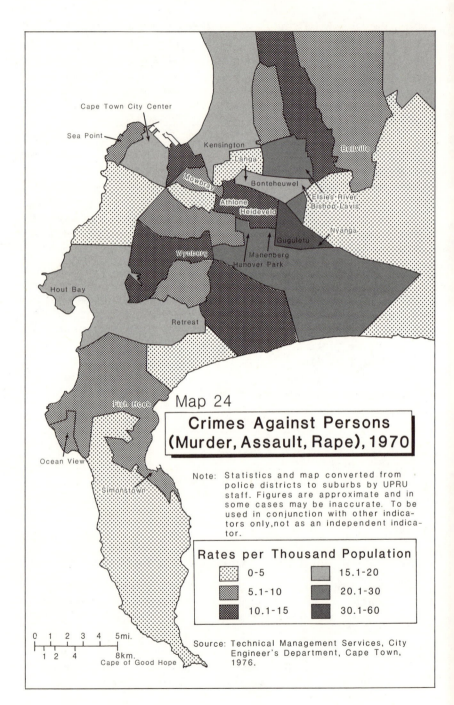

Map 24

**Crimes Against Persons
(Murder, Assault, Rape), 1970**

Note: Statistics and map converted from
police districts to suburbs by UPRU
staff. Figures are approximate and in
some cases may be inaccurate. To be
used in conjunction with other indica-
tors only, not as an independent indicator.

Rates per Thousand Population

░	0-5	▓	15.1-20
▓	5.1-10	▓	20.1-30
▓	10.1-15	▓	30.1-60

Source: Technical Management Services, City
Engineer's Department, Cape Town,
1976.

Cape Town City Center
Sea Point
Kensington
Langa
Bellville
Mowbra
Bonteheuwel
Athlone
Elsies River
Heideveld
Bishop Lavis
Nyanga
Wynberg
Guguletu
Manenberg
Hanover Park
Hout Bay
Retreat
Fish Hoek
Ocean View
Simonstown
Cape of Good Hope

0 1 2 3 4 5mi.
1 2 4 8km.

vate renters ($N = 6$) described such characteristics of their neighbors. Of the residents of the townships, living close together (that is, not surrounded by a private plot of land) with neighbors generally possessing fewer middle-class pretensions of reserve, only 21.6 percent ($N = 51$) talked of such distancing (that is, only half as many).

A young, white-collar home owner in Crawford, Mr. Delport, talked nostalgically of his Mowbray boyhood fifteen years previously and then made this point:

> I was really living then, now I'm not sure I am. I mean, I live for my job, that is, the money I can make so we can make the home comfortable for the family and to invite people in and be proud of it. But it's very rarely we can get up a party to go out dancing or to a movie. In Mowbray there was too much to be done outside—people would participate with you—here we live *too* much in our houses.

He had said earlier, "Kids don't play on the streets here, people're more worried about individual status."

Some of the new home-ownership tracts on the Cape Flats have much in common with Young and Willmott's pseudonymous Greenleigh, the out-of-town public housing estate to which Bethnal Greeners moved. Young and Willmott's (1962, p. 164) conclusions about the new distancing in Britain are applicable to Mr. Delport's upwardly mobile, young Crawford family:

> Negatively, people are without the old relations. Positively, they have a new house. In a life now house-centered instead of kinship-centered, competition for status takes the form of a struggle for material acquisition. In the absence of small groups which join one family to another, in the absence of strong personal associations [partly engendered by lengthy coresidence] which extend from one household to another, people think that they are judged, and judge others, by the material standards which are the outward and visible mark of respectability.

Distance from Amenities

After the three intangible effects had been mentioned, the next most frequent complaints were about the tangible, concrete impositions of removal. These impositions, of which 23 percent of the households complained, seem to affect home owners and council renters about equally. Eleven of forty-three home owners, and twelve of fifty-one council renters offered sentiments similar to Mrs. Aghardien's, who lived in Mount View (a home-ownership area).

It's isolated. You have to walk a long way to the bus because it's a new area, and there's no bus shelter. And it's very damp here, and when it rains. . . . And the buses are expensive, and you have to change at Wetton for Claremont, so it's twelve cents then another twelve cents, so that's twenty-four cents one way.

Noncommittal Attitude towards Neighbors

This response, from 20 percent of the households, was sometimes difficult to distinguish from "Here everybody minds their own business." At what point does the lack of intimate ties (and potentially demanding claims) to neighbors become something to be unenthusiastic about, instead of something to be more or less satisfied with? For example, a Coloured family man in his thirties told me nostalgically how good the situation was concerning neighbors in Mowbray, whereas "here in Silvertown I keep to myself; I greet them, but that's all. . . . On the other hand, there's the advantage that you don't find them running in and out and bumming off you." (On balance I decided to place this man's reply among these twenty noncommittal ones.) The home owner versus council renter variable does not appear to be germane here: eight of forty-three home owners, two of six private renters, and ten of fifty-one council renters offered these opinions.

Lack of Satisfaction with Neighbors

When it comes to the downright negative comments about neighbors, which 17 percent of all households expressed, unambiguous dissatisfaction was found among a much higher proportion of council renters than home owners: 25.5 percent ($N = 51$) of the council renters in my sample but only 9.3 percent ($N = 43$) of the home owners. A lot of this dissatisfaction was expressed in terms of place: that is, in the council schemes, removees (from Mowbray and, therefore, persons who claim respectability) were placed without being consulted next to persons from *other* places, who were stigmatized by those places' images in the social matrix of Cape Town. In a typical example, a young man in Duinefontein township told me that his neighbors next door and upstairs were from Newlands; next door and downstairs and also at the end of his apartment block from Maitland; then, in the flanking block, one family each from Constantia, Diep River, Woodstock, Athlone, Cape Town, and Claremont. Of these nine, at least six must have been removed to Duinefontein because of group areas development. In the absence of personal knowledge of these new neighbors such as would have grown through long coresidence in Mowbray, the man from Mowbray could only fall back warily on his images of their places of origin when he started to establish some kind of way of living with them.

Brendan Behan (1962, p.16), captured the fears of people involuntarily removed from inner Dublin to new, unknown neighborhoods and neighbors. He wrote about families such as his own

> when they were shifted out to Crumlin or Kimmage and set down in terrace houses mixing with God knows what muck from Irishtown, Ringsend, the Liberties and other parts south of the Liffey. I remember, when we got our notice to get moving, hearing one oul' wan moaning to my mother: "Oh, Mrs. Behing, jewel and darling! don't go out to Kimmage — that's where they ate their young." Four miles away it was, and no more, where this cannibalism took place.

Although one removed Mowbray woman may have thought that "the children here are animals," allegations of cannibalism were not forthcoming on the Cape Flats. The worst that was said, by five council renters, was that their neighbors were "trashy people" who were drunkards. A Muslim tailor in his forties complained of Heideveld:

> If you get into trouble, you're on your own. You've got to be alert from morning to the night. . . . We're respectable people—I'm from the imam's family [of Mowbray]. Why can't they keep us all together? I'm next to skollies from Maitland, alcoholics from Windermere [formerly a notorious shantytown, still partially uncleared]. There's noise till one in the morning. They opened the bar a year ago. There was a drunk being chased, ran into our house—I wasn't home, working late at the shop— he knocked my wife over. She had hysterics.

"My Parents Kept Me from Children Who Were Rough"

Another concomitant of dissatisfaction with neighbors was the next most common disapprobation expressed by 16 percent of all households: or, "Here a child can go astray." Only two of forty-three home owners (4.7 percent) and none of the private renters mentioned this complaint, but fourteen of fifty-one (27.6 percent) of the council renters did. A partially overlapping ten, all council renters, specifically said that they would not allow their children out of the yard to play on the street. In Bishop Lavis township, one person said, "Oh yes, this is not a good place at all for nobody's children. Different people move in from all kinds of places. A child picks it up very quick, though we keep them in." And Mrs. Davids said:

> The children are all mixed up here in Bonteheuwel. You have to keep them on a short lead. You must be worried when you send the children to the shops. Other ones take the money or stuff. Mowbray was safe. . . . But you've got to be satisfied, it goes like this in the townships.

Trying to Deal with Being Scattered

The three next most common complaints could not be differentiated according to housing status and were so straightforward as to preclude extended comment. Of the 100 households I contacted, 13 percent made remarks like "I've lost my friends, scattered I don't know where"; 12 percent stated that "we meet less frequently, it's more difficult now"; and 11 percent expressed sentiments like "Here we just make the best of a bad job."

To the first of these three ("scattered, lost friends"), I can append just one illustration, reported by Moodley (1975, p.264), for a parallel case, Indian removees from inner Durban.

> The extent of the impact of this single piece of legislation [the Group Areas Act] is summed up in a public wedding invitation, a form very seldom used by Indians: "Mr. and Mrs. . . . of . . . wish to extend a cordial invitation to friends and relatives with whom they have lost contact due to displacement under the Group Areas Act, on the occasion of the marriage of . . . ."

Moodley then explained that "Indians traditionally deliver wedding invitations personally from home to home, not relying on an impersonal postal service, to ensure a good turn-out at the wedding. *The Leader* (Durban) 20 July 1973."

"It's Safe Where We Live Now"

A different 11 percent of all the people I interviewed (different from that 11 percent "making the best of it") volunteered that where they were presently living was in fact a safe place. Of these eleven, ten were home owners and *only one* was a council renter. Two persons also said that they would walk at night where they lived; both were home owners. There was also the Muslim artisan in Silvertown, a well-established council estate, who said that he would walk at night but that his wife would not.

"We're Out in the Bush, the Wilderness"[2]

Only two home owners (4.7 percent of all those owning their own homes) but seven council renters (13.7 percent of renters) expressed such feelings. The imagery comes in part from the windswept, slightly undulating sandy expanses of the Cape Flats, dotted with Port Jackson scrub and vleis. (Captain Cook in 1776 described it as "the large plain that lies to the eastward of the town, which is entirely a white sand, like that commonly found on beaches, and produces only heath, and other small plants of various sorts.") When a southeaster blows during the summer, the sand makes life in the townships particularly unpleasant, and the photo of Heideveld center (note the prominence of its new tavern) explains in large measure more than one resident's description of it as "the desert" (Figure 28).

High Prices in the Cape Flats Stores

A different 9 percent of the households interviewed also complained that "here the shops are more expensive." The status of the interviewee's housing did not seem to be related to this complaint.

Figure 28. Heideveld Center, Summer 1975, Eleven Years after the Beginning of Construction of the Housing Scheme.

A Malay wholesale fruit merchant, a home owner in the Surrey Estate, said, "You wouldn't believe the prices we pay for meat out here to the Indians; we try not to buy here." (It may have been that business rivalry excited his comment.) And Mrs. Morkel, a housewife from Heideveld rental township, told me:

> For meat the shops are more expensive here. And lots of other things, too.
> . . . [I pressed her for a specific example.] Well, a bottle of fish oil I
> got on special offer in Athlone for sixty cents; here it's seventy cents.
> . . . It's because they've got a monopoly. In Athlone there are four or
> five in competition and the prices are lower. But you have to pay the bus
> fare: that's fourteen cents. And with this no conductor/pay as you enter
> nonsense [newly introduced at the time of this interview in August 1975],
> it takes much longer, the waiting. . . . Now, for something like a sauce-
> pan, I don't buy one every day. We'll wait till when we go in to Athlone
> or town for groceries, greens, and meat, on a Friday or Saturday, and do a
> lot of shopping there, like in Clicks or Woolworth's or OK Bazaars. For
> example, you won't find me running up to the shop here for a toilet roll,
> it's too expensive. I'll buy a lot of them all at once in town and they last
> me a while.

Whisson's August 1975 work in Ocean View township in the southern Cape Peninsula, to which Simonstown Nonwhites were forcibly removed, found the same. A careful comparison of prices for a shopping basket (compiled by an Ocean View household) was made between the township stores and the supermarket in [White] Fish Hoek, 8 kilometers distant. It was ascertained that, for any total purchase of R10 or more, it was more economical (although less convenient) for shoppers to travel those 16 kilometers and pay the fares.

Dissatisfaction with Housing Quality

Finally, 8 percent of the households made specific complaints about their present houses. Seven of these eight households were council renters. For example, construction of two-story maisonettes had begun in Bonteheuwel in 1974. The township's population density was thereby much increased (Figs. 29, 30). (Council tenants living in single-story cottages were not informed by the city council of its plan to construct the maisonettes "in their backyards" until shortly before construction began, which gave rise to a certain amount of resentment.) After living in his new maisonette three months, Mr. November, once of Mowbray, complained of the dampness; and the moisture was indeed visible on an inside wall. The interview took

Figure 29. Bonteheuwel, Original Cottages and New Maisonettes, 1976.
(Photograph used by permission of G. Ellis, UPRU.)

place in August (1975), during the winter rains. A month earlier, another ex-Mowbray household was interviewed in its new maisonette, which felt very dank, and there was mold on the inside of its apparently poorly constructed roof.

In Heideveld, also, in a ten-year-old, single-story cottage, the working housewife said, "These are damp, cold floors and damp walls. We have to whitewash them every year. And the walls are thin, you can hear their radio next door. And one kick at the door and you're through it. . . . Then there's the *sand*—the house is never clean." Five other people, all township renters (partially overlapping with the seven just considered), also complained about the sand. In Duinefontein (Manenberg), Mrs. Lennart said, "Here they said it was a vlei before. [This is correct.] It's always wet in the winter, you walk it into the house. You can't put white washing out for sand and dust in the wind, especially the southeaster. It blows it everywhere." And, in Bonteheuwel, one informant responded with these rhetorical questions: "Decent roads? Pavements [paved sidewalks]? In rainy weather we slide in through the sand and slide out again. What do we pay rent and taxes for?''

THE GEOGRAPHY OF STATUS

The Housing-Status Dimension

The foregoing recitation has underscored the importance of under-standing the relevance in the postremoval experience of the three types of accommodations available on the Cape Flats. On the one hand, there are the homes owned outright and rented privately (in home-ownership areas). On the other hand, there is the public housing occupied by council renters. Of these, two of the households I inter-viewed rented in Cape Divisional Council/Citizens' Housing League schemes (in Bishop Lavis Township), with the remaining forty-nine households in Cape Town City Council schemes. The people in my sample expressed:

1. feelings of present safety/lack of safety, or
2. satisfaction/dissatisfaction with neighbors, or
3. opinions on the reserved nature of their interactions with neigh-bors, or
4. disapproval of the children in their neighborhood, or
5. feeling of being "out in the bush," or
6. various specific complaints about their present houses.

All these reactions are related to whether the person interviewed was or was not a council renter.

This variable is connected to two others. (See Figure 19, again.) The first is religion. Table 7, in Chapter 7, showed that Muslims are more likely to be home owners than Christians. The second is age. If we draw the demarcation line at 50 years and above at the time of interviewing, then at removal these interviewees were 38 or 39 and above, a reasonable point for a young-old boundary.

Table 16
Age and Residential Status

Age	Home Owners	Council Renters	Total
Fifty and older at time of interviews	30	26	56
Under fifty	10	23	33

Table 16 shows the clear tendency for the older ex-Mowbrayites to be home owners. Using Yates's continuity correction, the value of chi square from this table fails by a small margin to demonstrate sig-nificance at the .05 level: 3.841 is required; 3.651 is computed. The

.05 significance level is attained when Yates's correction is not employed. Thus, any reference to housing status also has implications for religious and age status.

Now, some of the findings presented in Chapter 7 (pp. 179-84), in which removees characterized Mowbray's former qualities, when rapidly reexamined, reveal a number of other variables of the kind of 1 through 6. These also appear to be linked to housing status.

First, of that 36 percent of the households whose members said that they "would love to go back to Mowbray," the council renters make up an extraproportionate share. Only 16.6 percent of the private renters ($N = 6$) and 27.9 percent of the home owners ($N = 43$) said this, but 45.1 percent ($N = 51$) of the council renters did. Conversely, three households voiced their ambiguous feelings, saying that they were not sure whether they would like to return to Mowbray or not; all three were home owners. There were another three who said definitely they would *not* go back: "I far prefer here. The house is better, there it was right on the street, there was not a bit of ground, there was nowhere to park the car." Again, all three were home owners.

Second, of those twenty-one households who said that their present houses were better, two were private renters, fourteen were home owners, and five were council renters. That is to say, *one-third* of all home owners but only *one-tenth* of council renters expressed the feeling that their present physical accommodations were an improvement over those in Mowbray.

Third, 9 percent of all the households mentioned ease of accessibility. That is, 6 percent of the people I interviewed said that their new neighborhoods were as convenient as Mowbray; two were private renters and the other four were home owners. Another 3 percent said that their new locations were actually *more* convenient than Mowbray: one was a private renter and the other two were home owners. None of the council renters said their new places were as convenient as or more convenient than Mowbray.

Thus, to the list of six variables can be added three more that seem at least partially dependent on housing status:
7. wishing/not wishing to return to Mowbray,
8. feeling that the present accommodation was superior to that in Mowbray, and
9. feeling that Mowbray was no more convenient than the present location.

That these nine variables are related to housing status is an evaluation of the data's structure arrived at through my almost ponderously deliberate analysis. But a little imagination would suggest that it is hardly an unexpected finding. And, not surprisingly, many of the people I interviewed were well aware themselves of this differentiation among the Coloured people of the Cape Flats, and they had much to say about their area vis-à-vis others. Elements of internal social heterogeneity, somewhat disguised when the Coloured people lived in the Mowbray pockets, have become manifest in the new, status-specific spaces on the Cape Flats.

Expressed Opinions on Place and Status

Home Owners

Close to the top of the socioeconomic scale was Mr. van Wyk, late of Uitsig Close and in 1975 of Fairways. He said that there are

> a very middle-class kind of Coloured people in Fairways. Here's no skollies in Fairways [he chuckled]. Load of snobs here, posh houses built . . . but I'm not too happy walking here because of the Parkwood township toughs just over the way. All the beautiful areas we Coloured people have 've got mixed classes, the rougher types, nearby: Fairways next to Parkwood, Pinarty next to Hanover Park, Belhar next to Lavistown, Punts Estate next to Retreat.

(The role of the "Parkwood township toughs" was noted in Chapter 4 [p. 117] and Figure 5, with regard to the "exposed" corner of White Southfield.) It might be hypothesized that the usual target for lower-class Parkwood's aggressive frustration, or rather that of its skollies, would be the obviously affluent, elite Coloureds of adjoining Fairways. It would be safer to attack them (even though they are perhaps a surrogate) than to attack Whites or White property. However, during times of widespread civil unrest, when police surveillance is stretched and occupied elsewhere and especially when emotions are heightened through police overreaction, it is possible that any proximate Whites will be attacked. Mrs. Wheeler's home across the road from Parkwood, at the very edge of Southfield, was the most immediate such target that presented itself.

An older Coloured area of high status is the Walmer Estate, which some residents there (friends of mine) referred to tongue in cheek as "the Black Bishopscourt" (a nickname attached sometimes to Fairways and Syndeyvale). When I told another Coloured friend that a Mowbray family had removed to the Walmer Estate, his wondering reply was "How did they get in?!" Walmer Estate is close to the city center and is very desirable, having a similar "life-raft" function among the otherwise removed inner-city Nonwhite areas, just as Schotsche's Kloof has for Cape Malays.

At the time I talked with the ex-Mowbray Malay family there on 4 May 1975, Walmer Estate had not yet been proclaimed (it was on June 13, for Coloured and Malay occupation only). Thus was I told:

> We're living in an undeclared area. It's sort of frozen, you know what I mean? Now with all this Angola trouble and Mozambique we've got Portuguese coming in by the Holiday Inn there, even on the next street but one, Adelaide. I don't say anything against the government, but we don't like *that* at all.[3] From those places up there in Africa[4] they come down here and immediately start lording it over us like the natives up there, start off with cafes or as artisans, bringing in all that eating of fish —the poor man's food we call it here. Some Portuguese tried to move in across the street, but we managed to put a stop to it. We're going to call this Madeira Estate, not Walmer!

The Portuguese are disdained —clearly they are not "real Whites." The self-pride of these respectable Malays (they were one of the old Mowbray mosque's "anchor" families) was such that they could see the arrival of persons classified as White at the edge of their neighborhood as likely to lower its tone —quite an irony in South Africa!

A third high-status area, long established and close to excellent facilities, is lower Wynberg, an enclave today surrounded by White areas (Figure 31). Eight ex-Mowbray families managed to purchase homes there. One was a deputy school principal whose father was a Scot who had married a Coloured woman.[5] This gentleman went to great pains to emphasize his social and spatial distance from "those townships like Bonteheuwel —I don't know the names of those places. The most I ever see of them is when I'm driving out to the airport on the freeway, and that's enough for me. Never been there, never will." Notice how Bonteheuwel summed up for this man the supposed nature of *all* Cape Flats townships. Another ex-Mowbrayite mentioned two more recent townships: "I'm very lucky living in Wynberg; it's not Heideveld or Hanover Park." And yet another ex-Mowbrayite in Wynberg asserted respectability by telling me: "I don't go out into those other quarters. It's rough out there. . . . I *never* been to Athlone."

Private Renters

Just as Bonteheuwel means the Coloured townships in general for many Capetonians, so Athlone is sometimes a general synonym for the Cape Flats. The central area of Athlone is a home-ownership tract. Close to all the shopping, entertainment, and transportation facilities of central Athlone lived Mr. and Mrs. Du Toit, who privately rented one room. To the last question on my questionnaire, "What's life like here . . . ?" Mr. Du Toit replied:

> It's the same here [as it was in Mowbray] — if I was living in Bonteheuwel, it'd be a different story. We feel a bit close, a bit handicapped living in a room. We get crowded if we ask friends round, we don't have many since we've been in here. I'm looking for a house, but I don't want it out in one of *those* areas.

This couple had weighed the disadvantages of inadequate physical accommodation against those of the perceived environment of the council rental schemes and decided against chancing the latter.

Council Renters

Many residents in the townships are aware that their place has been stigmatized. For those renting in these tracts, their being from

Figure 30. Bonteheuwel Street Scene, 11 July 1978. Note the newer two-story maisonettes and the generally dilapidated air of the road surface, unpaved sidewalks, and loose trash. (Photograph used by permission of Struan Robertson, photographer.)

Mowbray was frequently a part of their self-definition; it was some respectability to hang on to. There were those who claimed that "they didn't sort us out, they put us next to District Six/Salt River /Maitland/Windermere/etc., people" and "you get the lowest type living around here" (Bonteheuwel)—those who were called by respectable ex-Mowbrayites "the mixed classes."

For some, space was still at least partially Mowbray centered. Some interviewees talked from the perspective of Mowbray and referred to "going farther out" to the Cape Flats, as if they were looking east from Mowbray, close beneath Table Mountain (Figure 32, Mowbray village center). And the mountain was always there, a visible reminder of how far they were moved (Figure 33). "There we were in the town, here we're out in the bush, the Flats." In Bonteheuwel "we're away from the main here." The aerial view of Figure 34 affords a general impression of the spreading Cape Flats housing tracts; the positions of Bishop Lavis and Bonteheuwel vis-à-vis Mowbray and Cape Town city center can be clearly seen.

Also, there was widespread dissatisfaction with the townships, for example, Kew Town: "The Bo-Dorp was very small. Mowbray was one big family, with the Malays, too. Here it's big, here you see a lot of people, you greet them, but you don't *know* them. You've got to

Figure 31. Lower Wynberg, an Older Home-Ownership Area, 1976.
Note the architectural influence of colonial India.

Figure 32. The Dorp, Mowbray, Close beneath Table Mountain, 1976.

Figure 33. Table Mountain Viewed from Bishop Lavis Township, 1976.
This is the same face of the mountain as that shown in Figure 32.

STATUS AND FEAR 253

be careful, things are much rougher here." In Duinefontein, an informant said, "There's lots of drink, there's lots of all kinds of people. We keep to ourselves. This place is not for us" (after ten years). A resident of Manenberg told me, "There's nothing much to see around here. At the weekend we get trouble in the streets, people running round with pangas [machetes]." Gerwel, a South African social scientist classified as Coloured, wrote (1974, p. 5) of "the socialpathological conditions of the communities of the Cape Flats." He put in academic terms what many of the people were telling me.

> There is also the antagonism towards the place, with many people having been forced to move to it in the first place. This initial antagonism is heightened because of the public image of the townships. Here the Press can play an important part:—it is unquestionably the duty of a newspaper to show up social evils where they occur, but excessive emphasis on problems could stigmatize the area, making it doubly difficult for residents to identify with their community.

A conventionally respectable Muslim, a florist, summed up his feelings about Bonteheuwel, to which he was forcibly removed from

Figure 34. The Cape from the East. The northern suburbs are in the lower left on one side of the rail line, the Cape Flats are on the other side, and the southern suburbs are in the upper left (Photograph used by permission of Terence McNally, photographer.)

Mowbray and from which he was trying to escape into a home-ownership area: "As far as I'm concerned, Bonteheuwel's just a roof over my head." Mr. Gierdien went on to try to refute the stigma of his address: "No, when you say you're from Bonteheuwel, some of them look at you down their noses, people from Fairways or Wynberg. I tell them there are decent people in Bonteheuwel, too. We've got social apartheid among ourselves, as well as the big thing."

This statement is a striking example of a spatial expression given to a social differentiation that was only immanent when people were still resident of Mowbray. Certainly, then, space is mirroring society in Cape Town, but the very visibility of space—the different housing areas with their various names—underscores more clearly than before the social divisions. Space *enhances* societal distinction; social structure in a sense mirrors space. From this comes the characterization of the society-space relationship as one of dialectical interdependency.

Mr. Gierdien's words also serve to illustrate a perception of Heribert Adam's concerning the parallel development of single-status Indian group areas in Durban.[6] Adam (1975, p. 308) believed that such spatial sorting of statuses is functional for continuing apartheid domination, namely:

> Worlds separate the houseowner in Reservoir Hills from the poor Indian in Chatsworth. Not only do different strata within an oppressed ethnic group increasingly perceive their situation in different terms, but their interests are objectively different. By allowing for individual economic advancement, although restricted by the overall caste arrangements, the system has provided escapes from political frustrations.

THE GEOGRAPHY OF FEAR

The Experience of Violence on Different Geographic Scales

A Bishop Lavis housewife (the view from her front window is shown in Figure 35) told me:

> This is a terrible place. We're very much living in fear in this place. Best of all we were very much safe in Mowbray. . . . Here there are too many shebeens. And once my chickens has disappeared. Three weeks back my eighteen-year-old third eldest son got stabbed in the head by skollies outside the house, and his nose broken—with a nail, the doctor said. You don't know who they are, and you'll never find out. The police don't take action. You're scared to walk. The people are in fear. If you see a rape, you stay indoors. If you see them stealing washing, you stay quiet, other-

wise they'll come and smash your home up. . . . The sand and dust blow into the house, you can't keep it out. There's no electricity here, and I don't believe they're going to put it in for us either. When we came here eleven years ago, they said they were going to, and what's happened?

The people I talked with had more to say about fear for their physical safety than about any other subject. This is hardly surprising when viewed in the light of both the crime statistics for the Cape Flats and for crimes of violence for South Africa in general. Midgley (1977, p. 81) informed us that, "even the United States, which has often been portrayed as a violent society, has a lower rate of criminal violence." He said that in 1970 there were an estimated 15,810 murders in the United States, for a population then of something over 200 million. Approximately 6,500 murders were reported to the South African police during the same year. So, with about ten times as many people, the United States recorded only two and a half times as many murders as South Africa. Or, as the homicide statistics in England and Wales (with over twice the population of South Africa during the relevant period) reveal, *contemporary South Africa has as many murders in a single year as were reported to the police in England and Wales during the fifty years between 1900 and 1949.* It is upon the poorer and the darker that the brunt of this violence falls. Adam (1971) quoted an anonymous Black African who said, "A lot of people die in Soweto, and not all of them are sick."

House and Yard

The comparison between crime in the urban environment in the United States and in South Africa can be continued. "Fear and the House-as-Haven in the Lower Class" was what Rainwater entitled his 1966 study on the infamous, now-demolished, Pruitt-Igoe public housing project in St. Louis. He pointed out that environmental threats for the lower class are *just* outside the front door in new public housing, where neighbors do not know or acknowledge each other (as opposed to the safety built up over time on the semipublic stoops and bystreets of the Mowbray village). Rainwater contrasted these fears outside the door with those fears that the more privileged possess: fear at the boundaries of their neighborhood. But "for the lower class, inside is private, outside is public and therefore dangerous" (Mercer, 1975, p. 111). As Ley (1974) showed in Black North Philadelphia, one's enemy is one's neighbor. Or, as Mr. Gierdien put it in Bonteheuwel, "Before I go to sleep, I go to the yard and check everything's locked, and the front door and the windows. . . . Inside it's good, but outside you can't say what goes on." A grandmother in Heideveld told me, "We keep the children in here. We buy them games to keep them in." Confidence may extend beyond the front door to the sandy yard, but, in the following case, this happened only when the yard had been rendered safe by stockading. A young father in Manenberg said, "There's nothing the kids can go to here. In Mowbray there was a park, the Liesbeek River, the Common. They play wild here. I only put on this [enclosed] yard last week so they can play inside."

The boundaries of safe and unsafe space change diurnally. Mrs. Daniels in Heideveld was quite prepared to take the most direct path (via a street with open ground on one side) to her nearest bus stop in daylight, but not at night. Mrs. Baatjies complained angrily:

> Instead of building a hospital in Bonteheuwel, they put a tavern. You see them waiting outside for it to open at ten in the morning. And I won't send the children along to the shops at the centre at night because they're all drunk outside the tavern there.

She did send them for bread in the daytime, though; it was perhaps 200 meters along well-traveled streets to the Bonteheuwel shopping center (Figure 38). When I parked my Volkswagen at the curb at Mr. and Mrs. Davids's house in Heideveld one night, someone always looked out from time to time to see that it was all right. On two occasions when I visited during the daytime, this was not deemed at all necessary.

The look of the council rental schemes being described can be seen in Figures 29, 30, 33, 35 and 36. When constructing the township cottages, flats (apartment blocks), and maisonettes, the Cape Town City Council put in facilities (for example, electricity and kitchen sinks) over and above what the government's minimum housing code required. The Department of Community Development has raised its standards since then, as I was informed by one of the city's chief housing officers in 1976: "They're more enlightened now," she said wryly, "they're now allowing burglar bars on downstairs windows." These defensive grilles can hardly be called a luxury extra, for at night in the townships fear approaches the walls of the house itself, reaches the burglar bars across the windows, and (especially when there are no burglar bars) may even penetrate into the home itself. In Heideveld, as Mr. Adams recounted:

> We never used to bother with burglar bars. Then about a year ago, I woke up in the night to hear movings about, five great big Africans armed with pangas were getting in through the window. They went into all the rooms

Figure 35. Apartment Blocks in Bishop Lavis, 1976.

Figure 36. A Typical Cape Flats Township Rental Cottage in Kalksteenfontein (Bonteheuwel), 1975. Fifty percent of this area's houses were set aside for group areas removees, like this ex-Mowbray woman.

—I was terrified, I just sat in bed motionless watching them—pulling out drawers, looking for money. I've a teenage daughter, one started molesting her and I was horrified, all the stories I'd heard of how they rape your wife or girls if they don't find any money. I had R60 in a dresser, took it, and gave it to them. I still thought they were going to go at my daughter, but one of them seemed sort of levelheaded. He said to the others, "Come on, let's go," and they all climbed quietly out again and moved away past the garden. It took me six months to get over it. I used to get up in the night and peer around the house. I've put bars on the door and windows now.

Even during the daytime, however, the "house as haven" is not necessarily wholly safe. In a sense, there is a measure of insecurity in simply being a *renter* in public housing. Officials can check up on the tenants any time they please to make sure that they are not breaking the rules and, perhaps, to impose sanctions when they are. Mrs. Ziervogel had something to get off her chest in this regard. Her pride in her evident respectability was affronted by invasions of her privacy such as when

they come in poking around, counting the beds, walking into all your rooms, out into the yard at the back, seeing how many lives there, why aren't you working, how old are your children, is there a grandmother here? They've got a nerve. If we pay the rent and are good tenants, what business is it of theirs, is it?

Clearly, the officials from the housing office are particularly concerned with the ubiquitous illegal overcrowding in the rental units.

The daytime is also insecure when a tenant's unfenced yard is continually violated, if only by local urchins. Even in a fenced yard, as more than one woman complained, washing can disappear. The house itself is not safe. One family was burgled in broad daylight one midmorning when they were not home. Another woman was knocked down by a drunk in her own house when he rushed in trying to escape his pursuers.

Not only does the threshold of safe territory tend to change diurnally, it also changes during times of civil unrest, as in Bonteheuwel in August and September of 1976. In late August, I recall seeing a Cape Town press photograph taken from inside a police "pickup" van, past the White driver and his fellow officer safe inside their capsule. The photograph also showed, in an upstairs window of a two-story block of flats, a Coloured woman and a child peering out, partially hidden behind the curtains, inside *their* capsule. Into the space between them, the open street, neither the police nor the residents would willingly venture: it was a no-man's-land.

Figure 37. Athlone, 1 September 1976. Two White men run the gauntlet of rock-throwing Coloured youths in Klipfontein Road. The top left of the windshield has already been hit (*Die Burger*, 2 September 1976).

Figure 38. Shopping Center, Bonteheuwel, 12 July 1978. (Photograph used by permission of Struan Robertson, photographer.)

Figure 39. Athlone, 1 September 1976. "Coloured youths disperse as teargas cartridges smoulder in Klipfontein Road, Athlone, today where anti-riot police confronted large stone-throwing mobs" (*Argus,* 1 September 1976).

From its starting at Arcadia High School, violence and arson spread. The police used pistols and tear gas in a confrontation with stone-throwing children. At least one person was killed. Bonteheuwel was described as "a battlefield" by a police spokesman (August 26); it was a place where "safe space" no longer existed, unless it was inside walls or a vehicle's closed doors (Figures 37 and 39). Making allowances for its usual breathless style, we read in the *Cape Herald* (31 August 1976) "They Said It Could Never Happen," by Maruwan Gasant:

BONTEHEUWEL, Wednesday August 25 1976 — a day to remember. A day people said would never happen. Soweto, yes. Guguletu, Langa, Nyanga, yes. But never a Coloured township. But then it happened.

And when the dust and teargas had cleared, a 15-year-old pupil lay critically injured among the spent shotgun cartridges, stones, broken glass and gas canisters in the no-man's land between angry rioters and hard-pressed regular and riot police.

. . . Pupils from [a second] high school then joined the crowd and the emotional tirade of cheers, jeers and boos was punctuated with blasts from single-barrelled shotguns.

Then four plainclothed detectives arrived in a small blue car. One jumped out and was assisted by another policeman in grabbing a demonstrator and dragging him to the car.

Women screamed and swore at the policemen as stones hailed down. One detective, baton in hand, gun in the other, opened fire.

The detectives then got into their car—and fled. . . .

Then the feelings that had built up in the crowd were unleashed. They stoned cars occupied by Whites. They ran in droves along the pavements as teargas was fired from passing trucks and vans.

Immediate "Turf"

During more normal times, the next expansion of safe territory is to a few local streets, well known and taken for granted, the way that the Valley and the Bo-Dorp were. However, the Valley and the Bo-Dorp had much greater temporal depth and (I suspect) a lower rate of residential turnover than Bonteheuwel and Heideveld. Also, the Mowbray Nonwhite pockets were in their visible fabric and especially in their visible inhabitants well defined; the edges of Nonwhite Mowbray space were clear. In Bonteheuwel and Heideveld, one small group of streets is not physically distinguishable from any other group in the extensive housing tracts, where, as a character in an Adam Small play exclaims in Gamtaal when he first sees the Cape Flats townships, *"Die hyse lyk ammal dieselfde"* ("The houses all look alike").

Nevertheless, the houses' physical uniformity does not preclude behavioral differentiations made by their residents. Five of the fifty-one council renters in my sample clearly separated their local zones of Heideveld and Bonteheuwel from their township in general, although to an outsider like me no visible differences in character were apparent. Thus, in Bonteheuwel: "Even here, it's only certain parts that are bad. There's no ruffians on this street, it's quite safe." "It's very rowdy here . . . but here we're on the main road so it's not *too* bad, but further in . . . ." And in Heideveld: "These are very quiet three streets, but you mustn't take chances late at night." In fact, I suspect that those residents who contrasted the relative safety of their particular streets with the danger of the township as a whole were prisoners of their own images of their environments. That is to say, on their own particular streets they knew neighbors, faces, children, dogs, and cars; they knew what to expect. Their fear was gradually being assuaged by familiarity. The image of their township as a whole, purveyed by the *Cape Herald* and confirmed weekly by frightening stories—like Mr. Adams's—being passed around (and embellished) by word of mouth, is one of the unforeseeable violence of strangers; these strangers may be fellow Heideveldians, but no one knows that they are—it is not as though they were fellow Mowbray people. An ex-Mowbrayite had no connection with fellow Heideveldians; they were from "all kinds of places."

The Broader Neighborhood

Rainwater (1966) posited that more privileged people have fears, not of their immediate vicinities, but at the boundaries of their neighborhoods. Such is perhaps the next larger scale of safety in Cape Town territory. However, neighborhood boundaries are permeable where police surveillance is not extensive. That is to say, the highly privileged (relatively speaking) Coloured people of home-ownership Fairways are, like Mr. van Wyk, afraid not of Fairways people—there a neighbor is not an enemy but a competitor—but of the "Parkwood township toughs" who live just beyond the neighborhood's boundary but who penetrate into Fairways. (There is apparently no adolescent Fairways territorial gang to challenge or rebuff the intruders.) Similarly, an ex-Mowbrayite living in privileged lower Wynberg told me, "I wouldn't dream of walking here at night; it's not the people that live here, but the people who come here from further out" (that is, from the Cape Flats, out along the main route of Wetton Road). We have already seen what Mr. McDonald of lower Wynberg thought about "those townships like Bonteheuwel" and heard Mr. Du Toit say "if I was living in Bonteheuwel, it'd be a different story."

For at least some ex-Mowbrayites living in home-ownership areas, fear was indeed at the borders of their neighborhoods, that is, in the public rental townships. Mr. van Wyk complained that all the high-status Coloured residential areas had townships adjacent, and he cited four legitimate examples. Those ex-Mowbrayites who were removed to the townships, disliked them intensely, and made enormous and eventually successful efforts to get out into "more respectable," "safer" home-ownership surroundings were especially fearful of intrusions into their new neighborhoods. One person who moved from Bonteheuwel to Squarehill, one from Bonteheuwel to Primrose Park (Figure 40), and one from Heideveld to Penlyn Estate all expressed to me their relief at escaping the townships. A number of others I met in the townships were striving to do the same (for example, the Mr. Adams who was burglarized in Heideveld).

Figure 40. Greenhaven-Primrose Park, 1976. This is an example of a new Coloured home-ownership area on the Cape Flats.

White City-Nonwhite Periphery

One more general scale of safe space in greater Cape Town can be designated: "race" space. For many Whites the fear is of *any* Coloured territory, anything subsumed under the "master identities" (as Suttles [1972] termed them) of "the Cape Flats" and "Athlone." Mr. Petersen, a churchman living in Crawford home-ownership area, told how the St. Peter's Church Mowbray Whites were afraid to come out to "Athlone." To the Whites the subdivisions *within* Athlone, for example between Mr. Petersen's comfortable Crawford neighborhood and the ill-reputed rental district of Bokmakierie, meant nothing. Their unease was not discriminatory; it was a blanket ignorance born of separation.

Such unease becomes active fear during times of tension. During the unrest in the Cape winter of 1976, the police, on a number of occasions, acted with excessively nervous caution, for example, when they dismantled makeshift barricades across Klipfontein Road's divided highway on the first of September. An eyewitness described the scene for me: a police van with a number of officers inside repeatedly approached the flimsy barricades and one officer then gingerly ran out, threw aside a rock, and leapt back into the van again; this performance was repeated until the road was clear. The policemen's behavior was like soldiers' fighting in hostile territory, even though they were within their own city. Similar jumpiness was reported of White National Guardsmen during the Newark, New Jersey, riots of July 1967.

> Since everything appeared quiet and it was broad daylight [Director of Police] Spina walked directly down the middle of the street. Nothing happened. As he came to the last building of the complex, he heard a shot. All around him the troopers jumped, believing themselves to be under sniper fire. A moment later a young Guardsman ran from behind a building. . . . [Asked by Spina] the soldier said "Yes," he had fired to scare a man away from a window. . . . [Spina asked him] "Do you know what you just did? You have now created a state of hysteria" (Kerner Commission, 1968, p. 2).

In such tense situations, reliable information is scarce, and people are prepared to believe farfetched rumors that under other circumstances would be laughable. For example, the *Argus* announced (16 September 1976), after there had been a great deal of arson, looting, violence, and death in Cape Town, that it had set up a "Fact not Rumour" service, which was "constantly busy with calls from anxious Cape Town people and yesterday it handled about 700 inquiries on its single line. . . . Rumours are dangerous. They make matters seem worse than they really are." And two days later (18 September 1976), the newspaper reported that

> the vast majority of calls came from worried people who wanted to know the best routes in getting from A to B, or whether it was safe to send staff home [clearly these callers were almost all Whites]; . . . many called about the activities of a totally fictitious mob that spent two entire days marching along De Waal Drive.

This last point is particularly interesting. On 21 March 1960 police opened fire on an unarmed crowd in Sharpeville, near Vereeniging in the Transvaal, killing 69 persons and injuring 186. On the same day in Langa 2 men were shot dead by police and 49 were injured. Then, ten days later in Cape Town a procession of over 30,000 Black Africans marched on Parliament, along De Waal Drive, one of the two main freeways into the city center, and caused great alarm. One of the Malay people I interviewed told me about how he had watched the marchers go by "silently, there were so many, they stretched for miles; I was scared I think." A visible embodiment of the *swart gevaar*, whose image is still so strongly etched in the Capetonian memory that it surfaced, *wholly a hallucination*, during the next period of civil unrest sixteen years later.

Map 25 shows, somewhat imperfectly, the locations of civil unrest in metropolitan Cape Town during August and September of 1976, in which at least 113 persons died. (There were other riots and deaths at the year's end.) Most of the casualties occurred in the Nonwhite residential areas (recall that it was only the eventual spread of riot from the ghettos to the "White" city center that seemed to alarm *Die Burger*.) It is difficult to evaluate the precise meaning of the rioting. There seem to have been anti-White expressions of frustration and resentment catalyzed by bitter anger at police heavy-handedness. Particular targets for riot and arson (by both Black Africans and Coloureds) were the symbols of the apartheid system, such as the Bantu Administration's offices, Black African beer halls ("drink keeps us down"), government schools, housing offices, civic centers, police stations, houses of policemen and suspected informers, and even the public library in Kew Town. Such unrest is basically spontaneous, as is its exploitation by skollie elements who loot, assault fellow township dwellers, and behave generally in an antisocial manner. (I left Cape Town one week before the 1976 riots began, so my information is secondhand, but much of it came from witnesses of the riots, both Whites and Blacks, through personal communications during 1976 to 1978 and conversations in Cape Town in 1978.) "Skollies" were blamed by Minister of Coloured Relations H. Smit on 8 September 1976: "I ask you not to judge the mass of Coloured people by the actions of a few people in the Cape Peninsula—people who have certainly run amuck under the incitement of certain elements—because then you will be making a mistake" (*Argus*, September 9). Mr. Smit was addressing the Orange Free State National Party Congress.

However, *Die Burger* of September 3 expressed concern over "the work of cunning people." In addition to spontaneity, a measure of organization was detectable in the riots, as was evident perhaps in the selectivity with which buildings were attacked but particularly in both the widespread locations of the demonstrations of Coloured high school students and the burden of what they were demonstrating about. The students were not only demonstrating for Coloured civil rights and against the separate institutions of apartheid, but they also claimed to be showing solidarity with Black Africans.

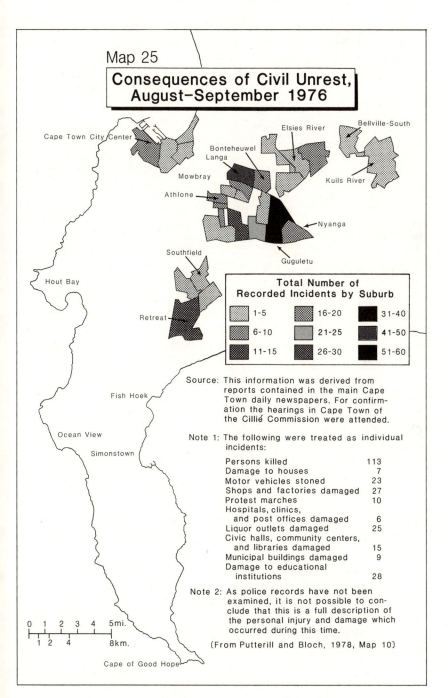

Map 25

Consequences of Civil Unrest, August–September 1976

Cape Town City Center

Elsies River

Bellville-South

Bonteheuwel
Langa

Mowbray

Kuils River

Athlone

Nyanga

Southfield

Guguletu

Hout Bay

Retreat

Total Number of Recorded Incidents by Suburb

1-5	16-20	31-40
6-10	21-25	41-50
11-15	26-30	51-60

Fish Hoek

Ocean View

Simonstown

Source: This information was derived from reports contained in the main Cape Town daily newspapers. For confirmation the hearings in Cape Town of the Cillié Commission were attended.

Note 1: The following were treated as individual incidents:

Persons killed	113
Damage to houses	7
Motor vehicles stoned	23
Shops and factories damaged	27
Protest marches	10
Hospitals, clinics, and post offices damaged	6
Liquor outlets damaged	25
Civic halls, community centers, and libraries damaged	15
Municipal buildings damaged	9
Damage to educational institutions	28

Note 2: As police records have not been examined, it is not possible to conclude that this is a full description of the personal injury and damage which occurred during this time.

(From Putterill and Bloch, 1978, Map 10)

0 1 2 3 4 5mi.
1 2 4 8km.

Cape of Good Hope

On 19 August students at Gordons High School, Somerset West [adjacent
to Cape Town] refused to go to classes after permission to hold a prayer
meeting in sympathy with the Blacks who had died, had been refused.
. . . On 23 August pupils at high schools in Bonteheuwel demonstrated
in sympathy with the students of Soweto and police were brought in to
disperse them (SAIRR, 1977, p. 72).

Coloured schoolchildren from Heideveld tried to march into Guguletu and Nyanga townships to show solidarity with the Black Africans there and were forcibly turned back by police at the only road
bridge (over the railway line that separates the Coloured and Black
African townships). The *Argus* (7 September 1976) reported that
"earlier today police opened fire with shotguns and service revolvers
into large groups of demonstrating Coloured youths . . . outside
the African township of Guguletu." And Stanley Uys, doyen of
political reporters from Cape Town, wrote in the *Guardian* (London
and Manchester) (2 September 1976):

> Today was the first time that Coloured pupils had linked up with Africans
> in a major display of solidarity. It was evident that the police have no real
> control over the Coloured and African townships around Cape Town,
> where they were able only to break up gatherings and restore order in
> trouble areas—until it all starts up again somewhere else.

> The pattern of unrest has become menacingly similar. Pupils gather at
> schools to demonstrate, the police arrive to disperse them with tear gas,
> the pupils retaliate by stoning the police and their vehicles, the police then
> make baton charges, parents protest and start shouting abuse at the police,
> and in no time the whole community is involved.

Such a situation had never been known before in Cape Town. Two
paradoxes should be considered: first, the Coloureds and the Black
Africans are removed from the city to a "safe" distance, thereby
losing their territorial roots and gaining only distanced space in the
sand dunes. Yet, some measure of spatial cohesion, of territorial
community (as Whisson observed of Belgravia during the rioting[7]),
may be being created again in the Cape Flats ghettos. Second, the
Coloureds and the Black Africans are spatially segregated from each
other, deliberately, by government group areas planners. Yet, young
Coloureds demonstrated for solidarity, redefining themselves as
Blacks to some degree. Eight years earlier, O'Toole (1973, p. 144)
reported about group areas:

> Although all the Coloureds consider this human removal humiliating at
> best and robbery at worst, there are some young militants who foresee

that the government's plan will backfire. "In Cape Town we thought of ourselves as Capetonians," a young man told me. "Whites lived in District Six and Woodstock, and Coloureds were scattered throughout the White neighborhoods. Now only Coloureds will be in one horrible slum. This will prove to my dense people once and for all where we stand in this country. The Sand Flats are natural breeding grounds for a revolution."

This I believe to be a very premature evaluation, but the two paradoxes nevertheless *do* seem to indicate that perhaps the manipulation of Cape Town's space by the government is not proceeding totally as planned.

Fear and the search for territorial safety are the bases of the contemporary pattern of Cape Town's space. The Whites have created group areas partially in an attempt to find security, which they associate with racial homogeneity of residential space. Most of the time, though not during the hours of darkness or during times of civil unrest, the Whites today feel themselves to be secure. This is not so for many Coloureds, for, even during the daylight hours during normal times of civil calm, many people living in the townships feel themselves to be at risk. To deal with this situation the Coloured inhabitants of the new Cape Flats housing estates need a measure of social cohesion.

The Mitigating Growth of a New Community Spirit?

Can the desired social cohesion be of the Mowbray kind: the warm, sentimental attachment to neighborhood and to neighbors who are often relatives—part of the image of a "natural" community? No—especially because of the short time elapsed since the townships' creation, their enormous scale compared with the Mowbray Nonwhite pockets, and their continual turnover in population (44 percent of the people I interviewed had moved again since they left Mowbray). A new kind of solidarity is needed, some conscious creation of a certain level of concerted action. One possibility is the creation of vigilantelike citizens' groups. To manage this, joint action among inhabitants is required, joint action that probably will eventually spill over into community goals other than defense. The following quotation concerns one of the newer council townships, where construction began on open ground in 1972 and whose name was fabricated in order to reassure its new inhabitants, many of them District Six removees, by reminding them of the name of their previous main street.

The 400 members of the Hanover Park Residents' Protection Union who call themselves the Peacemakers have proved that crime can never win if only people will get together and fight it. This time last year [mid-1974] the people of Hanover Park—which is in the middle of Athlone[8] —were living through a reign of terror. Assaults, robberies, car thefts, hooliganism, and gangs roaming the streets after dark made life intolerable. Husbands and fathers decided to act. They organized their own protection union and when they met in a classroom of a local school yesterday, Mr. Wilfred Schuter, vice-president of the union, said that crime and hooliganism in Hanover Park had been almost wiped out. He said that crime had been cut by 75% in the area. There were no more car thefts, their womenfolk could go out after dark without fear, and the gangs had been smashed, including the notorious "Mongrels" who had spread fear and alarm. [Mr. Schuter said] "We started by patrolling the streets three hours every night. But on Friday and Saturday nights our patrols are out all night from 8 pm to 5 am. All the men are volunteers . . . carrying a short baton . . . all family men . . . had the cooperation of the police.[9] . . ." They [the vigilantes] had their own badge and "uniform" [tracksuits]. . . . They planned to link up with other organizations in Manenberg, Heideveld, Bridgetown, and Lavender Hill.[10] . . . "This whole operation has done wonders for us. It has given us community spirit and has enabled people to get to know one another and take a greater interest in one another's welfare" (*Cape Times,* 26 May 1975).

Evidence of a growth of "community" in Hanover Park had been forthcoming before this report. The *Cape Times* (31 October 1974) reported that the (English-speaking) Churches' Urban Planning Commission organized a "Clean Up Hanover Park" antilitter campaign. Over 500 people participated and "a sense of belongingness was created in the area." A little earlier still (16 August 1974), the *Muslim News* editorialized:

Keep Hanover Park Dry. . . . That a bottle store [liquor outlet] is the last thing that the majority of the people are plumping for is evident by the protest raised by a band of women. . . . Hanover Park is most certainly not one of the more stable townships on the Cape Flats housing complex, and a bottle store with its availability of liquor can do nothing else but set the high crime rate soaring even further.

But such protests as this are reactive, not creative. Few things would have irked the *Muslim News* more than alcohol, and so one has no idea how large this reported "band of women" was. They protested the store, but the store was built; I assume that was the end of their organization, if such the "band" ever was. In a comparable situation, I attended a protest meeting in Manenberg in 1975 about increased bus fares; some locals let off steam, but the fares did not come down, a bus boycott was stillborn (in contrast to 1980; see my postscript), and no continuing organization resulted. The Peacemakers, however, went beyond mere reaction to negative stimuli, and they represent a concrete symptom of the growth of territorial community in the new estates, although Hanover Park is still plagued by crime.

Further indications of the new estates settling down have been shown in Table 15 in Chapter 8; new friends have been made out of unknown neighbors on the Cape Flats. To this can be added the information presented in Table 17, which shows that, of their "five best friends," over two-thirds of the households interviewed then had *more* new, post-Mowbray best friends than ex-Mowbray best friends. The implications of these figures are even greater when we realize that they are taken from a sample of 100, of whom 30 have lived in their present houses for only five years or less.

Table 17
Changing Composition of Best Friends after Removals

A Best Friend Who Had Lived in Mowbray	A *New* Best Friend	Number of Cases Reporting	Cumulative Percentage
0	and 5	18	19.1
1	and 4	25	45.1
2	and 3	21	68.1
3	and 2	14	83.0
4	and 1	3	86.1
5	and 0	13	100.0

It is unfortunate that the information in Table 17 on married couples was not differentiated (through my oversight) between husbands and wives. Husbands had some friends at work, while those wives who were not working (fifty-eight out of eighty-two: 70.7 percent) were much more involved in neighboring. For this reason, a dispute between Mr. and Mrs. Gierdien of Bonteheuwel arose as a result of their different commitment to the township. It was he who said that "as far as I'm concerned, Bonteheuwel's just a roof over my head"—he could not wait to get out to a respectable home-ownership estate. She, on the other hand, had cousins out in the country and was a woman of forceful character not prepared to be a mere housewife of the dependent Muslim variety. Her cousins brought in eggs, and vegetables and fruits in season, and she sold these in her immediate neighborhood in Bonteheuwel. She had all of her contacts set up, had dependable clients and suppliers. She said, "If we move, I'll have to start all over again." At the time of this conversation, they had been in Bonteheuwel a little over ten years.

Citing this example is not meant to imply that in general the men have no commitment to their new areas. They too have neighbors who have become friends. They may participate in vigilantelike associations, as in Hanover Park and Manenberg. Many of them spruce up the rather bare essentials the council presented them with in their township cottages. The concrete blocks may be disguised inside by wallpaper. Neatly painted white, wooden palings may replace the chain-link fences in the yard. A wooden porch may be added over the cottage's front door, although this has on occasion been construed as "unauthorized alteration of council property" and the porch officially torn off! Many people also care for their gardens. In Kew Town I was given a tour of the neat garden by a house-proud wife. At the front, an assorted flower garden and a tended grass lawn. In the back, there were oranges, figs, lemons, ginger, and chilies growing, plus eight chickens in their hutch and various decorative small plants growing in Nespray, Nesquick, Glenryck pilchards, and biscuit tins. The woman said, "You never see a piece of paper in front of our house. I clear it all up and burn it. . . . I want my front lawn and back yard to be as neat as the house inside—you can judge people by that, I say." This lady was concentrating purely on her own plot's appearance, but indirectly it could be claimed that her front flower garden was of communal worth to her corner of Kew Town. It is a constituent factor, however small, in the growth of pride in her new neighborhood.

Summary

Willmott (1967, p. 391) stated that, of those who had come to new public housing areas[11] in Britain,

> most people move for a house. In return, they often feel they have given up some qualities of their old life. . . . The main things that people "disliked" about their new environment or "missed" about their old were shopping, entertainment, or other amenities (mentioned by about half). The other main criticisms were of infrequent or expensive bus services (about a fifth or a quarter) and relatives or friends left behind (again about a quarter). With some people—wives more than husbands—the sense of loneliness is acute.

Certainly, there are parallels in the experiences of British residents moving to public housing with the experiences of ex-Mowbrayites who became home owners, but there is one important difference. Ex-Mowbrayites did not "move for a house." Very few of those in Britain of whom Willmott was writing could actually have been *forced* out of their original communities. *All* of those this study is concerned with were.

Marc Fried (1967, p. 98), who painstakingly controlled for all interlocking variables, concluded of the forced removees from Boston's West End:

> Hypothetically, relocation can be conceived as an opportunity for change, for greater assimilation, for social mobility. *However, the freedom to use these opportunities must first be achieved internally and become an aspect of the individual's adaptational potential* (Fried's italics).

In other words, for those who are ready for it psychologically, even the stress of enforced group areas removal can be turned to good account. Age is, of course, a highly significant factor, probably even more than postremoval residential status. When, like young Mr. Delport, removees are ready to make the transition that Young and Willmott (1962) called change from face-to-face relationships to those of window to window, they may well overcome the trauma of removal and only occasionally think of their past Mowbray with sentimentality. But, when they are old, they cannot start over, even when their housing has improved. All three of the elderly persons mentioned earlier who reportedly displayed the ultimate manifestations of grief for the lost Mowbray happened to have been home owners. So was an eighty-seven-year-old Muslim man from one of the "anchor families," whom the whole Dorp knew by his Mowbray nickname. In 1976, he lived in the lower Wynberg home-ownership area with his daughter and son-in-law's family. "I miss Mowbray," he said. "It was heartbreaking. I've forgotten—I choose not to go to Mowbray now." His grief did not permit him to say any more; he had not forgotten.

By far the greatest trauma of removal, general to all removees (and not just to the old), was fear. Fear did seem to lean more lightly on the home owners. The home-owning ex-Mowbrayites were more comparable to those who experienced "slum clearance" in Britain and the United States than the council renters, but their "opportunity for change, for greater assimilation, for social mobility" (per Fried) was definitely a circumscribed and segregated one. Certainly, there was great material advance, and their physical housing conditions did improve; but of assimilation there was none, and of social mobility only that which was permitted to occur within the flexible parameters of apartheid's system of control. (See Beinart, 1976.)

For the township renters the situation was worse. Most of those from relatively higher status Mowbray were probably not living after removal in physical housing measurably superior to what they occupied in Mowbray, as opposed to, say, a large proportion of District Six's removees. In fact, some ex-Mowbrayites in the townships were likely living in *less* acceptable housing. For all of them (perhaps excluding those seven households who had lived on Bruce Street), the nonmaterial surroundings in the townships were still far worse than in Mowbray, even though things had been improving somewhat with the passage of time.

Almost all removees lost an intangible quality of community when they left Mowbray and gained in return a climate of fear. And even though "times have changed everywhere," most ex-Mowbrayites believed, with reason, that "it's the moving that did it." The home owners found this loss at least partially outweighed by their material advance; nearly all the council renters did not. The renters were the real losers.

PART IV
PROSPECTS

CHAPTER TEN

The Shantytowns:
Trying to Keep the Lid On

Only last night it happened that about fifty of these natives wanted to put up their huts close to the banks of the moat of our fortress, and when told in a friendly manner by our men to go a little further away, they declared boldly that this was not our land but theirs and they would place their huts wherever they chose.

> Jan van Riebeeck's journal,
> Cape Town, 10 February 1655

The Government is beaten, because even the Government of England could not stop the people from squatting. The Government was like a man who has a cornfield which is invaded by birds. He chases the birds from one part of the field and they alight in another part of the field. . . . We squatters are the birds. The Government sends the policemen to chase us away and we move off and occupy another spot. We shall see whether it is the farmer or the birds who get tired first.

> Oriel Monongoaha,
> squatter leader,
> Johannesburg, 1947

OBSTACLES TO APARTHEID

The enormous efforts being made by the South African government to manipulate space and resettle people (in order to secure their kind of apartheid city) have encountered obstacles. One obstacle has been civil unrest, which in part has surely been engendered by the bitterness of the Coloured Capetonians at their removal; that is, the unrest, paradoxically, has been engendered by this very manipulation of space. The lid was kept on the Cape unrest only by a large-scale exercise of force, which depended on riot police flown to the area from other provinces of South Africa. Even then, as Stanley Uys noted, suppression was imperfect: the flames were controlled, but the smoldering has continued.

Another challenge to the structured features of the apartheid city, features that the government has worked so hard to build, is the existence of unplanned "spontaneous settlements," or squatter shantytowns. In 1977, between one-fifth and one-quarter of all the inhabitants of greater Cape Town were living in such areas. The settlements' peripheral distribution around the metropolis (that is, at a "safe" distance from the White core of the city) does not mean that they are not a threat or a problem. First, they are frequently contraventions of the Group Areas Act and other acts, in that they occupy land not set aside for "their" (Black African, Coloured[1]) official population groups. Greater Cape Town squatter shanties during the late 1970s were built on land zoned for Whites, for Coloureds, for Indians, for Black Africans, for industrial purposes, for border strips, and on unproclaimed land. Second, there is the perceived nature of the squatter camps and their inhabitants (not just their noncompliant geographical distribution). The government views them as a problem and, indeed, and "evil"[2] to be eradicated so that the lid can be kept on the regimented apartheid city.

There have probably been *pondoks* around Cape Town throughout this century. The immediate cause of their existence has been, naturally, a shortage of housing. The overarching reason for the shortage has been the political dispensation in South Africa during this same period. It is not surprising that the shortage of housing has been much greater for those who are not White, that is, those who are poor and so cannot purchase their own homes and those who have not had access to decision-making power over the allocation of government revenues for housing.   Although during the interwar depression some poor Whites built and lived in simple wood-and-iron shanties, a survey of the well over 200,000 shanty dwellers in the Cape Town metropolitan area today would turn up no Whites. Indeed, in October 1977 the Cape Town Metropolitan Planning Committee reported that there was an *oversupply* of residential plots for Whites and that 38,000 of these plots were vacant. However, in April 1977, Ellis, Hendrie, Kooy, and Maree estimated there were in the metropolis at least 120,000 and probably 180,000 Coloured squatters and about 51,000 Black African squatters. (The total metropolitan population of Cape Town in 1977 was about 1,100,000.) Map 26 shows the approximate spatial distribution of these settlements in 1976-1977.

Even in the difficult-to-administer "illegal" squatter situation, apartheid's distinction between Coloureds and Black Africans renders the experiences of the two groups at the hands of the law somewhat different. Until about April 1975, the settlements shown on Map 26 nearly all were characterized by various degrees of mixing between Black Africans and Coloureds. At that time, however, under the Divisional Council's prodding, Black Africans throughout the Cape Peninsula were urged to quit the camps where they were living among Coloured people and move to Crossroads. This, many did: Crossroads became an almost wholly Black African squatter camp as, to a lesser extent, did Modderdam, Unibell, and Werkgenot. (See Map 26). Nevertheless, some Black Africans have continued to live in numerous predominantly Coloured shantytowns. The government's policy toward these Coloured shantytowns can be generally characterized as one of containment; toward Black African shantytowns the policy is more one of expunction.

COLOURED SQUATTERS:
THE ATTEMPT AT CONTAINMENT

Of all the Coloureds in South Africa today 30 percent live on the Cape Peninsula; about a quarter of these people are squatters (Figure 41). In addition to the Coloureds' lack of political power, there are other causes for the discrepancy between housing provision and housing demand. These are: (1) the rapid rate of natural increase of the peninsula's Coloured population; (2) the continuing rural-urban migration to the peninsula; (3) the replacement of older, degenerated housing; and (4) the removals of Coloureds from housing during group areas enforcement. This fourth factor overlaps with the third in some areas—for example, in District Six; but it does not do so in other areas—for example, in Harfield and in most of Mowbray—where much of the ex-Nonwhite housing was and is sound.

The University of South Africa has estimated that the average growth rate of the Coloured population during the decade 1960-1970 was 3.29 percent per annum and that it fell during the 1970-1977 period to 2.35 percent per annum. The more recent estimate is still a relatively high figure—higher than the Whites' rate of increase both at present and during the 1960s—and it implies a doubling time of only twenty-nine years, were the rate to remain constant. Ellis and associates (1977) have calculated that between 3,300 and

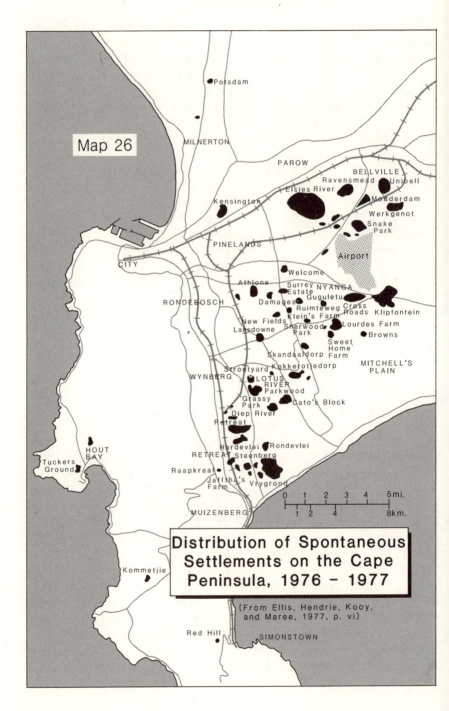

Map 26

MILNERTON

Potsdam

PAROW

BELLVILLE

Ravensmead Unibell

Elsies River

Kensington Modderdam

Werkgenot

Snake
Park

PINELANDS

Airport

CITY

Welcome

Athlone Surrey NYANGA
Estate

RONDEBOSCH Guguletu

Damages Ruimteweg Cross
Klein's Farm Roads Klipfontein

New Fields Sherwood Lourdes Farm
Lansdowne Park

Sweet Browns
Home
Farm

Skandaaldorp MITCHELL'S
PLAIN

Stroptyard Kokkerotjedorp

WYNBERG LOTUS
RIVER
Parkwood

Grassy Cato's Block
Park

Diep River

Retreat

HOUT Hardevlei Rondevlei
BAY RETREAT Steenberg

Tuckers Raapkraal
Ground

Jaffha's Vrygrond
Farm

0 1 2 3 4 5mi.

1 2 4 8km.

MUIZENBERG

Distribution of Spontaneous Settlements on the Cape Peninsula, 1976 – 1977

Kommetjie

(From Ellis, Hendrie, Kooy, and Maree, 1977, p. vi)

Red Hill SIMONSTOWN

Figure 41. Sunday Morning Checkers and Haircutting in Skandaaldorp, 1976.
This is a mainly Coloured shantytown on the southeastern perimeter of
Cape Town. (Photograph used by permission of G. Ellis, UPRU.)

4,300 new dwelling units were needed in the peninsula during the
1970-1980 period in order to meet the natural increase of the Coloured
population there. (The latest figures available for housing on the peninsula, from the March 1980 publication of the South African Institute
of Race Relations [SAIRR] *Survey 1979,* are for the year 1978.)

The immigration of Coloureds to the peninsula is of less overall
importance than the natural increase of those already living there.
Ellis and associates (1977) estimated that this immigration engenders
a demand for between 600 and 800 housing units per annum. The
move by Coloureds from the western Cape's rural areas (the *platteland*) to Cape Town, the closest large city, is a response to economic
pressures. In the *platteland,* the majority of Coloureds are wage
laborers, working on the farms where their ancestors worked as
slaves. As agricultural mechanization proceeded during the 1960-
1970 period, it has been calculated that, in the thirty-six administrative districts surrounding Cape Town, between 30,000 and 40,000
Coloured people were made redundant (Ellis et al., 1977). Further
mechanization continues today. Also, the wages are higher and work-

ing conditions are more attractive in Cape Town. If unhindered, rural Coloureds will continue to be drawn to the peninsula.

I have few figures for the clearance of old, substandard housing per se (as under the Slums Act) in greater Cape Town. Summing the 1971 through 1974 figures from the annual reports of the city's medical officer of health, I have found that a total of only 942 dwellings were demolished or recommended for demolition in the area controlled by the city council because they were considered substandard. This small figure—only 235 dwellings per year in a city the size of Cape Town—is a misleading indicator of the loss of housing to Coloured people. Slum clearance is confounded with the operation of the Group Areas Act, whereby much more housing is lost to Coloureds. Indeed, the city's medical officer of health himself wrote in his report for 1967:

> Since the Slums Amendment Act No. 55 of 1963 was promulgated I have been under pressure by the Department of Community Development to institute proceedings before the Slums Clearance Court in respect of a considerable number of residential properties in various parts of the Municipal area.
>
> After receiving reports from my Health Inspectoral Branch and by personal inspection, I satisfied myself that the primary object of such requests was the implementation of the removal of 527 persons in terms of the Group Areas Act.
>
> With the acute shortage of non-White housing, I have consistently refused to add to the burden of indiscriminately submitting reports to the Slums Clearance Court.
>
> However, during 1967, 21 properties . . . were reported to the Slums Court and were declared as Slums by that body. . . . The demolition of these units and the re-housing of tenants was not completed at the end of 1967.

When it removes persons from their homes under the Group Areas Act, the government attempts to have "alternative accommodation" ready for them, as was categorically prescribed by the minister of community development in 1962. Although there have been exceptions (see the *Argus,* 6 November 1975), this policy apparently has been followed. Hence, the minister's rather self-satisfied contention, which was reported in the *South African Digest* on 25 March 1977 under the heading "More Humane":

> The Department of Community Development used the Group Areas Act to relieve suffering and to resettle slum-dwellers in humane conditions, the

Minister of Community Development, Mr. Marais Steyn, said in the Senate.

Speaking on a private member's motion on slum clearance, Mr. Steyn said he preferred to use the Group Areas Act rather than the anti-slum laws because the Act placed a legal responsibility on the Government to provide alternative housing.

"The policy of my department is to act with the greatest compassion and full awareness of human dignity and the needs of the individual," he said.

By 1976, group areas removals were over three-quarters completed, as Table 4 showed. Thus, it can be anticipated that a declining proportion of new public housing is being set aside as the "alternative accommodation" for removees. In 1974, the minister of community development stated that 80 percent of all newly completed units were occupied for group areas removees, whereas in 1975 only 50 percent of new housing units built by local authorities were.[3] One such "50 percent" area in the Cape Town City Council's rental schemes in Kalksteenfontein, part of Bonteheuwel; Figure 36, photographed in 1975, shows a Valley removee living in Kalksteenfontein. Keeping in mind the figures just cited, note that from 1971 to 1974 the Cape Town City Council constructed 7,160 dwellings but only 3,581 of these were added to the housing stock because 3,579 were used by the Department of Community Development for resettlement of group areas removees.

In 1976, however, as Maasdorp and Pillay (1977, p. 174) have explained,

> In order to speed up the rehousing of squatters, the proportion allocated to group areas relocation was cut to 25 per cent although the Department of Community Development was apparently entitled to utilise 37.5 per cent of new dwelling units for this purpose. According to the Minister, however, the Department actually utilised only 19.6 per cent of all houses built by local authorities in 1976 for relocation. Of this 19.6 per cent, 93.3 per cent was allocated to squatters and slum dwellers and only 6.7 per cent to Group Areas Act resettlement. In other words, of all houses built by local authorities in 1976, only 1.3 per cent were allocated for group areas relocation.

Slightly different figures given in the SAIRR's *Survey 1976* confirm this general downward trend. Although there were still, at the beginning of 1977, about 8,000 Coloured families in Cape Town awaiting ejection from their homes by group areas enforcement, the government since the mid-1970s has considered the rehousing of Coloured squatters a greater priority. Thus, in 1975, only 289 Coloured families in the Cape Peninsula were rehoused because of group areas removals. Eventually, after having completed 80 percent of its planned group areas removals and being more concerned about the threat to White urban security that it perceives in the squatters and perhaps being prepared to make some tactical concessions to Coloureds in the wake of the 1976 rioting, the government may call a halt to some of the projected removals. During the late 1970s, actions affecting Salt River (anomalous area E, p. 111) and the modification and partial freezing of the Somerset West-Sir Lowry's Pass Village removals (about 25 kilometers southeast of the city's present edge) suggested such a change in priorities.

So far in this discussion, I have assumed that squatters will have to be reaccommodated in public housing for a number of reasons. First, the idea of squatters gradually "upgrading" their shanties in situ, as Andrew and Japha (1978) have shown to be both feasible and economical, seems to have been rejected by the government. (This despite the fact that in a number of locales on the Cape Flats, such as Gleemoor and Lotus River, such a process has been successfully occurring since 1927 and 1967, respectively.) Second, most Coloured squatters are poor and do not have the means to become home owners as yet, if ever. In 1975, of the squatters in the area controlled by the Cape Town City Council, 76.5 percent (of households) earned less than R160 per month (with *all* wage earners in the household included), 61 percent less than R120 per month, and 30 percent less than R80 per month. Third, bodies other than public housing authorities, such as the Citizens' Housing League and the Cape Flats Distress Association (CAFDA), that in the past have provided some low-income housing for Coloureds seem to have been squeezed out by government regulation (Ellis et al., 1977). Also, industry and employers have during the 1970s shown almost no interest in providing low-income housing for Coloureds.[4] Thus, such housing is almost totally public.

During the 1970s, the public sector did not produce enough housing units to meet the demand. Provision fluctuated greatly, and delivery did not measure up to official projections. Maree (1978) characterized the government's policy for Coloured housing as "stop-go." For example, in November 1972 Prof. S. P. Cilliers estimated that there was a shortage on the Cape Peninsula of at least 54,908 dewllings to house 314,623 Coloured people. In 1977 the same scholar showed, *using official figures,* that there had been *no change* in the backlog since 1972, despite a major building program.

Again, on 14 August 1971 the *Cape Times* quoted the then minister of community development, Blaar Coetzee, as saying that during the next three-year period 20,000 houses were to be built in the Cape Town metropolitan region. In fact, over that period the Cape Town City Council and the Divisional Council between them averaged only 3,000 per year, giving a total of slightly over 9,000 units and a shortfall for that period of 11,000 houses on the minister's 1971 estimate (Andrew and Japha, 1978). Another striking example of this was provided in 1976, when at the beginning of March the minister of community development announced that

> we are now building houses for the Coloured people at the rate of 13,000 to 14,000 a year and this is double the natural increase of the Coloured population of the country. We will have caught up the backlog in eight years from now and then there will be no more crises.

In 1976 there was a cutback in government funding (the economy was deep in a recession) and, as an example, in the Mitchell's Plain project, "the actual output for the year was 975 houses instead of [the anticipated] 6,000. Renewed funds made available later in 1976 have enabled the crash housing programme to be resumed." However, Ellis and associates, who wrote the previous sentence in April 1977 (p. 29), by now will have found that this "crash housing programme" once again did not live up to expectations. Official figures published in 1978 show that of the 4,960 dwelling units that were projected for Mitchell's Plain in 1977, only 2,139 were completed by September of that year. And, although the minister had claimed in March 1976 that the government would build between 13,000 and 14,000 dwellings each year, the 1977 total was only 10,231. The 1978 figure showed a tremendous improvement: 23,406 units.

Nevertheless, the overall impression is one of shortfalls or of dramatic fluctuations—unreliability in provision. And all the time these shortfalls were occurring, overcrowding in the existing housing estates continued unmitigated, physically forcing people out of the rental schemes and into shanty accommodations. Ellis and associates (1977) estimated that *the dwellings in the council schemes house about half again as many persons as they were planned to accommodate* (and they were not planned to be particularly spacious in the first place). They supported this contention with a veritable battery of figures from numerous sources, official, academic, and investigative, including CAFDA, NICRO (National Institute for Crime Prevention and Rehabilitation of Offenders, Cape Town), and BABS (Build a Better Society, Athlone). They also cited numerous statistics, with which I will not assault the reader. In an earlier survey, Mabin (1968) had found that already in Heideveld, which was at the most only four years old at the time of his research, 32 percent of the houses were overcrowded according to the national housing standards. Whisson and Kahn (1969, p. 27) observed that "managers in older estates suggested that this [32 percent] was not a particularly high figure and that a blind eye must occasionally be turned in the absence of any alternative accommodation for the excess tenants and family members." (Recall, however, Mrs. Ziervogel's [p. 259] indignation at her home being investigated for overcrowding.)

The minister of community development estimated that in all of Cape Province for 1978 12,519 dwellings would be constructed; most creditably, 19,770 units were in fact made available during that year, 13,170 of them in greater Cape Town. Nevertheless, his estimate of the housing shortage for Coloured people in Cape Province at the beginning of 1978 was 45,000 dwellings, 34,500 of which were on the Cape Peninsula.[5] Not only is this last figure lower than the "optimistic" (their adjective) estimate of Ellis and associates (1977) — 36,000 — and much lower than that of Cilliers (1977) — up to 55,000 — or that of the Cape Town Metropolitan Planning Committee — 60,000 — but also there is frequently a discrepancy between the announced official goals and the reality achieved during a year's housing construction. Thus, I am inclined to give credence to Ellis and associates when they said in April 1977 (p. 35) that, "unless the crash housing programme is substantially changed in character and magnitude, the coloured housing backlog will be with us for well over a decade." This backlog's direct result is an immensely long waiting list for council housing and severe overcrowding in the townships, which in turn directly results in a spillover into shantytowns. That overcrowding is a far more important cause of the shantytowns than any great rural-urban migration of Coloureds can be seen from the fact that *The Theron Commission Report* (1976) found that 75 percent of the peninsula's squatters were from Cape Town itself.

Those who find themselves forced to live in shanties are not those with some penchant for slum dwelling or predisposition to petty crime as most Whites commonly believe and — judging from official pronouncements — as the government does. From a survey of 3,794 squatter families conducted in sixteen settlements in 1975, it seems that most heads of household in squatter families are responsible workers and not shiftless layabouts. Not only was the employment rate of economically active adults 79 percent, but 82 percent of household heads also had worked on the same job for longer than one year; of these 58 percent had worked for longer than two years,

48 percent for longer than three years, 27 percent for longer than five years, and 9 percent for at least ten years.

The government's policy toward Coloured squatters has been one of unenthusiastic acceptance, or containment. That is to say, on 15 November 1974 the squatter population was "frozen" and all *pondoks* extant at that time were diligently enumerated—with numbers officially painted on their sides—and measured (to prevent subsequent additions to accommodate more inhabitants). These shanties have been allowed to remain; any new constructions have been demolished, without any alternative accommodation being provided for those rendered homeless. Such demolition, especially when bulldozers were used and during the rainy winter months of July and August, has become an emotional issue of high visibility in Cape Town since 1976-1977.[6] As further measures of control, the government also, during the 1976 and 1977 parliamentary sessions, gave itself more comprehensive and draconian powers under the Prevention of Illegal Squatting Acts, whose provisions we shall look at below.

BLACK AFRICAN SQUATTERS:
THE ATTEMPT AT EXPUNCTION

The Crossroads squatters' camp is not a unique case and not just another shantytown to be reported upon empirically. Its existence highlights the nature of grand apartheid in the Republic of South Africa. Also, Crossroads represents all of the peripheral Black African shantytowns that have been an important facet of Cape Town's social geography. One of the foundations of the contemporary political economy of the Republic of South Africa is the Whites' strict control of a cheap Black African labor force, which outnumbers the Whites four to one. It is around this factor that the discussion of the case of Crossroads and the other Black African shantytowns outside Cape Town will revolve.

Areas of dense Black African settlement were incorporated into the developing South African economic system during the nineteenth century. The eroded resource bases of these "native reserves" have progressively fallen behind in providing subsistence for an increasing population. Black Africans, therefore, had to sell their labor to the Whites in the burgeoning industrial nodes of the diamondfields and goldfields and in ports such as Durban and Cape Town. This continuing Black African urbanization, however, has meant that the Whites, who brought modern industrialism to southern Africa and who first established the cities, are increasingly being outnumbered in the cities by Black Africans. Black African labor is needed, but otherwise their presence is not wanted. How can this dilemma be "solved"?

A purported answer to the White government's "Black problem" is the institution of the homelands policy and migrant labor. These try to ensure, through the imposition of the Pass Laws, that the stream of Black African workers to the cities includes only male migrants who return to their homeland (formerly native reserve) each year. Their families are left behind in the homelands, thus lessening the numbers—the physical presence—of Black Africans in the "White cities." This migrant system also, supposedly, lessens the undesirable (to Whites) permanency of Black African labor in the "White cities." Furthermore, the migrant system also seems to promise a lessening of the urban Black African's political presence. The system offers a supposed (but shaky) base for the White government's attempts to justify the denial of franchise rights to the Black Africans in the urban areas of South Africa. Instead, a Black African's voting rights are to be exercised "at home." And "home" for Black African contract workers is not to be in the "White cities," where they spend at least eleven months of the year, but where their wives and children are. And the families of these workers are forced by the Pass Laws to remain in the rural homeland. There are in Cape Town other complicating factors, but, basically, the Black African squatters of Crossroads are living *as families* illegally in terms of the Pass Laws. Therefore, they directly challenge Afrikaner Nationalist government authority and policy. From this challenge comes the extreme disinclination of the South African government to permit Crossroads and other such Black African shantytowns to remain.

It is said that there are a handful of Coloured inhabitants among the approximately 20,000 people in the 3,038 shanties in Crossroads, but the settlement can be taken to be 99.9 percent Black African. What, then, is the position of Black Africans in Cape Town?

Today, 96 percent of those approximately 120,000 Black Africans officially enumerated in the Cape Peninsula are Xhosa. The government has estimated that there are another 90,000 "illegal" Black Africans in the area. Thus, there may be as many as 210,000 Black Africans in the metropolis. Initially, the Xhosa or their forebears came from the Cape border regions, over 800 kilometers to the east of Cape Town, where the Ciskei and Transkei homelands are now established. After a century of conflict, the final subjugation of the Xhosa and the collapse of their economy during the third quarter of the nineteenth century left them with little means of subsistence but their labor. This, many sold in Cape Town, and the pattern has persisted.

Numerous studies have established the feeble economy of the Ciskei and Transkei and have demonstrated how the abased quality of life there is a "push factor" in propelling Xhosa workers toward the cities. For example, Graaff and Maree's (1977) random sample of 211 legal Black African Cape Town workers in 1975-1976 showed that, of those with dependents in the Ciskei and Transkei, 40 percent owned no land whatsoever and more than 50 percent owned neither cattle nor sheep. A quarter of their homeland families *had no subsistence income at all* and relied wholly on remittances from the men's wage labor. And *none* of these homeland families, without the remittances, had enough income from subsistence agriculture even to reach the poverty datum line.[7] Another Transkei survey (Leeuwenberg, 1974) showed that 67 percent of the 757 households studied were never able to produce enough crops to feed themselves; another 24 percent had adequate crops only during good years. In one Transkei district, half the children were found to go through a period of severe undernutrition. In the Tsolo district of the Transkei, 12 percent of the children were found by Westcott and Stott (1976) to be suffering from malnutrition (as clinically defined by the Shakir strip method), whereas in Crossroads about a year later the same method revealed that only 1.9 percent of the children were malnourished (White, 1978). Most significant, a comparative study in 1977 of 800 mothers in the Transkei and in the Cape Town Black African settlement of Guguletu showed that 25 percent of all babies born alive in the rural group died during their first year but only 10 percent died in the Cape Town group (Knudzen and Bourne, 1977).

It is obvious that it is necessary for their *survival* that the Xhosa find nonagricultural income somewhere. They can look for wage employment in their homeland, say at Butterworth in the Transkei or at Dimbaza in the Ciskei, or they can seek it in nearby East London, a node for the "border industries" scheme. But it can be easily demonstrated that the number of employment opportunities in or adjoining the homelands is risible when compared with the demand for jobs. There is chronic unemployment in the homelands, and such growth in the number of jobs as occurs in these areas makes virtually no impact.[8] The Ciskei and Transkei cannot support their populations. In this way "pushed"—and "pulled" by the attraction of higher wages in the distant big city—Black African workers have gravitated toward Cape Town.

Their migration to Cape Town has not been unimpeded, however. Unlike the Coloureds, who since the Cape Colony Ordinance 50 of 1828 and the emancipation of the slaves in 1834 have been free to move throughout the land,[9] Black Africans must carry passes. In order to leave their homelands, they must have government permission, for they are traveling into what, according to the Pass Laws, is a de jure foreign country, "White South Africa." In coming to work in the cities of this country, Black Africans are to be made aware of the official policy that "the native should only be allowed to enter the urban areas, which are essentially the white man's creation, when he is willing to enter and to minister to the needs of the white man and should depart therefrom when he ceases so to minister."

This crisp enunciation of intent was made in 1921 by government commissioner Colonel Stallard.[10] In 1923, policies that were to implement this intention were foreshadowed in the Urban Areas Act, which gave (White) local authorities the power to segregate Black Africans into separate townships, and to deport those who were habitually unemployed or otherwise undesirable. The 1937 Native Laws Amendment Act tightened the regulations considerably in order to control the influx of Black Africans to the cities. A man then had only fourteen days in the "White city" to find work; if he found no work, he had to return home. A 1952 amendment reduced this limit to three days[11] and stated just which Black Africans had the permanent right to live in the prescribed White areas, which comprise over 86 percent of the total area of South Africa.

Section 10(1) of the Urban Areas Act as amended—the Pass Law—reads:

No Bantu shall remain for more than 72 hours in a prescribed area unless he produces proof in the manner prescribed [that is, a pass] that—

   (a)   he has, since birth, resided continuously in such area; or

   (b)   he has worked continuously in such area for one employer for a period of not less than ten years or has lawfully resided continuously in such area for a period of not less than fifteen years and has thereafter continued to reside in such area and is not employed outside such area and has not during either period or thereafter been sentenced to a fine exceeding one hundred rand or to imprisonment for a period exceeding six months; or

   (c)   such a Bantu is the wife, unmarried daughter or son . . . [being a minor] . . . of any Bantu mentioned in paragraphs (a) or (b) of this sub-section and *after lawful entry* [my emphasis] into such prescribed area, ordinarily resides with that Bantu in such area.

These are the circumscribed terms on which Black Africans are allowed to live in the cities of South Africa. Stallard's statement expresses the government's current policy on "influx control." In

August 1976, the minister of Bantu administration and development stated that the only reason for which Black Africans were permitted in "White areas" was to sell their labor. Indeed, their legal hold on permanent city residence has been eroded still further with the "independence" of the Transkei, Bophuthatswana, and Venda. Since these territories were accorded "independence" (in 1976, 1977, and 1979, respectively), all Black Africans whose origins go back to those homelands (even when they are third-generation city born) may officially be considered "foreigners" in "White South Africa."

A total of 381,858 Black Africans were prosecuted under the Pass Laws during the year 1975-1976. A very rough estimate would be that 1 in every 25 Black Africans in "White South Africa" was prosecuted. Furthermore, Black Africans working in Cape Town in particular have also been restricted by the establishment of the Coloured Labour Preference Area.

Those people who today are classified as Coloured persons had their origins and are still spatially concentrated in the western Cape. The government has attempted to perpetuate this pattern by giving automatic preference, since the 1960s, to Coloured people seeking work in that area. West of the officially delineated Eiselen Line,[12] which runs north from the coast near Port Elizabeth, any Black African—even when he or she is legally in the western Cape and even when classified a "borner" under subsection 10(1)(a)—cannot strictly speaking accept any job unless the prospective employer obtains a certificate from the Coloured Labour Department to the effect that there is no Coloured worker available to take the job.

The government's goal has not merely been containment, or freezing, of numbers but in fact diminution of the Black African presence in the western Cape; there are "too many" Black Africans there. In 1966 a policy of reducing their number by five percent per annum was announced. It has not proved capable of implementation. Ineluctable economic forces—a growing demand for labor and the poverty of the homelands—have actually increased the number of contract laborers in Cape Town. Maree in February 1978 reported Francis Wilson's finding that, even after three years of severe recession, there were still twice as many Black African laborers in Cape Town as there were in 1968.[13]

In the year 1968 another regulation was introduced, which made *all* Black African workers in Cape Town one-year contract laborers from that date. That is to say, even when a man spends forty-eight or forty-nine weeks in a year at his job in Cape Town, takes his annual vacation, and then returns to the same place of employment for another full year, his periods of employment cannot be summed; one plus one is not considered by the government to equal two. This prevents any more Black Africans from gaining subsection 10(1)(b) rights. In fact, the latest any Black African man now holding such rights could have come to Cape Town is the year 1959. Only such persons, and borners under subsection 10(1)(a), have permanent residence status in Cape Town.

Women and children must qualify *in their own right* under these two subsections. A husband who has qualified under subsection 10(1)(a) or 10(1)(b) is not permitted to bring in his family under subsection 10(1)(c) provisions, for subsection 10(1)(c) states that they may reside with him only "after lawful entry." Now, throughout the prescribed "White urban areas" of South Africa the central government's Bantu Affairs Board (now renamed Plural Relations) owns all the land on which Black African housing can be erected legally. Thus, the government oversees all legal accommodations for Black Africans in Cape Town. From this position of monopoly, it can simply refuse to provide any *family* housing in the townships. Therefore, "lawful entry" to families is refused. At the end of 1975, there was already a shortage of 1,440 *lawful* dwellings for Black African families in Cape Town (Granelli, 1977). Despite this fact and despite the natural increase in the number of Black Africans legally living in Cape Town, no new family housing whatsoever was provided from 1972 until the last year of the decade. Official housing ratios indicate that 79 percent of all Black African workers legally living in Cape Town are meant to be there *without* their families. Furthermore, particularly after Transkeian "independence," the possibility has been debated of officially declaring all the Xhosa living in Cape Town, for however long, to be "temporary residents."

There are two further elements in this draconian freeze policy especially directed against families. First, in 1975 a decision to relax restrictions a little on Black African permanent urban residency was made by the central government. Black Africans were to be allowed to buy their homes from the government on a thirty-year leasehold. However, the Cape branch of the National party was against this being allowed west of the Eiselen Line, and so in February 1976 it was announced that home ownership would not be permitted in the Cape area at all. In August 1978 the Cape leader of the National party, Minister of Defense P. W. Botha—who the following month became prime minister—persuaded the party's congress that this policy should be continued and that the western Cape should be strengthened and "protected" as a White and Coloured labor-preference area (*Cape Times*, 23 August 1978).

Second, in September through November 1979, the government granted a "precrackdown" grace period during which "illegal" Black African workers in the cities were permitted to regularize their status by registration, which many tens of thousands did. The provisions of subsection 10(1)(b) were, for this three-month period, relaxed; those who had worked illegally either for one employer for one full year or for more than one employer in any one district for three years would be permitted to gain legal urban residence rights.[14] *However, the western Cape was totally exempted from these concessions.*

These geographically discriminatory policies are symptomatic of an attempt to divide and rule Nonwhite South Africans by offering the Coloureds a superior place separate from the Black Africans, especially since Coloured loyalty to the Whites cannot now be automatically counted upon as it once was. Before the 1976 Cape riots, the situation was seen by most Whites in the way that Adam Small almost parodied it in 1971 (p. 24):

> We Coloureds, we have been on the side of the Whites for so long. I remember one history book which says, "At the time of Sharpeville, the casualties on the side of the Blacks were so many, I don't know how many, and on the side of the Whites it was one Coloured." This was true.

The Sharpeville shootings (in which sixty-nine Black Africans were killed) occurred in 1960. During the unrest sixteen years later, by contrast, many Coloured youths demonstrated for solidarity with Black Africans.

In addition, it could be speculated that there is the subconscious feeling that, if worse came to worst for South Africa's Whites, the western Cape might be a Masada, the last redoubt after a partition of the present republic. There they would not be outnumbered by Black Africans, who must in the meantime be kept out if at all possible. In the *Los Angeles Times* of 15 August 1977, we read:

> Another black [Black African] squatter village is scheduled for destruction this week and, in all, the influx-control program is expected to displace about 26,000 black squatters. . . . A government official said that black growth in Cape Town "is disturbing to our race ratio, and the freeze on blacks is to keep the Coloureds happy."

This last assertion is without foundation if we believe the government's *The Theron Commission Report* (1976), which found that the majority of Coloured people did *not* agree that the Coloured people had to be protected against Black African encroachment. Not only is the assertion false and not only is it trying to shift the responsibility for demolition partially from the White government's shoulders, it also has the goal of adding to the Black Africans' resentment of Coloureds, a resentment that certainly exists. Such resentment is functional in the maintenance of White hegemony over internally divided subjects.

From such governmental concerns stem regulations that mold the daily lives of Black Africans in Cape Town. The regulations' stringency is reflected in the fact that 44 percent of all those Black Africans living in Cape Town were in mid-1975 estimated by a government minister[15] to be "illegals." Many of these people were the wives and children of the men working in Cape Town. When a woman is arrested and found guilty, under section 10(4), of being in the area illegally, she may be put on a train within two weeks and shipped back to her homeland. Additionally, husbands in such situations have been found guilty of "illegally harbouring" their own wives and have been *fined*. A man working in Cape Town described the texture of lives lived under the conditions that the Pass Laws impose:

> A wife is important to each husband; the enforced separation can lead to adultery.[16] This means that the life of a migrant is not the life of healthy, normal people.[17] All this means that migrant labour and a jail term, as far as our conditions are concerned, are not very different—for even in our residence [barracks] we can hardly sleep because of the relentless raids by the police. All this means therefore that the day you are fortunate enough to get a contract, your life as a convict has begun.[18]

Now the significance of Crossroads is becoming obvious. The macroscale economic forces bringing Black Africans to Cape Town, the political forces creating a housing shortage and overcrowding, and the official "illegality" of work seekers and of most family life, all engender situations to which squatting appears to be a logical response. Consider three such situations.

First, when a Black African is working for a Cape Town employer who has already used up his or her official quota of permitted Black African labor (unrestricted White or Coloured labor is more costly), then the Black African's employment is against the law. In March 1976, for example, 224 Cape Town employers were convicted of having illegal employees. In such cases, the employer is fined and the worker may be expelled from the area, or "endorsed out." To avoid this, would it not make sense for the Black African to live illegally in a shanty on the sandy scrubland of the Cape Flats outside Cape Town? He is less likely to be caught there than if he stayed illegally in the barracks or the cottages of the official Black African townships of

Langa, Nyanga, and Guguletu, which are frequently raided by the police. Such raids resulted in more than 16,000 Black Africans being tried under the Pass Laws in the Langa Bantu Administration Commissioner's Court during 1976.

Second, the man is one of the approximately 4,000 officially unemployed Black Africans who were retrenched from Cape Town jobs during the recession (by August 1978). Without subsection 10(1)(a) or 10(1)(b) rights and if he looks for work in Cape Town for longer than seventy-two hours, he is an "illegal." Again and for the same reasons, he squats.

The third situation is the one faced by by far the largest single category of Crossroaders. A man legally working and living in the Cape Town area wants his "illegal" wife and children with him. He could leave and look for work, and he would be very fortunate to find it, in the Ciskei or Transkei, where the family could all live together legally. Or he could resign himself to seeing them for only one month a year, if he stays in Cape Town alone as a migrant contract laborer. Or he could have them live with him in Cape Town illegally. That this last course has been the one most frequently chosen for a long time is indicated by the fact that by 1977 the average length of time women in Crossroads had been in the Cape Town area was twelve years. Of Crossroads women 90.7 percent are "illegals." However, Crossroads has been in existence only since February 1975; therefore, most of these women must have been living illegally in Cape Town—in the townships or in live-in servants' quarters—dreading a pass raid for an average of *over nine years.* For a family, as for a single man, squatting on land not administered by the government's Bantu Affairs Board, as Crossroads is not, seems a little more secure than living inside the townships.

Indeed, when Crossroads first took shape, the people there called it Mgababa, which means loosely "where we are free of regulations." Recall that the Bantu Affairs Board, committed to a policy of reducing the number of Black Africans in the western Cape, is the only land owner in the Black African townships. Crossroads is on land not owned by the Bantu Affairs Board and is therefore in some measure under the local authority (Divisional Council) jurisdiction. Furthermore, many Crossroaders were encouraged to come there from their shanties all over the Cape Flats by Divisional Council (*not* Bantu Affairs Board) officials. Because of this, the Crossroaders assumed they had some measure of de facto recognition and, therefore, security.[19] On 29 June 1976, Crossroads was officially declared an emergency camp by the Divisional Council, thus gaining a measure of legal acknowledgment, at least temporarily. So in a Crossroads shanty all the family can be together under one roof with less fear, but in the townships the family unit is covert and they most likely will have to be split up and housed under a number of roofs.

The situation is graphically illustrated by a 1977 case. Frikkie Botha, chief Bantu affairs commissioner (western Cape), agreed to meet Kenneth Kewana of Crossroads. In 1961, Mr. Kewana, a Cape Town borner, married a woman who as a homelander was illegally living in Cape Town. For this reason, they and their children did not qualify for a house, so they squatted. During the meeting, according to the *Daily Dispatch* (East London) of 27 July 1978,

> Mr. Kewana [said]: "I was born in Cape Town and do not know the Transkei, but while I qualify under Section 10 to stay here, my wife who is from Lady Frere does not. What must I do—divorce her?"
>
> Mr. Botha [replied]: "You should have thought of the consequences before you married her."

All squatters, both Black African and Coloured and specifically those whose shanties were erected after 15 November 1974 (as Crossroads was), are subject to the Prevention of Illegal Squatting Amendment Acts of 1976 and 1977. The original act of 1951 was challenged in court, and a number of Crossroads residents eventually won their cases against expulsion on appeal.[20] The government's response, with its assured majority in Parliament, has simply been to instigate tighter legislation; the amendment of 1977 is even more tight than that of 1976; the former reads in part:

> An illegal squatter building or structure may be demolished, and the material and contents thereof may be removed, without any prior notice of whatever nature to any person. No person may seek a court interdict, order, judgement, or other relief against the demolition of a structure without first satisfying the court that he has title or right to the land on which the structure is situated.

This law is also fully retroactive: any previous court interdicts or orders were automatically nullified. When he introduced the bill, the minister of community development said that its purpose was to counteract "forces whose object it is to encourage and perpetuate squatting in order to foment dissatisfaction and racial hatred and to discredit the Government and South Africa." He also said that, since squatting is illegal, "we have no duty to consult with lawbreakers."

Hemmed in by this labyrinth of laws are 20,000 Crossroaders. By now it is surely clear that to describe them as "living in a police state"

Figure 42. A "Police Pick Up" in the Early Morning at Crossroads, 1978.
The White policemen have stationed themselves near one of the communal water
faucets to which the women—almost all of whom are "illegals"—must go to
get water. The police will catch them and demand to see their passes. Note that
the Chevrolet truck has chain mesh over the windshield and headlights as a
defense against stone throwing. (Photograph used by permission of P. Andrew,
UPRU.)

is not wholly hyperbole. Figure 42 gives an impression of the way
the police harassed the Crossroaders in 1978. Later that year, the
police made a number of midnight and dawn pass raids on the camp.
During the September 14 raid at least one Crossroader was killed;
a progovernment newspaper claimed that the raid was "to prevent
crime"[21] —presumably the crime of being in a "White area" illegally.
What profile have researchers drawn of Crossroaders, and how similar
is it to the government's descriptions?

A 1977 random survey was made by Maree and Cornell, who used
a sample representing 8.5 to 10 percent of Crossroaders, with the following results.
1. About 85 percent of all households were families with both par-
   ·ents present.
2. Of the heads of households (all males) 50 percent were legally living in the area, but only 9.3 percent of the females were. Similar
   proportions were found in the Unibell Black African squatter
   camp, which grew up in 1976 (Maree, 1978). Figure 43 shows the

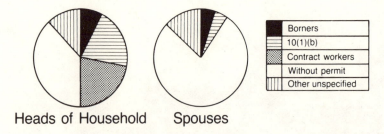

Heads of Household   Spouses

Figure 43. Crossroaders' Legal Status. (From Maree and Cornell, 1978.)

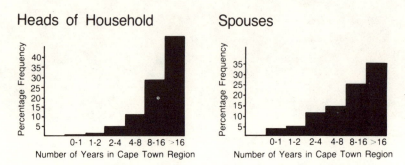

Figure 44. Distribution of Crossroaders' Period of Residence in Cape Town. (From Maree and Cornell, 1978.)

various modes of qualifying in Crossroads: 27 percent of the males qualified permanently under subsection 10(1)(a) or 10(1)(b) rights. Another survey,[22] representing 900 of the approximately 3,000 households of Crossroads, found this proportion to be 21 percent.

3. The *average* period of residence for the heads of household in the Cape Town region was 18.2 years; for spouses, 11.7 years. Figure 44 gives the details.

4. Crossroaders' prior residential areas are shown by Figure 45. Only 2 percent of the men and 17 percent of the women had come in to Crossroads from outside the Cape Peninsula. This is a lower proportion than those of Unibell and Modderdam (another Black African squatter camp that appeared in 1976). In Unibell it was found that 52 percent of all squatters had *not* moved in to the camp directly from outside the peninsula; in Modderdam, 54 percent.[23]

Despite the latter two camps' somewhat higher proportions of inmigrants, the figures in toto still contradict the official line—that

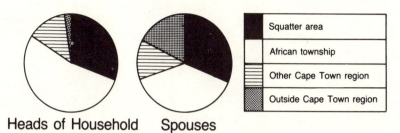

Heads of Household   Spouses

	Squatter area
	African township
	Other Cape Town region
	Outside Cape Town region

Figure 45. Crossroaders' Prior Residential Areas. (From Maree and Cornell, 1978.)

once it became known that Black Africans were getting away with living in these settlements illegally, others "stampeded"[24] in from outside the area. Therefore, regulations must be harsh, government thinking runs, otherwise "Crossroads and its population is a drop in the ocean as compared with what would follow, and conditions would become even more horrifying. People must not use Crossroads as a test case."[25] However, this spokesman's belief in the ability of stringent regulations to contain macroeconomic forces is ill founded, and his assumption that Crossroaders are new arrivals is false. His introduction of "horrifying conditions" leads us to another issue.

Crossroads, a five-year-old shantytown, is not beautiful, but what conclusions can be validly drawn from that fact alone? When considering District Six, we observed Marris's strictures against assuming social disorganization to be an inevitable outgrowth of visible physical squalor. The words of government officials on the topic of Crossroads illustrate Marris's point precisely. The minister of community development asserted in Parliament in May 1976 that the squatters' way of life tended to degenerate into a subculture out of which the people were unable to extricate themselves. Concerning the "sickly humanistic attack"[26] that "energetic leftists"[27] had mounted to defend the family life in Crossroads, another official[28] held the opinion that "the family broke itself up when the man came here and agreed to live in single quarters." He also stated, "The sanctity of family life, about which we all agree, is now being dragged into the campaign as a strong weapon, but in the parlousness of the squatter camps, the sanctity of family life is once more lost."[29] The undefined criticism in the phrase "the parlousness of the squatter camps" is spelled out more specifically by a National party member of Parliament speaking in support of the 1977 bill in Parliament: "In many cases they are criminals who prey parasitically upon society." In an attempt to give "The Case for Crossroads," the Cape Town *Argus* had to tell its readers that Crossroads "does not fit the popular notion of a squatter camp. There is no rampant disease, crime, poverty and despair and there are few vagrants. . . . [Crossroaders] are neither shiftless, lazy, nor destitute" (3 and 4 July 1978).

What more factual indications do we have of life in Crossroads? First, Crossroaders are not criminally inclined unemployables, nor are they peri-urban parasites. Most of them claim "respectability," and they play a necessary economic role in the metropolis. Figure 46 shows that almost three-quarters of all heads of household (legal or illegal) in Crossroads were employed in the formal Capetonian economy five or more days a week, and over a quarter of their spouses were also so employed. Another 20 percent of the spouses worked in the formal sector fewer than five days a week, for example, as domestic servants or chars.[30] The integration of Crossroads into the city's economy is reflected by the fact that the City Tramways established regular, well-patronized bus service between the camp and the city.

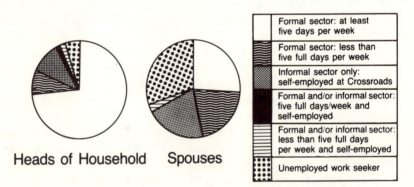

Heads of Household   Spouses

Formal sector: at least five days per week

Formal sector: less than five full days per week

Informal sector only: self-employed at Crossroads

Formal and/or informal sector: five full days/week and self-employed

Formal and/or informal sector: less than five full days per week and self-employed

Unemployed work seeker

Figure 46. Crossroaders' Employment Situation. (From Maree and Cornell, 1978.)

Second, a comparative study was made of Crossroads and the adjacent government-constructed township of Nyanga by Weichel, Smith, and Putterill (1978). Nyanga has been a permanent settlement for over twenty years, with rectangular, brick row cottages, paved roads, electric street lights, running water, et cetera. Crossroads, less than three years old at the time of the survey, was made up of tin shanties perched on raw sand dunes in a kind of makeshift squalor. Yet, it was found that Crossroaders expressed greater satisfaction[31] with their community in two important respects: eighteen out of twenty Crossroaders, but only seven out of twenty Nyangans, said that they felt relatively safe from crime in their area; seventeen out of twenty

Crossroaders, but only six out of twenty Nyangans, felt that solidarity existed among the residents. *The settlement with greater physical unsightliness may possess greater social cohesion, especially because it is a settlement of families and because it has had to create itself and its institutions by community participation.*

Because Crossroads has, in many respects, arisen outside the law, it has had to look after itself. Initiative and self-reliance are characteristics that in Black South Africans are generally stultified, if not actively discouraged, by the White minority's legislated and all-encompassing social, economic, and political power. Schlemmer (1976, p. 5) pointed out that with urban Black Africans "one finds massive evidence of feelings of alienation, of being an atom in a fragmented mass, . . . of being totally controlled by a bureaucratic machine." Passive, fatalistic acceptance of this situation has been attacked by Black consciousness advocates such as Biko, who actively promoted self-help programs.

Crossroads has organized its own self-government[32] by two committees, dividing the responsibilities between them, the male and the female. (Map 27 shows the electoral wards that have been established by the Crossroaders for these committees.[33]) For example, night caretakers, organized by the committees, control crime to the degree that it is lower than in many official Black African and Coloured townships.[34] Schooling is another self-established function. Although Crossroads children also crowd into the adjacent Black African township schools, many attend the Noxolo ("Peace") and Sizamele grade schools, built and staffed by Crossroaders. Also, there are adult literacy night-school classes. Various clubs operate from the schools: soccer, scouting, judo, and ballroom dancing, for example. There are many wood-and-iron churches.

The resourcefulness of the residents is manifest in the care that can go into making a shanty interior presentable (Figure 47) and also in the informal economy. [35] (See Figure 46.) Freed of the many official restrictions on petty trading in the townships, Crossroaders participate in buying and selling; in mending clothes, shoes, furniture, and transistor radios; and in similar services and even in manufacturing. One man makes metal travel cases in various sizes, another makes sjamboks[36] from plastic piping. Jobs are created: people operate vegetable stalls (some produce is homegrown in carefully tended Crossroads gardens, Figure 48), cooked food stands, small general stores, sorghum beer breweries and auto welding shops; people sew, crochet, raise chickens, and frame pictures; and they do many more things to make money. There is even a travel agency that arranges trips to the Transkei.

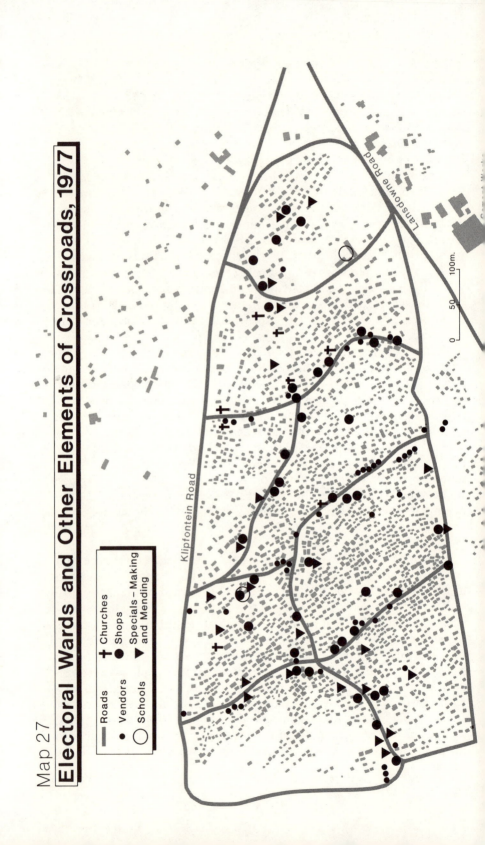

Map 27
Electoral Wards and Other Elements of Crossroads, 1977

Roads
Vendors •
Schools ◯

Churches +
Shops ●
Specials – Making ▼
and Mending

Klipfontein Road

Lansdowne Road

0   50   100m.

Figure 47. Well-kept Interior of a Crossroads Shanty, 1978. Note that the lack of electricity means that bottled gas and kerosene are used for cooking. The lack of piped water means that the bucket on the extreme right has been carried from one of the communal water faucets (as in Figure 42). (Photograph used by permission of P. Andrew, UPRU.)

Figure 48. Carefully Whitewashed Crossroads Shanty, 1978. Behind the fenced entrance grows a spinach and vegetable garden. (Photograph used by permission of P. Andrew, UPRU.)

Such vitality of life-style appears common to many other *informal* settlements in urban Black Africa. Contrasting the informal settlements in Lusaka, Zambia, to the official township housing schemes there, Andrew, Christie, and Martin (1973, p. 25) made a general point:

> The true significance of the squatters is not that they exist, but that they exist independently of the imposed colonial legal system which dominates the environment and life-style of those in authorised housing areas. By being outside the law they have shown the irrelevance of the law. They are evolving a new way of living that is related to Africa.

In this, surely, is a fundamental reason for the White South African government's insistence that "the squatting evil" and Crossroads are to be eradicated. From the government's standpoint, it is supine and pliant Black Africans that are needed, ones who obey "the law." Crossroaders do not, nor did those approximately 25,000 who lived in similar squatter settlements near Crossroads and whose camps—Modderdam, Unibell, and Werkgenot—were razed in 1977-1978.

At Modderdam, demolitions began on 17 February 1977. Held up in part by a South African Supreme Court order on March 8, demolition resumed on August 8. Armed police with dogs stood by while about forty dwellings were destroyed (Figure 49). During several confrontations with police, residents were bitten by police dogs. On August 9, police fired tear gas into a large crowd at the settlement, which included about a hundred Whites who had gathered to form a human chain to prevent the demolitions. On August 11, Rev. David Russell, Richard de Satgé, and a social worker were arrested for lying down in front of a bulldozer at the camp. Russell, a White South African, was subsequently "banned" and in 1980 sentenced to a one-year term in jail; de Satgé, who held a British passport, was expelled from the republic. The wife of an American diplomat was also among those present; this fact gave rise to murmurings in National party circles about the unseemliness of such a foreigner "meddling in the internal affairs of South Africa."

The SAIRR's *Survey 1977* (1978a, p. 453) reported on what happened after the August demolitions.

> A public meeting of over 2,000 was held in Cape Town on 14 August. A resolution was passed calling on the Government to stop the demolition of squatter shanties. By the end of August it was reported that a large number of squatter families from demolition areas were being accommodated at various church centres and at private homes in the white suburbs of Cape

Town. Police warned that white property owners accommodating the squatters were liable for prosecution. About 275 squatters were accommodated at the Anglican Church in Rondebosch in tents. . . . In August [there were] 2,000 residents living in 388 shanties at the Werkgenot squatter camp. . . . On 25 August government workers destroyed the camp. . . .

By early September more than 20 churches of different denominations all over the Peninsula were accommodating more than 1,000 squatters from Modderdam and Werkgenot camps. On 2 September divisional council workers, accompanied by police, pulled down 26 tents housing 230 squatters at an Elsie's River Catholic centre after serving a one hour notice requiring that the tents be taken down. Other temporary squatter camps on church property were raided. Over 130 squatters from St. George's Cathedral [in Cape Town city center] and the Rondebosch Anglican church were arrested, and charged with being in white areas illegally. Those convicted were fined up to R60 each. Squatters on white properties started moving out for fear of official action.

Figure 49. Police Supervise the Dismantling of a Shanty at Modderdam Road Squatter Camp, Winter 1977.

To where did they move? The evidence suggests that the majority of the homeless squatters did not leave the area but are lying low, still in Cape Town. In 1977, when asked what they intended to do in the event that *their* homes were demolished, 72 percent of the Crossroads inhabitants responded that they would try to erect a house elsewhere.[37] Or, as a Black African shanty dweller outside Cape Town said in 1976 (*Sunday Times Extra*, 4 April 1976), "My husband works here for many years. He could not find work in King Williams Town [Ciskei]. I look after the children. If they find me here and kick me out, I will build deeper in the bush. We are trapped. There is nowhere else to go." Although Unibell, too, was demolished, from 16 to 20 January 1978, it seems that the demolitions have solved nothing.

This fact may have influenced the government's decision to postpone the demolition of Crossroads, which was to have begun on 20 November 1978. Probably, however, the international cause célèbre that Crossroads had become—especially at a time when a depressed South African economy needed foreign investment and faced a strong, politically motivated disinvestment drive—stayed the government's hand for fear of worldwide adverse publicity.[38] An attempt to demolish the cohesive Crossroads community might well have proved a flash point for more widespread civil unrest, which would have harmed further South Africa's image overseas. There was probably some diplomatic pressure against demolition from the United States and the United Kingdom. Another factor is that the minister dealing with Black African affairs, Cornelius Mulder, disgraced in a government financial scandal, had just been forced to resign. His replacement, Piet Koornhof, is the least conservative of the members of the cabinet.[39] In a report in the *New York Times*:

> "I want to deal with the thing in a humane way, not with bloody bulldozers," Mr. Koornhof declared. . . . [It was] disclosed that Mr. Koornhof had intervened at the last minute to halt a Government plan to demolish the camp and put thousands of its residents on trains back to the Transkei tribal homeland, 700 miles away [where a resettlement camp was being prepared for them[40]]. . . . . He left no doubt that the government remained determined that the camp would eventually disappear. But he insisted that this was not a matter of rigidly enforcing the regulations of apartheid, but of removing what he described as a serious health and fire hazard" (*New York Times*, 1 December 1978).

Dr. Koornhof announced at the beginning of April 1979 that nearly all Crossroaders would be rehoused. This was to be done not by upgrading their makeshift housing, but by building new accommodations on an adjacent site in a Black African township zone.

The concessions that Dr. Koornhof has made to the Crossroads community appear, at first glance, to be very generous. Urban residence rights will be accorded to people qualifying under subsections 10(1)(a) and 10(1)(b); migrant workers laboring under legal contracts; people providing a legitimate service to the community (for example, a local shopkeeper or a shoemaker); a category of hard-luck cases; and, *in all cases, the wives and families* of those so qualifying. The right to stay in the area depends on the individual concerned retaining his or her qualifying status; for example, if employment were terminated or if the contract expired and was not renewed, residence rights would be ended.

The number of people who will be allowed to stay in the Cape Town area will depend on who is interpreting the conditions. Andrew (1979) claimed that the officials in the Department of Cooperation and Development (a new name for Bantu Administration and Development), as in all the governmental departments, are lagging somewhat behind the pace being set at the top by Prime Minister P. W. Botha's and Dr. Koornhof's "liberalization" efforts. Most of the middle-level civil servants are staunch party supporters—cast in the Verwoerd mold—and are ideologically and bureaucratically resistant to the sort of action being expected of them at this time. Hence, there is no sort of certainty about the future (relative) security of the inhabitants of Crossroads.

The cohesive power of Crossroaders has been so strong that their leaders were actually consulted on some matters affecting the future of the settlement. Emerging from the discussions between Dr. Koornhof and the Crossroads representatives were the following points: the residents were to be able to "afford" the houses and services to be provided by the state; the community representatives were to be "fully involved"[41] in the planning of the new development; and as many local people as possible were to be given jobs during the actual construction of the project. Andrew believed that these conditions have already (that is, from April [when Dr. Koornhof announced the concessions] to November 1979 [the time of Andrew's report]) been eroded to the point that they can be regarded as hardly existent. He also believed that it would take major intervention by Minister Koornhof to reinstate them to at least the level of his earlier promises. Crossroads residents themselves have also expressed dissatisfaction over the lack of "real consultations" and over the decrease (from 2,575 to 1,662) of the number of new homes to be built to rehouse Crossroaders (*Cape Times*, 30 April 1980).

In conclusion, I should note that for weeks before his April 1979 announcement, Dr. Koornhof and his department had been meeting with members of commerce and industry to reach an agreement over the responsibility of providing accommodation for Black African employees and the role that they, as employers, would be expected to play in adhering to influx control—and an agreement on the fines for default. Thus, at the same time he was announcing a reprieve for Crossroads, he was declaring that a greatly increased fine, of R500 per employee, would have to be paid by the employer of any person working and living in the western Cape "illegally." This crackdown, applying to all urban areas in "White South Africa," is an attempt to reinforce the grand apartheid homeland policy of separate development and influx control. So much for Dr. Koornhof's claim, on a 1979 tour of the United States, that "apartheid is dead."

The fact of the matter is that, although Prime Minister P. W. Botha (with Dr. Koornhof acting as one of his main lieutenants) is taking an apparently less dogmatic stance than his predecessors, *the basic apartheid concepts remain.* These are territorial separation of racial groups on a national and a metropolitan scale and complete economic and political dominance of all Nonwhite South Africans on both scales. 'Self-determination"—the "independence" of the Black African homelands—although perhaps a fine notion, cannot be authentic within a context of total dominance and one-way dependency. The present removal of certain elements of petty apartheid is the removal of relatively superficial categories of social control. But, when any commentators wondered whether the apparent about-face on the part of the government over Crossroads signaled any abandonment of the migrant labor system and influx control (grand apartheid), the Afrikaans-language press was quick to discount the possibility. "Crossroads may in no circumstances become a symbol of injudicious leniency. . . . Crossroads should become a symbol of 'so far and no further'" admonished Cape Town's *Die Burger* (4 April 1979). And *Rapport* (Johannesburg, 8 April 1979) made a point in underscoring that ". . . . the Minister states clearly that it is a single action—measures to prevent similar situations will be intensified." Such smoke screens cannot, however, disguise the fact that the Crossroads community has tested the limits of the government's power; and this in a state where such power is exercised both overtly and as a matter of course against the majority of its citizens.

CHAPTER ELEVEN

Apartheid in South Africa:
An Uncertain Conclusion

To survive these days you had to be either black or white. It
was no good being brown. No good at all.

> Shiva Naipaul,
> *North of South: An African Journey,*
> 1978, 1979

GROUP AREAS ACHIEVEMENT IN CAPE TOWN

This last chapter hardly merits the label "conclusion" because the
study of Cape Town's social geography cannot be neatly tied up,
especially when South Africa's sociopolitical future is so uncertain.
The future of South Africa is an area for speculation, which I do not
feel is at all my forte. As a social geographer, I pursued research in
Cape Town and then wrote an interpretative report on it. I offer no
prognostications. Nevertheless, I will briefly undertake a discussion
of some urban planning material that attempts to take account
of the various political futures of South Africa, for it is obvious that
the future of Cape Town will be inextricably bound to the future
political changes in the Republic of South Africa.

Group areas were introduced by the Whites for the Whites. It is
clear from all that has gone before that the Whites have benefited in
various ways, as in business and real estate. They have also gained a
measure of perceived security in the sense that the Nonwhites and
their problems, many of which (such as higher violent crime rates
and lower health standards) are like those of poor people in other
societies, have been put at a distance. This distancing is also supposed
to have lessened the potential for "friction" and thereby to have
"improved race relations" (which in a sense means that the exploitation of Nonwhites is still well oiled and that it proceeds without, so

far, too much overt resistance or dysfunction, such as sabotage and urban guerrilla warfare). However, it may be easier to argue the converse, that is, that group areas have *worsened* race relations and have exacerbated interracial tensions. The report of the government's Theron Commission (1976) strongly implied this possibility, and Maasdorp and Pillay (1977) stated it flatly to be the case; so did the Cape Town City Council in the winter of 1978, during the group areas controversy over the future of "controlled" Salt River. I too consider this to be so in Cape Town, and surely anyone who has read the words of the removees that have been quoted in this work can hardly doubt it. In the longest term, then, it would seem that such exacerbation of intrasocietal tension by the institution of group areas may actually be undermining the security of that shrinking minority in South Africa—the Whites.

For the majority of Capetonians who are Coloured people, the Group Areas Act has been a bane. Again, the official *Theron Commission Report* observed as much in its ninth chapter. And the South African Institute of Race Relations (1978b, p. 111) in addressing the government's Cillié Commission on the causes of the 1976-1977 civil unrest, declared that "no single Government measure has created greater coloured resentment, sacrifice and sense of injustice." This present work and many others amply document such a contention. Consider one of the main goals of the Group Areas Act: the strategic goal of clearly demarcating in both society and space the place of the Coloured people from, on the one hand, the Whites and, on the other hand, the Black Africans. Has the group areas conception succeeded in defining such a buffering, intercalary, separate group?

If we are looking for an enhanced solidarity among Coloureds, some enhanced self-consciousness of a nation in the making, we will find none in greater Cape Town.[1] But, if we are trying to find out whether the Group Areas Act has enhanced the separation in affect, the lack of empathy, between Coloureds and Black Africans or between Coloureds and Whites, we will find that generally it has. As Whisson (1971, p. 75) expressed it, "The policy of apartheid has been successful in creating self-sustaining barriers which make group attitudes of suspicion more likely and individual non-racist attitudes less likely." Both such suspicion, and the lack of certainty as to what "Colouredness" may consist of, are inherent in the following vignette.

One Sunday afternoon, I went round to Heideveld township to look up a family I had interviewed a couple of weeks before and who had asked me to come back. I walked in and found myself among a half-dozen men who were drinking bottled beer in the cottage's front room and in the mood for talking about sociophilosophy. The man who lived in the cottage explained who I was. "Oh, you're writing your thesis. . . . I see. Are you going to write about us here today?" This comment caused some laughter, but still I tried to explain what my study was about. "So you'll write it all down, and then the big boys overseas'll read it and that'll help," someone said. I expressed strong doubts about the likelihood of this happening. Another man said, "You be frank with us. What do you think about South Africa?" "I can't be frank now," I replied. "I don't know who you are, you don't know who I am. I'm here on a visa. I don't want to be chucked out, can't say just what I think." "Well, d'you mind if I speak freely? . . . Well, we don't trust the White man, *any* White man. Don't get me wrong, but who are you, what are you doing here? You say you just came here on a *social* call? [He expressed his extreme disbelief.] You say you're an exchange student. Got any proof? We can't just trust anyone, you know."

Another man said, "It's time the Coloured nation stood together." I asked, "Is there a 'Coloured nation'? I think it's something the White man calls you. If people want to be a nation, let them be a nation. But I think he's trying to force it on you." The youngest, most vociferous man in the party said, "No, we're all Blacks, against the Whites." An older man interjected, "Don't you call me a Black. You're not a Black, you're a bloody Jew, but your father married a Coloured woman. I'm not a Black. . . . And those *boere* saying they're pure, they want to be apart from us. They're not *real* Whites. Go up to the Transvaal and look at them!² No, I'm not against the Africans really, if a man's civilized, then I'll be friends with him. A doctor's a doctor. But everybody makes friends with their own kind: that's social apartheid—yes, that's social apartheid. But we should get paid for the job we do. Now I work—I'm a bricklayer—with a White man, but he gets more than me for doing the same thing. . . ."

The "in-betweenness" of the Coloureds was vividly brought out that afternoon in the Cape Flats cottage. *The Whites have always realized that they can exploit this "in-betweenness" for their own advantage.* One aspect of the British policy, for example, on the Cape's eastern frontier during the rebellions of 1799-1803 was to drive a wedge between the uprising proto-Coloured/Khoikhoi farm workers and the restive Xhosa. Thus, ". . . most of the Hottentots . . . not only ceased to be a peril to the Colony, but in due course became a reinforcement to it against the Kaffirs" (Walker, 1957, p. 135). Prime Minister Hertzog, an Afrikaner, in February 1929 expressed his wariness of policies that might end up driving the Coloured people "to rest in the arms of the Native." When in 1950 it was becoming clear that apartheid's implementation was going to attack Coloured status strongly, the *Star* (16 October 1950) warned against making "a million new enemies." As Patterson (1953) unerringly pointed out, the burden of this White newspaper's phraseology is that the other (then) nearly 9 million Nonwhites were already "enemies." This "them and us" viewpoint held by most Whites in South Africa runs very deep. Are the Coloureds (and Indians?) going to be *with* "us" *against* "them"? Wollheim (1963, p. 41) attacked apartheid legislation by noting that it might deprive Whites "should a clash occur between White and African, of 1½ million staunch and loyal allies almost as sophisticated as themselves." The *Star*'s message on 27 September 1969 was almost word for word the same, but by then the number of Coloureds had risen to 2 million.

Finally, one of the most recent examples concerns the South African Black Alliance, which was formed by Chief Gatsha Buthelezi's Inkatha movement, the (Indian) Reform party, and the (Coloured) Labour party at Ulundi in Zululand on 11 January 1978. Even though these three bodies can hardly be considered widely representative of Black South Africans, many Afrikaans-language newspapers reacted stridently, and the government fell back on the well-tried strategy of divide and rule. On 12 January, on its current affairs program, the South African Broadcasting Corporation talked of "The Inkatha Trap":

> Moreover, the Zulus have shown no interest in the past in the Coloureds far away in the Cape, and with their neighbour Indians in Natal relations have always been mutually suspicious and tense. Where does security and opportunity for the Coloureds and Indians really lie — as adjuncts to Chief Buthelezi's Inkatha; or in a dispensation in which they will each have their own parliament equal in status to the Anglo-Afrikaner nation's, and in which all three national communities will participate [note that Indian and Coloured representatives together add up to a number well below those of the Whites] at the highest executive level in decision-making?

SABC radio and the Group Areas Act are both creations of the White government. In fostering mutual suspicion among Nonwhites (the one by words, the other by space), the government is striving to maintain White hegemony.

Yet, in the excerpt from the Heideveld conversation (which took place in August 1975), the youngest person claimed Blackness. The Black consciousness movement began during the late 1960s, and one of its basic equations was "I am oppressed, therefore Black"; thereby, Coloureds are included should they wish to be. However, only a small proportion of Coloureds do wish to consider themselves Blacks, apparently, although the proportion is probably growing. To put this in perspective, observe what Dickie-Clark wrote after research with Durban Coloureds during the first half of the 1960s. He stated (1972, p.34) that there arose

> three very different broad possibilities: to strive after full equality with whites for themselves alone; to accept the separate and distinctive status the whites offer them; or to make common cause with the other subordinate groups and strive for equality for all. The Coloureds' marginal situation . . . prevent[s] any one choice . . . [and prevents] decisive action.

This is very much a reiteration of what the same scholar said in 1966, when he wrote (p.136) that

> clearly for Whites and Africans, and less clearly for Indians, there seem to be overwhelming reasons why certain courses of action are preferable and satisfying to these strata. In comparison, the Coloureds have good cause to be doubtful about all three of the broad choices offered them by their situation.

At the very end of the 1960s, Morse and Peele (1974), too, found, especially among middle-class Coloureds, a distinct disinterest in political activity—partly for the same reasons as Dickie-Clark proposed.

During the middle of the following decade, the Theron Commission found that most Coloured people were prepared, although without much enthusiasm, to identify with "their own group." Among those who did not want to so identify themselves—and this feeling was more prevalent in Cape Town than in any other area—there were three main categories. The smallest category included those who tended toward Black consciousness because they believed that all oppressed Blacks had to unite against White domination. The *Argus* (18 June 1976) summarized the commission's findings in this way:

> In the urban areas 44 percent were against it [a closer association with Blacks], 24 percent favoured it and 32 percent were uncertain. Those in favour of the proposition that the future of the Coloured people lay with the Blacks were mainly the young and the better educated.

The second of the three categories was comprised of a slightly larger number of Coloured people who tended toward a closer association with the Whites because they believed that culturally and historically they had a common destiny. Again, according to the *Argus* report:

> Among urban Coloured people the response was 41.3% in favour of this, 30.9% disagreed, and 27.8% were uncertain. In Cape Town the majority of the Coloured people did not think that their future lay with the White people. In the age group 18 to 24 the majority were aginst such an association and they were more sure of their viewpoint.

The third and largest category included those who, according to *The Theron Commission Report* (van der Horst, 1976, p.114):

> adopted the attitude that they wanted to be identified as South African only, because they are opposed to any form of ethnocentrism or racial prejudice. This category consisted mainly of people with a middle to a higher socioeconomic status, an urban background (especially Cape Town), and a Western-oriented system of values. They stood aloof from any sectional movements and group-oriented institutions.

This third standpoint is echoed in the feelings of the other group "in the middle," the Indians. Meer (1972, pp.5–6) reported that the overwhelming majority of Indians fear, more than White rule, a "genuine danger of Black Consciousness leading to Black racism" and, therefore, stand for mobilization "towards the goal of a common society."

The Theron Commission's findings confirmed the impressions I gained from conversations with ex-Mowbrayites and others in 1975 and 1976. However, most of those with whom I talked were older, and our conversations, (like the Theron Commission's investigations,) preceded the 1976 Cape riots. On my return to Cape Town in July and August of 1978, I sensed a much greater foreboding for the future (for example, the weighing of the emigration option), and a greater politicization among the educated young and a wish for solidarity with the Black Africans. Is that brash claim made in 1968 that "the Sand Flats are natural breeding-grounds for a revolution" going to come true? Will the group areas conception prove so goading an instrument of oppression that it will become its own nemesis? Or will it continue "successfully" to orchestrate division among the internally divided subjects of apartheid?

APARTHEID AND THE
CONTEMPORARY SOUTH AFRICAN CITY

Until the present time, it would seem that the advantages that have accrued to the Whites from the group areas conception have outweighed the disadvantages. It would be naive, then, to anticipate some kind of dismantling of group areas as an attempt at "liberalization" from Prime Minister P. W. Botha's administration. On the other hand, it seems equally inappropriate to imagine that the city-scale apartheid plans are totally cemented ideologically, totally rigid blueprints to be carried out at all costs. Apartheid has a certain ad hoc malleability about it, which must increase its potential longevity. If there seems to be a net advantage in the group areas conception for the Whites, they will continue to use group areas. If this advantage can be increased by relaxing *some* of the restrictive tenets of spatial segregation, then such "liberalization" will be permitted.

The *South African Digest* (5 October 1979) reported that Minister of Community Development Marais Steyn had announced that "all restaurants in South Africa can now open to all races without having to apply for permits." Any restaurant then had only "to apply to his department for a 'once and for all' exemption. He said, however, he reserved the right to withdraw an exemption to avoid racial friction or incidents. But, he said, he did not think this would happen." Note that no restaurant is obliged to desegregate and also that still, in the end, the restauranteur proposes but the minister disposes.

During 1979, also, Cape Town buses were desegregated. Another area of some change may be sea bathing, although I am still a little confused about the precise legal situation in this area. In 1978-1979, some Cape Peninsula beaches were formally desegregated, but there were reports over the Christmas 1979 summer holiday season of police escorting a total of over 800 Blacks off certain still-White beaches. In Simonstown, a Coloured man was convicted and fined for being on a Whites-only beach. What appears to have occurred in the Cape peninsula is that formerly Black African-only and Coloured-only beaches have been proclaimed open to all (permitting White use), while most White beaches are still segregated. Once again, the Whites are having their cake and eating it, too. In Durban in 1977, where beaches had been segregated since 1930 (long before the apartheid Afrikaner Nationalist government came to power in 1948), the beaches were redemarcated in order to move Nonwhite bathers farther away from White hotels and apartment complexes. Attempts in the Durban City Council to include a racially mixed beach in the zoning plans were defeated.

Another area of conflicting signals has been housing in Johannesburg. The minister of community development in 1978 made homes available for Coloureds to purchase by permit in Fleurhof, a White group area. Fleurhof, with 100 houses and 245 lots, had become almost empty of Whites; it adjoins Soweto. At the same time, in *central* Johannesburg, there was another White group area where there were also a great many vacancies—Hillbrow (and some adjacent tracts), just above the central business district. Hillbrow is an area with a very high population density since it is almost completely made up of high rises. Although Hillbrow once had a cosmopolitan character, many members of its floating population of young European immigrants who had not taken out South African citizenship left the country after the Soweto riots and when strict new conscription/permanent residency regulations for immigrant Whites were enacted. The acute shortage of Coloured and Indian housing, plus empty apartments gaining no revenue for property owners, resulted in the illegal renting of apartments to Coloureds and Indians.

What was the minister of community development's reaction? In April 1979, he said that the surplus in White group areas was a temporary one and that, when normal demand returned, racially qualified (White) people would want the accommodations, causing racial tension. In May 1978, Mr. Steyn had already stated that he

> intended clamping down on illegal residents. Acting on many complaints received, the Group Areas branch of the police were investigating. . . . Housing shortages [were going to be] eliminated and no laws could be flouted in the meanwhile. Speaking at the Cape Congress of the National Party later in the year, he said action would be taken against landlords who allowed other races to occupy flats in white group areas. . . . The PFP MP for the area appealed to the Government to turn a blind eye, as he had received no complaints. A snap poll by the *Star* in May revealed that seven out of every ten whites asked said they were not against neighbours of other races (SAIRR, 1979, p.389).

By April 1979, it had been estimated that there might be up to 10,000 Coloured and Indian people living in the White areas of Johannesburg (in *Race Relations News*, April 1979). (*Survey 1979* of the SAIRR subsequently reduced its estimate to between 2,000 and 3,000.) It does not seem that the government is going to give them permits to stay, contrary to its course in the Fleurhof case.[3]

On the other hand, the Community Development Amendment Act Number 19 of 1978 is a recent relaxation of group areas restrictions. The act abolished the payment of appreciation contributions under section 34 of the Community Development Act of 1966. Wollheim characterized the reaction of disqualified Nonwhite property owners to this provision as one of outrage.[4] However, in 1976 a reliable Cape Town conveyancing agent informed me, after consulting a number of colleagues, that no cases were known of appreciation contributions having been demanded by the Community Development Board in Cape Town. A very few cases were known of depreciation allowances having been paid out by the board. The SAIRR's *Survey 1978* (1979) reported that this was the general case, for there had been an official moratorium on the payment of appreciation contributions, which had continually been extended, in order to encourage sales by disqualified owners. Section 34 was a legal stick that had never, at least since 1974, actually been used, only brandished. With group areas removals about 80 percent completed, the government felt confident enough to remove the appreciation contribution clause while it retained the provision for depreciation allowances. Perhaps the government was thereby trying to appear magnanimous and conciliatory to the Coloureds, at little cost to its plans—as in the Salt River, Sir Lowry's Pass Village, and Somerset West/Gordon's Bay instances.

The most interesting recent developments in the implementation of the Group Areas Act have been those concerning the role of Indian traders in central cities, a relaxation in restrictions that has been somewhat fitfully proceeding since 1976. At a state occasion in September of that year, Sen. Marais Viljoen declared before a Coloured audience that Coloured and Indian traders would be allowed more freedom to trade outside their group areas. He also stated that general industrial areas would be opened to Coloured and Indian entrepreneurs and that these areas would not have a "group character." Later in the month, the executive committee of the Indian Council met with Minister Marais Steyn to ask for a clarification of the senator's statement. After the meeting, a member of the commitee, J. A. Carrim, described the concessions as "virtually meaningless." It appeared that it was only in terms of section 19 of the Community Development Act, which concerns permits for disqualified persons to trade, that the minister was to "allow more freedom": that is, the minister was prepared to grant more permits in the future, but he would clearly retain his discretionary power. In October, two Indian traders, whose application to trade in the central business district had been approved by the Krugersdorp (Transvaal) Town Council, were refused permission so to do by the Department of Community Development.

The next year (1977), the situation was clarified somewhat. The Group Areas Amendment Act Number 96 of 1977 was passed, which eliminated the Group Areas Act's restrictions on ownership, occupation, purchase, and use of land and property by disqualified persons in controlled areas zoned for industrial purposes (for example, in Salt River and parts of lower Woodstock). This relaxation of the restrictions did not apply, however, to zones where industrial areas were situated *within* proclaimed group areas, for example, at the borders of Woodstock with Salt River and Cape Town city center/foreshore (both areas proclaimed for Whites). The minister of community development said during the parliamentary debate on the amendment, however, that in some cases the government would consider deproclaiming group areas. This course was subsequently (November 1979) followed for the Salt River/Woodstock border tract. Also, in November 1977, under section 19 of the Community Development Act, a Coloured garage manager was granted a permit to trade as an individual in a White group area on the Cape Peninsula. The *Financial Mail* (November 4) reported this to be the first such permit granted since the Group Areas Act became law in 1950.

Again in 1977, the *Star* (July 20) reported that Minister Steyn had assured representatives of the Indian Council that Indian traders in the Transvaal, the eastern Cape, and Natal[5] would no longer be resettled according to the terms of the Group Areas Act. (On June 21, he had estimated the number of such traders to be 3,400.) Nine months later, in April 1978, in response to an opposition member's call in the House of Assembly for the opening of central business districts to traders from all population groups, the minister said that White traders in the centers of White urban areas could not in future be expected to retain a monopoly of trade among all races. Then, in June of that year, the minister made it official: he announced to the Senate that trader resettlement under the Group Areas Act would end everywhere in South Africa, except on the Transvaal *platteland*, where special circumstances made restrictions necessary to avoid friction, and in Ladysmith, where he was committed to other arrangements.[6]

Once again, such concessions have not been made by the government because of some access of philanthropy toward its Nonwhite subjects; they were made because the government is malleable enough to change its plans in an ad hoc manner when it perceives that it is to the Whites' advantage to do so. For, as the SAIRR's *Survey 1978* (1979, p. 386) informed us:

It was reported from various centres, notably Ladysmith, Louis Trichardt, Vereeniging and Pietersburg, that the local white business community was against the planned removal of Indian traders. Similar reasons were given in each case. Moral reasons aside, the traders attracted a lot of business including that of the local and surrounding black populations, to the towns' central business districts. This business would probably be attracted to the planned new centres outside the towns. This could detrimentally affect already depressed conditions in the central business districts, where many shops were empty, lowering property values and possibly leaving them as ghost towns.

Another point to bear in mind is that it is well known that, in central business districts proclaimed for Whites only, Whites have frequently acted as legal fronts for Indians who want to continue trading there instead of starting over again in their sometimes distant, new "Asiatic bazaars." Whites have received considerations of up to R100 per month in return for their being pseudomanagers. Wills and Schulze (1976) observed such subterfuge in Pietermaritzburg, Natal; and Patricios applied this pattern to all the larger South African urban areas.[7] There were numerous prosecutions under the Group Areas Act in 1977: of Indians charged with illegally occupying premises from which they were disqualified and of White firms for employing Indian managers (*Sunday Times*, 24 July 1977; *Star*, 29 July 1977; *Rand Daily Mail*, 4 August 1977).

This covert bending of the Group Areas Act is so common that it would be very difficult for the government to put an end to it completely. And, indeed, with his June 1978 statement, the minister of community development has had to come to terms with the economic rationale that gave rise to such bending. Indian traders are to be allowed to stay because the White traders want them to (presumably, the Whites *do not* want them to stay in the exceptions the minister mentioned, the rural Transvaal and Ladysmith). (Yet, in Ladysmith at least some of the local White businesspeople want the Indians to stay. So what exactly did it mean when the minister said he was "committed" to the removal of Indian traders in that city? To whom was he committed?) Are any of the traders who were removed before June 1978 going to be allowed to return? —presumably not. And, after the June 1978 announcement, many Indian traders were still very uncertain of their future security. Some asked whether, for example, in areas that had physically deteriorated because of uncertainty about their future (thus, there having been no investment or renovation by Indians there), the Slums Act might yet be used to continue removals. In his announcement, the minister did say that this would be the case "where necessary," and he identified Pageview, in Johannesburg, as such a target area. A few Indian traders are still (January 1980) being removed by the Group Areas Act in Cape Town.[8]

Nevertheless, the amendments, plus the substance of the minister's statement, do add up to a significant relaxation of group areas apartheid. During 1978, in fact, eight urban areas had been officially pinpointed under section 19 of the Act, where Coloured and Indian persons were to be allowed to carry on businesses outside their own group areas: East London, Ladysmith (so there is a contradiction with what has just been noted), Newcastle, Pinetown, Port Elizabeth, Pretoria, Roodepoort, and Vryburg. It was reported, furthermore, that the possibility of such relaxation was being reviewed for other urban areas, including Johannesburg and Durban—but not (yet?) Cape Town.[9]

THE FUTURE OF SOUTH AFRICA'S CITIES

It must be borne in mind that the magnitude of probable future growth in South African cities is staggering. A University of Cape Town urban planner, D. Dewar, recently estimated that as many new homes would have to be built before the year 2000 as had been constructed in the period from van Riebeeck's arrival in 1652 through 1977 (Dewar, 1977). Various speakers at "The Road Ahead" conference at Grahamstown, Cape, in July 1978, predicted that, if present trends continued, over 80 percent of the population (which would probably have doubled to 51 million) would be living in cities by the year 2000. Against demographic pressures on such a scale, I wonder what efficacy the influx control "crackdown" can have (it was about to be put into motion in January 1980).

At The Road Ahead conference, the professor of urban planning at the University of the Witwatersrand, N. Patricios (1978, p. 7) stated:

If forecasters are correct in their population projections and income inequalities between the races remain disparate, then at a national level the number of rich Whites in the inner cities will be more or less equal in number to the poor Browns in the outer cities. Of utmost concern should be the probability that the poorer urban Blacks will outnumber the Whites and Browns taken together by as much as three times or more. The inequalities will be aggravated by the unemployment problem, which to be overcome will mean that 1,500 new jobs will have to be created each working day until the year 2000 (*Financial Mail*, 1977). This should be seen against the 6% annual growth rate during the Sixties when only about 900 new jobs per day were created. Even with an optimistic outlook the real economic growth is unlikely to average more than 4% per annum between now and the end of the century.

Apparently, there will be a very large number of unemployed Black African urban dwellers. Their potential disaffection may give them political importance as leaven for changes in South Africa's system of government (although this is a very unpredictable matter). Depending upon the nature of such possible changes, Patricios, acknowledging his debt to the formulations of Hans Carol (1975), offered three contrasting scenarios for the future of South African cities.

The first scenario is the evolutionary possibility, that is, the continuance of White rule employing the same policies of grand apartheid and group areas. The ethic will be one of expansion—that is, maximum economic growth and free application of technology—in a capitalist framework. There will be, according to Patricios (1978, pp. 15-16), a "reasonably high increase" in wealth and a

> mixture of personal values oriented to advancement and gain, with some public action to offset deprivation among the low-income groups, particularly in the Black African and Coloured populations. . . . The form of South Africa's metropolitan areas and large cities will remain dualistic in structure. The difference from the present will be the utter [numerical] dominance of the segregated Brown and Black areas. The populous, poor outer city will overshadow the smaller rich inner city. There will be a lower proportion of shanty-towns than in Black Africa, due to the greater availability of capital to build low cost housing, but a larger proportion relative to the present figures for South Africa.

The second scenario is the revolutionary possibility, whereby South Africa could become an industrialized Marxist-Leninist state, "ostensibly . . . classless and racially integrated," although in practice there would probably be a small elite group. Group areas would be immediately abandoned, but unforced residential segregation would certainly continue. The numbers of the White population would be reduced and the homelands would be disestablished, but there would be, Patricios declared, a coercive policy keeping people in the rural areas.

Carol's original scheme included as a third scenario the reactionary possibility, whereby utter disillusion with industrialism and modernization would induce an African state to turn inward and withdraw to a subsistence level, predominantly rural economy. Although this might be a possible future for a Burundi, it can hardly be one for South Africa, so Carol's third scenario can be dismissed as inappropriate and his fourth scenario becomes Patricios's third, namely, the reformative possibility.

Patricios envisioned some kind of African socialism, which in the South African context would mean a reform movement away from apartheid's goal of separate development to the goals of achieving "a multiracial, egalitarian society, and redistribution of wealth in a mixed economy." South Africa would be part of an African common market, and its orientation would shift from regarding itself as part of the Western world to being part of Africa. Some residential areas would be racially mixed, while others would be voluntarily segregated into White, Black African, Coloured, and Asian areas.

In all three "possible" scenarios (which I have here greatly condensed), despite the great differences in political color, two characteristics of the envisaged city are always present. They should not surprise us. One is that residential segregation according to race and status would continue to exist, although not on the present scale, not through the use of force, and not necessarily as the norm for the society. The second is that the continued existence of shantytowns is foreseen. Shantytowns would be the most extensive if the reformative possibility came to pass. Even the White-dominated evolutionary possibility, however, would be unable to expunge them, despite any efforts they might make. I wonder, then, whether what I described in Chapter 10 is more representative of the coming Cape Town than what I described in Chapter 2. That is, is not Cape Town going to become increasingly Third World in character since most of the urban population increase is bound to be among the poorest people, the Black Africans? And is not Cape Town thereby going to diverge yet further from the postcolonial port and industrial city of 1948, when it was in the very broadest sense somewhat comparable in its social geography to the northern United States industrial cities of that time?

To make a still more general point, I could in the longest term think of Cape Town's predominant nature as passing from African to European to African, again. Before 1652, the settlements at Table Bay—Khoikhoi huts—were wholly of Africa. Then, Dutch and later British mercantile imperialism made the Cape Peninsula an outpost of empire. The Khoikhoi disappeared, and only hints of their previous existence could be seen in a few place-names and in the features of some Coloured slaves, whose culture, however, became unavoidably European. Since that time, two major themes are of relevance. The first is that the Whites themselves, especially the Afrikaners —by the very name they have adopted—have become more African and less colonial European: Africanity is not totally color specific. The second is that, since the nineteenth-century extension of British hegemony over most of southern Africa and since the attendant introduction of modern industrialism, the Republic of South Africa has contained a large Black African population. Originally, the Black Africans' slow southward migration down the continent's east coast brought them no nearer to Cape Town than 750 kilometers; their encounter at the time of the American Revolution with the Boers expanding from the other direction was at the Great Fish River on the eastern Cape border. But with the change in South Africa from a pastoral to an industrial economy, these hitherto-distant Black Africans have come to work and live in Cape Town. Despite the incredibly stringent restrictions on the Black Africans' presence in Cape Town, especially during the last thirty years, their numbers in the Mother City continue to grow; today, they may account for one-fifth of the city's population. Once the 350 years of White rule in South Africa has ended and a Black African government takes over and the Pass Laws are abolished (or certainly modified), the Black African mark on Cape Town is bound to become more and more pronounced. And, eventually, I presume, Cape Town will lose its Coloured-White character and become a fascinating variation on the more general pattern of African cities—perhaps as a Sante Fe is to a Chicago in the United States.

SOUTH AFRICA AND THE DIALECTIC
OF PERSON AND PLACE

The Mowbray Nonwhite community was at first tolerated but then it was expelled from a larger White community that held power. This can be seen as a move from containment to abolition. The application of the term "abolition," however, is specific to the inner-city/inner-suburb scale. On a slightly more general scale, that of the metropolis as a whole, it becomes clear that the abolition of Nonwhite Mowbrayites was in fact the same thing as the placing of Coloured (and Indian) people into a new container situated more toward the city's edge. The Coloured people are perfectly welcome to stay in the metropolis as long as they remain in their acceptable peripheral place, the White government seems to be saying. The Coloured squatters are similarly contained at the city's edge, or at least those whose shanties were erected before November 1974 are; and it even seems that those whose shacks were erected after that date will eventually be rehoused as part of the crash program and not evicted from the peninsula (that is, their presence will not be abolished).

However, the strenuous efforts made by the government concerning Black Africans on the peninsula are much more "abolitionist." Recall the 1966 policy statement aimed at reducing Black African numbers by 5 percent per annum or, failing that, toward a particularly tight version of containment, which included the enjoinment of most family life, the harrying of Black African women and children back to the Transkei, and the demolition of the Black African shantytowns.

A consideration of the next more general scale, the regional, includes the matter of the Eiselen Line. West of this line, the western Cape is to remain a Coloured (and, of course, White) labor preference area, a container advantageous to the Coloureds. This same area is the most confining container in South Africa for the Black Africans, where they can rent only in segregated townships on land owned by the White government or in small separate quarters on some White farms, for example, in the wine-growing Hex River Valley. They can never own land. Again, the Black African presence supposedly is to be gradually abolished in the western Cape, although presumably few South Africans now believe that there is any real possibility of this happening.

On the national scale, South Africa, within which over 86 percent of the country's land area is legally defined as "White South Africa" (or, more delicately, "the common area"), follows a policy of containment for Black Africans. The Pass Laws, the segregated townships, the migrant labor system are all visible evidence. And this containment is grudging. Only during the last five years have Black Africans gradually been permitted to buy their own homes within the segregated townships of the republic's urban areas, and that only on thirty-year, and recently ninety-nine-year, leasehold from the government. Only in 1978 did the government *officially* consider these townships as anything but "temporary" settlements.

Concurrent with containment, a policy of abolition of the Black African presence is clearly being implemented on a national scale in South Africa. The maintenance of grand apartheid—which involves the resettlement of up to *1.5 million Black Africans*,[10] the creation of "independent" Black states by the Pretoria bureaucracy, and the unilateral transference of the pseudocitizenship of urban Black Africans to these fictitious homelands—is clearly an attempt to abolish the urban presence of as many Black Africans as possible (those superfluous to industry's immediate labor needs). The three-month relaxation of Pass Law registration procedures in late 1979, followed more recently by a crackdown, is the policy of containment and abolition in one. Those who attain urban residence rights are contained; those who do not are "endorsed out," abolished. This policy constitutes another wedge that can be driven between the Blacks of South Africa in order to divide and rule. Urban Black Africans, with a circumscribed but nonetheless extant access to some of the material advantages of living in an industrial society (for example, consumer goods) can be played off against the poverty-stricken rural Black Africans in the legally "foreign" homelands. Why should the urban Black Africans make common cause with "them"? Why not hold fast to and accept the limited (but tangible) urban "privileges"—this especially so when one is in danger of being cast out in the future (once one retires or one's job ceases to exist during, say, an economic downswing)?

Why did not the Europeans, when they were conquering South Africa, simply avoid all their future problems by abolishing the Africans completely long ago? This, indeed, is what happened to the Khoikhoi and the San, who, like the American Indians of the eastern coast, were killed off by firearms, disease, and starvation, and their remnants absorbed by miscegenation, to leave virtually no native inhabitants. In America, those natives who were not simply erased were transported wholesale (as during the Cherokee Trail of Tears episode) out of their homeland west across the Mississippi, to a unilaterally declared Indian Territory (which Indians subsequently lost, as did the Griquas in South Africa). Could this have been done in South Africa? There were a number of reasons why it was not: the relatively small numbers of Whites, with the additional element of a degree of (sometimes restraining) control from London rather than control by local settlers; the relatively dense populations of the Black Africans encountered at the eastern Cape border; and the Black Africans' unwillingness to offer physical resistance, as during the costly Zulu Wars, the nine Kaffir Wars with the Xhosa, and the confrontations with the tenacious Moshesh in his mountain fastnesses of Sotho territory.

However, given the will to exercise the industrial-military force at its disposal, the British Empire during the nineteenth century could doubtless have removed the Black African nations from *all* of their land (rather than some of it), had it coveted all the land for White settlers. A fundamental reason it did not was neatly expressed by De Kiewiet (1941) in his classic history of South Africa written forty years ago. Why was there so little (European) immigration to South Africa, as opposed to Australia or Canada? Well, he declared, there *was* large-scale immigration when South Africa began to industrialize, but it was *Black African* immigration. In other words, the use to industrial capitalism of the labor reserve that these subjugated African nations[11] represented was greater than the utility of abolishing them (by war or by transportation to distant parts) and taking (all) their land for European settlement. Genocide was not so attractive a course as the continuing exploitation of the cheap labor of those who had been overwhelmed. The same is true today in the grand apartheid policy, which is the child of the native reserves of labor that the British Empire established during the latter part of the nineteenth century.[12]

The difficulty in all this for the Whites, of course, is whether they can now be sure that they can forever control the increasing numbers of Black *untermensch*. All of this can be turned on its head and looked at from the standpoint of Black Africans. With the retreat of overt political colonialism, Black Africa has been selectively abolishing or containing White residents. Tanzania has abolished the White coffee planters near Kilimanjaro; but the Ivory Coast, Kenya, and Zambia have chosen to contain a good proportion of their White settlers. Their reasons are that it makes apparently good economic sense, and, as long as any perceived negative sociopolitical ramifications of such continued White presence are outweighed by the profit they bring to the country, the Whites can stay if they choose. From the standpoint of Black Africa, the perceived negative sociopolitical role of minority Whites ruling in southern Africa must be abolished; and since 1974 the removal of White control in Angola, Mozambique, and Zimbabwe-Rhodesia, with possibilities of movement in Namibia, must give them heart.

Whether the existence of Whites per se (as opposed to Whites-only rule) must be abolished from the remaining goal — South Africa — is another matter. Most Black African nationalists do not adhere to the emotional rhetoric of "driving the Whites into the sea" as a statement of policy. Many are prepared to grant the evident historical right of White Africans to remain in South Africa, for Black African nationalism must surely realize that, if it can take over the reins of the South African state without too much destruction (and too much loss of White expertise), it will be the most powerful state in sub-Saharan Africa, rivaled only by Nigeria, and in a better position than Nigeria to dominate and develop the portion of the continent south of the equator. Therefore, a sage Black African strategy would not be the abolition but the containment of "its" Whites in the future Azania, the putting of them to their most productive use. And many of the Whites would stay under those conditions — given a measure of civil peace and security — for the majority of the Afrikaners, in particular, would surely want to remain in their only homeland.

In the meantime, however, the methods for achieving this future are most uncertain. The Whites' fear of retribution contributes to their reluctance to make fundamental changes in the direction of a more inclusive, power-sharing society. Such reluctance, naturally, gives rise to greater pressures for change from those who are subordinated, to greater tension, and to greater racially conditioned emotionalism: the situation feeds off of itself.

Since I feel I have been wandering from social geography into an area where I am not at all expert, I will draw this discussion to a close. I end by asserting that the tension and the fear that are the concomitants of the South African society's structure are reflected in the urban geography of Cape Town and that the manipulation of this urban geography itself has, in turn, created tension and fear in the society. Hence, the space-society dialectic that has run through this work. I foresee an increase in tension in Cape Town—an increase in civil unrest and perhaps also in sabotage and in urban guerrilla activity —rendering it a less and less pleasant place to live for all Capetonians. That is a personal opinion, but it is based on the feelings and ideas that Capetonians expressed to me and I have expressed to the reader throughout this book.

Humanistic geography, among other things, implies looking at the city through the texture of the lives of its inhabitants. Seen this way, the astonishing physical beauty of the Cape Peninsula is metamorphosed into a remarkably bleak experience of living for many Capetonians. The reader must have gained some sense of this, for the bleakness has been conveyed in the words of those who are experiencing apartheid's inhumanity. Not only is such an account distressing, it bodes ill for any peaceful future.

POSTSCRIPT

I wrote those last words in January 1980. In July 1980, unexpectedly, I was visiting Cape Town again. During the intervening six months, events had occurred on the Cape Peninsula that seemed to confirm my pessimism about its immediate sociopolitical future.

On February 12 the Coloured students of Mountview High School in Hanover Park boycotted classes for one day in a protest against conditions at their school. Official assurances were given that corrective steps would be taken, but a month later (March 13) the dissatisfaction of parents and students at Mountview High and at Crystal High (also in Hanover Park) surfaced again: neither school had electricity; there were not enough textbooks and stationery; broken fixtures and windows were left unrepaired (some since the 1976 unrest). Separate and inferior "gutter education" was being protested. By mid-April a boycott of classes over these issues spread throughout the Cape Flats schools and then rapidly to other areas of South Africa (and to some degree to other Nonwhite racial groups). There were soon somewhere between 20,000 (Minister Marais Steyn's estimate) and 100,000 (that of the *Argus*, 21 April 1980) pupils involved. At first there were marches and peaceful demonstrations, and then the police used tear gas and batons (there was a report of their using dogs as well). Steyn threatened to close the schools and declared that the question was not one of education but one of "children being influenced by propaganda."[13] He said that the government could not countenance "the misuse being made of schoolchildren by agitators." The pro-government newspaper the *Citizen*[14] editorialized on April 22:

> Education, however, is only one area in which we are running into trouble with our Coloured folk.

> They have rejected the representative and administrative machinery with which they controlled their own affairs.[15]

> They have become more radical.

> Far too many Coloured people have thrown in their lot with the Black militants, instead of regarding the Whites as friends and natural allies, as people with whom they can link hands to ensure a peaceful and prosperous future for all.

> The fact that there is a new militancy among Coloured students, a linking up of Coloured youth and Black school radicals, is warning enough that we risk losing the support not only of the older, but of the younger generation of Coloureds as well. . . .

> [The government] must act, as a matter of some priority, to bring the Coloured people back into the special relationship they had vis-à-vis the Whites.

> We stress: The alienation of the Coloureds must not be allowed to continue unchecked.

This Cassandra-like editorial had no visible effect on governmental policy. The school boycott continued, and concurrently a series of strikes in various parts of the country (in Cape Town at a food-processing factory and among meat workers) heightened tensions. On May 24 some of the boycotting high school students (who had until then acted with restraint) disrupted supermarkets in Cape Town city center and in Bellville. Police baton-charged them; 134 arrests were made. Incidents of stone throwing began to grow in number, and on May 28 police fired on a crowd during a vehicle-stoning incident in Halt Road, Elsies River (Map 28). Two people were killed, and sentiments were further polarized. (On June 1 African National Congress saboteurs exploded devices at the strategic oil-from-coal plant at Sasolburg in the Orange Free State, doing about $8 million of damage.) On June 2 the funeral procession for the two youths shot in Halt Road, 2 kilometers long, consisted of over 12,000 mourners. On June 3, in protest against higher fares, a bus boycott began on the Cape Flats and was adhered to widely. Over 250 persons had by then been arrested and held without trial (and in some cases incommunicado) by the police under the security laws (*Argus*, 3 June 1980). Extra riot police were flown in from other provinces of South Africa.

Then, the anniversary of the start of the Soweto rioting, June 16, approached. Every year since 1976 the government has had to steel itself against civil unrest on this day. And in 1980 it was in Cape Town, not on the Rand, that the greatest demonstration of popular disaffection occurred. According to the *Cape Times*, the Nonwhite commemorative work boycott was 70 percent successful throughout the Cape Peninsula on June 16, and somewhat less widespread on the following day. This was by far the most successful one-day general strike in any of the republic's cities. David Curry, of the (Coloured) Labour party, explained that in his view "the root of the present unrest and yesterday's massive stay-away in the Peninsula was the Group Areas Act" (*Cape Times*, 17 June 1980).

It was on this and the following days (June 17 and 18) that the worst violence occurred, centered again around Elsies River. At least forty-two people were shot dead by the police, most of them stone throwers, arsonists, and looters. There is no doubt that, as during the 1976 unrest, unruly skollie elements precipitated the rioting. But there can also be no doubt that the widespread disorder—which was not confined to Elsies River—expressed the bitterness of the popular mood. A middle-aged Coloured man employed in Elsies River was quoted as saying, "There is an anger in the young people that bullets won't shoot down." (*Sunday Times* [Johannesburg] , 22 June 1980). Map 28 shows where incidents of civil disorder—not including student boycotts—occurred in the Cape Peninsula during the one-month period from May 24.

Widespread civil violence had subsided by the end of June, although the bus and red-meat boycotts continued (by then the midyear vacations had arrived for the Coloured schools). To be in Cape

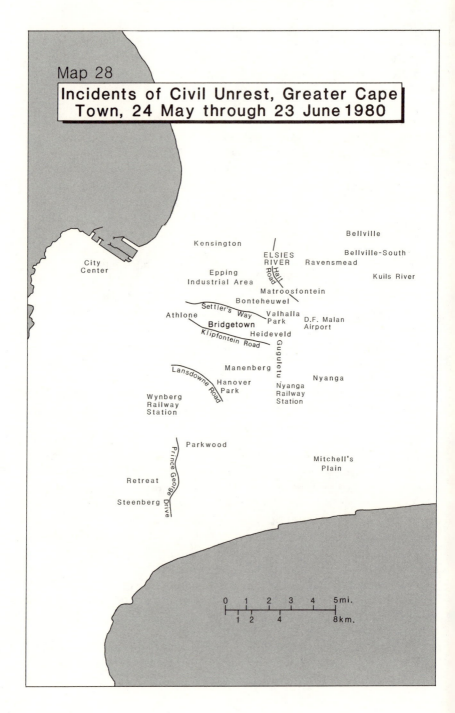

Map 28

Incidents of Civil Unrest, Greater Cape Town, 24 May through 23 June 1980

Town at this time, as I was, was to apprehend a sort of grayness of spirit in the city. *Place*—a sense of pride in living on the Cape of Good Hope, which Sir Francis Drake on rounding it in 1580 deemed "a most stately thing and the fairest cape we saw in the whole circumference of the earth"—has clearly been a focus of unifying sentiment for Capetonians. Yet now, after decades of legislated inequality imposed according to color, it seems that *race* is becoming a more important element of self-definition, especially for many among the young.

Philadelphia, September 1980

NOTES

Notes

Chapter 1

1. There are, for example, many valid insights in Oscar Newman's (1972) *Defensible Space: Crime Prevention through Urban Design.*

2. This phrase is John Friedmann's, a professor of urban planning at UCLA. I encountered it when I was one of his students in 1972, and it also appears in his published academic writings.

3. Dr. Hendrik Verwoerd was minister of native affairs from 1954 to 1958 and prime minister from 1958 until his assassination (by a crazed White man) in 1966. A brilliant social psychologist, he is widely credited with being the efficient architect of many apartheid measures, especially the Bantustan, or Homelands, policy. (See pp. 66-69.)

4. The Khoisan peoples were obliterated during the northward and eastward extension of the White frontier out from Cape Town from the mid-seventeenth to nineteenth centuries. The Dutch and Huguenot farmers (Boers) wiped them out with firearms and diseases. As late as 1879, a British Cape magistrate referred to them as "game."

5. It is only fair to note that the three or four excerpts from Olive Schreiner's writings that I employ in this section are not wholly representative of the complexity of her view. That is, she was far ahead of her time in calling for a common South Africanness and was prepared to wield a cudgel on behalf of "the underdog," be they Boers, Blacks, or women; yet, at the same time, she subscribed to the then-current Social Darwinist idea, which today would be labeled racist by many. (See, for example, First and Scott, 1980, pp. 258-61, 277, 293, 304, 322-23, and 337-40.)

6. The municipal washhouses of the era before washing machines were places where, as one Coloured person interviewed told me, "for 5^d a tub we did the Europeans' washing. There wasn't room in our own backyards to hang it out, they were too small. So we did it up there" (that is, at the Mowbray washhouse, which was still being used in 1976).

7. Tavern of the Seas is an old nickname for Cape Town.

8. Diminutive of *Mogamat*, not surprisingly a very widespread forename among the Islamic Cape Malays. "G" in Afrikaans sounds like the "ch" in the Scottish word "loch."

9. This is, as noted, a catchall term subsuming *all* the Cape Flats townships. Its first family having moved in as long ago as May 1961, Bonteheuwel now is certainly *not* the least pleasant of the townships to inhabit.

10. The parallels throughout the colonial world are legion. Mannoni (1956) reported that the Malagasy alleged precisely the same of children of Malagasy-French unions. The Anglo-Indians or Eurasians of imperial India were by the English "traditionally said to have acquired the worst characteristics of both races" (Allen, 1975, p. 104).

11. Tokai is a southern exurban area of greater Cape Town of the highest socioeconomic status.

Chapter 2

1. Kanaaldorp is known today as District Six, a name conferred after a local government reorganization in 1867.

2. Schotsche's Kloof is popularly known as the Malay Quarter.

3. These are the words of J. S. Marais (1939) in his authoritative history, *The Cape Coloured People, 1652-1937.*

4. This estimate is based on Batson's (1947) criteria for a "mixed" residential area—that it should be less than 75 percent European and less than 75 percent non-European.

5. The Gardens area of Cape Town was so named because it is adjacent to the place where the Dutch East India Company established its vegetable plots.

6. M. G. Whisson, personal communication, 1977.

7. *Bungalow* comes from Gujarati *bangalo* and Hindi *bangla*, "of Bengal."

8. That is, pertaining to the British raj in India, not to Eurasians.

9. M. G. Whisson, personal communication, 1977.

10. This word is perhaps misleading. Many of these "obsolescent" houses were renovated into bijou Chelsea cottages for Whites after the Group Areas Act's removal of their former inhabitants. (See Chapter 7.)

11. Confirmation of this characterization of White/Nonwhite neighboring comes from Margo Russell's (1961) study of a Durban mixed residential zone. See especially pp. 171-200.

12. The date was 1902 according to Wilson and Mafeje (1963, p. 3). Saunders (1978, p. 29) reported that this occurred in February 1901.

13. The epidemic was vividly recalled by one older ex-Mowbrayite I interviewed: "They were dying like flies down in District Six. . . ." The epidemic did not spare Nonwhite Mowbray either, as Simcox (1975, p. 7) noted. The official figure, which Marais (1939) deemed "a guess," was that half a million Nonwhites died. This figure would have included more than one in nine Nonwhites in South Africa, which seems incredible.

14. These figures are from Wilson and Mafeje (1963, pp. 56-59).

15. Kuper, Watts, and R. J. Davies followed this quotation (p. 158) with a finely argued and instructive consideration of just what constitutes "voluntary" and "involuntary" racial residential segregation.

16. "Low grade" is defined as housing priced (in 1950-1952) at under £2,000. (South Africa changed to its present system of decimal currency in February 1961.)

17. Thus, Observatory, where the Whites were largely blue-collar workers, was an area where professional Coloureds could find housing. Compare this situation with the situation in the United States, where Susskind (1973, p. 300) observed: "Racial integration . . . will be most feasible when there are no significant class differences between the races, or when minority racial groups are of higher status than the whites." The extra point earned for having higher socioeconomic status is counterbalanced by the point lost for not being White. Russell's (1961) study in Durban revealed much the same situation.

18. For example, this last point was made by a letter entitled "Coloured Penetration" in the *Cape Times* of 14 July 1949.

Chapter 3

1. This depends on the White government's final plans. Under its Final Consolidation Proposals of March 1975 the proximate homeland would be South Ndebele. Under a 1979 plan by Prof. R. P. Botha, a member of the Prime Minister's Planning Advisory Council, the proximate homeland would become Lebowa. Another homeland blueprint, put out in 1977, was prepared by the government-aligned South African Bureau of Racial Affairs.

2. N. N. Patricios, personal communications, 1977.

3. This phrase is from the celebrated words of the Stallard (Transvaal local government) Commission of 1922 concerning the role of Black African labor in South African cities. (See Chapter 10.)

4. It was David M. Smith's article in *Antipode* (July 1974) that brought to my attention this most quotable of quotes for a geographer studying South Africa. The lie is given to it by the bizarrely tragic story of a White woman in Cape Town who in the period between 1977 and 1979 had a disease that turned her skin brown; the change had far-reaching effects on the woman's social and family life.

5. Such euphemisms are so typical of pronouncements by government spokesmen that the *Economist* (London, 21 June 1980) dubbed them "apartheidspeak" and offered as an example the minister of community development's characterization of the Group Areas Act as a "friend of the people" (because it aids in slum clearance—see p. 283). Further examples of phraseology of this kind will be encountered throughout this book.

6. The Union of South Africa, founded in 1910 by the merger of the British Cape Colony and Natal with the Afrikaner (until 1900) South African Republic (Transvaal) and the Orange Free State, became the present Republic of South Africa in 1961.

7. The House of Assembly is the lower house of South Africa's Westminster-style Parliament. The upper house is the Senate. This bicameral system is about to be changed (1980).

8. There were perhaps a handful of Black Africans who, as registered voters under the tattered remnants of the old Cape franchise, continued until 1959 to be "exempted persons" in terms of the Native Laws Amendment Act of 1937. They could live and even occupy their own property *outside* those parts of urban areas designated for Black Africans. Wilson and Mafeje (1963, p. 7) considered that these persons' rights would be negated, and they themselves removed, by the Group Areas Act.

9. Marais (1939, p. 282) wrote of the "unshakeable belief in the essential inferiority of the Coloured man's 'blood.' . . . It leads to the passionate aversion to miscegenation—the contamination of pure with bad blood—which is the primary article of faith of the South African nation." Marais was, of course, referring here, with undisguised selective perception, to the *White* South African nation! Olive Schreiner (1923, p. 139) in the 1890s had written: "All that we are qualified to assert in the present infantile state of our knowledge is, that there is a danger, and we believe that it is a very great danger, of reversion to the lower primitive type where two widely severed varieties cross, that humanity may by that process lose the results of hundreds of years of slow-evolution. . . . It is all important, socially, both as individuals and collectively as a society, that the mingling of our breeds . . . is almost always distinctly anti-social."

10. L. Kuper, personal communication, 1977.

11. An Indian group area to be established near Mitchell's Plain (the southern extremity of greater Cape Town; see Map 19) was mooted in 1978. Further details, such as its precise delineation, are lacking.

Chapter 4

1. Sen. William Proxmire, 7 July 1977, referred to "healthy, diverse communities with a mix of race, age, and income" during hearings before the Commission on Banking, Housing, and Urban Affairs in Washington, D.C.

2. See "Displacement: City Neighborhoods in Transition," pp. 2, 25. National Urban Coalition, July 1978, Washington, D.C.

3. Except ethnic differentiation among Whites, which was discussed in Chapter 3.

4. Prof. R. J. Davies, interviewed in Cape Town, 7 August 1978.

5. For example, Indians attend the same high schools as Coloureds in many places, as in East London and Cape Town. If the Indians had made up a larger proportion of the total population of the area in question (in the Cape Town metropolis, it is only 1 percent), they would have been provided with their own high schools. Since they do not and since they must receive high school education somewhere, they are assigned not to White schools, nor to Black African schools, but to Coloured schools—apartheid education planners presuming that their greatest affinity lies with the Coloureds. (I have just learned [1980] that Indian students in Cape Town now have a high school of "their own" in Rylands. Whether all Indian students throughout the metropolis now commute to this school or whether some of them still attend Coloured high schools nearer home, I do not know.)

6. Certain cities—for example, Pretoria—no longer permit having live-in Nonwhite servants in any new White developments.

7. Strictly speaking, Asiatics, but there are so few Chinese or other Asiatics that they have been subsumed under the heading Indians. All these population groups are those defined by apartheid legislation.

8. The name Mother City was, of course, given to Cape Town by Whites; it refers to the place where Whites first came to South Africa. Cape Town is equally the Mother City of the Coloured people. The Black Africans, who are historically somewhat "strangers" in the western Cape, can hardly be expected to feel that it is *their* mother city, and I would surmise that Indians would have such an affective tie to Durban, rather than to Cape Town. Because it is the dominant group's continually employed term, however, it seems that Mother City is accepted general usage for Cape Town. Note that the local Black African soccer team in Langa has called itself Mother City (Wilson and Mafeje, 1963, Plate 10, facing p. 132).

9. Even the government's own Theron Commission, reporting in June 1976, concluded that this is so. (See van der Horst, 1976, p. 9.)

10. This is a statement incapable of measurement, but I do not believe it to be misleading.

11. This phrase is not used idly. Celebrated historical antecedents of apartheid were the Statutes of Kilkenny, enacted in 1366 to maintain social separation between the English colonizers of the Pale around Dublin and the outnumbering, lower-status (to English eyes) Irish. No speaking of Gaelic, no intermarriage, no foster parenting of English children with Irish families or vice versa, and various other prohibitions—all were enacted because the English perceived themselves to be at risk as an enclave of "civilization" surrounded by a sea of barbarity. The statutes proved to be unenforceable.

12. I was informed of this by a reliable senior academic source involved with the Mitchell's Plain project.

13. Compare the situation in Epping with the situation in Philadelphia exemplified by a "letter to a newspaper written by a proud resident of Kensington, a staunchly White working class community. Here, the writer defines the boundaries of his neighborhood to exclude the location where a crime was committed: '. . . reporting a hold-up that happened on the 4500 block of Frankford Avenue and calling it Kensington is indeed an injustice to our area. . . . In future reporting, make certain that the following boundaries are adhered to: Lehigh Avenue to the south; Torresdale or Eric Avenue to the north; Richmond Street to the east, and Front Street to the west. This is Greater Kensington as we know it'" (Muller, Meyer, and Cybriwsky, 1976, pp. 26-27). This represents the existence of what I might term uncodified group areas.

14. In a personal communication (1977), Whisson informed me that "there are 191 lettings in Schotsche's Kloof, plus 20 in the restoration scheme plus a small number of private houses. . . . Multiply this by 6.5 [the rule of thumb for present Coloured/Malay household size in Cape Town], and it equals plus or minus 1,750 persons."

15. Perhaps another candidate for this label is the location of shanties next to some ostentatiously substantial homes of Indian business people in Rylands. This latter gradient, however, does not cross the White/Nonwhite divide but is a more purely economic one.

16. Cars on this section of Prince George Drive were attacked by stone throwers during the June 1980 unrest, too.

17. This figure and that for Black Africans excludes the Cape Flats squatters, for whom information is incomplete. They are living in group areas zoned for Coloureds, Indians, border strips, industrial use, and Whites and on unproclaimed land and Black African space (not strictly the group areas' domain). (See Chapter 10.)

Chapter 5

1. The July proposals included one for a Chinese group area, which was discussed, reformulated, discussed again, and eventually dropped.

2. Horrell was at that time (and through 1977) senior research officer of the politically liberal South African Institute of Race Relations.

3. For example, a memorandum had been submitted by the Association of Building Societies of South Africa pointing out that property values would depreciate in districts zoned as possible group areas for Coloured people; this would affect the builders since they held a number of bonds in such areas (where presumably some Whites were already living).

Chapter 6

1. And it is wholly a White group area.

2. The administrative capital of the Republic of South Africa is Pretoria, but the legislative capital is Cape Town. Come the parliamentary season at the beginning of each calendar year, and ministers and upper-echelon civil servants, with files and documents in hand, have to travel the 1,500 kilometers between Pretoria and Cape Town.

3. Recall that 600,000 South Africans have been or are to be removed, of whom only 1 percent are Whites.

4. Winter (1971) wrote, "We had not been in Simonstown for more than a week when we were warned by a fellow countryman [that is, an Englishman] about having too much contact with the Coloureds. 'You can catch disease from their sweat, you know,' he remarked cheerily as we drank a cup of tea together." This remark was made in 1959.

5. One can speculate with interest about the possibility of a study like Alex Haley's written by a Coloured South African—perhaps most likely by a Cape Malay who could trace his or her line back to Sheikh Joseph or another exiled political figure, and thence back to some village in Java.

6. In Afrikaans *stompie* means, literally, "cigarette butt" or (in Britain) "fag-end." Figuratively, it can refer to a person of small stature ("shorty").

7. My thanks to Cosmo Pieterse and Val Wagner for helping me with the nuances of translation of both this poem and the one quoted on p. 154.

8. Edelstein was one of only two White people killed in the Soweto rioting that began on 16 June 1976. Hundreds of Black Africans died.

9. The APO was founded in 1902 and faded away during the 1950s. Its major figure was Dr. Abdurahman, a Cape Malay who died in 1940.

10. This refers to the four legal subcategories of "Coloured": "Cape Coloured," (Cape) "Malay," "Griqua," and "other Coloured." Of these four subcategories, "Cape Coloureds" officially make up (1970 census) over 93 percent. "Asiatics" are not included in these statistics.

11. Most of Woodstock had been proclaimed for Whites on 31 January and 20 February 1958, and the city center so on 11 June 1965.

12. The National Monuments Commission is involved in the "preservation" of parts of the Malay Quarter.

13. Is this preserve supposed to depict picturesque poverty? It seems similar to the "Save Arniston" campaign over the western-Ireland-like appearance of a Coloured fishing village about 200 kilometers from Cape Town. Little was said about the material conditions of life of the Coloured families. The concern was more with the site and fabric of their whitewashed, aesthetically appealing thatched hovels.

14. See the pamphlet published by the Centre for Intergroup Studies, University of Cape Town, in December 1979 entitled "District Six," especially pp. 3-4.

15. The Shell Company of South Africa, after a 1978 arrangement to obtain land for a service station in District Six, the next year abandoned the project and expressed concern about future plans for the area.

Chapter 7

1. One of the treasured possessions of the ex-Mowbray Muslims is the deeds, on vellum, for the plot for the Mowbray mosque and the adjacent imam's (priest's) house, handwritten, signed, and sealed by Her Majesty's Governor of the Cape of Good Hope Sir Philip Wodehouse. The mosque's land is still owned by the Muslims, but they were dispossessed of that portion of the plot on which the house (renovated and lived in by Whites) stands by the eminent domain clauses of the Group Areas Act. To see the Muslims' impressive document and then to realize its utter negation by "notwithstanding anything to the contrary contained in any law or deed . . ." is to appreciate the monopoly of power mandated by the Group Areas Act.

2. This interviewee graduated from Trafalgar High School in District Six and had become a schoolteacher. "Houses" refers to the originally British secondary school organization of intramural sports and other activities.

3. M. G. Whisson, personal communication, 1975.

4. Another interviewee used the phrase "the wrong side of the line" to indicate which members of a Pass-White family had remained Coloured.

5. The reference is to Marc Fried's (1963) work of the same title, which concerned removees forced from Boston's West End.

6. If members of what had been the same nuclear family in Mowbray were living in separate households (for example, parents and grown son; full siblings [both grown]) at the time of my survey, only one person was interviewed for the sample. Other members of the dispersed family were often interviewed, but not added in to the sample unless the relationship was uncle/aunt, nephew/niece, cousin, or another relationship more distant. The questionnaire I used has not been included as an appendix to this book, but a copy can be obtained by direct communication with me.

7. This, however, was using a somewhat different occupational status scheme devised by the Centre for Intergroup Studies (University of Cape Town) for its 1975 Mobility study.

8. M. G. Whisson, personal communications, 1976 and 1977.

9. This figure (which I came across in Maasdorp and Pillay, 1977, p. 180) originated with the *Daily News* (Durban) report (22 August 1974) of a statement made by Sen. L. E. D. Winchester.

10. Strictly speaking, these terms refer to the rate at which the central government lends money to the Cape Town City Council for housing construction. In fact, only families whose principal wage earner was receiving (at the time of interview) less than R100 per month (on 1 June 1976 this rose to R200) were eligible for the subsidized—that is, "subeconomic"—housing. Additionally, in Heideveld "subeconomic" refers to various details in the house's construction, such as its having curtained passageways from one room to another (no doors). Since real incomes have been rising among the Coloured people, it can be appreciated that the demand for economic housing is growing while that for subeconomic is declining.

11. This is one method for computing a poverty datum line for South Africa. (See SAIRR, 1978a, pp. 202-3.)

12. Throughout Chapters 7, 8, and 9, the number of cases in each respect—be it regarding where the interviewee's job was when he or she lived in Mowbray or where he or she went shopping or to the movies—will vary from 100 on down. For example, there are only 19 comparisons (that is, before and after removal) of costs of travel to high schools because in only 19 households were there children attending high school both before and after group areas removals *and* traveling by public transportation (as opposed to walking or going in a parent's car) whereby comparative costs could be computed. Through the action of many such detailed constraints, N will vary continually. In *this* case (that is, preremoval job location), a number of interviewees were already retired when group areas development came to Mowbray, one man was disabled, et cetera.

13. In 1960, the life expectancy of the average Coloured male was 44.82 years; of the average female, 47.77 years. The average for 1970-1975 had risen to 50.54 and 57.22 years, respectively.

14. Of the fourteen heads of household who employed the image "Mowbray was like one big family," seven were Muslim and seven were not. This is a disproportionately high number of Muslims to Christians—that is, 50:50 instead of 35:64—perhaps because, to many Malays, Mowbray *was* one big family.

15. It appears that Muslims did not participate in the City and Suburban League.

16. With the rise of Black consciousness there has come an increased boycott of White sports. However, Nonwhite attendance at White sporting events offered certain possibilities. If the reader considers the reference to South Africa's national sport an exaggeration, he or she might consider rugby's symbolism, especially for the Afrikaners. In 1974, the British Lions touring team was humiliating the (Whites-only) South African Springboks. Certain White sensibilities were tender. Nonwhite spectators at these matches have long had the habit of shouting for the opposition against the White Springboks, as I found when I watched the British Lions play the Springboks in Johannesburg; the Nonwhites in their separate enclosure booed the Springboks. The Port Elizabeth Nationalist newspaper *Die Oosterlig* editorialized in mid-July 1974 that such behavior by Nonwhite spectators could be likened to that of "terrorists" on "South Africa's borders"—presumably meaning the northern borders of Namibia. The paper apparently in all seriousness called for a ban on Nonwhite spectators at Boet Erasmus Stadium in Port Elizabeth during international test matches *or for a screening system that would differentiate between genuine rugby aficionados and those who wished only to express anti-White feelings*! (See *Argus*, 18 July 1974 and a particularly hilarious cartoon in the *Cape Herald*, circulating mainly on the Cape Flats, on 27 July 1974.) "Multiracial" sport is now gradually becoming more and more officially tolerated in South Africa.

17. Because of its Cape Flats bus feeders, the Mowbray railway station was in 1965-66 (at the time of the removals) the fourth busiest in the metropolis, after Cape Town, Langa, and Salt River.

18. This game is makeshift billiards played with checkers, instead of billiard balls.

19. This verb implies a shade of maliciousness.

20. That is, the mechanical task of sewing the pieces of cloth together.

21. Some St. Helenans have been classified as Coloured, others as White. A White St. Helenan still lived in Mowbray after removals; this couple was removed.

22. O. D. Wollheim, personal communications, 1979.

23. Mr. G. Seeff, property consultant, kindly provided these figures through the good offices of Dr. M. Putterill, then (1977) head of the Urban Problems Research Unit at the University of Cape Town.

24. Even this exception proves the rule. Case 2 is the only case of the twenty transactions in which both B (the Nonwhite seller) and C (the White buyer and subsequent seller)

were people of comparable status and who knew each other from long coresidence in the Dorp. C, in other words, was a Pass-White household; therefore, this deal was the only one between White-Nonwhite putative equals.

25. In fact, among those who live there today are persons who have been harassed for their strong antigovernment political views; one was "banned" (analogous to house arrest) and another fled the country in fear for his safety. I insert this here *not* to point a finger but to convey to the reader the *impossibility* of living in South Africa without being in some way party to legally imposed racial and economic injustice. I am fully aware that this inevitably applies to my own case as a visiting researcher.

26. In implementing the Group Areas Act, the government has wisely seen fit to recognize the Muslim claim that, once a plot has been sanctified for worship, it is forever sanctified; therefore, mosques are not being demolished. In a celebrated Port Elizabeth case, this very consideration influenced the construction of a freeway.

27. She died in Heideveld in September 1975.

Chapter 8

1. Eid is short for Eid-ul-Fitr, an important Muslim festival at the end of Ramadan; it is also known on the Cape as Labarang, a term of Malay origin.

2. It is accepted that most of the old White Cape families must have varying degrees of Coloured "blood." In Cape Town's earliest days, marriage between Europeans and Khoikhoi was allowed. The surgeon and explorer Pieter van Meerhoff married the sister-in-law of a Khoikhoi chief, and the marriage celebrations were paid for by the Dutch East India Company. Another such marriage between an early governor's parents rendered Simon van der Stel a person who today would be classified as Coloured. The possibilities for such retrospective racial classification are, naturally, endless. A row erupted in the Dutch Reformed Church in May 1975 when it was stated that *Christ's* identity document would have been that of an Asiatic, for he was "olive skinned" and had a "forked beard." Dr. Koot Vorster, a brother of the then prime minister and a former moderator of the church, denounced this view as "sheer nonsense" and said that Christ was a "supranational figure" who could not be racially classified (*Cape Times*, 22 May 1975).

3. But I was not addressed as Mister John by the younger members of the family. To the five-year-old grandson I was "White Uncle John" as opposed to his father's brother John, whose skin color was similar to mine!

4. Such relatives included first cousins, but not parents, say, a White father and a Coloured mother.

5. M. G. Whisson, personal communications, 1979.

6. Peter Hain is an active organizer in London's Anti-Apartheid League who has been responsible for many demonstrations, especially those dealing with the partially successful sports boycott of "White South Africa."

7. Yet, during World War II, they were not placed with the Coloureds but in the Indian and Malay Corps.

8. This point is apparently still at issue. See Chapter 11.

9. See, for example, *Ahmed Jawoodien* vs. *the Secretary for the Interior* (X.R. 259/68) in the Supreme Court of South Africa (Cape of Good Hope division).

10. S. P. Cilliers, personal communication, 1976.

11. All distance are straight-line distances, unless they were between places on opposite sides of Table Mountain; that is, when a journey between Heathfield and Sea Point was mentioned, the distance was computed by measuring *around* the mountain, which forces all routes to skirt it. There were few such journeys; the one most often mentioned was Wynberg/Grassy Park to Cape Town city center.

12. Marris (1961) noted similar grounds for complaint in Lagos.

13. N. N. Patricios, personal communication, 1977.

Chapter 9

1. The raw data are from C. Barac (of the Urban Problems Research Unit, University of Cape Town), 1977.

2. These responses appear identical to those of many of Marris's Lagos informants, who had experienced a similar removal to the city's periphery. (See Marris, 1961, p. 101.)

3. Such anti-Portuguese sentiments are wholly shared by many (non-Portuguese) White South Africans. (See Watson, 1970, p. 48; and Adam, 1971, pp. 129-30.)

4. Clearly "those places up there in Africa" are perceived by Capetonians as a different, distant land from the Cape Peninsula.

5. A fascinating situation now exists. Having been a successful professional man, Mr. McDonald traveled widely and went "home" to the Orkney Islands more than once. Through his father, he owned a one-sixteenth share in the family lands there, which had appreciated in value enormously since North Sea oil production began. He looked like a middle-class Spaniard with silver hair, and he said in 1978 that he was planning (although this may have been a fantasy) to retire to Orkney in 1979 and live the rest of his years with his "family." He was a bachelor.

6. Moodley (1975) and Maasdorp and Pillay (1977) published similar findings for Indians removed to new group areas in Durban.

7. M. G. Whisson, personal communication, 1977.

8. This is an excellent example of a "master-identity" Athlone, analogous to the East End of London and the West Side of Chicago. Hanover Park is not "in the middle of Athlone" properly speaking but 4 kilometers to the southeast. However, the *Cape Times* assumed (correctly) that the majority of its White readership had no idea of the precise location of Hanover Park and therefore needed some guidance.

9. This is so, although there was apparently some controversy among the police because some felt it reflected badly on the police that they were not capable of maintaining peace themselves; others were concerned lest the vigilantes come to take the law too much into their own hands. (See, for example, Bloch, 1977, in which a measure of doubt is cast on the aptness of so uncritically enthusiastic a depiction of the Peacemakers as the *Cape Times* offered.)

10. Lavender Hill is another old name with District Six connotations given to a new Coloured Cape Flats township. So, together with the naming of Hanover Park, we see another quasi-official recognition of the sentimental claims that Cape Coloured people have on District Six.

11. The people moved to "new towns" and "expanded towns," therefore, moved both voluntarily *and* by assisted passage, as it were, under the aegis of city housing authorities.

Chapter 10

1. This includes Malays. There may also be a very few Asiatic (Indian) squatters.

2. "The squatting evil" was a phrase used in an official notice from the Department of Community Development to local authorities in August 1977, as reported in the *Cape Times*, 10 August 1977. The phrase was used again, by L. Fouché, secretary for community development, in his paper of 6 July 1978, "The Resolution of the Squatter Problem in South Africa," p. 2.

3. See Maasdorp and Pillay, 1977, p. 174.

4. According to Maree, 1978, p. 5.

5. By August 1979 the deputy minister of community development estimated the metropolitan housing shortage for Coloureds to be about 30,000 units (*Argus,* 14 August 1979).

6. For example, a furor arose over the destruction (although it was done during the summer) of some shanties in southern Cape Town. "At the end of January the houses of 26 Coloured families (about 150 individuals) on Klip Road in Grassy Park were demolished by the Cape Divisional Council and the inhabitants were left in the open on the site. Makeshift structures were constructed and three weeks later Divisional Council workers again moved in to destroy them. After several nights in the open, the families were permitted to move to Lourdes Farm, a Divisional Council site-and-service area where there were already 670 squatter families living. . . . The fact that squatter shanties were demolished with bulldozers was raised in Parliament. The Minister of Community Development gave an assurance that bulldozers were not used but he subsequently admitted that earth-moving equipment was used" (SAIRR, 1978a, p. 450). That there is a distinction between bulldozers and other earth-moving equipment, such as the front-end loaders frequently used for shanty demolition, is true. It is also a very misleading distinction, as the minister must have known. It also, of course, makes very little difference to the shanty dwellers which of these large machines was used to destroy their homes.

7. The poverty datum line is an index widely used in studies of South Africa dealing with standards of living. For a discussion of its computation, see, for example, SAIRR, 1978a, pp. 202-3.

8. Among many others, see Fair and R. J. Davies, 1976, pp. 153-54; Cilliers, 1975, pp. 42-52; Adam, 1971, pp. 93-94.

9. Maree (1978, p. 9) is of the opinion that "the purpose of Section 3C of the Prevention of Illegal Squatting Amendment Act [1977] is also to introduce a form of influx control on Coloureds. It has been made an offence for an employer in the Cape Town Region, Stellenbosch, Paarl, Somerset West and Strand to employ Coloured people from outside unless the employer obtains a certificate from a local authority that 'proper housing' is available for them." However, there are no Coloured homelands to which Coloureds could be "repatriated," and the minister of community development, Marais Steyn, has said (*Cape Times,* 26 February 1977) that the authorities "have no intention" of applying influx control to Coloured people. Two days later, the *Argus* reported that the Cape Town Chamber of Industries had been told that "lodging or staying with friends will be regarded as suitable accommodation" and that there was no need for a certificate for a worker who would commute from outside the area. But why insert a section in an act if the intention is truly never to use it?

10. In the Transvaal Province report of the local government commission (Stallard), Pretoria, 1922, paragraph 267.

11. It was reported in February 1980 that Dr. Piet Koornhof, minister of cooperation and development (Bantu administration renamed), had initiated the experiment of dropping the seventy-two-hour rule temporarily in Bloemfontein and Pretoria (*Christian Science Monitor* [Boston], 8 February 1980). As far as I am aware, this experiment was stopped shortly thereafter.

12. The line was named after Werner W. M. Eiselen, who proposed the measure while serving as the secretary of Bantu administration.

13. Maree (1978, p. 7), referring to Francis Wilson's article "Die Plakkers: wat sê ons vir die vader?" *Rapport,* 14 August 1977.

14. However, if such employment were terminated, then the right to remain in the area would also end.

15. Punt Janson, deputy minister of Bantu administration, as reported in *Cape Times,* 26 September 1975.

16. In the Ciskei, Dr. Trudi Thomas found that 80 percent of the malnourished children there had been deserted by their fathers, most of whom had gone to work in the cities and had established other liaisons there. Conversely, 90 percent of the well-nourished children were supported by their fathers (Thomas, 1974, p. 17). Another example, from KwaZulu, is found in Clarke and Ngobese (1975, p. 31).

17. One government spokesman has inadvisedly opined that, in fact, Black Africans do not esteem family life as much as other South Africans and so the government need not be overly concerned about the migrant labor system.

18. The quotation is from the education workshops organized by the Extra-Mural Studies Department of the University of Cape Town in January 1975.

19. This was one of the points of issue in the trial of Amelia Ndamase, a Crossroader who won her case on appeal.

20. The shortcomings of the original legislation were implicit in the case of Lilian Peter of Crossroads in 1975-1976 but more clearly explicit in the February 1977 case of a Mr. Fredericks, a squatter whose home at Kraaifontein near Cape Town was bulldozed. Both people won their cases. Mr. Fredericks's home was rebuilt for him.

21. Such were the words of *Die Burger* (Cape Town), 18 September 1978.

22. Black Sash records, as referred to by Graaff and Robb (1978, p. 22).

23. Maree, 1978, p. 2. The source of the information he provided on Modderdam was Thomas, 1977, Tables 4 and 5.

24. The word choice of Brigadier J. H. van der Westhuizen, chairman of the Peninsula Bantu Administration Board, in *Argus*, 16 August 1978.

25. A quotation from Brigadier J. H. van der Westhuizen, *Die Burger*, 22 December 1975.

26. Words of Dr. Willie Vosloo, deputy minister of plural relations, at the National Party Congress in East London, 22 August 1978.

27. From *Beeld*, 18 September 1978.

28. Brigadier J. H. van der Westhuizen, in an interview with *Financial Mail*, 20 February 1976.

29. Brigadier J. H. van der Westhuizen, *Die Burger*, 22 December 1975.

30. Maree and Cornell, 1977. (See also Graaff and Weichel, 1978.)

31. This is not an unprecedented finding. In many instances, shanty dwellers have expressed much greater satisfaction with their housing situation than people living in public housing, who feel more hemmed in by regulations and more vulnerable to officialdom's whim. (For an example, see Hollingshead and Rogler, 1963, pp. 229-45.)

32. Lest this sentence and the previous one give the impression that self-organization in squatter camps is a new phenomenon (an outgrowth of Black consciousness, perhaps), it should be pointed out that similar self-organization was manifest in, for example, the Black African squatter camps near Johannesburg during the late 1940s. (See Stadler, 1979, p. 94.)

33. "The unofficial 'mayor' of Crossroads, Mr. Johnson Ngxobongwana, was set upon yesterday by several camouflaged policemen and beaten unconscious when he questioned their methods 'of hitting and shooting the people' [during the raid of 14 September 1978]. Mr. Ngxobongwana is head of the two Crossroads committees which govern the internal affairs of the squatter camp, and commander of the homeguard vigilante force . . . [of] about 100 men. . . . A witness to the assault was Miss Jackie Gulliver, . . . who said she saw about six policemen at one stage 'hurl Mr. Ngxobongwana through the air.' He was bludgeoned unconscious at one stage and regained his senses as he was being put into the police van. . . . Brigadier J. F. Rossouw, Divisional Commissioner of Police for the Western Cape, said last night, 'I don't believe it at all. If he was beaten by one of my chaps, he is at liberty to go to the police and lay a charge of assault.'" *Cape Times* (15 September 1978).

34. Various reports support this assertion; for example, *Argus*, 3 July 1978; *Cape Times*, 27 July 1978; *Argus*, 3 August 1978.

35. Examples from Durban of the role of the informal economy in squatter life appear in Maasdorp and Humphreys (1975, p. 44).

36. Ceremonial whips carried as symbols of status.

37. SAIRR, 1978a, p. 454; Ellis et al., 1977, pp. 44-46; Maree and Cornell, 1977, Table 17, p. 18.

38. For example, *Die Burger* (4 April 1979) published its opinion that Crossroads "has —mainly because of the efforts of people whose motives are highly suspect—become an emotional issue in South Africa and further abroad . . .; it [the demolition] would have evoked the mightiest action abroad at a time when South Africa can least of all afford reactions like this." Piet Koornhof himself, in a television interview on the BBC in December 1978, has said much the same thing.

39. His lack of conservatism, of course, is relative to the spectrum of Afrikaner Nationalism. Nevertheless, Steve Biko perceived some humanity in Koornhof, which he did not see in other Nationalist politicians. (See Woods, 1978, p. 108.)

40. These somewhat covert preparations gave rise to another furor, namely: "Reports that PRAD [Plural Relations and Development—a new euphemism for White administration of Black Africans] was building a township for the Crossroads squatters amongst others on Bridge Farm in the Bolotwa-Gwatyu area near Queenstown and bordering on Transkei led Chief K. Matanzima to protest to the SA government. The farm was one of 20 which had been expropriated by the SA Development Trust for eventual incorporation into Transkei. Chief Matanzima sent a telegram to the SA government demanding an explanation and accused the government of trying to create 'a slum' in Transkei territory. In commenting Dr. Vosloo [deputy minister of plural relations and development] said that the Crossroads squatters would not be resettled in one township but would be assisted to return to their own areas. Some might go to Bridge Farm. All plans for the development of the township were scrapped after talks were held in Queenstown between Chief Matanzima and a SA delegation under Mr. Pik Botha, minister of foreign affairs. Chief Matanzima in commenting on the talks said it was agreed that the settlement be removed" (SAIRR, 1979, pp. 354-55).

41. As reported by P. Andrew, of UPRU, University of Cape Town, in a personal communication, November 1979.

Chapter 11

1. The sense of a specifically Coloured identity among those persons so classified was at its weakest in Cape Town, as opposed to other areas where Coloured persons constituted a minority group in their immediate environment (whereas in Cape Town they outnumber all other groups).

2. Afrikaner poet Breyten Breytenbach, now imprisoned for plotting the overthrow of the present government, said in 1973, "We are a bastard people with a bastard language. Our nature is bastardy. Well and good . . . [but] we felt threatened. We built walls. Not cities, but city walls. And like all bastards—uncertain of their identity—we began to clutch at the notion of purity. That is apartheid."

3. A report in January 1980 tells of the resignation from the bench of Mr. Justice Mervyn King, "young . . . and highly regarded . . . 'because of a conflict of conscience' about having to apply certain of the government's discriminatory race laws. One case involved an Asian couple who were taken to court because they were living in an apartment in a technically 'white' area of Johannesburg. The judge told them in court that he was legally obliged to have them evicted because 'as a judge in a court of law, I am obliged to give effect

to the provisions of an act of Parliament.' But he added most significantly: 'Speaking for myself, and if I were sitting as a court of equity, I would have come to the assistance of the appellant'—meaning the Asian couple. 'Unfortunately,' he said, he could not do this because of the law" (*Christian Science Monitor* [Boston] , 21 January 1980).

4. O. D. Wollheim, personal communications, 1979.

5. No Indian traders have ever resided in the Orange Free State, and only a very few have yet to be moved in the Western Cape (so all of South Africa is thus accounted for).

6. His statement according to the SAIRR (1979).

7. N. N. Patricios, personal communications, 1977.

8. For example, the removal of a Mr. Khalfey from his store in Newlands (*Cape Times*, 24 January 1980).

9. SAIRR, 1980, p. 466.

10. For more details on such removals, which lie outside the scope of this book, see Maré (1980), a very informative account.

11. Under the category of subjugated African nations one could with some justification include the Boers of South Africa, for two decades or so after 1900.

12. It is most interesting to note that, when many of the apartheid policies were being formulated by Stellenbosch academics prior to the 1948 election, certain of them " . . . realised that the Reserves were inadequate; indeed, [Professors] Eiselen and [Andries] Cilliers proposed that the Union's eight million Africans should be pushed bodily northward of the Limpopo River, though they did not say whether this should be into Southern Rhodesia or the Belgian Congo." (Walker, 1957, p. 770).

13. In August 1980 (effective October 1980) Steyn was removed from his position as minister for community development, apparently because of his less-than-deft handling of the Coloured schools boycott during mid-1980. He became South African ambassador in London.

14. Among the revelations made in the 1978-1979 Department of Information scandal in the republic, it emerged that the government had covertly spent millions of rands from public funds to establish and to financially prop up the *Citizen*. (See the SAIRR, 1979, p. 4; and SAIRR, 1980, p. 7.)

15. This is a reference to the ill-fated Coloured Persons' Representative Council (CPRC, later CRC) in Bellville-South, which eventually attracted so much disdainful ridicule and boycott from those persons classified as Coloured that it proved unworkable. Accounts can be found in Whisson (1971), M. Simons (1976), and South African Institute of Race Relations (1979, 1980).

BIBLIOGRAPHY

Bibliography

Adam, H. (1971). *Modernizing Racial Domination*. Berkeley and Los Angeles: University of California Press.

Adam, H. (1975). "Internal Constellations and Potentials for Change." In L. Thompson and J. Butler (eds.), *Change in Contemporary South Africa*, pp. 303-26. Berkeley and Los Angeles: University of California Press.

Allen, C. ed. (1975). *Plain Tales from the Raj*. London: André Deutsch and British Broadcasting Corporation.

Andrew, P., Christie, M., and Martin, R. (1973). "Squatters and the Evolution of a Lifestyle." *Architectural Design*, 43 (1), pp. 16-25.

Andrew, P., and Japha, D. (1978). *Low Income Housing Alternatives for the Western Cape*. Cape Town: Urban Problems Research Unit (UPRU), University of Cape Town.

Baker, S., and Katzen, B. (1972). *Looking at Cape Town*. Cape Town: Howard Timmins. (Photographs by Katzen.)

Baldwin, J. (1963). *The Fire Next Time*. New York: Dial Press.

Banton, M. (1967). *Race Relations*. New York: Basic Books.

Batson, E. (1947). "Notes on the Distribution and Density of Population in Cape Town, 1936." *Transactions of the Royal Society of South Africa*, 31 (4), pp. 389-420.

Behan, B. (1962). *Brendan Behan's Island*. London: Hutchinson.

Beinart, W. (1976). "Recent Occupational Mobility of Coloured People in Cape Town." In H. W. van der Merwe and C. J. Groenewald (eds.), *Occupational and Social Change among Coloured People in South Africa*, pp. 84-113. Cape Town: Juta.

Berry, B. J. L. (1973). *The Human Consequences of Urbanization*. New York: St. Martin's Press.

Bloch, C. (1977). *Vigilante Groups on the Cape Flats*. Cape Town: NICRO.

Board, C., Davies, R. J., and Fair, T. J. D. (1970). "The Structure of the South African Space Economy: An Integrated Approach." *Regional Studies*, 4, pp. 367-92.

Botha, D. P. (1960). *Die opkoms van ons Derde Stand*. Cape Town: Juta.

Brand, D. (1971). "Blues for District Six." In C. Pieterse (ed.), *Seven South African Poets*. London: Heinemann Educational.

Branford, J. (1978). *A Dictionary of South African English*. Cape Town: Oxford University Press.

Breytenbach, B. (1973). " 'n Blik van Buite." Paper read at Die Sestigers Conference, University of Cape Town Summer School.

Brink, A. (1975). *Looking on Darkness*. New York: William Morrow. (First published in 1973 as *Kennis van die Aand*. Cape Town: Buren.)

Butler, G. (ed.) (1959). *A Book of South African Verse*. Cape Town: Balkema.

Carol, H. (1975). "Geographical Scenarios for an Underdeveloped Area: Alternative Futures for Tropical Africa." In R. Abler, D. Janelle, A. Philbrick, and J. Sommer (eds.), *Human Geography in a Shrinking World*, pp. 217-36. North Scituate, Mass.: Duxbury Press.

Centre for Intergroup Studies (1979). *District Six*. Occasional Paper No. 2. Cape Town: Centre for Intergroup Studies, University of Cape Town.

Chombart de Lauwe, P.-H., et al. (1960). "Un Essai d'observation expérimentale." In *Famille et Habitation*. Paris: Centre National de la Recherche Scientifique.

Cilliers, S. P. (1972). "Facing the Crisis in Housing for the Coloured People." Paper read at a meeting of the Cape Town Chamber of Commerce, 21 November 1972, Cape Town.

Cilliers, S. P. (1975). "The Social, Political and Economic Implications of Industrial Progress, with Particular Reference to the Position of the Coloured Population." *Social Dynamics* 1 (1), pp. 42-52.

Cilliers, S. P. (1977). "The Urban Situation — A Re-assessment of Objectives." Paper read at the Conference on Media and Change, winter school, University of the Witwatersrand, Johannesburg.

Clarke, L., and Ngobese, J. (1975). *Women without Men: A Study of 150 Families in the Nqutu District of KwaZulu*. Durban: Institute for Black Research.

Cooke Taylor, W. (1842). Notes of a Tour in the Manufacturing Districts of Lancashire.

Davids, A. (1974). "Residential Apartheid with Special Reference to District Six." Cape Town: unpublished paper.

Davies, W. J. (1971). *Patterns of Non-White Population Distribution in Port Elizabeth with Special Reference to the Application of the Group Areas Act*. Series B, Special Publication No. 1. Port Elizabeth: Institute for Planning Research, University of Port Elizabeth.

Dennis, N. (1958). "The Popularity of the Neighborhood Community Idea." *Sociological Review*, 6 (2), pp. 191-206.

Deskins, D. R. (1973). "Residence-Workplace Interaction Vectors for the Detroit Metropolitan Area: 1953 to 1965." In M. Albaum (ed.), *Geography and Contemporary Issues: Studies of Relevant Problems*, pp. 157-74. New York: John Wiley and Sons.

Dewar, D. (1977). "An Evaluation of Low Income Housing Policy in South Africa." *International Conference on Low Income Housing-Technology and Policy*, vol. 1. Bangkok, Thailand: Asian Institute of Technology.

Dickie-Clark, H. F. (1966). *The Marginal Situation*. London: Routledge and Kegan Paul.

Dickie-Clark, H. F. (1972). "The Coloured Minority of Durban." In N. P. Gist and A. G. Dworkin (eds.), *The Blending of Races: Marginality and Identity in World Perspective*, pp. 25-38. New York and London: John Wiley and Sons.

Doman, E. J. (1975). "The In-Betweeners: A Look at the Coloured People of South Africa." *Optima*, 25 (3), pp. 131-51.

Du Plessis, I. D. (1944). *The Cape Malays*. Cape Town: Balkema.

Durant, R. (1939). *Watling: A Survey of Social Life on a New Housing Estate*. London: P. S. King.

Effrat, M. (1973). "Approaches to Community: Conflicts and Complementaries." *Sociological Enquiry*, 43 (3-4), pp. 1-32.

Ellis, G., Hendrie, D., Kooy, A., and Maree, J. (1977). *The Squatter Problem in the Western Cape: Some Causes and Remedies*. Johannesburg: South African Institute of Race Relations.

Engels, F. (1844). *The Condition of the Working-Class in England in 1844*. (1962 edition.) London.

Evans-Pritchard, E. E. (1940). *The Nuer*. Oxford: Clarendon Press.

Fair, T. J. D. (1969). "Southern Africa: Bonds and Barriers in a Multi-racial Region." In R. M. Prothero (ed.), *A Geography of Africa*, pp. 325-79. London: Routledge and Kegan Paul.

Fair, T. J. D., and Davies, R. J. (1976). "Constrained Urbanization: White South Africa and Black Africa Compared." In B. J. L. Berry (ed.), *Urbanization and Counter-Urbanization,* pp. 145-68. Beverly Hills, Calif.: Sage.

Findlay, G. (1936). *Miscegenation.* Pretoria, South Africa: Pretoria News Publishers.

Fouché, L. (1978). "The Resolution of the Squatter Problem in South Africa." Paper read at the Road Ahead conference, Grahamstown, Cape, 6 July 1978.

First, R., and Scott, A. (1980). *Olive Schreiner.* New York: Schocken Books.

Fried, M. (1963). "Grieving for a Lost Home." In L. J. Duhl (ed.) (with the assistance of J. Powell), *The Urban Condition, People and Policy in the Metropolis,* pp. 151-71. New York: Basic Books.

Fried, M. (1967). "Functions of the Working-Class Community in Modern Urban Society: Implications for Forced Relocation." *Journal of the American Institute of Planners,* 33 (2), pp. 90-103.

Gans, H. J. (1972). *People and Plans.* Harmondsworth, Middlesex: Penguin Books.

Gerwel, J. G. (1974). "The Social-Pathological Conditions of the Communities of the Cape Flats." Paper given to the symposium A Programme for Social Upliftment for the Cape Flats Communities, 28 July 1974, in Athlone, Cape.

Glass, R. (1955). "Urban Sociology in Great Britain: A Trend Report." *Current Sociology,* 4 (4), pp. 5-19.

Glazer, N. (1965). "The Renewal of Cities." *Scientific American,* CCXIII, 3, pp. 195-204.

Graaff, J., and Maree, J. (1977). *African Workers in Cape Town.* Cape Town: Southern Africa Labour and Development Research Unit (SALDRU), University of Cape Town.

Graaff, J., and Robb, N. (1978). "Crossroads—The Facts." *South African Outlook,* 108 (1280), pp. 21-23.

Graaff, J., and Weichel, K. (1978). *Employment Survey of Black Workers Living in Crossroads.* Cape Town: South African Institute of Race Relations; and Urban Problems Research Unit (UPRU), University of Cape Town.

Granelli, R. (1977). *Urban Black Housing: A Review of Existing Conditions in the Cape Peninsula with Some Guidelines for Change.* Cape Town: Urban Problems Research Unit (UPRU), University of Cape Town.

Graves, L. M., and Fletcher, A. H. (1941). "Some Trends in Public Housing." *American Journal of Public Health,* 31, pp. 65-71.

Halpern, J. (1965). *South Africa's Hostages.* Harmondsworth, Middlesex: Penguin Books.

Hannerz, U. (1969). *Soulside: Inquiries into Ghetto Culture and Community.* New York and London: Columbia University Press.

Hiemstra, V. G. (1953). *The Group Areas Act.* Cape Town: Juta.

Hillery, G. A., Jr. (1955). "Definitions of Community: Areas of Agreement." *Rural Sociology,* 10, pp. 111-23.

Hillery, G. A., Jr. (1968). *Communal Organizations: A Study of Local Societies.* Chicago: University of Chicago Press.

Hollingshead, A. B., and Rogler, L. (1963). "Attitudes towards Public Housing in Puerto Rico." In L. J. Duhl (ed.), *The Urban Condition,* pp. 229-45. New York: Basic Books.

Holzner, L. (1971). "Soweto-Johannesburg, Beispiel einer südafrikanischen Bantustadt." *Geographische Rundschau,* 23 (6), pp. 209-22.

Horrell, M. (1956). *The Group Areas Act—Its Effects on Human Beings.* Johannesburg: South African Institute of Race Relations.

Jackson, B. (1972). *Working Class Community.* Harmondsworth, Middlesex: Penguin Books.

Keppel-Jones, A. (1947). *When Smuts Goes: A History of South Africa from 1952-2010; First Published in 2015.* Pietermaritzburg, Natal: Shuter and Shooter.

Kerner Commission: See United States of America.

King, A. D. (1976). *Colonial Urban Development.* London: Routledge and Kegan Paul.

Knudzen, V. K., and Bourne, D. E. (1977). "The Reproductive Efficiency of the Xhosa." *South African Medical Journal*, 57, p. 392.

Kuper, H. (1947). *The Uniform of Colour*. Johannesburg: Witwatersrand University Press.

Kuper, H. (1972). "The Language of Sites and the Politics of Space." *American Anthropologist*, 74 (3), pp. 411-25.

Kuper, L. (1956). "Techniques of Social Control in South Africa." *The Listener*, 31 May 1956.

Kuper, L., Watts, H., and Davies, R. J. (1958). *Durban: A Study in Racial Ecology*. London: Jonathan Cape.

Leeuwenberg, J. (1974). *Transkei Study Project, January-March 1974*. Cape Town: mimeographed report.

Levy, P. R. (1978). *Queen Village: The Eclipse of Community*. Public Papers in the Humanities No. 2. Philadelphia: Institute for the Study of Civic Values.

Ley, D. (1974). *The Black Inner City as Frontier Outpost*. Monograph Series No. 7. Washington, D.C.: Association of American Geographers.

Lorenz, K. (1966). *On Aggression*. New York: Harcourt, Brace, and World.

Lynch, K. (1960). *The Image of the City*. Cambridge, Mass.: Massachusetts Institute of Technology Press.

Maasdorp, G. (1976). "The Development of the Homelands with Special Reference to KwaZulu." In D. M. Smith (ed.), *Separation in South Africa: 2. Homelands and Cities*, pp. 21-36. Occasional Papers No. 7. London: Department of Geography, Queen Mary College, University of London.

Maasdorp, G., and Humphreys, A. (eds.) (1975). *From Shantytown to Township*. Cape Town: Juta.

Maasdorp, G., and Pillay, N. (1977). *Urban Relocation and Racial Segregation: The Case of Indian South Africans*. Durban: University of Natal, Department of Economics.

Mabin, D. S. (1968). "Patterns of Low Cost Housing." Unpublished masters of science thesis, University of Cape Town.

McGee, T. G. (1967). *The Southeast Asian City*. London: Bell.

Mannoni, O. (1956). *Prospero and Caliban: The Psychology of Colonization*. New York: Praeger. (First published in French in 1950.)

Marais, J. S. (1939). *The Cape Coloured People, 1652-1937*. London, New York, and Toronto: Longmans.

Maré, G. (1980). *African Population Relocation in South Africa*. Johannesburg: South African Institute of Race Relations.

Maree, J. (1978). "African and Coloured Squatters in the Cape Town Region: 1975-78." Paper read at a history workshop, The Witwatersrand: Labour, Townships, and Patterns of Protest, 3-7 February 1978, University of the Witwatersrand, Johannesburg.

Maree, J., and Cornell, J. (1977). "A Sample Survey of Squatters in Unibell, September 1977." Working Paper No. 14. Cape Town: Southern Africa Labour and Development Research Unit (SALDRU), University of Cape Town.

Maree, J., and Cornell, J. (1978). "A Sample Survey of Squatters in Crossroads, December 1977." Working Paper No. 17. Cape Town: Southern Africa Labour and Development Research Unit (SALDRU), University of Cape Town.

Marris, P. (1961). *Family and Social Change in an African City: A Study of Rehousing in Lagos*. London: Routledge and Kegan Paul.

Marris, P. (1974). *Loss and Change*. London: Routledge and Kegan Paul.

Marris, P. (1977). "Community as Ideology." Paper given at School of Architecture and Urban Planning, 27 January 1977, University of California at Los Angeles.

Matoré, G. (1966). "Existential Space." *Landscape*, 15, pp. 5-6.

Meer, F. (1972). "The Natal Indian Congress." *Reality* (July 1972), pp. 5-6.

Meer, F. (1976). "Domination through Separation: A Resume of Major Laws Enacting and Preserving Racial Segregation." In D. M. Smith (ed.), *Separation in South Africa: 1. People and Policies*, Occasional Papers No. 6. London: Department of Geography, Queen Mary College, University of London, pp. 17-24.

Mercer, C. (1975). *Living in Cities*. Harmondsworth, Middlesex: Penguin Books.

Midgley, J. (1977). "Crime in South Africa." *South African Journal of Criminal Law and Criminology*, 1 (1), p. 87.

Millin, S. G. (1924). *God's Stepchildren*. New York: Boni and Liveright.

Montagu, A. (ed.) (1968). *Man and Aggression*. New York: Oxford University Press.

Moodley, K. (1975). "South African Indians: The Wavering Minority." In L. Thompson and J. Butler (eds.), *Change in Contemporary South Africa*, pp. 250-79. Berkeley and Los Angeles: University of California Press.

Morse, S. J., and Peele, S. (1974). "Coloured Power or Coloured Bourgeoisie? A Survey of Political Attitudes among Coloureds in South Africa." *Public Opinion Quarterly*, 38, pp. 317-34.

Muller, P. O., Meyer, K. C., and Cybriwsky, R. A. (1976). *Metropolitan Philadelphia: A Study of Conflicts and Social Cleavages*. Cambridge, Mass.: Ballinger.

Nel, A. (1962). "Geographical Aspects of *Apartheid* in South Africa." *Tijdschrift voor Econ. en Soc. Geografie*, 53 (10), pp. 197-209.

Newman, O. (1972). *Defensible Space: Crime Prevention through Urban Design*. New York: Macmillan.

O'Toole, J. (1973). *Watts and Woodstock: Identity and Culture in the United States and South Africa*. New York: Holt, Rinehart, and Winston.

Pahl, R. E. (1965). "Trends in Social Geography." In R. J. Chorley and P. Haggett (eds.), *Frontiers in Geographical Teaching*, pp. 81-100. London: Methuen.

Pakenham, T. (1979). *The Boer War*. New York: Random House.

Patricios, N. N. (1975). "A Planning and Design Investigation into Family Housing for Black Mine-Workers." Working Report. Johannesburg: Department of Town and Regional Planning, University of Witwatersrand.

Patricios, N. N. (1978). "Cities in the 21st Century." Paper read at the Road Ahead conference, 3-7 July 1978, Grahamstown, Cape.

Patterson, S. (1953). *Colour and Culture in South Africa*. London: Routledge and Kegan Paul.

Pieterse, C. (1971). *Seven South African Poets: Poems of Exile Collected and Selected by Cosmo Pieterse*. London: Heinemann Educational Books.

Pinnock, D. (1980). "District Six: Historical Vignettes." *South African Outlook*, 110 (1303), pp. 9-11.

Popenoe, D. (1973). "Urban Residential Differentiation: An Overview of Patterns, Trends, and Problems." *Sociological Enquiry*, 43 (3-4), pp. 35-36.

Putterill, M. S., and Bloch, C. (1978). *Providing for Leisure for the City Dweller*. Cape Town: Urban Problems Research Unit (UPRU), University of Cape Town.

Rainwater, L. (1966). "Fear and the House-as-Haven in the Lower Class." *Journal of the American Institute of Planners*, 32 (1), pp. 23-31.

Rive, R. (1980). "Growing Up in District Six." *South African Outlook*, 110 (1303), pp. 6-8.

Russell, M. J. (1961). *A Study of a South African Interracial Neighbourhood*. Monograph No. 3. Durban: Institute for Social Research, University of Natal.

Saunders, C. (1978). "Not Newcomers." *South African Outlook*, 108 (1280), p. 29.

Schlemmer, L. (1976). "Research Analysis of Problems, Grievances and Development Priorities of Black Urban Communities." Durban: Institute of Social and Economic Research, University of Natal.

Schnore, L. F., and Evenson, P. C. (1966). "Segregation in Southern Cities." *American Journal of Sociology*, 72 (1), pp. 58-67.

Schreiner, O. (1923). *Thoughts on South Africa*. London: T. Fisher Unwin.

Scott, P. (1955). "Cape Town, A Multi-racial City." *Geographical Journal*, 121, pp. 149-57.

Selwyn, P. (1973a). "Industrial Development in Peripheral Small Countries." I.D.S. Discussion Paper No. 14. Brighton: Institute of Development Studies, University of Sussex.

Selwyn, P. (1973b). "The Dual Economy Transcending National Frontiers: The Case of Industrial Development in Lesotho." I.D.S. Communication No. 105. Brighton: Institute of Development Studies, University of Sussex.

Shell, R. (1975). "The Establishment and Spread of Islam at the Cape from the Beginnings of Company Rule to 1838." Unpublished bachelor's degree honours thesis, Department of History, University of Cape Town.

Simcox, R. W. (1975). *Mowbray Frontier Town*. Mowbray, Cape: Lions Club of Mowbray.

Simons, H. J., and Simons, R. E. (1969). *Class and Colour in South Africa, 1850-1950*. Harmondsworth, Middlesex: Penguin Books.

Simons, M. (1976). "Organised Coloured Political Movements." In H. W. van der Merwe and C. J. Groenewald (eds.), *Occupational and Social Change among Coloured People in South Africa*, pp. 202-37. Cape Town: Juta.

Small, A. (1971). *A Brown Afrikaner Speaks: A Coloured Poet and Philosopher Looks Ahead*. Munger Africana Library Notes No. 8. Pasadena: California Institute of Technology.

Small, A., and Jansen, C. (1973). *Oos Wes Tuis Bes: Distrik Ses*. Cape Town and Pretoria: Human and Rousseau. (Photographs by Jansen.)

Smith, D. M. (1974). "Race-Space Inequality in South Africa: A Study in Welfare Geography." *Antipode*, 6 (3), pp. 42-69.

Smith, D. M. (1977). *Human Geography, a Welfare Approach*. London: Edward Arnold.

Soja, E. W. (1976). *Spatial Inequality in Africa*, Comparative Urbanization Studies. Los Angeles: School of Architecture and Urban Planning, University of California.

Sommer. R. (1969). *Personal Space*. Englewood Cliffs, N.J.: Prentice-Hall.

Sorokin, P. A. (1964). *Sociocultural Causality, Space, Time*. New York: Russell and Russell.

South African Institute of Race Relations (1977). *A Survey of Race Relations in South Africa, 1976*. Johannesburg: SAIRR.

South African Institute of Race Relations (1978a). *A Survey of Race Relations in South Africa, 1977*. Johannesburg: SAIRR.

South African Institute of Race Relations (1978b). *South Africa in Travail: The Disturbances of 1976/77*. Johannesburg: SAIRR.

South African Institute of Race Relations (1979). *A Survey of Race Relations in South Africa, 1978*. Johannesburg: SAIRR.

South African Institute of Race Relations (1980). *A Survey of Race Relations in South Africa, 1979*. Johannesburg: SAIRR.

Stadler, A. W. (1979). "Birds in the Cornfield: Squatter Movements in Johannesburg, 1944-1947." *Journal of Southern African Studies*, 6 (1), pp. 93-123.

Stone, G. L. (1972). "Identity among Lower-class Cape Coloureds." In M. G. Whisson and H. W. van der Merwe (eds.), *Coloured Citizenship in South Africa*, pp. 28-47. Cape Town: Abe Bailey Institute, University of Cape Town.

Strauss, A. (1959). *Mirrors and Masks: The Search for Identity*. Glencoe, Ill.: Free Press.

Susskind, L. (1973). "Planning for New Towns: The Gap between Theory and Practice." *Sociological Enquiry*, 42 (3-4), pp. 291-310.

Suttles, G. D. (1968). *The Social Order of the Slum: Ethnicity and Territory in the Inner City*. Chicago and London: University of Chicago Press.

Suttles, G. D. (1972). *The Social Construction of Communities*. Chicago and London: University of Chicago Press.

Theron Commission: See van der Horst.

Thomas, T. (1974). *The Children of Apartheid: A Study of the Effects of Migratory Labour on Family Life in the Ciskei*. London: The Africa Publications Trust.

Thomas, W. H. (1977). *Opname van Plakkergemeenskap van Modderdam*. Bellville-South, Cape: Institute for Social Development, University of the Western Cape.

Tilly, C. (1973). "Do Communities Act?" *Sociological Enquiry*, 43 (3-4), pp. 209-40.

Tuan, Y.-F. (1977). "Sacred Space: Explorations of an Idea." Paper presented at the annual meetings of the Association of American Geographers, 25 April 1977, Salt Lake City.

United States of America (1968). *Report of the National Advisory Commission on Civil Disorders* (Kerner Commission). Washington, D.C.: United States Government Printing Office.

Unterhalter, B. (1975). "Changing Attitudes to 'Passing for White' in an Urban Coloured Community." *Social Dynamics*, 1 (1), pp. 53-62.

van den Berghe, P. L. (1962). "Race Attitudes in Durban, South Africa." *Journal of Social Psychology*, 57, pp. 55-72.

van den Berghe, P. L. (1966). "Racial Segregation in South Africa: Degrees and Kinds." *Cahiers d'Etudes Africaines*, 6 (23), pp. 408-18.

van der Horst, S. T. (ed.) (1976). *The Theron Commission Report: A Summary*. Johannesburg: SAIRR.

van der Ross, R. E. (1979). *Myths and Attitudes: An Inside Look at the Coloured People*. Cape Town: Tafelberg.

Walker, E. A. (1957). *A History of Southern Africa*. London, New York, and Toronto: Longmans.

Watson, G. (1970). *Passing for White: A Study of Racial Assimilation in a South African School*. London: Tavistock. (Preface by H. J. Simons.)

Webber, M. M. (1964). "The Urban Place and the Non-place Urban Realm." In J. W. Dyckman, M. M. Webber, et al., *Explorations into Urban Structure*, pp. 79-153. Philadelphia: University of Pennsylvania Press.

Webber, M. M. (1968). "The Post-city Age." *Daedalus*, 97 (4), pp. 1091-110.

Weichel, K., Smith, L. C., and Putterill, M. S. (1978). *Nyanga and Crossroads: Some Aspects of Social and Economic Activity*. Cape Town: Urban Problems Research Unit (UPRU), University of Cape Town.

Westcott, G. M., and Stott, R. A. P. (1976). *A Study of Child Malnutrition in Tsolo District*. Cape Town: mimeographed report.

Whisson, M. G. (1971). "The Coloured People." In P. Randall (ed.), *South Africa's Minorities*. Occasional Publication No. 2. Johannesburg: Study Project on Christianity in Apartheid Society (SPROCAS).

Whisson, M. G. (1972). *The Fairest Cape?* Johannesburg: SAIRR.

Whisson, M. G. (1973). "The Legitimacy of Treating Coloured People in South Africa as a Minority Group." Paper read at the First Congress of the Association for Sociology in Southern Africa, Swaziland.

Whisson, M. G., and Kahn, S. (1969). *Coloured Housing in Cape Town*. Cape Town: Diocese of Cape Town, Board of Social Responsibility.

White, N. (1978). "The Nutritional Status of Children of Crossroads and Nqutu." *South African Outlook*, 108 (1288), pp. 147-48.

Wild, J. (1963). *Existence and the World of Freedom*. Englewood Cliffs, N.J.: Prentice-Hall.

Willmott, P. (1967). "Social Research and New Communities." *Journal of the American Institute of Planners*, 33 (5), pp. 388-93.

Wills, T. M., and Schulze, R. E. (1976). "Segregated Business Districts in a South African City." In D. M. Smith (ed.), *Separation in South Africa: 2. Homelands and Cities*. Occasional Papers No. 7, pp. 67-84. London: Department of Geography, Queen Mary College, University of London.

Wilson, M., and Mafeje, A. (1963). *Langa: A Study of Social Groups in an African Township.* Cape Town: Oxford University Press.

Winter, C. (1971). *Just People.* London: SPCK (Society for the Propagation of Christian Knowledge).

Wollheim, O. D. (1963). "The Coloured People of South Africa." *Race,* 5 (2), pp. 25-41.

Woods, D. (1978). *Biko.* New York: Vintage Books.

Young, M., and Willmott, P. (1962). *Family and Kinship in East London.* Rev. ed. Harmondsworth, Middlesex: Penguin Books.

Zorbaugh, H. (1929). *The Gold Coast and the Slum.* Chicago: University of Chicago Press.

INDEX

Index

Population Registration Act, 77, 209
Port Elizabeth, 11, 36, 121, 231, 320, 342
n26; comparison of with Cape Town
prior to Group Areas, 56-57; comparison
of with Cape Town regarding Group
Areas public hearings, 132-33; Group
Areas planning for, 88-106 passim;
possibility of Malay Group Area in, 78;
slum clearance in, 143
Portuguese, 31, 77, 249
Post offices, desegregation of, 61
Presbyterian Church (Mowbray), 204
Pretoria, 66, 89, 122, 125, 320, 338 n6,
344 n11
Prevention of Illegal Squatting Acts, 287,
296
Primrose Park, 263, Figure 40
Prince George Drive, 117, 339 n16, Figure 5
Princess Vlei, 99-100
Proclamation of Group Areas, 89, 122, 129-
33; of Mowbray as a White group area,
196, 215; outline of, 71
Progressive Federal Party, 125, 193, 316
Property market, in Cape Town (1963-
1972), 189, 192, Figure 14
Prostitution, 26, 146
Protea Village, 40
Pruitt-Igoe (St. Louis, Mo.), 255
Punts Estate, 248

Race Classification Board, 80, 215
"Racial" differentiation, as defined by
Group Areas Act, 9, 78
Railway lines, as demarcations in Group
Areas planning, 84, 93, 103-18 passim,
123-25, 129, 131, Figure 4
Rand, The, 96, 140, 151, 329
Ravensmead, 113
Rebellion of 1799-1803, 311
Reform Party (Indian), 312
Religious affiliation: among Coloureds in
South Africa, 169; and degree of inter-
religious social contact in Mowbray, 204-
6; among ex-Mowbrayites, 169-70;
relationship of with other social indi-
cators within Mowbray community, 174-
76, Figure 19
Removal, forced. See Group Areas Act
Renovation. See Chelsea cottages
Rent control and decontrol, 194-95

Reservation of Separate Amenities Act, 80
Reservoir Hills (Durban), 254
Resettlement of Black Africans, as part of
grand apartheid, 324, 347 n12
"Respectability": as attribute of Coloured
Mowbrayites, 148, 166; as attribute
claimed by Crossroaders, 300, Figures
47, 48
Retreat, and Group Areas planning, 118,
248
Rhodes, Cecil, 13-14; statue of, 140
Rhodes Recreation Ground (Rosebank),
177
Rhodesia, 69. See also Southern Rhodesia;
Zimbabwe
Riots. See Civil Unrest
Rive, Richard, 145
Riverlea (Johannesburg), 37
Roggebaai, 96
Rondebosch, 39, 145, 193, 231, 305
Rondebosch Common, 177, 256
Rondebosch and Mowbray Cottage Hospi-
tal, 177, 199, 224
Rondevlei, 99-100
Roodepoort (Transvaal), 320
Rosebank, 40, 161, 164, 165, 221, Figure 9
Rossouw, Brig. J. F., 345 n33
Rowen, Leonard M., 131
Rugby, 341 n16. See also Perseverance
Rural-urban migration: of Black Africans,
287; of Coloureds, 49, 281-82, 286; of
poor Whites, 80
Russell, Rev. David, 304
Rylands, 82, 113, 123, 182, 214, 215, 338
n5, 338 n15

Safety: as a quality of Mowbray, 179-80; as
a quality lacking on the Cape Flats, 236-
37, 241, 254-64, 269-70, 274, Figure 35.
See also Crime rates
Saint George's (Anglican) Cathedral (Cape
Town city center), 140, 305
Saint Helenans, 183, 196, 341 n21
Saint Louis (Mo.), 255
Saint Peter's Church (Anglican) (Mowbray),
161, 204, 224, 228, 264
Salt River, 32
Salt River (neighborhood), 33, 38, 46, 111,
123, 137, 159, 164, 219, 221, 230, 231,
251, 310, Figure 6; Coloured "penetra-

Born in England, John Western was educated at
Oxford University, the University of Western Ontario,
and the University of California, Los Angeles, where
he earned his Ph.D. *Outcast Cape Town* is based on
field work he conducted as a research scholar at the
Centre for Intergroup Studies, University of Cape
Town. Western is now an assistant professor of
geography at Temple University.